Smoothie with Orange and Celery
Page 23

Wholesome Bread
Page 37

Zucchini Walnut Bread
Page 38

Caribben Holiday
Watermelon, page 246

Chocolate Cookies, page 41

Ways To Make Oatmeal for Breakfast, page 193

Crumble Rhubarb-Banana Crisp
Page 46

Creamy Dipping Sauce with
Prawns, page 53

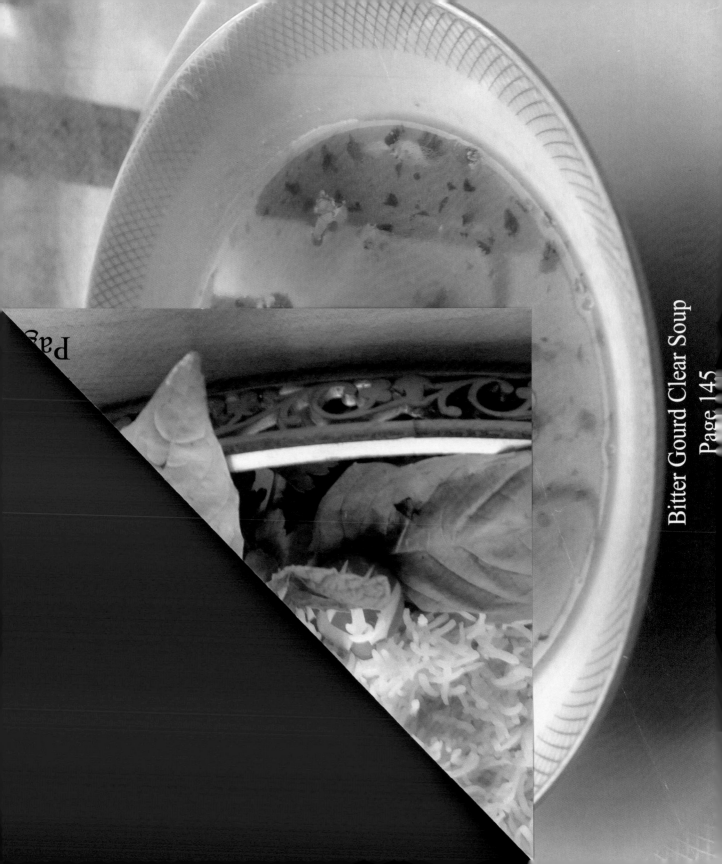

Chicken with Mushrooms and wine,
Page 70

Pecan Crusted Halibut, page 58

Honest Vegetable Pizza
Page 101

Tofu, page 14

Ways to make classic guacamole dish, page 16

Star Vegetable Fish Dish
Page 60

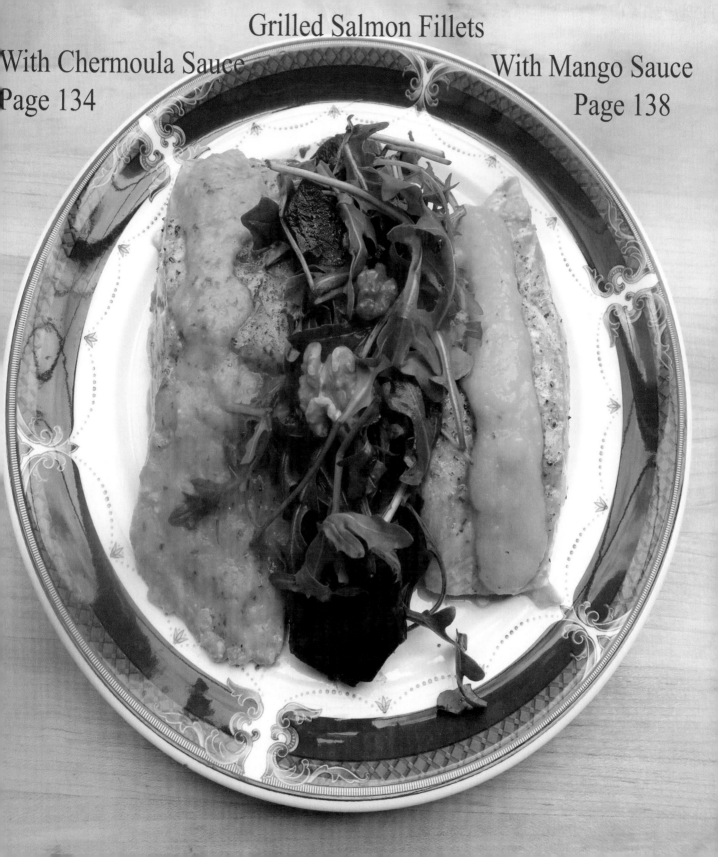

Grilled Salmon Fillets

With Chermoula Sauce
Page 134

With Mango Sauce
Page 138

Seasoned Chicken Patties
Page 82

Spark like Tuna
Page 59

With grace and joy our ancestors were satisfied with a simple organic meal (eggs, flat bread, onion, salt and spring water).

Enlightened Home-Chef

"Green Pharmacy"

RECIPES: A unique health handbook of "*natural cuisine*" with 200 recipes to balance and emphasize the elements of taste, simplicity and sound nutrition

TIPS: Seasoning mixes for international recipes

GLOSSARIES: Key uses of 150 herbal plants with their essential benefits and therapeutic properties

MEDICINAL HERBAL TEA PLANTS: More than 60 ancient treasures of aromatic teas

MEDICINAL HERBAL FOOD PLANTS THAT MAY HELP: Herbs to help us "*wealth-up*" body-mind health

PHILOSOPHY: Ancient and authentic wisdom on food and "*green pharmacy*" to enhance world peace with meditation and rejuvenated spiritual thoughts

Tea Wise

Pen and ink drawing of a tea set, by Gloria Sampson

A cup of good tea not only brings cheer to our face,
it also helps us to sustain good health.
A reflection of sky, sunlight and stars is captured in our eyes as lovely "*Tea Wise*".

Foreword
Enlightened Home-Chef Green Pharmacy

I have known Parisa Ambwani for 15 years. She has great talents in the world of cookery and authorship. Parisa brings deep compassion and a wealth of information to her writing that will greatly benefit her readers.

Parisa is a professional Chef who has prepared many delicious meals for me which I thoroughly enjoyed at her home near San Francisco. She has natural ability in her cooking talents. Parisa has visited me in Florida too several times. She also participated in a 'Culinary Tour of Ireland', which I organized in 2006. The 'Tour' was sponsored by several Irish Government Food Boards and Baileys Irish Cream.

I am delighted to see Parisa has now written a book about the world of herbs and spices. It is of considerable interest to me as I grew up in India, a country famous for their use of herbs and spices to impart delicious, nutritious healthy flavors to food. By the simple addition of herbs and spices, food can be transformed from mundane into a *Culinary Masterpiece*.

I was thrilled to hear Parisa has visited India to research and extend her knowledge on the fascinating range of natural healthy seasonings. Therein lies a great adventure into the exciting world of food. Her book is a Masterpiece. It is an inspiring journey through the use of cookery in the "Enlightened Home-Chef Green Pharmacy".

Noreen Kinney
Honorary Culinary Ambassador of Ireland to the USA. -1996-2020
Published author and commissioned journalist
Culinary Entrepreneur, Executive Chef & University Instructor
Honorary Life Member of ACF -American Culinary Federation -2009
Honorary Life Member of AAC –American Academy of Chefs -2011
Recipient of the President's Gold Medallion -ACF- 2008
Pioneer -New Irish Cuisine 1960-1986. Organized 'Culinary Tours' nationwide in Ireland
Director - Cordon d'Or -Gold Ribbon Annual International & Florida *'Culinary Academy Awards'*
Graduate of Cambridge University, UK
AmbassadorNoreen@tampabay.rr.com

Enlightened Home-Chef

"Green Pharmacy"

The theme of TRILOGY continues its journey
(Old herbal remedies provide natural nourishing traditions that can often gently heal
with almost no side effect).

A handbook of descriptions, uses and benefits of savory, flavorful and
medicinal herbal tea plants that makes it easy to understand
how to use nature's gentle green
pharmacy to enjoy, a
healthier, happier
and fuller
life.

****

By Parisa Z. Anvari Ambwani

2016

Published by Celestial Arts-Creative Cooking Publications

Glossary, Medicinal Herbal Tea Plants and Food Plants That May Help editor: Dr. Elson M. Haas, MD and Nutritionist www.ElsonHaasMD.com
Contributing editor: Antonia Allegra, Symposium for Professional Food Writers
Contributing philosophy editor: Dr. Dan Brinton
Contributing book editor: Betty Jacobsen
Contributing poem editor: Deema K. Shehabi
Contributing editorial assistant: Dr. Branzie Dabney
Technical consultant and support: Shawn D. Ambwani
Book cover layout: Suzanne Barnes
Book cover photos: Parisa Z. Ambwani
Philosophy and photography, and interior design: Parisa Z. Ambwani

Library of Congress Control Number: 2015909482
ISBN   978-0-9753840-5-3
Printed in the United States of America

Please address all inquiries to:
Celestial Arts-Creative Cooking Publications
P.O. Box 3571, Danville, CA 94526-9998, USA

Disclaimer

The information in this book reflects the author's personal opinion and experience. It is not intended to replace individualized professional advice. All recipes (including philosophy, introduction, heading and footnotes, tips, glossary, herbs, spices, fruits, vegetables and medicinal herbal plants) are used at the risk of the consumer. We cannot be responsible for any hazards, loss or damage that may occur as a result of any use of this information without proper consultation with a health care provider. It is not intended as a substitute for any treatment that may have been prescribed by your doctor. For all matters pertaining to your health, a qualified health professional must be consulted.

Enlightened Home-Chef
"Green Pharmacy"

This Book is dedicated to my husband Dr. Durga Das S. Ambwani.
His never-ending love and support inspired me to follow my dream.
"True happiness shines from the heart where *love and peace are our goal*
and our deeds of actions reflect that truth".

****

I'd like to give heartfelt thanks to my editors, herbalists, and farmers
who have preserved and kept the traditional organic herbal seeds
alive for the next generation to come.

****

America is a noble land of nature with opportunity to learn and grow. I am
honored to have met wonderful people all around the world, along with having my rich cultural
background from Persia. I would like to give back my thanks through writing "***TRIOLOGY*** "
(Food of the body, mind, and spirit in a state of harmony and balance).

Overall, we as the root of one planet, are to enjoy the benefits of enlightenment on *"human-unity"*
Humanity, the core of humanity is a divine spiritual love we are holding in our heart. It is
connected to *"the universal Source"*; it will never change; it will never end; and it will always be there.

Ultimate Guide to Natures and Best Natural Foods

Food consumption is a major component for survival of human life. Food of the body, mind and the emotions have an interconnected relationship. Nourishing ourselves with **wholesome food** in peaceful surrounding and Spirit of Love while we are eating, can bring joy and blessing our body with vital nutrition. Our body nutritional requirements have extreme ability to cope with psychological stress (tension, depression and anxiety). Consequently, a balanced diet is the foundation of good physical and emotional well-being that can lead to peace, happiness and success.

****

This timely book was written based on "Ancient Herbal Wisdom", that may be an alternative to modern medicine. It is a great companion to keep on your coffee table or take on the road.

Table of Recipe Contents

(Natural cuisine recipes)

A traditional home wooden churn
A skimmer is used to lift off the *sweetest and freshest cream* which is churned into butter.
Churning still is used, in rural parts of developed countries
and in some small family dairies.

Lemons (Citrus lemon)

CHAPTER 1
The Food Safety Factor and Herbal Wisdom

Important Notice: This book is intended as one for sumptuous eating and as a reference for ideas and suggestions only, **not as a medical advice manual.** *The author's book is concerned with good dietary food habits, but she has no clinical experience with herbal medicinal treatments.* Therefore, if you plan to use herbs or food for medical treatment, seek out a professional herbalist or a medical doctor for attention and guidance. The main purpose of these writings, ideas, and suggestions is to draw attention to the importance of home-grown food, and consuming more vegetables and fruits, in the hope that all people, especially parents and their children, will be encouraged to *plant organically-grown foods, and inspired to cook and eat them for a most wholesome diet.*

Herbs and spices have long histories of use and have been around for millennia. They have endured the test of time. During World War II, herb shortages caused production of new medicines by scientists inventing synthetic drugs. Many studies by researchers worldwide clearly shows how herbal plants can be valuable to us, but the popularity and use of herbal plants have grown over many years.

The United Nations and WHO (World Health Organization) have encouraged the use of Traditional Herbal Medicines alongside Western Medicine.

Herbal strength depends on plant genetics, growing conditions (soil, water and climate), maturity at harvest, length of storage and other safety factors. Herbs and spices always should be chosen and used cautiously. And we should have a basic understanding of herbal safety issues, either using individual plants or blending herbs, so it does not cause damage to our body rather than healing. If these plants are used improperly and we are not sure about herbs and/or spices for our particular medical condition or history, it is wise to consult with a doctor who can assess your history and health condition.

The standard medical advice warns that if you have any problems including kidney or heart disease, diabetes, allergies or hypersensitivity to plants, or are pregnant or breast-feeding, it is not recommended to use herbs and spices for health benefits without professional consultation and supervision. Herb teas are mostly suggested for adults and not for children. And they can interact with some drugs as well.

PLEASE NOTE: This book is written and sold with the understanding that the author, publisher, and other participant are not engaged in giving medical, health, and dietary advice.

In this book I am explaining basic and simple information regarding what I call the "*Home Green Pharmacy*", and not "*Home Treatment Remedy.*" The latter ideally needs a prescription and guidance in how to take them from *a health provider, physician, and/or an experienced naturopathic doctor.* In the tea section I provide valuable information for my readers regarding the "*Home Green Pharmacy*" that a normal person can use with knowledge and some caution to prevent diseases and maintain health, not for necessarily for curing existing diseases or illness.

Please check with your healthcare practitioner and/or traditional naturopathic doctor for any question you have and specifics about herbal therapy, and study carefully the benefits and safety of herbal plants before you start to use them.

Some herbal plants, including herbal teas, can occasionally cause adverse reactions in some people, especially pregnant or breast-feeding women, young children (under 13), those with allergies, those taking certain medications, and/or people with medical problems. You need to check with your physician prior to using plants in recipes or tea and/or as a dietary supplement (vitamins, minerals, or other nutritive content) as part of your medical care. The body needs a steady, regular supply of nutrients, preferably from a good diet, to nourish the cells and tissues. At the same time, we can avoid many toxins in our world to protect our health. Dietary nutritional supplements should not be viewed as an instant solution. Although nutritional supplements may help to protect against some illnesses, they alone cannot always cure diseases.

Always look for healing herbs by their *Latin binominal names (the Latin name signifies the official medicinal herb so you can have more confidence in choosing an effective herbal remedy*). Each plant, food, and animal has been given a genus (family) and species (specific) name to identify them and their qualities. Read labels carefully and look for the key ingredients that may enhance benefits and have the ability to improve mental clarity, memory, and mood. Choose organically grown foods (if it is possible) such as grass-fed meat, pasture-raised eggs, wild fish, milk products, vegetables and fruits, like our ancestors used for many centuries from the living earth. Healing herbs and spices can have both pleasurable and medicinal values, but they are not the same for everyone as individuals vary; we are all unique although the same genus and species, as *Homo sapiens*. Therefore, have respect for your body's individuality and strength as you choose the right ones. And of course, be aware, pay attention, to the effects anything you take has on your health and wellbeing.

Medicinal herbs should be used with good knowledge and understanding so that their effectiveness and benefits are safe, as individual results may vary, as do individual products. **Herbal teas should not be consumed on a regular basis. The wisest way is to incorporate herbal teas with your healthcare doctor's approval and monitor your responses carefully.**

The Benefits of Herbal Plants....

Herbal plants are praised throughout the world for flavorful taste and health benefits.

During olden times, the *"Herbs and Spices Road"* or *"Silk Road"* or *"Caravan Road,"* went from Asia to Egypt and transported more than 200 herbs, including almond, anise, clove, caraway, coriander, juniper, saffron, sesame seeds, turmeric, willow, cardamom, chamomile, cinnamon, fennel, fenugreek, garlic, ginger, mint, onion, sage, thyme, rosemary, burdock, roses, aloe, dill, marjoram, rhubarb, and more.

Today, medical problems like cancer, diabetes, high cholesterol, high blood pressure, and obesity are leading killers according to health experts. Stress, toxicity, lack of relaxation, sleep and a poor diet can leads to all kinds of health problems, can upset hormone balance, influence circulation, increase tension and lead to physical and mental problems. Obesity is a great concern as it significantly increases the risk of developing diabetes and coronary heart disease. According to health-care practitioners, obesity cannot be fixed totally with medicine until our diet is changed and fixed.

Most of the chemicals used for spraying crops to control pests and weeds are toxic. If they are accidently ingested, they must be processed and eliminated from the blood and body with the help of the liver and kidneys. Toxins also are sweated out in exercise or with saunas. Excess toxins can stress the liver, cause kidneys damage, skin rashes, and alter moods and energy levels. The detoxification process can really help us reduce many symptoms and medical complaints.

We are masters of our own destiny; we can choose what we eat; and the bowels (intestines) can absorb what they are able to, based on our overall digestion. We can help them greatly with good chewing). If we want our body to function well, we may want to focus on learning more about herbal plants and nutritious foods from nature's oldest "*green pharmacy*". Not only the taste, and visual presentation of food that we are serving is important; we also need to maintain a healthy diet, low in fats, and high in vegetables, fruits, beans and grains, along with moderate daily exercise for self-care and prevention of possible diseases. As we know most of us want to live a healthier life to enjoy later years as comfortably as possible.

"Although we cannot stop our ageing," we can slow it down and stay healthy and vital. It begins with our diet, for which we have the greatest control.

....Continuing to Change the World.

The health of individuals and society is our greatest goal, and this health is where our nation's real wealth lies.

Yet, we are challenged with the lifestyle of modern days, with all the junk foods, fast foods and processed foods, stress, poor sleep and more. That's why we need to get back to Nature and eat fresh local and seasonal foods and use herbs to support wellness and healing.

A long time ago, before over-the-counter medication and prescription drugs came on the scene, herbal plants proved to be powerful healers. Benefits can be achieved only after evaluating a person's physical and mental status and then learning to use herbal plants correctly. Based on ancient's records and the knowledge passed on through generations, many scientists believe "*herbal healing plants*" can provide beneficial remedies. These records date back over several thousand years from succeeding generations in such cultures as ancient Egypt, Persia, India and China. This is especially true for India and China where herbs are used in conjunction with yoga (deep breathing) and meditation for prevention of many common health issues and sustainable wholesome living.

An enlightened home-chef needs to learn the value of holistic nutrition through herbal plants, our "*green pharmacy*" in order to improve and sustain the health of their family and others. Consuming good food contributes to healthier cells, improved digestion, physical strength and consistent energy. In fact, many natural foods with their many essential nutrients are necessary for the proper functioning of the organs in growing children and to sustain us as adults (Using whole food and avoiding sugary and/or refined foods during the early years will help children develop and maintain their taste for natural foods). *Deficiency of natural foods in early childhood may result in weakened organs, low function, and poor health.*

I remember, as I was growing up with our family of seven children, that my parents had a small "*green pharmacy cabinet*" used to make herbal teas for health benefits in our home. They were used to treat and prevent minor health problems. Our parents tried to keep prescription and over-the-counter medicines to a minimum because of their potential side effects and interaction with some food. Of course, if there were any serious health problems and/or an emergency, my parents took us to see a doctor. *"Please do not use herbal medicine to avoid seeing a physician for persistent or emergency medical problems." Western medicine has some gifts yet it is most important that we learn what it takes to Stay Healthy, says my medical ally, Dr. Elson Haas* (See www.ElsonHaasMD.com)

Enlightened Home-Chef

"Green Pharmacy"
(Your health is your best security for a happy meaningful life.)

This is an essential handbook for everyone who wants to gain the benefits of healing herbs
from a wholesome diet to meet our body's nutritional requirements and maintain
the balance of hormones. These benefits, when combined with knowledgeable
use of medical care, will enhance our potential health and improve
our ability to cope with psychological stress, tension, anxiety and
depression. It is wise to follow the father of natural
medicine, *Hippocrates, the foremost Greek
physician of the fifth century B.C., who
emphasized a vegetarian diet, physical
exercise, music, and meditation.*

For several decades, the author, **Parisa Z. Anvari Ambwani,** has done extensive research on
worldwide cuisine (including herbs and spices, and their benefits and uses). Her work is highly
respected for its warmth and simplicity. Her endearing holistic works can be enjoyed with grace
in day-to-day life.

She has written a series of books. Her books include:

FOOD FOR THE BODY: *Recipes from the Heart,*
Recipes from the Millennia, and
Enticing Tasty Treats (cooking with children)

FOOD FOR THE MIND: *Seeds of Celestial Love and Peace*

FOOD FOR THE SPIRIT: *Human-Unity (Humanity)*

********** * *

www.enlightenedrecipes.com
www.culinaryartsandphilosophy.com
www.seedsofcelecialloveandpeace.com
www.human-unity.com
www.recipesfromthemillennia.com
www.enticingtastytreats.com
www.enlightenedhome-chefgreenpharmacy.com

"In Enlightened Home-Chef Green Pharmacy, Parisa Ambwani has produced another beautiful food, recipe and herb book.

Her food is delightful, sumptuous, elegant, and healthy. Enjoy!"

Elson Haas, MD (www.ElsonHaasMD.com)

Integrative Family Physician and Author of many books including Staying Healthy with the Seasons, the Detox Diet, and Staying Healthy with Nutrition.

Sunflowers

Please see, Glossary, sunflower seeds, page 243

Carrots (Daucus carota)

CHAPTER 2
Natural Cuisine Home-Chef Recipes

Growing Herbal Plants and Blessing Your Food Plants,
Will Spice up Your Cooking for Health and Beauty

Choose a variety of herbs for your planter.
Freshen your meals with these health promoting mint herbs.

Appetizer, Side Dish
And Snack

Tofu, recipe on page 14

A Flavorful Side Dish of Seasonal Red Chili Beans

Serves 4-5

1 cup small red chili beans

8 cups cold water, divided

1 cup tomato basil sauce (see "*Tomato basil sauce*", below)

½ teaspoon advieh-poloye (see Tips, "advieh-poloye", page 185)

¼ teaspoon sea salt OR to taste

1 dash black cumin seeds

1 pinch hot chili powder

1 pinch black pepper, freshly ground

1 teaspoon honey OR turbinado raw sugar

1 tablespoon lemon juice, freshly squeezed

Soak beans in 4 cups water overnight, drain and replace water at least once during soaking. Add beans and 4 cups fresh water to heavy based stock-pot*. Let the mixture come to a simmer, reduce the heat and simmer for 2-3 hours or until beans are completely tender. Drain off any liquid and return beans to stock-pot, add remaining ingredients (tomato basil sauce, advieh-poloye, and salt, cumin, chili powder, black pepper, honey and lemon juice). Continue to cook for 35 minutes or until desired thickness. Serve warm as a side dish or store in a sterilized non-metallic, tightly sealed container in the refrigerator, and gently reheat prior to serving.

Tomato Basil Sauce:

1 small onion, finely chopped

4 cloves of garlic, finely chopped

4 tablespoon extra-virgin olive oil

4 cups ripe red tomatoes, peeled, chopped

½ teaspoon raw sugar

1 dash each of ground oregano, basil, salt and black pepper

In a large saucepan, fry onion and garlic in heated olive oil for 3-4 minutes or until golden brown, stirring constantly. Add tomato, sugar, oregano, basil, salt, and pepper. Cover saucepan and simmer over medium heat, for 8-10 minutes or until sauce thickens, stirring occasionally to prevent burning. Let cool and puree in blender. Sauce can be added to dishes such as green beans, vegetables and pasta.

Note: Small red chili beans hold their shape better after cooking and have a slightly smoother texture than larger beans.

*You may use an electric, ceramic-crock-pot, at low temperature setting, instead of stock-pot.

Braised* Mushrooms

Serves 4

    1 onion, finely chopped
    4 cloves of garlic, finely chopped
    1 teaspoon ginger root, peeled, finely chopped
    ¼ cup extra virgin olive oil
    1½ pounds crimini mushrooms, cleaned, sliced
    ½ teaspoon sea salt OR to taste
    ¼ teaspoon black pepper, freshly ground
    ¼ teaspoon of the following ground spices
    (coriander, curry powder, turmeric, cinnamon,
    paprika, cayenne pepper and cumin)
    1 (Laurel) bay leaf, dried, bruised
    4 sweet-petite red pepper, chopped
    2 large heirloom red tomatoes, cut into small pieces
    2 tablespoons agar agar
    2 tablespoons water (to dissolve agar agar)

Mini Crimini mushrooms

Garnish:
¾ cup strained plain Greek OR Persian yogurt
2 tablespoons cilantro OR basil, chopped

In a large heavy-based pot sauté onion, garlic, and ginger in heated olive oil for 3 minutes. Add mushrooms and stir-fry until mushroom are slightly golden brown. Sprinkle with mixture of salt, pepper, coriander, curry powder, turmeric, cinnamon, paprika, cayenne pepper and cumin. Stir once. Add bay leaf, and red pepper, stir once and remove pot from heat. To a medium size saucepan add tomatoes and agar agar mixture and stir at low-medium heat until agar agar is dissolved. Let the mixture come to a simmer. Simmer in covered saucepan for a few minutes or until the sauce thickens to 1 cup. Combine sauce with onion-mushrooms mixture and gently heat until warm (2 minutes). Remove the bay leaf, and transfer food onto serving dish and garnish with yogurt and cilantro. This authentic vegetarian dish can be served either as a side dish or with warmed pita (flat) bread.

*Braising: A combination method of cooking in two steps: a) Food first is browned in fat. b) Then food is cooked in small amount of liquid, in covered pot, over low heat. Usually, this method is used for meat and vegetables.

Braised Sweet Potato

Serves 4

For braising this vegetable dish, Tagine* stone ware is my preference

    4 large shallots, peeled, thinly sliced

    4 cloves of garlic, chopped

    ¼ cup olive oil

    1 cup prunes, pitted

    1½ pounds sweet potatoes, peeled, cut in 1-inch cubes

    2 carrots, peeled, cut in 1-inch sections

    ½ teaspoon sea salt OR to taste

    ¼ teaspoon black pepper, freshly ground

    ¼ teaspoon black cumin

    ½ teaspoon cinnamon

    ¼ teaspoon cardamom

    1 cup chicken broth

    Juice of 1 lemon, freshly squeezed OR dried lemon

    1 tablespoon lemon zest, freshly grated

Garnish:

    ½ cup walnuts (slightly toasted, and cut in half) and ¼ cup raisins (optional)

In a heavy-based deep frying pan, stir-fry shallots and garlic in heated olive oil for 3 minutes. Add prunes, sweet potatoes and carrots, and stir-fry for a few minutes until shallots are slightly golden brown. Sprinkle with mixture of salt, black pepper, cumin, cinnamon and cardamom and stir a few times. Add chicken broth and bring to a simmer in a very tight covered frying pan (or Tagine). Simmer for 15 minutes or until sweet potatoes are fork tender but still firm. Add lemon and lemon zest; stir once. Garnish with walnut, and raisins.

This flavorful dish can be used to make a sandwich with flat Turkish bread or served with plain steamed rice.

*__Tagine__, a shallow earth-ware dish with a unique, tight-fitting, conical shaped lid that helps to circulate moist air gently as it slowly simmers, vegetables, meat and dried fruits. Tagine is a beautiful invention and cornerstone of the *Moroccan kitchen* for making great stews. Tagine cooking requires a small amount of liquid.

Braised Okra with Tomatoes

(An easy Moroccan-style side dish.)

North Africa cooking from Morocco, Tunisia, Algeria, Libya, and Egypt, where ancient history and sophisticated cultured meet provide a magnificent tasty cuisine.

Serves 4

1 pound okra, rinse, pat-dry, trim the bottom and leave cone-shaped top

1 cup vinegar (white vinegar is preferable)

¼ cup olive oil

1 large onion, julienned (thinly sliced)

4 cloves of garlic, finely chopped

1 pound tomato basil sauce

½ teaspoon paprika

½ teaspoon cumin seeds, ground

¼ teaspoon sea salt OR to taste

1 dash black pepper, freshly grounded

Garnish:

2 tablespoons parsley, chopped

Place okra in a bowl and cover with vinegar and set aside. After 30 minutes drain okra, rinse well with water, gently pat-dry and set aside. In a large saucepan heat olive oil and stir-fry onion and garlic until onion are translucent, about 3-4 minutes. Add okra and stir for a few minutes. Add tomato basil sauce, paprika, cumin, salt and pepper. Let the mixture come to a simmer and cover saucepan. Simmer gently over low heat for 15-20 minutes or until okra is tender. Garnish with chopped parsley and serve.

Children's Goat Cheese Snacks

Serves 2

2 tablespoons of creamy goat cheese

¼ teaspoon lemon zest, freshly grated

2 slices of "*sprouted cinnamon raisins*" bread, lightly toasted

Mix creamy cheese with lemon zest, spread on a slice of the toasted bread to make a sandwich. Cut sandwich in half or if you wish quarters for snacks.

Alternative: Snack or Appetizer, spread one tablespoon of creamy cheese/almond butter on a slice of bread, and top with apricot jam or one Japanese persimmon (choose a persimmon that is fully ripe and sweet; remove skin, mash and spread on almonds butter), cut into quarters and serve open face or form into a sandwich and enjoy.

Crunchy Garbanzo Snacks

Serves 6-8

Preheat oven to 325 degree F.

     1 tablespoon olive oil

     1 tablespoon lemon juice, freshly squeezed

     1 clove of garlic, grated

     ½ teaspoon sea salt

     ¼ teaspoon peppercorn (black pepper), freshly ground

     ½ teaspoon brown mustard seeds, ground

     1 teaspoon turbinado raw sugar (optional)

     1 cup organic dried garbanzo beans, nearly cooked

In a small mixing bowl, mix olive oil, lemon juice and garlic together. In another mixing bowl mix salt, pepper, mustard and sugar together. Combine wet and dried ingredients with garbanzo beans. Place mixture evenly on grilling tray in single rows. Transfer into oven and cook for 25 minutes or until garbanzo beans are completely cooked, stir once while it is cooking.

Variation: Seasoned garbanzo Beans, in a mixing bowl combine 2 cups very well cooked garbanzo with ½ cup olive oil, ¼ cup plus 1 tablespoon balsamic vinegar, ½ teaspoon sea salt, ¼ teaspoon black pepper, and add the following dried herbs (2 teaspoons basils, 2 teaspoons mint, ½ teaspoon rosemary, ¼ teaspoon savory and ¼ teaspoon thyme). Mix all ingredients and adjust the seasoning if needed. Refrigerate in sterilized jar for 24 hours before serving. Serve as a side dish or toss with green salad of your choice.

Easy Appetizer with Tomato and Cheese

Ingredients for 1 person:

     1 green lettuce leaf (butter lettuce is my preference), cut slightly larger than tomato

     1 thinly sliced red tomato (about 1½-inch in diameter)

     1 thinly cut round Mozzarella cheese

     1 green basil leaf

     2 drops of olive oil

     2 drops of balsamic vinegar

On a serving plate, layer lettuce, tomato, and cheese.

Top with a basil leaf and drizzle with olive oil and balsamic vinegar.

Grilled Chicken Liver

(Experience the flavors of Mediterranean food as an appetizer or side dish.)

Serves 8

Preheat oven to 350 degree F.

1 onion (shredded) OR 6 shallots, peeled, chopped

4 cloves of garlic, chopped

¼ cup olive oil + 2 tablespoons

1 ½ pounds fresh organic chicken liver, rinsed, drip-dry completely

½ teaspoon sea salt

¼ teaspoon black pepper, freshly ground

¼ cup white wine OR cherry wine

2 teaspoon arrowroot powder, mix with wine

1 pound crimini mushrooms, wipe-dried with a clean cloth

1 cup Italian parsley leaves, cleaned, pat-dried, chopped

4 wheat pita bread, cut into halves OR 8 small flat bread, warmed

½ cup brown mustard*

Garnish:

1 cup sprouted radish

Stir-fry onion and garlic in heated olive oil using a large heavy-based frying pan, for a few minutes and add livers. Pan-fry chicken livers for 2 minutes on each side or until slightly golden brown. Sprinkle with salt and pepper. Add wine and arrowroot mixture from the corner of pan. Bring to simmer over medium heat, stir gently with wooden spoon over medium heat until almost all the liquid evaporates (1-2 minutes). Remove from heat and let cool.

On a grilling tray with screen on top (or roasting rack), arrange mushrooms in single layer. Place tray on the middle rack of oven. Bake for 15 minutes or until mushrooms dry slightly. Remove mushrooms from oven and let cool for a minute. Place mushrooms in food processor and add liver mixture. Pulse 5 times. Transfer mixture into serving bowl, add parsley, gently toss and serve. Spread mustard inside of each pita bread, top with liver mixture and garnish with sprouted radishes. Enjoy this wonderful tasty and wholesome appetizer.

*The stone ground, organic, brown mustard made with apple cider-vinegar is my preference.

Marinated Mushrooms

Serves 6

      1 pound mini mushrooms (about 28)

      ½ cup extra virgin olive oil

      ½ cup red wine vinegar

      4 cloves of garlic, crushed

      ½ teaspoon thyme

      ½ teaspoon oregano

      ½ teaspoon sea salt OR to taste

      ¼ teaspoon black pepper, freshly ground

      ¼ teaspoon paprika

      2 shallots, quartered

Clean mushrooms carefully*. In a medium saucepan, bring ½ gallons spring water to rolling boil. Add mushrooms to boiling water and cook for 1 minute (uncovered). Immediately drain mushrooms, rinse with cold water and drain again. In a large mixing bowl, combine remaining ingredients except shallots (oil, vinegar, garlic, thyme, oregano, salt, pepper and paprika). Stir in shallots and mushrooms. Refrigerate for 24 hours in air tight container prior to serving. You may use marinated mushrooms as an appetizer or condiment with main dish.

*You may wipe mushrooms with a damp cloth.

Please see Glossary, Mushrooms, page 229

Power Snacks

(Super gluten free snacks)

Serves 12 +

A) **Raw Vegan Mix**

    1 cup sweet almonds

    ¼ cup raisins

    ½ cup golden mulberries

    ½ cup goji berries

    ¼ cup pistachios, shelled

    ¼ cup walnuts, shelled

    ¼ cup sun dried cherries OR dates OR prunes OR apricot OR figs (pit, and cut into small pieces)

    ¼ cup carob chips (optional) OR cacao nibs

Mix all dried nuts and fruits together along with carob chips to make a nutritious and delicious snack.

B) **Super Berry Mix** (naturally sweet, tart and tasty)

    12 oz. golden mulberries

    8 oz. goji berries

    4 oz. dried blue berries

Mix all ingredients together.

C) **Super Almond Mix**

    16 oz. (about 3 cups) sweet almonds

    8 oz. gooseberry (golden berries)

    1 cup golden mulberries

    ¼ cup pistachio, shelled

Mix all dried ingredients together and use as a snack.

D) **Symphony of Seeds and Colors**

    Preheat oven to 275 degree F.

    12 oz. pine nuts

    12 oz. pumpkin seeds

    12 oz. sunflower seeds

Oh, my favorite snacks!
Ju-lian Toh

Combine all ingredients. Spread in a single layer on an oven-proof tray. Place on middle rack of oven and toast for 5 minutes. Remove from oven, stir, return to oven and continue to toast for a few minutes more or until the color changes to slightly golden brown. Enjoy a tasty snack.

Side Dish with Asparagus and Carrots

Serves 4

Dressing:

2 tablespoons toasted sesame seeds oil

2 teaspoons organic tamari OR soy sauce

2 teaspoons sugar

2 teaspoons ginger root, peeled, crushed

2 teaspoons garlic, peeled, crushed

Vegetables:

1 pound asparagus, cleaned, cut into 2 ½-inch length

2 carrots, peeled, cut into Julian 2-inch length

3 tablespoons olive oil

Place sesame oil, tamari, sugar, ginger root and garlic in blender and blend until smooth. Stir-fry asparagus and carrots in heated olive oil for 1 minute; cover the pan and steam for 3 more minute. In a serving dish toss together asparagus, carrots and dressing.

Stuffed Mushrooms

Serves 8-10

Preheat oven to 350 degree F.

Pastry Dough Ingredients:

3 cups unbleached all-purpose flour (organic flour is my preference)

2 teaspoons baking powder (aluminum-free)

1 dash sea salt (sift together flour, baking powder and salt twice)

½ cup turbinado raw sugar, ground OR

¾ cup sweet butter (1½ sticks), cut into small pieces and chill

2 large eggs at room temperature (slightly whisk with lemon zest)

1 lemon zest (about 1 tablespoon grated lemon peel)

Mushroom Filling Ingredients:

1 red OR yellow onion, chopped

2 teaspoon ginger root, finely chopped

4 cloves of garlic, crushed

¼ cup olive oil

1 pound cremini "*button mushrooms*", cleaned and pat-dried

½ cup carrot, shredded OR julienned

1 pinch sea salt OR to taste

1 pinch black pepper, freshly ground

1 cup parsley, cleaned, chopped

1 teaspoon mint, dried

2 tablespoons arrowroot powder, to be dissolved in white wine

½ cup white wine

How to Make Pastry Dough to Wrap Mushrooms, please see Tips, "*pastry dough*", page 177. Roll out dough and cut into 2 ½-inch squares. One by one, fit each square of dough into small ramekin (to get some form). Add 1 teaspoon of sauté mushroom filling*. Gather the four corners of pastry wrap, pinch or twist dough to seal (use egg wash if needed to secure seal) and remove from ramekin. Place each mushroom wrap in a small muffin tin. Continue above directions until all dough squares are used. Place muffin tin in oven and bake for 8-10 minutes or until wraps are golden brown. Serve while still warm. You can offer some shredded cheese on the side.

*How to Sauté Mushroom Filling:

In a heavy-based skillet, lightly sauté onion, ginger, and garlic in heated olive oil. Then add mushroom, carrot, salt and pepper, parsley, and mint. Stir a few times until mushroom turns slightly golden color. Mix arrowroot with wine and add from corner of skillet. Simmer for a few minutes and stir until liquid evaporates (watch carefully to prevent food from burning). Let it cool and follow directions above for wrapping.

Variation: Cut two mini baguettes (French bread) in half lengthwise. Hollow inside of baguettes by scooping out half of bread to form baguette shells. In a heavy-based skillet, lightly sauté 2 shallots (finely chopped), and 2 cloves of garlic (finely chopped), in heated 3 tablespoons olive oil. Then add ½ pound cleaned cremini "*button mushrooms*" (sliced) and continue stir-fry for 3 minutes. In a small bowl mix together (2 teaspoons arrowroot powder in ¼ cup sherry wine, 1 cup milk, 1 teaspoon paprika, 1 pinch of nutmeg, ¼ teaspoon sea salt and ¼ teaspoon black pepper (freshly ground). Stir this mixture into mushroom pan. Let the mixture come to a simmer and simmer for 5-7 minutes over medium-low heat until sauce is thickened. Occasionally stir to prevent from burning. Arrange baguette shells on cookie sheet, spoon in mushrooms mixture and sprinkle with 1 tablespoon chopped basil leaves, and top with 1 cup shredded mild cheddar cheese (with smooth and creamy flavor). Place baguettes in preheated 400 degree oven and cook for 2 minutes or until cheese is melted and baguettes edge are slightly golden brown. Garnish with 2 teaspoons snipped chives (optional).

Tasty Seasonal Red Chili Beans

Serves 4

    1 cup small red navy beans, cooked

    1 cup "*tomato basil sauce*", see Tips, page189

    ½ teaspoon "*advieh-poloye*", ground, see Tips, page 185

    ¼ teaspoon sea salt OR to taste

    1 dash black cumin seeds

    1 pinch hot chili, ground

    1 pinch black pepper, freshly ground

    1 teaspoon paprika (optional)

    1 teaspoon honey OR turbinado raw sugar

    1 tablespoon lemon juice, freshly squeezed

In a pot, add all ingredients (navy beans, tomato basil sauce, advieh-poloye, salt, cumin seeds, chili, and black pepper, paprika, and honey and lemon juice). Simmer gently over medium heat in covered pot for 35 minutes or until it reaches desired thickness. Serve warm as a side dish.

Tofu

(A fabulous tofu dish for a fresh vegetable platter.)

Serves 4

    ¼ cup vegetable oil

    1 onion, chopped

    ½ inch ginger root, peeled, chopped

    4 cloves of garlic, chopped

    12 ounce extra firm tofu, drained and cut into 12 pieces (tofu made organically from sprouted soy beans is my preference)

    ¼ cup rich chicken broth (see Tips, chicken broth, page 178)

    2 teaspoons soy sauce OR to taste

    2 teaspoons rice vinegar (mix with soy sauce)

    Garnish: ¼ cup baby arugula, cleaned, pat dried

    2 tablespoons sesame seeds, slightly toasted

Heat a wok over medium heat until hot. Add oil, swirling to coat pan. Sauté onion, ginger and garlic in heated oil until nearly golden brown. Add tofu and continue to stir-fry for 2 minutes. Lower heat to low-medium. Add chicken broth and cover the wok. Let mixture simmer in covered wok for a few minutes until tofu is tender, but still crisp and firm. Stir in a mixture of soy sauce and rice vinegar. Transfer tofu to serving plate, garnish with baby arugula and sprinkle with sesame seeds.

Tasty Seasonal Okra

A simple but stunning side dish that can be used as a condiments with main dish.
Best made just before serving.

Serves 4

> 1 pound green okra
> 2 tablespoons chickpea (garbanzo) flour
> 1 teaspoon paprika flour
> 1 teaspoon sea salt OR to taste
> 1 dash peppercorn (black pepper), freshly ground
> 1 pinch cayenne powder
> ½ teaspoon cumin, ground
> 1 dash nutmeg, freshly ground
> 1 red onion, chopped
> 1 teaspoon ginger, freshly chopped
> 1-2 clove of garlic, chopped
> ¼ cup olive oil
> 1 mango, peeled, pitted, flesh cut into small pieces
> Juice of 1 lemon, freshly squeezed

Rinse the okra, pat-dry and trim top and bottom ends. Using a sharp paring knife, slice each okra pod lengthwise into 3 thin slices. In a small bowl combine and mix chickpea flour, paprika, salt, pepper, cayenne, cumin and nutmeg. Sprinkle the flour and spice mixture over the okra. Toss to coat okra slices and prevent them from sticking together. In a large heavy-based frying pan, stir-fry onion, ginger and garlic in heated olive oil for 2-3 minutes or until onion is translucent. Add okra and stir for 2 minutes over medium heat until the mixture turns slightly golden brown.

Blend mango and lemon juice in blender for a few seconds to puree, add to frying pan and mix with vegetables mixture. Cover the pan and let simmer over low-medium heat for 8 minutes or until okra is cooked. Stir occasionally to prevent burning. Serve immediately.

Note: When buying okra, please be sure it is fresh, firm and pods are under 4-inch long (larger pod can be very tough). Fresh and brightly colored green okra has sufficient moisture to mix well with spices during cooking.

Vegetable Dish with Carrots and Parsnips

Serves 6

Preheat oven to 300 degree F.

    1 extra-large onion cut into 8 sections OR 12 mini-onions
    4 cloves of garlic, chopped
    ¼ cup olive oil
    2 parsnips, peeled, thinly sliced
    4 carrots, peeled, thinly sliced
    2 extra-large tomatoes (heirloom tomatoes is preferable), peeled, diced
    ½ cup red drinking wine
    2 teaspoon flour (mix with red wine)
    1¼ teaspoon sea salt
    ¼ teaspoon black pepper, freshly ground
    ¼ teaspoon thyme
    2 rosemary sprigs

In a heavy-based frying-pan, sauté onion, garlic in heated olive oil. In an oven-proof casserole pot add sautéed onions, along with remaining ingredients (parsnip, carrot, tomatoes, wine and flour mixture, salt and pepper, thyme and rosemary). Bring content to simmer. Transfer covered pot into oven and cook for 25-30 minutes or until done. Stir gently prior to serving.

Ways to Make Classic Guacamole Dish
(A cold chunky mixture of avocado, vegetables, herbs and spices served as a side dish.)

Serves2-3

    2 large ripe Hass avocado, pitted, peeled, diced
    2 tablespoons red onion, diced
    2 medium red tomatoes, diced
    2 tablespoons lime OR lemon, freshly squeezed
    2 cloves of garlic, grated
    2 tablespoons, cilantro leaves, chopped
    ¼ teaspoon black cumin seeds, ground
    ¼ teaspoon sea salt OR to taste
    ¼ teaspoon black pepper, freshly ground
    1 teaspoon extra virgin olive oil

Gently mix all ingredients together and serve immediately to prevent discoloration of avocado.

Beverage

A Cold Beverage with Chia Seeds

(Seed your soul with vita-blend chia seeds)

This is a national Persian drink to celebrate "*ancient grain of the future*" during the summer. Chia seeds are from the mint family and have a pleasant nutty flavor. They are a nutrient-rich source of omega-3 fatty acids and dietary fibers. Chia seeds can be used in small amounts in beverages, sauces and soups.

(Please read **Chapter one**, page vi, for safe use).

Serves 2

    1 tablespoon certified organic, whole grain chia seeds, cleaned

    2 cups purified water + 1 cup for soaking chia seeds

    1 tablespoon sugar OR to taste

    1 teaspoon rosewater.

Soak chia seeds with 1 cup fresh water for 15 minutes or until chia-water mixture become gelatinous. In a medium saucepan, add 2 cups of water and sugar, bring to a boil and stir until sugar is dissolved and a light syrup forms. Remove from heat, add chia-water mixture and rosewater, cover saucepan and allow to cool. Adjust the thickness and sweetness with a few ice cubes and serve.

Variation: Chia-Ginger Drink, in a medium saucepan, bring 2 cups purified water and 1-inch ginger root (cut ginger in half) to boil. Remove the saucepan from heat, remove ginger, add 1 tablespoon (certified organic, whole grain) chia seeds, cover saucepan and allow to cool. Stir in juice of one lemon (freshly squeezed) and ½ pinch cayenne powder, prior to serve.

A Delightful Summery Beverage

Serves 2

    1 banana, thinly sliced

    1 mango, cut flesh into small pieces

    1 cup frozen watermelon balls (scoop watermelon flesh and freeze)

    1 tablespoon rose water

    1 teaspoon turbinado raw sugar powder (optional)

Blend all ingredients (banana, mango, watermelon, rosewater and sugar) in blender for a few seconds and serve.

Chocolate Milk

Serves 4

    4 cups milk
    8 mint sprigs, divided
    4-inch strips organic orange rind
    ½-inch cinnamon bark
    4-5 tablespoons semi dark chocolate, shaved

Chocolate milk to share

Place all ingredients except chocolate (milk, 4 mint sprigs, orange rind and cinnamon bark) in a medium size saucepan. Gradually bring content to simmer. Turn off heat and cover the saucepan for 4 minutes. Remove the mint sprigs, orange rind and cinnamon bark and stir in chocolate until completely dissolved. Pour into mugs, garnish with remaining mint sprig and serve hot.

Cooling Sunrise Lemonade

Serves 2   Preheat oven to 350 degree F.

    2 organic lemons, thinly sliced
    1 vanilla string beans
    2 teaspoons turbinado OR raw sugar
    2 cups spring water

Place sliced lemons and vanilla beans in a large pan. Sprinkle with sugar and add water. Transfer to oven. Cook for 10-15 minutes. Strain the liquid, cool and serve.

Cucumber Drink

Serves 2

    ½ cup cucumber, peeled, grated
    ½ cup coconut milk
    ½ cup plain yogurt
    1 dash sea salt
    1 dash black pepper OR cayenne pepper
    1 dash thyme
    ½ teaspoons brown sugar

Blend all ingredients (cucumber, coconut milk, yogurt, salt and pepper, thyme and sugar) together in a blender for a few seconds until smooth. Chill and enjoy this natural drink.

Note: You can make an excellent blended drink from cucumber, apple, and celery/carrot.

Cucumber and Avocado Smoothie

Serves 2

    1 cucumber, peeled, diced

    1 avocado, peeled, pitted, diced

    Juice of 1 lemon OR lime, freshly squeezed

    1 dash sea salt

    1 dash cayenne

    ½ cup of each assorted vegetables (kale, baby bok choy and broccoli floret)

Blend all ingredients (cucumber, avocado, lemon juice, salt, cayenne, kale, baby bok choy, and broccoli) together in blender for a few seconds or until smooth. Chill prior to serving.

Cucumber and Spinach Smoothie

Serves 2

    1 medium cucumber, peeled, diced

    1 cup spinach leaves, cleaned, chopped

    1 cup plain yogurt (unflavored)

    1 teaspoon ginger root, peeled, chopped

    1 dash sea salt (optional)

Blend all ingredients (cucumber, spinach, yogurt, ginger and salt) together in blender for a few seconds until smooth. Chill prior to serving.

Cucumber and Pear Smoothie

Serves 2

    1 cucumber, peeled, cut into small pieces

    2 pears, peeled, cored, diced

    2 cups spinach, cleaned, chopped

    Juice of 1 lemon, freshly squeezed

    Zest of 1 organic lemon, freshly grated

    ½ inch ginger root, peeled, finely chopped

Blend all ingredients (cucumber, pears, spinach, lemon juice, lemon zest, ginger) together in blender for a few seconds until smooth. Chill prior to serving.

Cooling Punch with Borage for Hot Day

(Try this blended herbs punch on hot days)

Serves 10

    10 cups fresh spring water

    2 lemon balm sprigs

    1 mint sprig

    ½ inch cinnamon bark

    1 medium organic orange peel*

    2 teaspoons borage dried leaves**

    Juice of 1 lemon, freshly squeezed

    1 tablespoon honey OR to taste

    Garnish: 2 mint sprigs

In a large saucepan bring water to a boil. Stir in all ingredients except lemon juice and honey (lemon balm, mint, cinnamon bark, orange peel and borage). Cover the saucepan tightly and let it cool completely (about 45 minutes). Strain mixture into pitcher, add lemon juice and honey and mix. Refrigerate for several hours. When you are ready to serve, pour into tall glasses with several ice cubes and garnish with mint.

*Peel freshly harvested orange in circle pattern.

**You may wrap borage dried leaves in muslin cloth, tie tightly and place in boiling water. They will be removed when mixture is strained.

Fruit and Carrot Puree Blend

Serves 2

    1 ¼ cups apple cider

    2 large apples, peeled, cored, diced

    2 carrots, peeled, sliced, diced

    2 pears, peeled, cored, diced

    2 teaspoons rosewater

    1 dash cardamom

Blend ingredients (apple cider, apples, carrots, pears, rosewater and cardamom) in power-blender for 30 seconds, chill, and serve.

Variation 1: To power blender, blend together two banana, 1 mango, 1 teaspoon acai powder, and 1 teaspoon rosewater. Garnish with shaved dark sweet chocolate.

Variation 2: To blender, blend together 1 cup apple cider, 2 apples (peeled and diced), juice of 1 orange and ½ lemon, and 1 pinch of each (cinnamon, turmeric, cayenne). Chill and serve.

Fruity Puree Blend

Serves 2

> 1 cup orange juice, freshly squeezed
>
> 1 cup apple puree
>
> 1 cup pear puree
>
> 1 cup banana puree
>
> 1 cup blueberries
>
> 1 teaspoon lime juice, freshly squeezed

Blend orange juice, purees (apple, pear and banana), blueberries, and lime juice together in blender for a few seconds until smooth. Chill prior to serving.

Fruit and Herbal Blend

Serves 2

> 1 pear, peeled, cored, diced
>
> 1 cucumber, peeled, diced
>
> 1 cup parsley, cleaned, chopped
>
> 1 sprig of each herb (sage, thyme, mint and rosemary OR lavender flower)
>
> 1 pinch sea salt (optional)

Blend all ingredients (pear, cucumber, parsley, sage, thyme, mint, rosemary and salt) together in blender for a few seconds until smooth. Chill prior to serving.

Lassi with Yogurt

Serves 2

> 1 cup plain yogurt (unflavored yogurt), strained OR Greek plain yogurt
>
> 2 cups water
>
> ¼ teaspoon sea salt
>
> 1 dash black pepper, freshly ground
>
> 1 dash black cumin seeds, freshly ground
>
> 1 teaspoon chocolate mint
>
> 1 teaspoon ginger root, peeled, chopped
>
> 1 teaspoon fruit sugar OR honey

Place all ingredients (yogurt, water, salt, pepper, cumin, chocolate mint, ginger, and sugar) together in blender and run until light and smooth; chill and shake prior to serving.

Persian-style Quince-Lime Drink

Persian cooks often create luxurious beverages and cuisine creations for a dining feast.
Quince not only has a wonderful aroma and taste it also provides medicinal benefits.

Serves 8

>   8 cups spring water
>   4 quinces, peeled, quartered*
>   ¼ cup culinary rose petals
>   2 tablespoons honey OR turbinado raw sugar to taste
>   Juice of 1 lime, freshly squeezed

In a 4 quarts pot, bring water to boil. Add quince, rose petals, cover the pot and reduce the heat to medium-low heat. Simmer for 1½ -2 hours or until quince is fork tender. Strain off the liquid and discard the solids. Add honey, and lime juice to liquid and continue to cook for 5 more minutes. Check the consistency and sweetness and make adjustments if necessary. Let cool and serve with ice cubes. Enjoy a royal homemade quince drink.

*For easier cutting you may wrap quince in aluminum foil, place in ovenproof dish and transfer into preheated 200 degree F. oven and bake for 45 minutes (to soften without cooking the quince).

Note 1: Instead of cooking on the stove top, you may cook quince with water in a 4 quarts ovenproof pot in a 300 degree F. oven for a shorter period of time.

Note: 2: If you blend cooked quince pulps (without skin and seeds) with a little sugar and *"quince-lime drink"* in a power blender and freeze, the mixture you have is called quince sherbet.

Smoothie with Mango

Serve 4

>   2 mangos, peeled, seeded, cut into small pieces
>   1 cup cherries, pitted, halved
>   1 pear, peeled, seeded, cut into small pieces
>   ¼ cup almond flour
>   ¼ cup hazelnut flour
>   1 teaspoon Arabic gum (optional)

Place mango, cherries, and pear into blender and run for a few seconds to make juice. Pour into a heavy-based saucepan. Mix almond flour, hazelnuts flour and Arabic gum together and add to saucepan. Place over low-medium heat and bring to a simmer; simmer for 25 minutes or until done; stir occasionally at the beginning and more frequently as mixture thickens. Cool and serve.

Smoothie with Orange and Pineapple

Serves 2

   4 ice cubes

   1 orange, peeled, seeded, cut into small pieces

   1 slice freshly cut pineapple (½-inch round from center of pineapple), peeled, cored, cut into small pieces

   1 small banana, peeled, cut into small pieces

   1 cup baby spinach leaves, cleaned, pat-dried

   1 pinch sea salt

   ½ cup celery, cleaned, cut into small pieces

   2 tablespoons lime juice, freshly squeezed

   ½ teaspoon honey OR another sweetener (optional)

Place all ingredients in power-blender. Blend for a few seconds until smooth. Chill and serve.

Variation: Smoothie with Pineapple and Almond milk: In power-blender add 1 cup pineapple juice, ½ cup almond milk, 1 banana (cut into small pieces), ½ teaspoon acai powder and 1 dash vanilla powder (optional). Blend for a few seconds until smooth. Chill and serve.

Smoothie with Orange and Celery

(This is my whole day energizer drink)

Serves 4

   4 ice cubes, crushed

   Juice of 3 oranges

   2 celery stalks, cleaned, sliced

   6 oz. baby spinach, cleaned

   1 avocado, peeled, pitted, sliced

   1 cup almond slivers

   1 cucumber, peeled, sliced

   1 pinch sea salt

   1 pinch cayenne pepper

   1½ tablespoons lemon juice, freshly squeezed

   1½ teaspoons acai powder

Place all ingredients (ice cubes, orange juice, celery, spinach, avocado, almond, cucumber, salt, cayenne pepper, lemon juice and acai powder) in power-blender. Blend for a few seconds until smooth. Chill and serve. Refresh your thirst with this bright green super nutrition beverage.

Smoothie with Carrots and Ginger

(Irresistible beverage in color, taste and vitamins)

Serves 3-4

> 2 carrots, peeled, sliced and diced
> Juice of 2 oranges, freshly squeezed
> 2 ice cubes, crushed
> 1 teaspoon ginger root, peeled, diced
> 1 apple, peeled, cored, diced
> 1 mango, peeled, pitted, diced
> Juice of 1 lemon, freshly squeezed
> 1 organic lemon's peel, freshly peeled, cut in small pieces

Place all ingredients (carrots, orange juice, ice cubes, ginger, apple, mango, lemon juice and lemon peel) in power-blender. Blend for a few seconds until thick and smooth. Chill and serve. This delicious smoothie gives you a natural boost.

Smoothie with Almonds and Carob

Serves 2

> ½ cup almond milk OR regular milk
> ¼ cup + 1 tablespoon almond flour/meal
> 2 teaspoons carob powder
> 1 teaspoon mint, dried
> ½ teaspoon brown sugar

Place all ingredients (almond milk, almond flour, carob powder, mint, and brown sugar) in blender and blend for a few seconds or until smooth. You may serve warm or chill.

Smoothie with Almonds and Flax seeds

Serves 2

> 1 cup strawberries, cleaned, stemmed, pat-dried, halved
> Juice of 1 medium orange, freshly squeezed
> 1 tablespoon almond flour/meal
> 1 apple, peeled, cored, diced
> 1 teaspoon flax seeds, freshly ground
> 1 dash sea salt
> 1 teaspoon culinary rose petals, dried

Blend all ingredients (strawberries, orange juice, almond flour, apple, flax seeds, salt, rose petals) in blender. Blend for a few seconds or until smooth. Chill and serve.

Smoothie with Grapes and Parsley

Serves 2

  1 cup grapes (sour green grapes are my preference)
  1 cup Italian parsley, green leaves, cleaned, chopped
  1 apple, peeled, cored, diced
  1 avocado, peeled, pitted, cut into small pieces
  2 kiwi, peeled, thinly sliced, divided
  1 dash sea salt

Blend all ingredients except a few kiwi slices (grapes, parsley, apple, avocado, kiwi and salt) in blender for a few seconds or until smooth. Chill, garnish with sliced kiwi and serve.

Smoothie with Lettuce

This recipe may help the body detoxify itself more efficiently by giving superior nutrients to enjoy for amazing energy and natural healing power.

Serves 2

  4 ice cubes
  1 orange, peeled, seeded, cut into small pieces
  Juice of ½ lime, freshly squeezed
  1 teaspoon olive oil
  1 clove garlic, chopped
  1 clove ginger root, chopped
  1 tablespoon basil, chopped
  1 dash sea salt OR to taste
  1 dash black pepper, freshly ground
  1 teaspoon lemon verbena, chopped
  1 teaspoon culinary dried rose hips
  1 teaspoon honey
  1 cup parsley leaves, cleaned, chopped
  2 cups heart of Romaine lettuce, chopped

Place all ingredients (ice cubes, oranges, lime juice, olive oil, garlic, ginger root, basil, salt, black pepper, lemon verbena, rose hips, honey, parsley and lettuce) in power-blender, blend until smooth and serve.

Smoothie with Mango and Kale

Serves 4+

  6 ice cubes, crushed
  1 cup mango, peeled, pitted, diced
  1 cup pineapple, diced
  2 apples, peeled, cored, diced
  ½ cup coconuts meat, shredded
  6 oz. kale leaves, cleaned
  ½ dash sea salt

Place all ingredients (ice cubes, mango, pineapple, apples, coconut, kale and salt) in power-blender. Blend until smooth and serve.

Smoothie with Strawberries and Peaches

Serves 2

  2 cups strawberries, wash, pat-dry, stemmed, thinly slice, and freeze for 2 hours
  1 cup peaches, peeled, pitted, diced
  1 large apple, peeled, cored, diced
  1½ cup mango, peeled, pitted, diced

Blend all ingredients (strawberries, peaches, apples, and mango) in blender for 30 seconds and serve *"fruity nectar"* chilled.

Smoothie with Fruits and Oat-Crumbs

Serves 2 +

  1 red apple, peeled, cored, diced
  Juice of 1 small orange, freshly squeezed
  1 small red mango, peeled, pitted, diced
  2 teaspoons lemon zest, freshly grated
  2 tablespoons lime juice, freshly squeezed
  ¼ cup *"oat-crumbs"*, divided. See Tips, page 181

Place all ingredient except oat crumbs (apple, orange juice, mango, lemon zest, and lime juice) in blender. Run for 30 seconds or until thoroughly mixed and smooth, chill for one hour prior to serving.   Fill two glass with chilled smoothie and top each with 2 tablespoons *"oat-crumbs"*.

Spinach and Lime Smoothie

Serves 2-3

     1½ cup coconut milk (see coconut milk page 78)

     1 tablespoon kaffir lime, bruised OR 2 teaspoons organic lime zest, freshly grated

     ½ teaspoon ginger root, chopped

     2 medium apples, cored, diced

     1 cup baby spinach leaf, chopped

     ½ cup baby kale leaf, chopped

     1 tablespoon fresh mint leaf, chopped

     2 tablespoons fresh basil leaf, chopped

     1 dash sea salt OR to taste

     1 dash black pepper, freshly ground OR cayenne

     Garnish: A few sliced apple OR basil sprig

Place the first 4 ingredients (coconut milk, kaffir lime, ginger root and apples) in power blender. Blend for a few seconds until smooth to make a smoothie base. Add all other ingredients (spinach, kale, mint, basil, salt and pepper). Blend again until smooth. Taste and adjust seasoning if necessary. Cool and garnish with sliced apple and serve. Enjoy a unique and satisfying beverage.

Strawberries and Orange Smoothie

(Enjoy this refreshing, savory sorbet with its beautiful color and granular texture)

Serves 2

     4 ice cubes

     1½ cups strawberries, cleaned, stemmed, sliced, frozen for 2 hours

     Juice of 1 orange, freshly squeezed

     Zest of ½ lemon, freshly graded

     1 tablespoon turbinado raw sugar OR to taste

     Garnish:

     2 tablespoon pistachio, coarsely chopped OR your favorite nuts topping

     A few orange blossom (optional)

Place ingredients (ice cubes, strawberries, orange juice, lemon zest and sugar) in power-blender (such as Vita-mix). Blend for a few seconds or until semi smooth. Pour in glass and garnish with pistachio and orange blossom and serve immediately.

Summery Cool Drink

Serves 2

    2 ice cubes

    2 cups natural carbonated mineral water (Perrier natural water is my preference)

    Juice of 1 lime, freshly squeezed

    ½ teaspoon honey (optional)

Combine ingredients and pour into tall glasses. Enjoy!

Sunshine Cool Drink

Serves 2

Sunshine cool drink

    4 ice cubes

    3 carrots, peeled, grated

    1 teaspoon ginger root, grated

    1 banana (about 1 cup), thinly sliced

    1 ripe mango (about 1 cup), peeled, pitted, chopped

    1 tablespoon maple syrup (optional)

    1 teaspoon mint, chopped

    Garnish: 2 mint sprigs

Place ingredients (ice cubes, carrots, ginger, banana, mango, maple syrup and mint) in power-blender. Run until juiced. Pour into tall glasses and garnish with mint sprig.

Tasty Treat Watermelon Drink

Serves 2

    1½ cup frozen watermelon balls (scoop watermelon flesh and freeze for several hours)

    Juice of 1 lime, freshly squeezed

    1-2 teaspoons powdered sugar (turbinado raw sugar is my preference)

    1 teaspoon rosewater

    1 teaspoon kaffir lime leaves, chopped

Place ingredients (watermelon, lime juice, sugar, rosewater and kaffir lime) in power-blender. Run until juiced. Pour into glasses and garnish with basil sprig (optional).

Breads and Breakfast

Breads are a major energy source in many countries; most are highly nutritious,
providing protein, iron, calcium, and B vitamins.

Breakfast is the most important meal of the day. When you start your day with a
good breakfast containing 100% rye bread* it gives you energy
that last through the morning and into the next meal.
*Several study from researchers show that
using whole-grain rye-bread
increases the feeling of
lasting fullness,
compared to
other
whole grains
such as wheat bread.
Whole wheat bread contains almost twice as much soluble
fiber as white bread (fiber helps increase intestinal mobility).

Ways to make "*oatmeal*" for breakfast, Tips, page 193.

This hot cereal that is made from highly nutritious grain
(oats kernel), is excellent for breakfast and
your kitchen library today
and tomorrow!

Buckwheat Pancake-Bread

Buckwheat groats* one of world's real amazing food
You can have lovely pancake/bread from buckwheat *gluten free flour*

Serves 3-4

> 1 cup buckwheat flour
> ½ cup oat flour
> 1 cup goat milk
> 2 egg whites, slightly beaten
> 3 tablespoons olive oil plus olive oil for brushing the pancake pan OR skillet
> ¼ teaspoon sea salt

Whisk all the ingredients (buckwheat flour, oat flour, milk, eggs whites, olive oil and salt) vigorously until the batter is completely smooth (or alternative use blender). Refrigerate overnight. Next day heat a non-stick-griddle, over low-medium heat; when it is hot, add ½ cup of batter to the center of pan and swirl quickly until the bottom of pan is covered with batter. Cook the pancake for a few minutes or until the top is slightly moist and underneath is golden brown. With small wooden spatula loosen the edges. With a larger wooden spatula slide under pancake and then gently flip it over, and cook for a few more minutes or until done. Repeat this with the remaining batter until finished.

Variation: Crepe (thin pancake) with Cheese/Chocolate/Jam Filling: If you would like to make crepe, add ¼ cup more milk to the above batter and blend well. Follow the same procedure as for pancake (you may use a square non-stick-griddle). After crepe is done, place a small amount (2-3 ounces) of shredded cheese (or shaved chocolate or jam) in the center of crepe, and fold up the edges (four sides) of the crepe onto the cheese. Transfer crepe onto platter and serve while still warm.

Buckwheat Groats, are fruit seeds that you can substitute for grains. Whole buckwheat like all grains should be rinsed thoroughly under running water before cooking, and any dirt or debris should be removed. In general when you are cooking, for 1 cup of buckwheat, add 2 cups boiling spring water/broth and a small amount of sea salt. After the liquid comes to a boil, turn down the heat, cover and simmer for 20-25 minutes or until done (almost cooked like rice). You can cook and serve buckwheat in many different ways. One way is to cook and serve as an alternative to rice, another way is to make into a porridge.

Breakfast with Ancient Grain Millet

Serves 4

> 2 cups cooked millet*
>
> 2 cups milk
>
> 2 pears, peel, core, and grate (Bosc pear is preferable)
>
> ¼ teaspoon cardamom seeds, ground
>
> ¼ teaspoon vanilla extract
>
> 1 dash cinnamon
>
> 1 teaspoon honey or another sweetener (optional)

In a medium size saucepan combine all ingredients except honey and simmer for 10 minutes or until well cooked. Add honey and mix together or blend in blender to make a nice pudding.

*Millet cooks like rice, in a large saucepan add 1 cup cleaned millet, 2 ½ cups spring water, and 1 dash of salt. Let the mixture come to a simmer and simmer in covered pan at low temperature for 25 minutes or until millet is cooked. Stir occasionally to prevent burning.

"Haleemy Oat" for Good Breakfast

Serves 6

> 1½ cups rolled oats OR precooked steel cut-oats
>
> 4 cups spring water
>
> 5 cups (condensed) milk
>
> 8 soft dates (medjool-soft date is preferable), pitted, cut into small pieces
>
> 6 tablespoons carob powder
>
> ¼ cup hazelnuts, ground
>
> ¼ cup coconuts, shredded
>
> 1 dash salt
>
> 1 tablespoon brown sugar
>
> 2 tablespoons rosewater
>
> **Garnish:** A few pistachio nuts and chocolate mint sprigs (optional)

Rinse lightly rolled oats with spring water. In a large saucepan bring milk to simmer and stir in oats, dates, carob powder, hazelnuts, coconuts and salt. Simmer in partially covered saucepan for 10 minutes over low-medium heat and stir occasionally. Add sugar and rosewater. Simmer for a few more minutes. Adjust the seasoning and thickening if needed. Garnish with pistachio and mint.

Oatmeal Fruity Breakfast

Serves 2-3

> 1 cup old fashioned rolled oats
> 1 pear, peeled, cored, cut into small pieces
> 1 red apple, peeled, cored, cut into small pieces
> 1 cup blueberries
> 1 teaspoon honey
> 1 teaspoon rosewater
> 1 dash cardamom
> 1 dash sea salt OR to taste
> 4 cups water

Place all ingredients in a medium saucepan. Bring to simmer, and simmer over low-medium heat. Stir occasionally for 8-10 minutes or until done. Serve warm, to give kids a lift!

Porridge with Chocolate Topping

Serves 6

Preheat oven to 275 degree F.

> 5 cups spring water
> 1½ cups Scottish oat, lightly toasted (see Glossary, oat, page 231)
> 1 pinch sea salt
> 4 cups milk, concentrated (heat milk slowly, without boiling until reduced to 2 cups)
> ¼ cup almond meal/flour
> ½ cup raisins
> 1 tablespoon raw honey
> 2 tablespoons rosewater
> 1 dash cardamom seeds, ground
> **Topping:**

¼ cup +2 tablespoons semi sweet dark chocolate, shaved

In a large sized ovenproof pot, bring water to boil. Add oatmeal and salt. Bring contents to simmer over low-medium heat. Continue simmering while stirring occasionally to prevent burning. Meantime, in a medium-sized mixing bowl, mix together milk, almond meal, raisins, honey, rosewater and cardamom. Add this to partially cooked oatmeal mixture and stir well. Bring the content to simmer, transfer uncovered pot into oven and cook for 30 minutes. After 15 minutes, remove pot and stir with a wooden spatula; test for consistency, adjust if needed, and continue to cook in the oven for 10 more minutes or until done. Remove from oven and spoon porridge* into individual bowl, top with chocolate and serve while still warm.

***Porridge**, is a thick pudding like dish, made with oatmeal (a cereal grains from the grass family that yield an edible seeds), milk and/or water and sugar. Often eaten hot for breakfast.

Quinoa with Oat and Chocolate

(A good breakfast pudding for longevity)

Serves 6

Quinoa with oat and chocolate

    4 red apples, peeled, diced
    4 cups milk
    4 dates, pitted, diced
    ½ cup quinoa whole grain flour,
    see Glossary (GF grains), page 219
    ½ cup rolled oat
    2 eggs, slightly beaten
    1 cup semi dark baking chocolate, shaved
    2 tablespoons maple syrup
    1 tablespoon olive oil
    1 teaspoon vanilla extract
    1 dash salt

Garnish: 2 fresh strawberries (sliced), 2 tablespoons almond slivers, and mint sprigs

To the power-blender add all ingredients (apples, milk, dates, quinoa flour, oats, eggs, chocolate, maple syrup, olive oil, vanilla and salt), blend for 1-2 minutes or until soft creamy liquid is formed (you may do several batches for convenient blending). Pour into top of double boiler and fill bottom 2/3 full of water. Bring water to a boil and lower the heat, place lid on top of double boiler. Let the mixture come to simmer and cook over medium-low heat for 20 minutes or until pudding is done; stirring gently occasionally. When done, pour into small bowl and garnish with sliced strawberries, almonds slivers and mint.

Variation: Quinoa Thin Flat Bread: In a small mixing bowl, mix ¼ cup of quinoa whole grain flour and 1/3 cup whole milk, ¼ teaspoon sea salt and ¼ teaspoon black seeds (nigella). Blend together to make a smooth batter and let mixture rest for a 30 minutes. Stir in 2 teaspoons olive oil. On a hot non-stick griddle, add quinoa batter to the center of griddle and level it. Wait until some small bubbles appear, flip it over and cook for a few minutes or until done.

Sunrise Flat Bread

Chapatti/roti is a common flat bread in India. It is made of whole wheat flour with natural fibers. It is nutrition, tasty and easy to make. The flour is called "atta"*.

Serves 4-5

    1 cup atta* flour, plus extra flour for rolling chapatti
    ½ cup spring water, plus extra water for rolling chapatti

In a medium size bowl, sift flour, gradually add water to make dough. Knead by hands for 1 minute and be sure flour is fully and evenly hydrated; dough should be medium soft and not sticky (if sticky, knead in a little more flour). Form dough into ball and place in bowl, cover loosely and let dough rest for several minutes.

Lightly floured board surface (or a raised marble stone), and slightly moisten your fingers. Cut a piece of dough (the size of gulf ball), place in palm of your hands and form into a ball. Dip dough lightly into flour and roll out from center to sides to make about a 5-inch round. Fold dough, dip lightly into flour, make a ball and roll again to form chapatti. Cut off another piece of dough and repeat process until all the dough is used.

Heat tava** until hot. Let chapatti cook on tava for 30 seconds; turn over with the help of tongs and cook for another 30 seconds. Quickly rotate chapatti back and forth on the tava a few times so it browns evenly on both sides until done (you may with a tong, gently, push the edge to help bread to puff up during cooking). Your chapatti bread should be light, fluffy and soft. Place chapatti in "chapatti warmer" and cover until next one is ready.

Variation: Thin Flat Bread: In a small mixing bowl, mix ¼ cup atta* flour/quinoa flour, and ½ cup whole milk, ¼ teaspoon sea salt and ¼ teaspoon black seeds (nigella). Blend together to make a smooth batter and let mixture rest for 30 minutes. Stir in 1 teaspoon olive oil. On a hot non-stick, 9-inch, griddle, add batter to the center of griddle and level it. Wait until some small bubbles appear, flip it over and cook for a few minutes or until done.

*Atta: It is a very fine-milled whole wheat flour, with a high ratio of gluten to starch. It is available at Indian markets.

**Tava: A cast-iron frying-pan (a round single handle griddle of cast iron with smooth surface called "tava"; traditionally is used to make chapatti bread.

Note 1: Deep fried chapatti/roti is called "*puri*". If you stuff roti prior to cook and fill in with a small amount of cooked mashed potatoes and onion or other similar vegetables and brushed vegetables lightly with ghee (clarified butter), then fold and roll out again and fry; it is called "*aloo paratha*".

Sweet Potato for Breakfast
(Fast, easy and tasty)

Serves 3

> 3 eggs, slightly beaten
> 1 tablespoon onion, chopped
> ¼ cup sweet potatoes, partially cooked, peeled, grated
> ½ teaspoon ginger root, grated
> ¼ teaspoon sea salt OR to taste
> 1 dash black pepper, freshly ground
> ¼ cup olive oil

In a small mixing bowl, mix all ingredients except olive oil (eggs, onion, sweet potato, ginger, salt and pepper). Pour batter, all at once into a frying-pan (about 6-inch round) containing heated olive oil. Cover the pan for a few minutes until set, and the edges are slightly golden brown (watch carefully so it does not burn). Remove the cover, divide omelet into quarter for easier turning. With a flat and small spatula turn omelet over and let it cook on the other side for a few more minutes. Excellent.

Sweet Potato Pancake

Serves 2-3

> ¼ cup sweet potato, partially cooked
> ¼ cup milk
> 2 tablespoons olive oil, OR vegetable oil, divided
> 2 eggs, slightly beaten
> 1 teaspoon rice flour
> 1-inch ginger root, peeled, grated
> 1 teaspoon lemon zest, freshly grated
> 1 dash cinnamon and 1 dash sea salt
> 2-3 tablespoons pure maple syrup

To a blender add potato, milk, 1 tablespoon olive oil, eggs, rice flour, ginger, zest, cinnamon, and salt. Blend for 30 seconds or until all ingredients are thoroughly mixed. Refrigerate for 30 minutes. Heat a heavy-based pancake pan/skillet over high heat until hot. Remove from heat and add 1½ teaspoon vegetable oil, swirl oil around the pan; return pan to heat and pour in half the batter (with the help of pitcher). Cover the pan and cook for 1 minute over medium-high heat. Uncover and continue to cook for 4 more minutes. Turn pancake over and cook 2 more minutes. Serve warm with maple/honey syrup. Repeat with second pancake.

Sweet Quinoa Bread

(Divine Sweet Bread)

Serves 8-10

Preheat oven to 350 degree F.　　Grease and lightly flour two 9 ½ x 5 x 3-inch loaf pans.

- 2½ cup whole grain quinoa flour
- 2 teaspoons baking soda
- ½ teaspoon baking powder (optional)
- ¾ teaspoon sea salt OR to taste
- ½ teaspoon cinnamon, ground
- 1½ cup apple sauce (see Tips, how to make "*apple sauce*", page 177)
- 1 medium green apple, peeled, grated (about ½ cup)
- ¼ cup olive oil
- ¼ cup brown sugar, packed
- ½ cup raisins, cleaned
- ½ teaspoon vanilla extract
- 3 medium eggs, slightly beaten
- ½ cup walnuts, coarsely ground

In a large mixing bowl, mix dry ingredients (flour, baking soda, baking powder, salt, and cinnamon). Sift twice. In another mixing bowl, mix wet ingredients except walnuts (apple sauce, apple, olive oil, brown sugar, raisins, vanilla and eggs) together. With a wooden spoon stir dry ingredients into wet ingredients; make sure mixture is smooth and free from lumps. Fold in walnuts. Pour into loaf pans, level the top and allow to stand for a minute. Place loaf pans on middle rack of preheated oven and bake for 35-40 minutes or until toothpick comes out clean. Cool for 10 minutes prior to removing from pan.

Note: If bread appears to be rising unevenly, rotate loaf pan.

See Glossary, apple, page 201

Wholesome Bread

(Morning Star Breakfast)

Serves 8-10

Preheat oven to 350 degree F.   Grease and lightly flour a 9 ½ x 5 x 3-inch loaf pan.

Bread:

2 cups unbleached all-purpose flour (organic flour is my preference)

1 teaspoon baking powder

½ teaspoon baking soda

¼ teaspoon sea salt OR to taste

½ cup (1 stick) sweet butter, softened

½ cup turbinado raw sugar

3 medium eggs, slightly beaten

1 tablespoon, squeezed lemon juice

Zest of 1 organic lemon, freshly grated

½ teaspoon vanilla extract

2 large red apples, skinned, cored, minced (about 3 cups)

Topping:

2 tablespoons all-purpose flour

1 tablespoon Ceylon cinnamon, ground

¼ teaspoon nutmeg

1 tablespoon butter, cut into very small pieces

1 tablespoon turbinado raw sugar + 2 tablespoons brown sugar

To prepare the bread: In a mixing bowl, combine dry ingredients, flour, baking powder, baking soda and salt. Sift 2-3 times and set aside. Cream butter and sugar until light and fluffy, mix in eggs, lemon juice, lemon zest and vanilla. Gradually spoon flour mixture into butter mixture (you may use stand mixer instead of hand mixer) until all ingredients are incorporated and moistened. Gently stir in apples until all ingredients are combined and mixed well.

To prepare the topping: Combine all ingredients except brown sugar, in a small bowl mix (flour, cinnamon, nutmeg, butter and raw sugar) until it resembles bread crumbs, set aside. Spoon ½ of bread batter into loaf-pan, sprinkle with ½ of topping mixture. Spoon remaining bread batter into pan. Evenly sprinkle the batter with remaining topping mixture and 2 tablespoons brown sugar. Place pan on lower-middle oven rack and bake for 55-60 minutes or until a wooden toothpick inserted in the center comes out clean. Remove immediately and cool.

Zucchini Walnut Bread

(The bread is less sweet than most quick breads. The zucchini adds a lovely color and texture)

Serves 10   Grease and lightly flour 9 x 5 x 3-inch loaf-pan.

Preheat oven to 350 degree F.

> 4 tablespoons turbinado raw sugar, divided
>
> 1 tablespoon cinnamon, divided
>
> 2 eggs, slightly beaten
>
> 2 tablespoons olive oil
>
> ¾ cup sour cream OR Greek yogurt
>
> 1 ½ teaspoons baking soda (to be mixed with sour cream for 10 minutes)
>
> ½ teaspoon vanilla extract
>
> 1 ½ cups organic zucchini, trim off ends, brush the skin and rinse under water, pat-dry, shred
>
> 2 cups all-purpose flour (organic, unbleached flour is my preference)
>
> 1 teaspoon sea salt OR to taste
>
> ½ cup walnut, coarsely chopped

Mix 1 tablespoon sugar and ½ tablespoon cinnamon together, evenly sprinkle half of this mixture over the greased bottom of loaf-pan; tap to remove any excess.

In a medium mixing bowl combine and mix wet ingredients (eggs, olive oil, sour cream mixture, vanilla and zucchini), set aside. In a large mixing bowl, sift dry ingredients (flour, sea salt, remaining half of sugar and cinnamon mixture and 3 tablespoon sugar). Gradually stir dry ingredients into wet ingredients. Fold in walnuts. Spoon batter into loaf-pan and spread evenly. Place on the middle rack of preheated oven and bake for 40-45 minutes or until a toothpick inserted in the center comes out clean. Let cool in the loaf pan for 10 minutes before removing. Cool completely on cooling rack prior to slicing. Take this beautiful bread to your neighbor and friend.

Note: If bread appears to be rising unevenly, rotate pan. A sliced of zucchini bread can be toasted very well.

Cake and Cookies
Persian-style Diamond Cake

Serves 18-20

Preheat oven to 350 degree F.   Grease and lightly flour 8 x 8 x 2-inch square baking pan

¾ cup sweet butter (1½ sticks)

2 cups (turbinado) raw powdered sugar, divided

4 eggs, beat egg whites and egg yolks in separate bowls

1 cup plain yogurt (unflavored yogurt), at room temperature

1 teaspoon honey

1½ cup pastry flour OR unbleached all-purpose flour

½ cup rice flour (super fine flour)

1 tablespoon baking powder

½ teaspoon cardamom powder

Syrup:

1 cup water

1 tablespoon rose water

Garnish: ¼ cup of powdered sugar, and ¼ cup unsalted pistachio

Cream butter and 1 cup sugar in a stand mixer bowl, using flat beater/dough hook (starting at low speed and gradually increasing speed to #4) until light and fluffy. Stir in egg white and egg yolks alternately with yogurt and honey. Mix and sift pastry flour, rice flour, baking powder and cardamom; gradually spoon flour mixture into butter mixture (start with low speed first, scrape the bowl with wooden spoon as needed) until all ingredients incorporate. Pour batter into baking pan, bake on lower rack for 30 minutes then transfer to middle rack, bake for 5 minutes or until the top is golden brown and a wooden toothpick inserted in the center comes out clean and if gently pressed springs back. Remove cake from the oven immediately.

Meanwhile, in a heavy based saucepan, place 1 cup of water and 1 cup remaining sugar. Cook over medium heat, stirring often and let simmer for 10-15 minutes or until sugar dissolved and the syrup concentrated down to about 1 cup. Add rosewater and bring to boil. Boil rapidly for 2 minutes then cool syrup by placing pan in cold water-bath.

Spoon cooled syrup over hot cake. Cool thoroughly and cut into diamond shapes. Sprinkle with powdered sugar and press one pistachio in the center of each piece and serve.

Almond Cookies

Serves 10

Preheat oven to 350 degree F.   Medium size oven proof flat tray with holes in the bottom (so the air can circulate around cookies while baking)

> 2 cups sweet almonds, blanched (see Tips, almond blanching, page 172)
>
> 4 tablespoons turbinado raw sugar
>
> 1 tablespoon maple sugar
>
> 2 teaspoons vanilla extract (see note 1)
>
> 1 dash sea salt
>
> 1-2 large egg white, whisk, used for egg-wash
>
> 1 cup almond slivers

To processor or power-blender, add blanched almonds (see note 2), sugar, maple syrup, vanilla, and salt. Blend for a few minutes, starting at low speed and gradually increasing speed until thoroughly mixed and all ingredients are grounded to a soft dough and almond paste is formed. Remove almond paste with a long wooden spatula and transfer into a bowl.

Take 2 tablespoons of paste, roll between your palms of your hands to form an oval shape cookie. Bend slightly in the middle. Dip each rolled cookie into egg white and roll in almond slivers. Press the top of each cookie gently to flatten. Place on ovenproof flat tray. Bake on the middle rack of oven for 20 minutes or until the edges are slightly golden brown. Watch carefully so cookies do not burn.

Note 1: Instead of vanilla, you may use 1 tablespoon rosewater and ¼ teaspoon ground cardamom.

Note 2: Blanched almonds will mix better if used immediately after blanching and before they dry out.

Variation: Fruity Almond Cookies, Mix and sift 2 cups all-purpose flour, ¼ cup almond flour, 1 teaspoon baking soda and ½ teaspoon sea salt. In a mixing bowl softened ½ cup unsalted butter and gradually add ½ cup (turbinado raw) sugar until mixture is light and fluffy. Combine the following ingredients and gradually add to the butter mixture and mix well after each addition: ½ cup dairy sour cream, 1 cup medjool soft dates (cut into small pieces), 2 teaspoons organic orange zest, ¼ cup orange juice (freshly squeezed) and 1 large beaten egg. Gradually combine sifted dry ingredients alternately with wet ingredients until well mixed (you may use food processor). On a cookie sheet, drop about 1½ tablespoons of dough mixture and bake in on middle rack a preheated 350 degree F. oven for 10-12 minutes or until inserted toothpick comes clean. Remove from oven and let it cool and store in airtight sterilized cookie container. Enjoy cookies with a cup of your favorite tea.

Chocolate Cookies
(Gluten free chocolate cookies)

Serves 6

Preheat oven to 350 degree F.

> 1½ cup rolled oats
>
> 4 ounce semi-sweet dark chocolate, shaved
>
> ¼ cup turbinado raw sugar
>
> ¼ cup unsweetened coconut, finely shredded
>
> ¼ teaspoon sea salt
>
> 1 whole egg, lightly beaten and 2 egg white, beaten to soft peak
>
> 1½ teaspoons olive oil
>
> 2 teaspoons organic lemon zest, freshly grated
>
> ½ teaspoon vanilla extract

Place (oats, chocolate, sugar, coconuts and salt) in food processor. Pulse processor a few times (on and off) until dry ingredients are thoroughly mixed. With the processor running and the help of pitcher gradually add remaining ingredients (whole egg, egg white, olive oil, lemon zest and vanilla) through the feeding tube and run for 30 seconds until soft dough ball is formed that cleans the bowl. Form dough into small balls and flatten or cover a wooden board with a sheet of clear plastic wrap, place cookie dough on the plastic wrap and cover with another plastic wrap. With your hand press the dough gently to create a smooth flat surface and roll the dough gently about ¼-inch thick with a rolling pin. Remove top plastic wrap and using a small circular cookie cutter that has been dusted with flour, cut the dough. Place formed cookies onto parchment paper lined cookie sheet about ½ inch apart. Bake cookies in the middle rack of oven for 8-10 minutes or until toothpick inserted into center comes out slightly moist but clean.

Cinnamon Pumpkin Cookies

(Gluten free cookies)

Serves 12

Preheat oven to 375 degree F.　Lightly grease a large cookie sheet

Nothing is more important than love of our children and feeding them nicely.

> 4 tablespoons sweet butter
> ½ cup granulated sugar
> 2 eggs, slightly beaten
> 1 teaspoon vanilla extract
> ¼ cup olive oil
> 1½ cups cooked pumpkin, mashed
> 1 teaspoon ginger, minced
> 1¾ cups sorghum flour
> 2 tablespoons almond meal
> 2 teaspoons baking powder
> ¼ teaspoon sea salt
> 1 teaspoon cinnamon
> ½ teaspoon nutmeg
> 1 dash clove
> 1 cup seedless, dark raisins
> ¼ cup walnuts, coarsely chopped
> 2 tablespoons sorghum flour (for dusting raisins and walnuts)
> **Garnish** (optional):
> 20 walnut halves

Eating baby, Ju-lian Toh

In a medium bowl cream butter and sugar thoroughly, add eggs, vanilla, olive oil and stir vigorously until well blended. Stir in pumpkin and ginger. In a large mixing bowl sift twice 1 ¾ cup sorghum flour, almond meal, baking powder, salt, cinnamon, nutmeg, and clove.

In a small bowl dust raisins and walnuts with 2 tablespoons sorghum flour and combine with sifted flour mixture. Gradually add dry ingredients (flour mixture) into wet ingredients (liquid mixture) until well mixed. Drop 2 tablespoons of mixture onto cookie sheet 1-inch apart. Bake on the middle rack of oven for 12-15 minutes or until toothpick inserted into center comes out clean and the top is slightly golden brown. Remove from oven and insert a walnut half into each cookie's top while still hot. Place cookies on rack to cool.

Desserts
Caramel Topped Custard

Serves 8

Preheat oven to 350 degree F.   You need 8 ½-inch soufflé dish OR 8 ramekins

    ¾ cup sugar, powdered (turbinado raw sugar is my preference)

    8 ounces (1 package) cream cheese, softened

    ¼ cup + 1 tablespoon sugar (to make custard)

    1 teaspoon vanilla extract

    2 teaspoons organic lemon zest

    5-6 eggs

    2 cups milk, condensed

Caramel Topping: In a heavy based saucepan over medium-low heat, melt ¾ cup sugar; cook gradually and stir occasionally until sugar starts jiggling, melting and caramelized to golden brown color and pleasant taste (about 10-15 minutes). Quickly pour into soufflé dish, tilting to coat the bottom evenly; let stand for 10 minutes.

In a large mixing bowl, beat the cream cheese until smooth. Stir in ¼ cup +1 tablespoon sugar, vanilla and lemon zest. Add eggs, one at a time, and beat mixture at medium speed until smooth after each addition. Gradually blend in milk at very low speed until thoroughly combined. Pour mixture over caramelized sugar. Place baking dish into a larger baking pan and transfer both onto oven. Carefully, pour boiling water into larger pan to a depth of 1-inch (see Tips, Bain-marie/water bath, page 173). Bake in the oven for 50-60 minutes or until center is just set and a toothpick inserted in the center comes out clean (mixture will jiggle). Remove dish from larger pan. Let it cool for 1 hour. Refrigerate overnight. To unmold, run a dull knife, around the edges and invert onto larger rimmed serving platter. Cut into wedges or spoon into dessert plates; spoon remaining sauce over each serving.

Note: If you plan to serve immediately remove "*caramel topped custard*" from oven and let sit for a few minutes, then immersed dish in a shallow pan of warm water for 30 seconds to make it easier to remove.

Crustless Butternut Squash Pie

(Gluten free pie)

Serves 6-8

Preheat oven to 400 degree F. Grease and lightly flour a 9-inch pie pan

> 4 cups butternut squash, cooked, grated
>
> 4 eggs, slightly beaten
>
> 2 tablespoons turbinado raw sugar
>
> Zest of 1 organic lemon, freshly grated (about 1 tablespoon)
>
> 2 teaspoons tapioca flour
>
> 1 teaspoon olive oil
>
> 1 teaspoon baking powder
>
> 1 dash sea salt
>
> 1 dash nutmeg, freshly grated
>
> **Garnish:** ¼ cup strawberries OR raspberries jam-spread (optional) and fresh strawberries

Place ingredients (butternut squash, eggs, sugar, lemon zest, tapioca flour, olive oil, baking powder, salt, and nutmeg) in food processor. Process until all ingredients bind together and are smooth (about 1 minute). Pour batter into a pie pan and place on middle rack of oven. Bake for 10 minutes. Turn heat down to 350 degree F. and bake 25 minutes more or until a toothpick comes out clean and top of pie is a nice golden brown color. Cool completely. With the dull edge of a small knife go around the pie pan and loosen the edge of the pie. Spread strawberries jam around edge of pie, cut into 8 pieces and serve garnished with strawberries. Excellent.

Crustless Butternut Squash Pie
A flavorful dessert, perfect for every occasions.

Crumble Cracker Fruit-Bars

(A delightful fruit-bar, easy to make and great to taste)

Serves 12

Preheat oven to 275 degree F. It is easier to use a "Sushi-Maker" for making this recipe

Crumble crackers:

1 cup rolled, old fashion, oats

¼ cup flour

1 teaspoon cinnamon

1 tablespoon butter

1 dash sea salt

Fruit filling:

14 medjool-soft dates, pitted, chopped

10 dried Turkish apricot, chopped

¼ cup orange juice

1 teaspoon orange zest

Garnish: 1 tablespoon pistachio, chopped

To Make Crumble Crackers: To food processor, add crumble crackers ingredients (oats, flour, cinnamon, butter and salt) and process for 30 seconds. Spread mixture on cookie sheet lined with parchment paper. Place in oven and toasted for about 6-8 minutes. Cool and use crumble crackers for the top and bottom of fruit-bars.

To Make Fruit Filling: In a saucepan, add medjool dates, Turkish apricots, orange juice and orange zest. Simmer for 10 minutes. Cool, place in food processor and process until smooth.

On a flat surface, spread clear plastic wrap. Place Sushi-Bar-Frame in the center of the plastic. Loop a generous-size piece of plastic wrap into Sushi-Maker-Frame. Fill the frame with small layer of crumble crackers followed by a layer of fruit filler, finish with a top layer of crumble crackers to make a fruit-bar (Sushi-Maker-frame should be about 2/3 full). Cover fruit-bar with another generous sheet of plastic over-lapping the frame. Press Sushi-Bar (wide side down) gently to level the ingredients. Carefully remove the Sushi-Maker-Frame and Sushi-Bar. Wrap the fruit-bar tightly in plastic wrap and place in zip-lock-bag. Freeze fruit-bar overnight. When you are ready to serve, unwrap fruit-bar, garnish with chopped pistachio. Use a small sharp knife and slice fruit-bar. Save any uncut fruit-bars in the freezer.

Crumble Rhubarb-Banana Crisp

Serves 5-6

Preheat oven to 400 degree F.   Grease and lightly flour a 9-inch pie pan

Filling:

3 tablespoon sweet butter

2 cups rhubarb (about 1 pound), trimmed, cut across the ribs into ¼-inch slices

¾ cup dark brown sugar, packed

2 tablespoons orange juice

Zest of 1 organic orange, freshly grated

½ teaspoon sea salt, divided

½ teaspoon cinnamon, divided

1/8 teaspoon nutmeg, freshly grated

2 medium banana, peeled, sliced into ½-inch sections (about 2 cups)

Topping:

1¾ cup rolled oats (slightly toasted)

2 tablespoons sweet butter, cut to small pieces

¼ cup dark brown sugar

1 teaspoon baking powder

½ cup almond slivers, divided, plus 1 ¼ cup vanilla yogurt

In a medium saucepan, melt 3 tablespoons butter slowly over low heat. In a mixing bowl combine rhubarb, brown sugar, orange juice, orange zest, ¼ teaspoon salt, ¼ teaspoon cinnamon, nutmeg and banana. Add this into saucepan and let the mixture come to a simmer and simmer over low heat in covered saucepan for 8-10 minutes stirring occasionally to prevent burning. Remove saucepan from heat and transfer rhubarb mixture to pie pan and set aside. To food processor add rolled oats, 2 tablespoons butter, and brown sugar, remaining ¼ teaspoon cinnamon, remaining ¼ teaspoon salt, baking powder and ¼ cup almonds. Blend together until it resembles crumbs. Sprinkle over rhubarb mixture. Cover pie pan tightly with aluminum foil. Bake on middle rack of oven for 20 minutes, remove foil and bake for 4 minutes more or until topping is slightly golden brown. Cool *crumble rhubarb-banana crisp* in pan for 30 minutes. Serve with vanilla yogurt and remaining ¼ cup almond slivers.

Variation: Strawberries and Rhubarb arrive in the garden about the same time in spring; by adding sugar to strawberries and rhubarb, it sweeten and balances the rhubarb's tart flavor. Instead of bananas substitute 2 cups sliced strawberries and 2 tablespoons sugar to the recipe above, and follow directions; bake strawberries-rhubarb pie in pastry dough shell (Tips, 177).

Elderberry Sherbet with Agar Agar

Serves 4

    ½ cup apple juice
    ½ teaspoon agar agar (seaweed gel)
    1 cup blackberries
    1 cup raspberries
    1¼ cup elderberries
    ¼ cup cherry wine
    3 tablespoons honey or sugar

In a double boiler, mix apple juice and agar-agar. Bring to a boil, reduce heat and simmer 5 minutes or until agar agar dissolved.

Add the remaining ingredients (blackberries, raspberries, elderberries, cherry wine, and honey) to the apple juice-agar agar mixture. Let the mixture come to a simmer and simmer for 4 minutes over medium heat. Let cool slightly.

Place ingredients in blender and blend for a few seconds or until smooth. Freeze sherbet for several hours in freezer, beating vigorously several times during freezing. Alternative, you can use an ice-cream machine maker.

Elderberries, see Glossary, page 216

Flaxseed Pudding

(Gluten free)

Serves 4

    ¼ cup flaxseeds, soaked overnight

    ¾ cup spring water, for soaking flaxseeds

    1½ cups blueberries, rinsed

    1 dash sea salt

    3 red apples, peeled, cored, diced

    2 tablespoons almond meal

    2 tablespoons concentrated pomegranate syrup

    2 tablespoons rosewater

    2 tablespoons turbinado raw sugar

    2 teaspoons acai powder

    ½ teaspoon spearmint, dried

Garnish:

    ½ cup shaved semisweet chocolate, divided

    ¼ cups ground pistachio (optional)

Place (soaked flaxseeds, blueberries and salt) in power-blender. Blend for 1 minute until smooth. Add apples, almond meal and continue blending until puree. Pour mixture into medium saucepan. Let the mixture come to a simmer and simmer for 5 minutes while stirring. Add pomegranate syrup, rosewater, raw sugar, acai powder and spearmint. Stir and simmer about 5 minutes. Taste and make adjustments if necessary. Pour into ramekins, let pudding cool and refrigerate for several hours. Garnish with chocolate and pistachio.

Instant Banana Sherbet

Serves 2

    1 cup ice cubes

    1 banana, peeled, cut into small pieces

    1 teaspoon honey OR another sweet OR to taste

    A few drops vanilla

Crush ice first in a power-blender, add remaining ingredients and blend for a few seconds. Place in freezer container and freeze for one hour or until firm. Beat vigorously several times during freezing.

Mango Dessert

(Artfully simple and incredibly delicious)

Serves 2

    1 cup strained yogurt

    1 tablespoon sugar

    2 large mangoes, skinned, pitted, pulp diced, divided

    Garnish: A few mint sprigs

Mix yogurt and sugar and place in refrigerator to chill. Puree 1 cup of mango cubes in blender until thick and fluffy. Pour chilled yogurt mixture into serving glass to form a base. Gently spoon mango puree over the yogurt. Top with remaining mango cubes and garnish with mint.

Millet Pudding

Serves 3-4

You need 4 small ramekins for molding

    2 ½ cups apple cider OR apple juice

    1 cup millet flour

    2 tablespoons rose water

    2 tablespoons olive oil

    2 tablespoons maple syrup

    1 dash sea salt

    1 dash cardamom

    1 dash saffron

Asian gluten free millet pudding

    Garnish: 1 persimmon (peeled and divided), top with 1 teaspoon strawberries jam and mint sprigs OR 1 tablespoons shelled pistachio, coarsely ground and divided

In a medium saucepan, bring apple cider to boil, turn off the heat and gradually add millet flour, rose water, olive oil, maple syrup, salt and cardamom while stirring constantly for 1 minute. Let mixture cool slightly and place mixture into power-blender. Blend for 30 seconds, return creamy mixture to the saucepan, and add a little apple cider juice if needed. Add saffron, place over low heat and simmer for 5-8 more minutes or until pudding thickens slightly. Pour into ramekins or small individual cup, let pudding cool and refrigerate for several hours or overnight until firm. With the dull edge of a small knife go around the perimeter of pudding, place serving plate up-side-down on ramekin top, and flip over so pudding is on serving plate. Enjoy!

Popsicle with Banana and Kudzu Root Starch

Serves 4

You need 1 set of Popsicle molds

      2 tablespoons kudzu (see Glossary "*kudzu root starch*", page 225)

      ¼ cup cold water

      1 banana, peeled, sliced

      1 mango, peeled, pitted, sliced

      ¼ teaspoon rosewater

      1 teaspoon comb honey, raw

Dissolve kudzu root starch in cold water. In a mixer/blender liquefy ingredients (banana, mango, rosewater, and honey). Add dissolved kudzu and blend again. Pour mixture into heavy medium saucepan. Let the mixture come to a simmer and reduce the heat. Simmer over low heat while stirring constantly for 8 minutes or until a medium thick pudding is formed. Let cool to room temperature and fill Popsicle mold, about ¾ full with mixture. Add Popsicle sticks. Place in the freezer and freeze overnight or until completely frozen.

Note: To remove Popsicles more easily, place mold in hot water for a few seconds. Once you unfreeze Popsicle, please do not refreeze.

White mulberry

See Glossary, page 229

Ricotta Cheese Light Dessert

(Dessert dream)

Serves 4

     1 pound ricotta cheese (16 oz.)

     2 tablespoons (turbinado) sugar OR to taste

     1 tablespoon lemon zest, freshly grated

     1 teaspoon maple syrup

     1 teaspoon amaretto liqueur (optional)

     1 teaspoon pure vanilla extract

     ½ dash sea salt

     Garnish:

     8 Pistachios, OR walnuts OR almond, coarsely ground

     8 Strawberries OR raspberries OR blueberries

Blend all ingredients (ricotta cheese, turbinado sugar, lemon zest, maple syrup, amaretto, vanilla, and salt) in blender and blend for 30 seconds or until texture is smooth and creamy. Taste and adjust seasoning if necessary. Transfer creamy cheese to a glass serving dish. Cover and refrigerate until thickened (about 2 hours). Garnish with pistachio and fresh strawberries.

Note: Ricotta cheese is one of my favorite cheeses, it is low in fat and when very fresh the flavor shines through.

Ricotta Cheese Light Dessert

Starburst Fruit Tart

Serves 8+

Tart Pastry Shell (See Tips, "*pastry dough*", page 177):

3 cups unbleached all-purpose flour

2 teaspoons baking powder

1 dash sea salt

½ cup granulated sugar

¾ cup sweet butter (1½ sticks), cut into small pieces and chill

2 large eggs

Zest of 1 organic lemon, freshly grated

Vanilla Pastry Cream (see Tips, "*vanilla pastry cream*", page 193):

2 cups milk

3 large egg yolks, slightly beaten

6 tablespoons brown sugar

Zest of 1 organic lemon, freshly grated

1 teaspoon vanilla extract

1 tablespoon of each wheat flour and cornstarch, sifted together

¼ cup + 1 tablespoon sweet butter, softened

Fruits:

1 pound strawberries, slice in half lengthwise

6 kiwis, peeled, sliced

2 cups blackberries

1 cup raspberries

1 cup blueberries

Glaze: ½ cup quince glaze OR strawberries glaze (see Tips, "*quince clear glaze*", page 192)

Spread "*vanilla pastry cream*" over the bottom of baked tart shell. Arrange the fruit in circles, starting at the outside edge and working inward with strawberries first, then kiwi slices slightly over lapping each other. Then arrange the blackberries, blueberries, and raspberries in the center; add any additional fresh fruits you wish like oranges or grapes.

Glaze: Apply clear glaze over fresh fruits lightly with a pastry brush; a shining glaze gives a professional artistic-look and beauty to the tart. Refrigerate tart at least for 2 hours before serving.

Dips

Creamy Dipping Sauce with Prawns

Serves 6

    1 onion, finely chopped

    2 cloves of garlic, finely chopped

    2 teaspoons ginger root, finely chopped

    6 tablespoons olive oil, divided

    1 teaspoon turmeric

    ½ teaspoon black cumin, powder

    ½ teaspoon coriander, powder

    ½ teaspoon paprika, powder

    ½ teaspoon gram-masala

    1 dash cayenne pepper

    1 teaspoon cornstarch

    1 teaspoon sugar

    1 dash sea salt

    1¼ cups concentrated milk

    ½ cup coconut milk

    1 pound prawns, deveined, cleaned, pat-dried

    Garnish: 1 sage sprig

In a medium saucepan, stir-fry onion, garlic, and ginger in 3 tablespoons heated olive oil until onion are translucent (3 minutes). Turn off the heat. Add spices (turmeric, cumin, coriander, paprika, gram-masala and cayenne), stir until fragrant (1 minute) set aside. In a bowl, mix together cornstarch, sugar, salt, concentrated milk and coconut milk. Add this mixture to onion-mixture in saucepan; let it cool and blend in blender for 30 seconds. Transfer into saucepan, bring to a simmer while stirring to prevent burning. Simmer for 5-6 minutes or until thickened. In a separate frying-pan sauté prawns in 3 tablespoons heated olive oil, cover the pan for 2-3 minutes, allow the prawns to cook. Remove cover and stir gently until shrimp turn pink and the edges are curled slightly (about 2-3 minutes). Garnish creamy dipping sauce with sage and serve with prawns as an appetizer or side dish.

Avocado Dip

Serves 2

      2 large, ripe avocado, pitted, peeled, chopped

      2 tablespoons shallot, peeled, chopped

      2 cloves of garlic, chopped

      2 tablespoons lime juice OR lemon juice, freshly squeezed

      2 teaspoons olive oil

      ¼ teaspoon sea salt OR to taste

      ¼ teaspoon black pepper, freshly ground

      2 tablespoons Chinese parsley, cleaned, chopped

      1 teaspoon lime zest, freshly grated

To the blender, add all ingredients except Chinese parsley and lime zest (avocados, shallot, garlic, lime juice, olive oil, salt and pepper). Blend for 30 seconds or until desired consistency is reached. Blend avocado mixture with Chinese parsley, and lime zest. Serve as a dip or spread on bread to make a nice sandwich.

Sprouted adzuki beans,
dried adzuki beans, mung beans and
fenugreek seeds.
(Please see Tips, beans/seeds are sprouting, page 173)

Herb Seasoning Dip

Serves 4

  ¼ teaspoon basil

  ¼ teaspoon oregano

  ¼ teaspoon thyme, dried

  ¼ teaspoon coriander seeds, ground

  1 pinch cayenne pepper

  4 cloves of garlic, chopped

  1 tablespoon brown mustard seeds, ground

  ¼ cup sesame seeds, lightly toasted, ground

  ¼ cup + 1 tablespoon wine vinegar

  2 tablespoons lemon juice, freshly squeezed

  Zest of 1 organic lemon, freshly grated

  1 cup extra virgin olive oil

  ½ teaspoon sea salt OR to taste

  ¼ teaspoon black pepper, freshly ground

Blend all ingredients (basil, oregano, thyme, coriander, cayenne pepper, garlic, mustard, sesame seeds, wine vinegar, lemon juice, lemon zest, olive oil, salt and pepper) in blender for 30 seconds or until smooth and well mixed. Refrigerate for several hours prior to use. This dip can also be used to marinate cooked garbanzo beans and chopped scallions to be used as a side dish.

Thai Kaffir Lime Dipping Sauce

Serves 6

  2 kaffir lime leaves, cut into small pieces OR 2 teaspoons organic lime zest

  1 tablespoon ginger root, freshly grated

  3 medjool dates, pitted, chopped

  2 tablespoons olive oil

  ½ teaspoon sea salt OR to taste

  ½ cup almond butter

  ¼ cup spring water

  Juice of 3-4 limes, freshly squeezed

  1 dash of each herb Thai chili and cayenne OR to taste

Blend all ingredients in a power blender until thick and creamy. Use for dip, celery sticks.

Robust Flavorful Dipping Oil

Serves 10

¾ cup extra virgin olive oil

¼ cup balsamic vinegar

¼ teaspoon sea salt OR to taste

1 dash red chili pepper, crushed OR black pepper, freshly ground

2-3 cloves of garlic, chopped

1 teaspoon lemon juice, freshly squeezed

½ dash oregano, dried

Garnish:

A few mint sprig

Blend all ingredients (olive oil, vinegar, salt, pepper, garlic, lemon juice and oregano) in blender for 30 seconds or until creamy dip forms. Garnish with mint sprig and serve. Dip your favorite bread into freshly made dipping oil and enjoy. This dip can also be used for marinating meat, fish, and poultry.

Spinach Dip

Serves 10

1 onion, shredded

4 cloves of garlic, chopped

4 tablespoons olive oil

2 bunches spinach, washed, pat-dried and chopped

2 cups plain yogurt, strained to 1 cup yogurt

1 tablespoon fresh sweet basil-mint, cut with scissors

¼ teaspoon sea salt OR to taste

1 dash black pepper, freshly ground

Garnish:

A few small sliced red onion OR mint sprig (optional)

In a frying pan, sauté onions and garlic in heated olive oil and set aside. In a saucepan with a few tablespoons water, simmer spinach slowly, until leaves are wilted but still bright green, drain. Add remaining ingredients (yogurt, basil, salt and pepper) into spinach and mix. In medium bowl combine and mix all ingredients (onion/garlic and spinach/yogurt mixtures), and refrigerate for 1 hour so flavor can blend. Garnish with sliced of red onions.

Fish Dishes

(True Foods such as Sea Foods)

Grilled salmon fillets one with chermoula sauce (page 134) and one with mango coconut sauce (page 138).

New study shows that the type of unsaturated fat present in fish are more health-promoting than those found in animals. Wild ocean fish such as king salmon, halibut and tuna, offers not only a good balance of protein, they are the best source of omega 3s fatty acids; it seems to act as a natural anti-inflammatory for "*joints and muscles pains*" in a healthy diet.

Grilled Tuna

Serves 1-2

> ½ pound Ahi-tuna (Sushi grade tuna)
> 2 tablespoons olive oil
> ¼ teaspoon sea salt and black pepper OR to taste
> ¼ cup raw sesame seeds (black and white)
> ¼ teaspoon dried thyme to be mixed with sesame seed

Brush tuna with olive oil, season with salt and pepper. Cover tuna with sesame seeds mixture on both sides. Grill/barbeque for 2-3 minutes each side. Slice, and transfer onto serving dish. Top with "*barbeque sauce with basil leaves*", page 133. Enjoy firm, flaky textured, and tender tuna with grilled asparagus and corn.

Note: Wild ocean fish can be expensive but worth the price to enjoy a healthy food twice a week.

Pecan Crusted Halibut

Serves 3

Preheat oven to 400 degree F.

       3 halibut fillet, skinned, rinsed, pat-dried

       2 tablespoons olive oil

       1/3 teaspoon sea salt OR to taste

       ¼ teaspoon black pepper, freshly ground

       ¼ cup pecans, finely chopped

       Garnish:

       1 bunch watercress, rinsed, pat-dried

       1 lemon, cut into wedges

Brush both side of halibut with olive oil, sprinkle with salt and pepper. Place the halibuts on a small grilling-tray, top with pecans and cover tightly with heavy aluminum foil. Transfer onto middle rack of oven. Bake halibut for 10-12 minutes or until nearly done. Lower the heat to 350 degree F; remove the aluminum foil from the tray, and return fish to the oven. Roast for 5 more minutes or until pecans turn golden brown (watch carefully so they do not burn). Place watercress on serving plate, top with halibut and add lemon wedge. You may serve this lovely tasty fish with steamed rice. Enjoy!

Variation 1: Salmon with Mango Sauce Topping: To the blender add 1 cup fresh mango (chopped), 1 tablespoon olive oil, 1 tablespoon lemon zest, ¼ teaspoon ginger root, ¼ teaspoon sea salt, and 1 dash cayenne. Blend until sauce is puree. Set aside. Drizzle 2 salmon filet with 1 teaspoon olive oil and sprinkle with salt and pepper. Sauté salmon in heated 2 tablespoon olive oil for 4-5 minutes each side or until done. Serve salmon with mango sauce topping.

Variation 2: Salmon with Pineapple Sauce Topping, to the blender add 1 cup fresh pineapple (chopped), 1 tablespoon olive oil, 2 tablespoons basil leaves (chopped), salt and pepper. Blend until sauce is puree. Set aside. Poke 2 salmon filet with fork several places and drizzle with 1 tablespoon olive oil and sprinkle with salt and pepper. Bake salmon in preheated 400 degree F. oven for 10-12 minutes or until cooked. Serve salmon with pineapple sauce topping and beet salad.

Beet Salad: Bake 4-5 baby beets, slice and cut into bite-size pieces. Place beets in a salad bowl, drizzle with mixture of 1 tablespoon olive oil, 1 teaspoon balsamic vinegar, 1 teaspoon maple syrup, 1 dash salt and pepper and juice of 1 orange. Add ½ pound baby arugula leaves and ¼ cup walnuts, and gently toss together.

Shrimp with White Wine and Tomatoes

Serves 4-5

> 1 red onion, chopped
> ¼ cup olive oil
> 4 cloves of garlic, chopped
> 2 medium tomatoes, peeled, cut into small pieces
> 3 cups homemade "*tomato-basil-sauce*" (see Tips, page 189)
> ½ cup dry white wine (Chardonnay is preferable)
> ½ pinch cayenne powder OR hot chili powder
> ½ teaspoon thyme
> ½ teaspoon basil
> ¼ teaspoon Italian seasoning
> 2 teaspoons granulated sugar
> Juice of 1 lemon, freshly squeezed (about ¼ cup)
> 1 pound extra-large shrimp (prawns), shelled, veined, cleaned

Garnish:

> A few rosemary sprigs

In a large heavy-based stock pot stir-fry onion in heated olive oil for 2 minutes add garlic and continue stirring for 1 more minute or until onion is slightly golden brown. Add tomatoes and tomato-basil-sauce. Bring to simmer and simmer for 20 minutes. Add remaining ingredients except shrimps to tomato mixture (wine, cayenne, thyme, basil, Italian seasoning, sugar, and lemon juice). Let the mixture come to a simmer and simmer for 10-15 minutes in covered stock pot. Reduce the heat add shrimps and cook uncovered for 2-3 minutes or until shrimp are done. Garnish with rosemary sprig and serve.

Note: You may serve this sauce with chicken breast (cut into small pieces) or mussels instead of shrimp.

Fish Variation: Spark like Tuna. In a large pan, lightly sauté 2 shallots (thinly sliced), 6 mushrooms, (thinly sliced), in heated 4 tablespoons olive oil. Arrange mushrooms and shallots on the sides of frying-pan; making room for tuna. Sprinkle ½ teaspoon sea salt on 1 pound fresh tuna and place in the center of pan. Continue to cook for 2-3 minutes or until the bottom of tuna (about ¼-inch) is cooked and leave the top uncooked and red. Serve tuna on the bed of baby mixed salad greens such as lettuce, chard, arugula, spinach and radicchio along with mushrooms and shallots. Top tuna with "*vinaigrette mustard sauce*", page 131.

Star Vegetable Fish Dish

Serves 4 +

Preheat oven to 325 degree F.

 1½ cups chicken broth, cooled

 1 teaspoon flour OR cornstarch flour

 1 large onion, chopped

 1 sweet potato, peeled, sliced ¾-inch thick

 1 large leek, cleaned, sliced ¾-inch, divided

 4 carrots, peeled, cut into 1-inch sections

 2 lemongrass, cleaned, chopped

 ¼ cup olive oil, divided

Ground Seasoning:

 1 teaspoon sea salt OR to taste, divided

 ¼ teaspoon black pepper, divided

 1 dash cayenne

 ¼ teaspoon cumin seeds

 ¼ teaspoon coriander

 1 pinch cardamom

 1½ pounds salmon fillet

Garnish:

 1 tablespoon chive leaves, sniped with scissors

 A few tarragon sprigs

 1 lemon, cut in wedges

In a small bowl stir chicken broth and flour together and pour into an ovenproof casserole dish and top with layers of onion, sweet potatoes, carrots, and half of leek. Place the other half of leek and lemongrass in food processor and run for a minute until finely chopped. Add to casserole dish and spread over vegetables. In a small bowl combine ground seasoning (½ teaspoon salt, 1 dash black pepper, cayenne, cumin, coriander and cardamom) and sprinkle over vegetables. Finally add and drizzle top with 2 tablespoons of olive oil. Transfer casserole dish into oven and cook for 45 minutes.

Meantime, sprinkle salmon with remaining ½ teaspoon salt and 1 dash black pepper. Sauté in 2 tablespoons heated olive oil. On the serving plate, place cooked vegetables, top with salmon and garnish with chives, tarragon and lemon wedges. Excellent!

Fruit Dishes

Fruits are considered nature's perfect food and
Wholesome pomegranate fruit considered a natural antioxidants fruit.

A ripe pomegranate has a large number of edible seeds and ruby in color.

(Please see Tips, how to cut and section "*Pomegranate*", page 175)

Baking Rhubarb with Strawberries Sauce

Serves 4-6

Preheat oven to 350 degree F.   Grease generously and lightly flour a pie-pan

> 2 cups rhubarb (about 1 pound), trimmed, cut across the ribs into ¼-inch slices
>
> 2 cups strawberries light sauce*
>
> ½ cup + ¼ cup turbinado raw sugar
>
> 2 tablespoons kudzu
>
> ¼ cup spring cold water (for dissolving kudzu)
>
> 1 cup toasted bread crumbs, unseasoned OR
>
> 1 pastry crust (please see Tips, page 177)
>
> ½ cup shelled walnuts, finely chopped
>
> 2 tablespoons lemon zest, freshly grated
>
> **Garnish:**
>
> Whipped cream** and strawberries (optional)

Baking Rhubarb with strawberries

Place rhubarb slices in medium saucepan, and pour "*strawberries light sauce*" on rhubarb to cover. Transfer covered saucepan into oven and bake for 20 minutes or until the rhubarb shows no resistance when pierced with the tip of a sharp knife. Remove from oven and cool completely.

In a small bowl, dissolve kudzu in water to form a smooth paste and gradually stir into cooled stewed rhubarb.

In a pie-pan arrange a thin layer of bread crumbs topped with a layer of mixed chopped walnuts and lemon zest. Pour rhubarb mixture over walnuts mixture and bake in the oven for 20-25 minutes or until done. Remove from oven, cool, cover with foil and chill for several hours or overnight. Next day when you are ready to use, remove foil, garnish with whip cream and arrange sliced strawberries in a design.

*Strawberries Light Sauce: Blend 2 ½ cups (about 1 pound) strawberries (washed, pat-dried, caps removed and sliced) with ½ cup + ¼ cup turbinado raw sugar in blender, strain and use 2 cups liquid as a sauce (the finer the strainer, the smoother the sauce).

**Whipped Cream: Whip 1 cup chilled heavy whipping cream in a large chilled bowl with electrical beater until it begins to thicken. Add ¼ cup turbinado powdered sugar and ½ teaspoon vanilla extract; continue to beat until it is firm to hold its shape. Squeeze the cream through a pastry tube in decorative swirls, add strawberries.

Chilled Strawberry Fruit Combo

Serves 4

> 1½ cups strawberries, washed, pat-dried, caps trimmed, sliced
> 1 cup plain yogurt
> 1 medium size banana, sliced
> 1 medium size tart apple, diced, OR ½ cup blueberries
> 1 tablespoon raw honey OR 3-4 tablespoons maple syrup
> 1 tablespoon almond meal (optional)

Combine ingredients (strawberries, yogurt, banana, apples, honey and almond meal) in blender and blend for 30 seconds. Chill and serve as side dish.

Peaches for Dessert

Serves 3-4

> 1 cup water
> 4 teaspoons brown sugar
> 4 pods cardamom, bruised
> 4 teaspoons lemon juice, freshly squeezed
> 4 teaspoons rosewater
> 4 medium organic peaches (in season), pitted,
> thinly sliced
> 5-6 soft dates, pitted, cut in ½-inch pieces
> **Garnish:**
> 4 shelled walnuts, coarsely chopped

In a saucepan, add water, sugar, cardamom, lemon juice, and rosewater. Let the mixture come to a simmer and simmer for a few minutes until a thickened syrup forms and is reduced to about half cup. Turn off the heat and remove cardamom pods from syrup.

Add peaches and dates to syrup and toss gently. Transfer fruits into classic dish and garnish with walnuts.

Sweet and Sour Fruit Salad

(This fruit salad can be the sweetest moment of your day!)

Serves 2-3

Honey Dressing:

1½ teaspoon honey

1½ teaspoons lemon juice, freshly squeezed, divided

1 teaspoon poppy seeds

1 dash salt

¼ cup orange juice, freshly squeezed

A few drops vanilla extract

Fresh Fruits:

1 red apple, cored, diced

1 banana, peeled, thinly sliced

1 avocado, peeled, pitted, sliced

1 mandarin orange, cut into smaller pieces

Garnish:

¼ cup raisins

¼ cup walnuts, coarsely chopped

Honey Dressing: Blend ingredients (honey, 1 teaspoon lemon juice, poppy seeds, salt, orange juice, and vanilla). Place in covered jar and refrigerate for 35 minutes.

In a serving bowl combine fresh fruits (apple, banana, avocado and mandarin orange). Sprinkle with ½ teaspoon remaining lemon juice to prevent fruits from discoloring. Add honey dressing and gently toss; sprinkle with raisins and walnuts prior to serving.

Fruits, Ju-lian-Toh

Variety of Seasonal Fruits

(With mint vinegar dressing)

Serves 2

>2 peaches, pitted, sliced
>
>2 pears, cored, sliced
>
>1 papaya, skinned, seeded, sliced
>
>2 cups green lettuce, cleaned, pat dried, cut into bite-size pieces
>
>¼ cup cherries, pitted OR red grapes, sliced
>
>¼ cup "*mint vinegar dressing*"*

For individual serving, alternate slices of peaches, pears, and papaya, on top of green lettuce. Scatters with cherries, and serve with "*mint vinegar dressing*" on the side.

***Mint Vinegar Dressing:** In a small saucepan, add ½ cup water, and ¼ cup apple cider. Bring to simmer. Stir in 2 tablespoons turbinado raw sugar, and 4 mint sprigs. Simmer for several minutes or until reduced to ¼ cup. Adjust sweetness and mint flavor if needed. Remove mint and cool prior to use.

Organically grown fruits market where the use of natural home remedies
is a core value of American cultural heritage to cherish.

Wonderful Fruity Lamb Dish

Enjoy dried fruits (apricot, dates, prunes, raisins and preserved lemons),
almonds, olives, variety aromatic herbs (onions, garlic, ginger and cayenne) and ground spices (saffron, cinnamon, cardamom and cumin) in chicken/lamb stew dishes made in Tagine cookware.
The use of fruits, herbs and spices with chicken/lamb is a good example of the ***Ancient Persian*** influences in North Africa cuisine.

Serves 6

Experience the authentic tastes of traditional Moroccan cuisine with its beautiful invention Tagine cookware.

1 cup dried apricot
1 cup dried prunes, presoaked, pitted
½ cup raisins
1 teaspoon lemon zest, freshly grated
1 teaspoon orange blossom water
2 tablespoons brown sugar
1 teaspoon cinnamon
½ teaspoon black cumin powder
1 teaspoon sea salt
¼ teaspoon peppercorn, freshly ground
1 large onion, chopped
1 tablespoon ginger root, grated
¼ cup olive oil
2 pounds boneless grass fed lamb, remove all visible fat, cut into 2-inch pieces
1 cup spring water
2 teaspoons organic cornstarch, dissolved in 1 tablespoon cold water
Garnish: ¼ toasted almond slivers

In a medium bowl soak cleaned apricot, prunes and raisins for 2 minutes, drain. Add lemon zest, orange blossom water and brown sugar and set aside. In a small bowl mix seasoning (cinnamon, cumin, salt and pepper) and set aside. In a large skillet, stir-fry onion and ginger in heated olive oil until onion is translucent (about 2-3 minutes). Add lamb and stir-fry until slightly golden brown (about 3-4 minutes). Turn the heat down to medium-low, add seasoning and stir for 30 seconds. Stir in spring water and cornstarch mixture. Add lamb mixture to the bottom of tagine and cover tagine with its lid. Bring to simmer and cook for 1 hour until meat is half cooked. Spread apricot mixture on top of meat. Continue to cook at a slow simmer for 20-25 minutes or until meat is cooked. Taste and make adjustment if necessary. Garnish with almonds. Serve with steamed rice. Enjoy the fruits of your labor with good food.

Main Dishes
A Special Persian Dish with Chicken and Rice
(This super delicious "*Persian-style meal with herbs and spices* "is called "*Tahchine*")

Serves 8

For the Marinade:

1 tablespoon, ginger root, grated

¼ cup mint leaves, chopped

¼ teaspoon mild chili pepper, chopped

1½ teaspoon sea salt

1 teaspoon Persian-style herb mixture "*advieh-poloye*" (see Tips, page 185)

1 cup strained yogurt

2 egg yolks, slightly beaten

2½ pounds chicken breast, skinned, boned, cut into 2-inch cubes

Rice: (See "*basic steamed basmati rice*", page 106)

3 cups long grain basmati rice

10 cups spring water

2 tablespoons sea salt

A few drops olive oil

¼ cup boiling water

1 onion (Julian's cut), sautéed in 2 tablespoons olive oil

¼ cup olive oil

¼ teaspoon ground saffron

Garnish: 2 tablespoons green onion (optional), chopped

To Marinate: In a bowl, blend all ingredients (ginger, mint, chili pepper, salt, advieh-poloye, yogurt and egg yolks) together until well blended. Cover chicken completely with marinate, place in covered container and refrigerate overnight. When you are ready to cook bring chicken to room temperature, with tong remove chicken, set aside and discard marinate. Cook the rice up to step 6 (page 106). Place an inch layers of strained rice at the bottom of ovenproof pot, add marinated chicken and cover with sautéed onion and top with remaining rice. Drizzle ¼ cup olive oil over the rice and sprinkle the mound with ground saffron, and follow step 7-8. Garnish with green onion and serve chicken-rice with plain yogurt.

Chicken Pot Pie with Crust Topping

(A delicious one-pot meal French-style)

Serves 8

Preheat oven to 375 degree F.

4 chicken legs (about three pound), skinned, defatted, rinsed and cut into drumsticks and thighs, OR 2 pounds, chicken breast halves, skinless, boneless and cut each half into quarters (this will reduce the cooking time from 25 to 20 minutes).

6 cups water OR 5 cups water plus 1 cup chicken broth

½ cup white wine

Herb Bouquet-garni:

2 bay leaves (Laurel)

2 Italian parsley sprigs

2 thyme sprigs

2 rosemary sprigs

2 tarragon sprigs OR ½ teaspoon dried tarragon

2 whole allspices

4 whole peppercorn

¾ teaspoon sea salt

Vegetables:

3 carrots, peeled, diced

1 stalk celery, cleaned, diced

30 pearl onions (about 1½ pounds), peeled OR two large onions, peeled, chopped

Stock Thickener:

2 teaspoons arrowroot powder

2 tablespoons fresh water to be mixed with arrowroot for thickening

Crust Topping:

2 cups all-purpose flour

1 teaspoon baking powder

½ teaspoon salt

¾ cup milk

1 tablespoon olive oil

1 egg yolk slightly beaten

1 egg white, whisk, used for egg-wash

In a 4 quart stock pot, add chicken, water and wine. Make a bouquet-garni by placing fresh herbs (bay leaves, parsley, thyme, rosemary and tarragon) along with spices (allspice, peppercorn) and salt in several layers of cheese cloth; tie securing with a string and add to stock pot.

Cover the pot and bring to a simmer. Simmer for 25 minutes over low-medium heat or until the chicken is fork tender. Remove chicken from stock pot and let it cool slightly (so you can handle), debone and cover chicken pieces to prevent chicken from drying out. Continue simmering the stock uncovered until the liquid is reduced to 2½ cups (about 35 minutes). Strain the stock, discard the herb bundle and add vegetables (carrots, celery and onion) and arrowroot mixture. Continue simmering until carrots are tender (about 10 minutes). Transfer chicken into a casserole dish; arrange vegetables to cover the chicken.

To Prepare Crust Topping: In a medium bowl, mix sifted dry ingredients (flour, baking powder, and salt), with liquid ingredients (milk, oil, and 1 egg yolk). Knead lightly. Roll out with flour dusted rolling pin to shape of casserole dish; brush the surface with egg-wash and cut into 8 pieces. Gently remove each piece and place lightly on top of chicken and vegetables in casserole dish (please do not press down). Bake in the oven uncovered for 10-15 minutes or until the crust topping is golden brown. **Enjoy!**

Lavender, see Glossary, page 226

Chicken with Mushrooms and Wine

(This fabulous dish brings us a heart warm feeling).

Serves 6-8

You need 4 quart heavy-based stove top pot

> 1 large white onion, chopped
>
> ½ cup olive oil + 2 tablespoons for sautéing garnish mushrooms
>
> 6 chicken thighs (2½ lb.), skinned, defatted
>
> 2 ½ teaspoons mixture of spices (combine and freshly grind ½ teaspoon of each whole spices: Cardamom, black cumin seeds, coriander seeds, peppercorn, and fennel seeds)
>
> 1½ teaspoons sea salt OR to taste
>
> ¼ teaspoon black pepper, freshly ground
>
> 1 dash cayenne pepper
>
> 1½ cups white drinking wine
>
> ½ cup chicken broth (see Tips, chicken broth, page 178)
>
> 2 tablespoons brown sugar
>
> 2 pounds crimini mushrooms, cleaned, pat dried and sliced
>
> 2 tablespoons arrowroot powder (to be mixed with mushrooms, see note)
>
> **Garnish:** A few mushrooms, shallots (sliced and sautéed in 2 tablespoons olive oil), ¼ cup pomegranate syrup and rosemary sprig

In a large pot, stir-fry onion in ½ cup heated olive oil for 3 minutes. Add chicken and stir while browning until both sides are lightly golden brown (a few minutes). Remove chicken from pot and sprinkle with spice mixture, salt and black pepper and set aside in covered dish. Turn off the heat/gas flame (to prevent the alcohol from igniting), add wine, broth and brown sugar. Cover the pot and bring the content to simmer over medium heat. Return chicken to pot, cover and simmer slowly over low-medium heat for 20 minutes. Add 2 pounds crispy mushrooms and cook for several minutes or until chicken is done (watch carefully as liquid will evaporate during cooking and may need to be replaced with water to prevent burning). Transfer food to a serving dish, garnish with mushrooms and shallots, pomegranate syrup and rosemary sprig. Serve with steamed rice.

Note: In a mixing bowl, toss together (2 pounds mushrooms and 2 tablespoons arrowroot). Line a heavy aluminum foil rimmed cookie sheet and arrange mushrooms in a single layer. Transfer onto lower rack of 400 degree F., preheated oven and bake for 6-8 minutes or until the edge of mushrooms are golden brown color and mushrooms become slightly dry. Remove from oven.

Chicken with Various Vegetables

(An exotic and authentic Persian dish, made with chicken, vegetables, herbs and spices, is called "***Morgh-tursh***").

Serves 5-6

Preheat oven to 300 degree F.

      4 cups Italian parsley, chopped

      ½ cup fenugreek green leaves, chopped OR ¼ cup fenugreek dried leaves

      ½ cup young leek OR chives, chopped

      1 young fennel bulb, chopped

      12 tablespoons olive oil, divided

      1 large onion, chopped

      2 large chicken breast (about 2 pounds), skinned, visible fats removed

      1¼ teaspoons sea salt OR to taste

      ¼ teaspoon black pepper, freshly ground

      1 pinch saffron

      1 teaspoon turmeric

      Juice of 1 lemon OR Seville orange (mix with 1 honey)

      1 teaspoon honey

      ½ cup water

      Garnish: (optional)

      5 okras, washed, pat dried, ends trimmed, thinly sliced

      1 small sweet red pepper, seeded, thinly sliced

      2 tablespoons olive oil

Parsley, fenugreek, leek, and fennel need to be washed, pat-dried and finely chopped ahead of time (you may use food processor). In a heavy-based frying pan, stir-fry them in 6 tablespoons heated olive oil for 5-6 minutes and set aside.

In a large heavy-based ovenproof pot, stir-fry onions in 6 tablespoons heated olive oil for 2 minutes or until nearly golden brown. Add chicken and continue to stir-fry for 3 minutes or until chicken is slightly browned; sprinkle chicken with salt, pepper and saffron. Add fried vegetables and sprinkle with turmeric and stir for 30 seconds. Sprinkle lemon-honey mixture on top of vegetables and add water to the bottom of pot. Cover the pot, bring to simmer and transfer pot into oven for 45 minutes or until done.

Sauté okra and bell pepper in 2 tablespoons heated olive oil for a minute. Cover the pan and set aside to use for garnishing. Serve this beautiful food with basmati rice.

Chicken with Vegetables

Serves 6-8   Preheat oven to 375 degree F.

Seasoning:

½ teaspoon of each dried herb (rosemary, sage, oregano, and thyme)

1 teaspoon dried basil leaves

2 teaspoons sea salt and ½ teaspoon black pepper, freshly ground

1 lemon, thinly sliced, seeded

Chicken and Vegetables:

4½ pounds whole chicken, cleaned and pat dried (see note)

¼ teaspoon ground saffron mixed with 1 teaspoon boiling water

6 shallots OR 2 onions, quarter

3 carrots, peeled, sliced (1-inch segments)

2 parsnip, peeled, sliced (1-inch segments)

1 turnip, peeled, cut in quarters

1 sweet potato, peeled, cut in 8 pieces

2 teaspoons olive oil and ½ teaspoon sea salt

Zest of 1 organic lemon, freshly grated

Whole chicken with vegetable mix.

Garnish: A few red radish, and lemon (thinly sliced)

In a small bowl mix together seasoning except lemon (rosemary, sage, oregano, thyme, basil, salt and pepper) and divided into half. With your fingers loose the skin along the chicken breast and rub half of the herb mixture under the skin. Rub the outside skin generously with the remaining half of seasoning mixture and slide lemon slices under the skin and tie legs together with kitchen string. Put chicken in a heavy plastic bag, close the bag and refrigerate for a few hours. Remove plastic and place chicken breast side up in a roasting pan and cover it loosely with heavy aluminum foil and transfer onto middle rack of oven. Roast chicken for 1: 30 minutes or until the thigh reaches 165 degree F. on meat thermometer. Remove from oven, brush skin with saffron-water and return to oven. Roast the top uncovered for 5 more minutes. Meantime, in a large mixing bowl mix together vegetables (shallots, carrots, parsnips, turnip and sweet potato) and sprinkle with olive oil, salt and lemon zest. Toss vegetables together and arrange on an ovenproof baking sheet. Cover tightly with a heavy aluminum foil. Transfer onto lower rack of oven. Cook vegetables for 45 minutes or until done.

Transfer chicken and vegetables to serving plate. Garnish with radish and lemon slices. You may offer (onion) pickles on the side. Enjoy lovely wholesome food.

Note: Remove the giblets, cut and trim away all excess fat, leaving the skin on.

Chicken Curry

Serves 4

1 large onion, chopped

1-inch ginger, peeled, chopped

4 cloves of garlic, peeled, chopped

¼ cup olive oil

4 whole chicken legs, skinned, defatted, cut into thighs and drumsticks

1 large red heirloom tomato, skinned, chopped

¼ cup plain yogurt

2 teaspoons sea salt and ¼ teaspoon black pepper, freshly ground

1 dash red chili OR jalapeno, seeded, chopped

2 teaspoons coriander

1 teaspoon cumin seeds

1 teaspoon paprika

½ teaspoon gram masala (please see Tips, page 184)

1 teaspoon brown sugar

Zest of 1 lemon and juice of 1 lemon and 1 teaspoon corn starch

Garnish: A few red onion rings, and thyme sprigs

In a large and deep frying pan, stir-fry onion, ginger and garlic in heated olive oil until onion are slightly golden brown. Add chicken and continue stir-fry until brown. Reduce the heat, add tomato, cover the pan and let chicken cook for 20 minutes, remove chicken only from pan and save in a covered bowl. Mix together yogurt and seasoning (salt, black pepper, red chili, coriander, cumin, paprika, gram masala, sugar, lemon zest). Blend corn starch in lemon juice, and mix with yogurt-seasoning. Stir liquid in saucepan and simmer until sauce is thickened. Slit chicken flesh in a few places and return chicken back into saucepan, cover the pan and cook for a few minutes. Serve with rice.

Elegant Turkey Meatball (Kofta)

(With herbs and Turkish apricots)

Preparing this dish is time consuming but yields a wonderful fragrance of herbs and great taste
to strengthen your body physically, mentally, and emotionally like a "*herbal tonic*".

Serves 10-12

Main Ingredients:

Rice and Parsley Cooking:

1 cup basmati rice, washed, drained

2 cups fresh water + add ¼ teaspoon sea salt

1 cup Italian parsley, cleaned, chopped

Crisp Fried Onion and Split Peas:

2 onions, thinly shredded

¼ cup olive oil

½ cup split peas

1½ cup fresh water

Presoaking Apricot and Cranberries/Zereshk:

16-20 Turkish dried apricots divided

¼ cup dried cranberries/zereshk

Assembling Meatball:

1½ pounds turkey, ground

1 egg, slightly beaten

2 tablespoons dill, dried

1 tablespoon of each dried herb (mint, basil, savory, tarragon)

1 teaspoon sea salt OR to taste

½ teaspoon black pepper, freshly ground

¼ teaspoon saffron, ground

Stock Making:

4-5 cups fresh water

½ cup tomato paste (see Tips, Tomatoes, page 189)

1 cup fennel bulbs, chopped

½ teaspoon sea salt

Juice of 1 lemon+ 2 tablespoons turbinado raw sugar

Rice and Parsley Cooking: In a medium sized pot, add Basmati rice with 2 cups fresh water and ¼ teaspoon salt and parsley. Bring contents to boil, stir twice, and reduce the heat. Cover the pot and simmer gently until the water is nearly all absorbed and the rice is soft and firm (half-cooked). Leave to cool in covered pot.

Crisp Fried Onion and Fried Split Peas: Stir-fry onions in heated olive oil until crisp and golden brown. Set aside half of stir fried onions for making stock. Add split peas into remaining fried onion and stir-fry for 1 minute or until split peas develop a slightly nutty aroma. Place the split peas-onion mixture in a medium-sized saucepan; cover peas with 1 ½ cups fresh water. Bring to a boil, turn down the heat and simmer in partially covered saucepan, about 20 minutes or until peas are half cooked; drain and mash. Cool in covered pot.

Presoaking Apricots and Cranberries/Zereshk: In a mixing bowl, presoak Turkish dried apricots and cranberries/zereshk with fresh water (the water should be enough to cover them nicely). After 15 minutes, drain off the water and pat-dry.

Assembling meatball: In a large mixing bowl, break ground turkey into smaller pieces with fork, add partially cooked rice and split pea mixture, egg, dill, mint, basil, savory, tarragon, 1 teaspoon salt, black pepper, and saffron. Knead ingredients together with your fingertips (it is important to mix by hand for several minutes; knead until mixture sticks together and forms a cohesive, pliable concoction). For each meatball take about 1/3 cup of this mixture and make a ball. Insert 1 apricot and a few cranberries/zereshk in the center of each ball; seal the seam and re-round. Make all of the mixture into meatball and set aside.

Stock Making: In stock pot, add fresh water, remaining stir-fry onions and tomato paste, fennel and ½ teaspoon salt. Bring the contents to a rolling boil. Carefully add meatballs into boiling liquid (be sure liquid completely covers each meatball); reduce the heat to a slow simmer. After a few minutes of cooking, uncover the pot, let meatball simmer about 45 minutes; add lemon juice and sugar to the simmering liquid and continue to simmer for 10 more minutes or until done. On an oval shape platter, arrange meatballs and decorate the top of each meatball with one Turkish apricot. This traditional meal makes a beautiful impression for any gathering.

Grilled Spicy Chicken

Serves 4

Preheat oven to 350 degree F.

> 1 teaspoon arrowroot powder
> 1 teaspoon sea salt OR to taste
> 2 tablespoons curry powder (see Tips "*Indian-style curry powder mixture*", page 183)
> 1 egg, slightly beaten
> 4 pieces chicken breast, skinned, deboned, cut lengthwise into thin strips, rinse and pat-dry
> 4 pita breads
> ½ cup plain strained yogurt OR Greek yogurt, divided
> **Garnish:** 1 cup sprouted radish

In a small bowl add arrowroot, salt, curry powder, mix well. Place slightly beaten egg into separate bowl. Dip chicken into egg and sprinkle with spices on both side.

On a broiler tray with screen on top, arrange chicken in single layer. Transfer broiler tray onto middle rack of oven. Cook for 25-30 minutes or until chicken is done. For each sandwich place one-fourth of the chicken on warmed pita bread, sprinkle with 2 tablespoons yogurt and garnish with sprouted radish. Fold pita like a sandwich and enjoy.

Lamb Shank Tagine

Serves 4

Preheat oven to 325 degree F.   Use a Tagine OR a tightly covered oven-proof dish

    1 large onion, chopped

    ¼ cup olive oil

    2 pounds grass fed lamb shank, visible fat removed, cut in half

    2 large tomatoes, peeled, minced (2 cups)

    2 tablespoons garlic, chopped

    2 tablespoons organic orange zest, freshly grated

    1 teaspoon sea salt OR to taste

    ¼ teaspoon black pepper, freshly ground

    2 tablespoons *"Moroccan-style mixed spices"*
    (see Tips, page 188)

    4 small carrots sticks, peeled, sliced 1-inch sections

    4 small parsnips, peeled, sliced 1-inch sections

    2 tablespoons green bell pepper, chopped

    8 dried prunes, presoaked, pitted

Lamb Shank Tagine

Garnish:

    A few red onion rings, cilantro and lemon wedges

Stir-fry onion in heated olive oil for a few minutes until translucent. Add lambs and continue to stir-fry until both sides of lamb are slightly brownish.

Combine tomatoes, garlic, orange zest, salt and black pepper in blender and blend for a few seconds or until puree. Add tomato mixture to the bottom of Tagine dish. Place lamb shank-onion mixture in center, sprinkle lamb-shank with Moroccan mixed spices. Arrange carrot, parsnips, green bell pepper, and prunes around lamb shank. Cover the Tagine and place on lower rack of oven and cook for 1½ -2 hours or until lamb is fork tender and fall off from the bone easily. Garnish lamb-shank with onion rings, cilantro and lemon wedges and serve with green vegetables of your choice.

Marinated Chicken to Skewer for Barbeque (BBQ)

Serves 6

Marinating sauce:

1 tablespoon tamari sauce

1 tablespoon brown sugar

1 tablespoon olive oil

2 tablespoons rice vinegar

4 cloves of garlic, minced

1 tablespoon lemon juice, freshly squeezed

¼ teaspoon sea salt OR to taste

¼ teaspoon black pepper, freshly ground

¼ teaspoon dried rosemary

¼ teaspoon dried thyme

¼ teaspoon dried basil

1 dash oregano

Chicken:

2 pounds chicken breast, without bone, cut into bite size pieces

Marinate chicken with sauce overnight in refrigerator. Next day strain off marinate and skew 2-3 pieces of chicken breast on each wooden skewer or rosemary branch and barbeque. Serve with grilled/roasted bell pepper*, onion, tomatoes and *"steamed basmati rice"* (see page106).

*Roasting Bell Pepper,** choose 2 different color of bell peppers. Cut in half, remove seeds and membranes. Cut in 2-inch sections. Place in the bowl, sprinkle with ¼ teaspoon sea salt, and 1/8 teaspoon black pepper, and 1 teaspoon olive oil. Mix together. Arrange peppers in single layer (skin side down) on a foil-lined shallow baking pan. Place pan uncovered in pre-heated 425 degree F. oven and cook for 15-20 minutes or until the edges slightly blackened on all sides, turning peppers once to avoid burning. Serve as a side dish with your main barbeque dish.

Note: The barbequed chicken can also be used in a green salad.

Variation: Marinating Sauce with Blended Herbs, in a small bowl mix ½ teaspoon of each **_minced_** herb (green leaf parsley, chervil, fennel, thyme, sweet marjoram, sage, and basil), with 2 shallots (chopped), ¼ teaspoon sea salt or to taste, ¼ teaspoon black pepper (freshly ground), ¼ cup apple cider, ¼ cup olive oil. Blend all ingredients to make sauce and marinate 2 pounds chicken breast (without bone and cut into bite size pieces) overnight. Follow above recipe for skewing and barbequing.

Prawns with Coconut Milk

(Thai-style dish)

Serves 4

4 ounces coconut meat, finely ground (about 2 cups)

1 cup boiling water

1 pound prawns, OR jumbo white shrimp OR Scampi, cleaned

1 cup pastry flour

1 teaspoon sugar

¼ teaspoon paprika

½ teaspoon sea salt OR to taste

¼ teaspoon black pepper, freshly ground

½ teaspoon curry powder

2 eggs, slightly beaten

1 cup unsweetened coconut, finely ground

4 tablespoons olive oil

Garnish:

1 tablespoon cilantro, chopped

Coconut Milk: Remove coconut meat from coconut shell with a sharp knife, grate finely in blender or food processor. Add boiling water to coconut meat and allow it to stand for 10 minutes. Blend the mixture until pureed. Strain the puree through double thickness of cheesecloth, squeezing it by hand to remove liquid (coconut milk); discard the solids.

Peel and devein prawns; leaving tail on. Lay each prawn flat on a cutting board and cover with heavy duty plastic food wrap. With a wooden hammer gently pound the prawns twice so they become flat like butterflies.

In a small bowl, mix flour, sugar, paprika, salt and pepper and curry. Set up four small bowls. Add 1 cup coconut milk to the first bowl, the pastry flour mixture to the second bowl, eggs in the third bowl, and 1 cup fine coconut (unsweetened) to the fourth bowl. Dip prawns and coat with coconut milk, then the flour-mixture, then eggs, and finally the fine coconut.

Fry the coated prawns in heated olive oil for 2-3 minutes watching carefully to prevent burning. Garnish with cilantro and serve with vegetable salad as a great main dish.

Note: You may place prawns in a single layer on a greased cookie sheet and bake in a 325 degree F. oven for 6-8 minutes instead of frying them.

Roasted Chicken with Various Spices

Serves 6

Preheat oven to 375 degree F. Use an unglazed clay roasting pot (called a Roman-pot*)

- 4 cloves of garlic, crushed
- 2 teaspoons granulated sugar
- 2 teaspoons lemon juice, freshly squeezed
- 2 teaspoons sea salt, divided
- ¼ teaspoon black pepper, freshly ground
- 4 pounds whole chicken, skin on
- 1 teaspoon tarragon, dried
- ¼ teaspoon paprika powder
- ¼ cup teaspoon coriander powder
- 1 dash brown mustard powder
- 2 tablespoons olive oil
- 1 dash saffron powder

In a small mixing bowl, combine and mix garlic, sugar, lemon juice, 1 teaspoon salt, and pepper to make a paste. Coat the inside of the chicken with this mixture. Combine and mix tarragon, remaining (1 teaspoon) salt, paprika, coriander, and mustard. Rub the chicken's skin generously with this herb and spice mixture.

Place chicken, breast side up in prepared (water soaked) Roman pot and place in oven. Bake in the oven for 10 minutes. Reduce the heat to 325 degree F. and cook for 1 hour and 15 minutes. Remove chicken from the oven and test for doneness, insert an instant- read thermometer into the meatiest part of the chicken. It should read 165 degree F. or higher.

Increase the oven temperature to 400 degree F. Mix olive oil with saffron. Brush the skin side of the chicken gently with the oil-saffron mixture. Return chicken uncovered to the middle rack of the oven. Roast for another 5 minutes or until the skin is golden brown color and crispy.

*Roman-pot has a special serrated bottom that keeps the food raised out of the liquid and provides moisture throughout the roasting period; poultry, meat, and vegetables have extra moisture and tenderness when prepared in these pot. Before using the Roman pot in the oven, it is extremely important to submerge both the clay pot and the lid in warm water for 15 minute. This will prevent the pot from cracking. When food is done, take the lid off; otherwise, the food will continue to cook until it has cooled.

Root Vegetable Casserole

(This classic dish makes a delicious first course, or a light super vegetable dish in its own right).

Serves 8

Preheat oven to 325 degree F.

1 medium yam/sweet potato

2 parsnips, remove woody part of older parsnip (if there is any)

4 small young red beets

2 small turnips

2 small rutabaga (Swiss turnip)

8 young carrots

10 mini shallot, peeled

4 cloves of garlic, chopped

1 teaspoon sea salt OR to taste

¼ teaspoon black pepper, freshly ground

2 sprigs rosemary, cleaned

½ cup chicken broth, thickened

½ cup (high quality) white drinking wine

2 tablespoons olive oil

1 tablespoon arrowroot powder (to be dissolved in 4 tablespoons cold water)

Juice of 1 lemon, freshly squeezed

¼ cup "*saffron-zereshk-jam*" (optional), see Tips, page 186.

All vegetables (yam, parsnips, beets, turnips, rutabagas, and carrots) need to be properly cleaned, peeled, and cut in about 1-inch pieces.

In a large 4-quart ovenproof casserole pot, arrange one layer of each vegetable roots (yam, parsnip, beet, turnip, rutabaga, carrot, shallot and garlic). Sprinkle with salt and pepper and top with rosemary sprigs. Add chicken broth and wine to the pot and drizzle with olive oil. Cover the pot and bring to simmer over medium heat on stovetop. Place the covered pot into oven and cook for 45 minutes. Remove from oven, stir gently. Sprinkle mixture of arrowroot-water and lemon juice over vegetables and add "*saffron-zereshk jam*". Return to oven and cook for 30 minutes more or until the vegetables are fork tender. Remove the rosemary branches prior to serving.

Sandwich with Crimini Mushroom

(It is delicious, nutritious and easy to make)

Serves 4

Preheat oven to 350 degree F.

16 oz. crimini button mushrooms (about 16), wipe-dried with a clean cloth, halved

4 medium shallots, peeled, quartered

2 teaspoons olive oil

¼ teaspoon thyme

¼ cup walnuts, coarsely chopped

¼ teaspoon sea salt OR to taste

1 dash black pepper, freshly ground

½ cup parsley leaves, cleaned, stemmed, finely chopped

1 cup radish sprouts OR another spicy sprout

¼ cup mustard* divided

4 small wheat pita breads** OR lavash OR another flat-bread

In a medium mixing bowl, add mushrooms and shallots; drizzle with olive oil and sprinkle with thyme. Gently mix together. Place a grill-screen over a baking tray. Arrange mushrooms and shallots on screen in single layer and place on middle rack of oven***. Bake for 15 minutes until mushrooms become slightly dry. Remove tray and let mushrooms cool for a few minutes.

Place walnuts in a food processor, and pulse 4 times, add the roasted mushrooms and shallots, salt, and black pepper. Pulse the processor for a few times until mixture is coarsely chopped. Transfer into serving bowl, add parsley and radish sprouts, and gently toss.

Spread mustard on each warm pita bread, top with mushroom mixture and fold to make a wonderful tasty sandwich. Enjoy!

*The stone ground, organic, brown mustard with apple cider vinegar, is my preference.

**Pita and Lebanese flat bread usually is called pocket bread and is made with wheat flour.

***Any drippings from vegetables will fall on tray and your oven will remain clean.

Note: Crimini mushrooms have more flavor and are firmer than white button mushrooms.

Seasoned Chicken Patties

(This may be the perfect dinner dish; elegant, delicious and best of all easy to make)

Serves 4

Preheat oven to 400 degree F.

>   3 large shallots, chopped
>   4 cloves of garlic, chopped
>   ½-inch ginger root, peeled, grated
>   1 tablespoon mild red bell pepper, chopped
>   ¼ cup extra virgin olive oil
>   6 crimini button mushrooms, cleaned, chopped
>   1 tablespoon lemongrass*, chopped, minced
>   ½ pound lean chicken, ground
>   ½ teaspoon salt OR to taste
>   1 dash black pepper, freshly ground
>   ¼ teaspoon of each herb rosemary and thyme, ground
>   1 teaspoon basil, ground
>   1 dash Italian seasoning OR oregano, ground
>   **Garnish:** ½ pound kale and ½ pound snow peas and lemon wedges

Seasoned chicken patties

In a large frying pan, stir-fry shallot, garlic, ginger and bell pepper in heated olive oil for a few minutes until onion is translucent. Combine mushrooms and lemongrass and add to shallots mixture and continue to stir-fry for 4 minutes or until the mushrooms color change slightly and mixture appears dry; watch carefully so mixture does not burn. Let it cool.

In a mixing bowl combine and mix all ingredients (shallot mushroom mixture, chicken, salt, pepper, rosemary, thyme, basil, and Italian seasoning). With hands knead the ingredients (about one minute) until thoroughly mixed. Refrigerate at least 1 hour and when you are ready, form into 8-10 patties. Arrange patties on broiler pan and place on the middle rack of oven. Bake for 10-12 minutes or until slightly golden brown. Turn over patties, and bake for 5 minutes more or until done. Serve these delicious patties on bed of lightly steamed kale and snow peas, and garnish with lemon wedges.

*Lemongrass, is an aromatic grass that has an essential oil also found in lemon peel; it has a sour lemon like flavor and fragrance. Fresh lemongrass is used in *Thai and Vietnamese cuisine*. Wrap fresh lemongrass tightly in a plastic bag and store in refrigerator for one to two weeks. When you are ready, use only white base (up to where leaves begin to branch and stem becomes woody) and then bruise the stem, slice, chop and mince.

Note: If lemongrass is not available use freshly made zest from 1 organic lemon.

Seasoned Turkey Taco Filling

Serves 4

    1 pound turkey, ground
    ¼ teaspoon sage
    ¼ teaspoon thyme
    ¼ teaspoon cinnamon
    ¼ teaspoon sea salt OR to taste
    ¼ teaspoon black pepper, freshly ground
    ½ teaspoon ginger root, finely chopped
    2 tablespoon olive oil

To a mixing bowl, add all ingredients except olive oil (turkey, sage, thyme, cinnamon, salt, pepper, and ginger). Knead ingredients for 30 seconds until thoroughly mixed. Cover the bowl and refrigerate overnight. Next day, in a medium size skillet, brown turkey mixture in heated olive oil. Break up ground meat into smaller pieces as it browns (turkey is done when it turns brown and is no longer pink). Use with shredded green lettuce and pickles to fill taco-shell.

Sage is the herb of wisdom as you age, a symbol
of infinite spirit, and is high in nutrients
(Please see Glossary, sage leaves, page 239)

Spicy Oven-Fried Chicken

Many Asian recipes call for marinating meat, poultry, and sea food before cooking. A marinate is a mixture of natural tenderizers such as lime, Seville orange, kiwi, pomegranate juice, soy sauce, tamari sauce, tamarind, *yogurt and herbs and/or spices*. Marinating raw meat etc. produces a delightful taste when cooked.

Serves 4

Preheat oven to 350 degree F.

> 1 cup plain yogurt
> ¼ cup Dijon mustard
> ¼ tablespoon ginger root, grated
> 6 cloves of garlic, crushed
> 4 whole chicken legs, skinned, rinsed, pat-dried, cut into drumsticks and thighs
> 2 cups unseasoned bread crumbs
> 1 teaspoon sea salt OR to taste
> ¼ teaspoon sage
> ¼ teaspoon oregano
> 1 teaspoon black pepper, freshly ground
> ¼ teaspoon paprika OR saffron
> ¼ teaspoon turmeric

In a mixing bowl, mix yogurt, mustard, ginger and garlic. Add chicken pieces and stir until chicken is thoroughly coated, refrigerate overnight. In another mixing bowl combine and mix bread crumbs, salt, and herbs and spices (sage, oregano, pepper, paprika and turmeric). Drain marinated chicken pieces and roll in bread crumbs mixture to coat. Arrange in single layer on grilling-pan and transfer into oven. Bake uncovered, on the middle rack of oven for 35 minutes. Turn chicken pieces over and continue baking for 8-10 minutes or until the chicken is cooked through and evenly browned on top. The result is a moist succulent chicken which can be served with steamed basmati rice and a green salad of your choice.

Variation: Spicy Oven-fried Chicken Breasts, to a power-blender add 1 cup plain yogurt, 1 teaspoon ginger root (chopped), 1 teaspoon garlic (chopped), 1 teaspoon turmeric, 1 teaspoon sea salt, ½ teaspoon gram-masala, 1½ teaspoon coriander, ¼ teaspoon saffron powder, ¼ teaspoon black pepper and 1 dash chili powder). Blend together. Pour marinate on 2 large chicken breasts (boneless, skinless and deep slit chicken flesh in a few places), stir to coat and refrigerate overnight. Next day drain marinated chicken pieces and arrange in single layer on grilling-pan, transfer into oven and follow above recipe for baking.

Sweet and Sour Moroccan Dish

Serves 4

Preheat oven to 350 degree F.   Use an ovenproof Tagine OR a tightly covered dish

    1 large onion, finely shredded

    1 teaspoon ginger root, peeled, finely chopped

    ¼ cup extra virgin olive oil

    2 pounds chicken breast

    (4 chicken breast halves), skinned, boned

    1 teaspoon sea salt, divided

    ¼ teaspoon of each ground spices (black pepper,

    cayenne, coriander, cinnamon, turmeric and fennel)

    2 tablespoons tamarind paste

    2 tablespoons brown sugar

    1 ½ tablespoon tomato paste

    ¼ cup chicken broth

    ¼ teaspoon dried orange peel

    1 tablespoon arrowroot powder

    2 tablespoon cold water (arrowroot to be completely dissolved in this water)

    2 carrots, peeled, sliced ½-inch diagonally

    10 mini potatoes, brushed, rinsed

Elegant Moroccan Style Dish

Garnish: Roasted bell pepper (see, roasting bell pepper, page 77) and cilantro
In a large skillet, stir-fry onion and ginger in heated olive oil just a few minutes. Cut each chicken breast half in half and slit a few places with scissors and add to onion mixture and continue to stir-fry for 4 minutes until the color of chicken on both sides slightly change. Remove chicken from skillet and sprinkle with ¾ teaspoon sea salt, cover and set aside. Stir in ¼ teaspoon of each ground spices (black pepper, cayenne, coriander, cinnamon, turmeric and fennel) and ¼ teaspoon remaining sea salt into mixture of onion and remove skillet from the heat. In a small bowl mix together, tamarind, brown sugar, tomato paste, chicken broth and orange peel and stir in arrowroot-water mixture for preparing sauce. Arrange carrots and potatoes on the bottom of tagine, place chicken on top of the vegetables (carrots and potatoes) and pour sauce mixture on top of chicken. Cover Tagine and place in the oven and cook 15-20 minutes or until chicken is fork tender. Garnish with roasted bell pepper, and cilantro. Serve with steamed rice and yogurt (optional). Enjoy!

Tasty Chicken Curry

Serves 4

Preheat oven to 350 degree F.

    ¼ teaspoon whole coriander seeds

    ¼ teaspoon whole black cumin seeds

    ¼ -inch cinnamon bark

    ½ whole clove

    1 laurel bay leaf

    1 dash thyme

    1 dash hot chili powder

    1 dash black pepper, freshly ground (optional)

    1 teaspoon sea salt OR to taste

    6 onions, finely chopped

    6 cloves of garlic, finely chopped

    ¼ -inch ginger root, peeled, chopped

    ¼ cup extra virgin olive oil

    1 whole chicken (remove giblets, bone, and skin, de-fat and cut in pieces)

    12 small red potatoes, washed thoroughly

    6 medium tomatoes, peeled, sliced

Bay Laurels
(Laurus Nobilis)

Ju-lian Toh
See Glossary, Laurel bay leaf, page 204

Add coriander and cumin seeds, cinnamon bark and clove to a heated heavy-based skillet. Gently swirl skillet over medium heat as you dry-toast spices (no oil), until you smell their fragrance (about 1 minute). Immediately remove from the heat. Allow spices to cool and grind. In a small bowl, mix freshly ground spices with remaining seasoning (bay leaf, thyme, chili pepper, pepper and salt) and set aside.

In an oven proof pot, stir-fry onion, garlic and ginger in heated olive oil until golden brown. Add chicken, and seasoning mixture and stir for 2 minutes. Add potatoes and tomatoes, cover and place in oven for 45 minutes or until chicken and potatoes are done. Remove bay leaf. Serve with plain yogurt and flat bread or steamed basmati rice.

Note: Instead of whole chicken you may use 2 pounds of chicken legs (find the joint of the legs and cut each leg into thighs and drumsticks).

Pasta
Noodles Chow-mein-style
(Master recipe)

Serves 6

Sauce to Marinate Chicken:

1 teaspoon olive oil

1 teaspoon brown rice vinegar

1 tablespoon soy sauce

1 dash white pepper

1 dash sugar (optional)

1 teaspoon cornstarch (dissolve in 1 tablespoon cold water)

1½ pounds chicken breasts, skinned, boned, tenderized, thinly cut in strips

Chow Sauce:

2 tablespoons soy sauce

1 tablespoon cornstarch (dissolve with 2 tablespoon cold water)

¼ cup chicken broth

½ teaspoon sugar

½ teaspoon sea salt and pepper to taste

Rice Noodles:

10 ounces Chinese noodles

5 quarts boiling water with dash of salt

1-2 teaspoons olive oil, divided

Stir-fry:

5 tablespoons toasted sesame oil, divided

2-3 cloves of garlic, minced

1-inch ginger root, minced

4 scallion bulbs (the white parts of the tips), finely chopped OR 1 onion

¼ cup red cabbage, shredded

2 carrots, thinly sliced diagonally, julienned

1 stalk celery, sliced diagonally, julienned

½ red bell pepper, seeded, julienned

Garnish:

½ cup green part of onion, chopped

Sauce to Marinate Chicken: In a bowl, mix olive oil, rice vinegar, soy sauce, white pepper, sugar, and cornstarch, cover chicken with mixture and refrigerate for 30 minutes.

Chow Sauce: In a small bowl mix ingredients (soy sauce, cornstarch mixture, chicken broth, sugar, salt and pepper). Set aside.

To Prepare Rice Noodles: Soften the noodles by placing in boiling water (with a dash of salt) for 1-2 minutes until noodles are soft but not mushy. While separating as many strands as possible (with the help of chopsticks or fork) pour into colander and rinse with cold water for a few seconds to stop the cooking process and remove any extra starch. Drain thoroughly. Sprinkle with 1 teaspoon olive oil to keep noodles moist and prevent sticking. Set aside.

Stir-fry Chicken: Warm wok over high heat (preferably on a gas stove). Add 1 tablespoon sesame oil. Stir-fry chicken strips for 2 minutes or until chicken is nearly cooked through and remove from wok. Place in a container, drizzle with 1 teaspoon olive oil, cover and set aside.

Stir-fry Vegetables: Heat wok to very hot*, add 2 tablespoons sesame oil. Stir-fry garlic, ginger and scallion for 2 minutes in heated sesame oil. Add cabbage, stir-fry for 1 minute, remove and set aside. Stir-fry carrots, celery, and bell pepper in 2 tablespoons heated sesame oil for 2 minutes.

Complete Stir-fry: Add chicken and cabbage to vegetables in wok, make a "well" in the middle, add chow sauce and stir quickly (thirty seconds) to thicken sauce. Add rice noodles and gently combine everything together with sauce. Cover the wok, turn off the heat and let steam for 30 seconds. Garnish with scallions and serve warm.

*In general, Chinese cooking requires a great deal of food preparation time, however, the actual cooking time may only take a few minutes. A wok is heated very hot prior to cooking, and vegetables oil such as sesame oil is used (I use olive oil for gentle stir-fry and sesame oil as a seasoning). You may use cornstarch as a thickener; dissolve ½ tablespoon cornstarch in 1 tablespoon cold water and use as a thickening for stir-frying.

Note: The main distinction between "*Lo-mein*" and "*Chow-mein*" are:

a) The type of noodles that are used. Lo-mein noodles are soft while chow-mein noodles are crisp.
b) Lo-mein means tossed noddles and chow-mein means fried noodles. In both dishes, the noodles used are made with egg noodles or wheat flour noodles and eggs.
c) Fresh egg noodles are best for lo-mein, and either fresh/dried noodles can be used for chow-mein.
d) The most important ingredient of any "lo-mein" or "chow-mein" dish is the SAUCE, it is the key ingredients in these two dishes. Normally lo-mein recipes have a little more sauce (because soft lo-mein noodles soak up more sauce than crispy fried noodles of chow-mein). Overall the main difference between these two comes down to frying time. The crispier chow-mein noodles requires adding a little more oil and increase the frying time.

Pasta Baked with Chicken, Zucchini and Tomatoes

Serves 4

Preheat oven to 350 degree F.   Greased and lightly floured a large oven proof -pan

Chicken and Seasoning:

½ pound, lean ground chicken

¼ teaspoon sea salt

1 dash black pepper

¼ teaspoon rosemary

1 dash Italian seasoning

¼ teaspoon thyme

1 teaspoon basil

1-inch lemongrass, finely chopped OR 1 tablespoon organic lemon zest (freshly grated)

Zucchini and Seasoning:

2 medium zucchinis, thinly sliced

½ teaspoon sea salt OR to taste

¼ teaspoon black pepper, freshly ground

¼ teaspoon thyme

Frying Onion Mixture:

2 medium onion, thinly shredded

4 cloves of garlic, peeled, minced

1-inch ginger root, peeled, grated

¼ cup olive oil

Noodles Cooking:

6 oz. brown rice noodles, partially cooked with 2 teaspoons sea salt, and 4 drops olive oil (cook noodles for 7 minutes), drain

Completing Pasta Bake:

3 medium tomatoes, thinly sliced, discard tomatoes juice

2 teaspoons lemon juice, freshly squeezed

Garnish:

¼ cup goat cheese, crumbled

2 tablespoons basil leaves, chopped

In a small bowl season chicken with a mixture of salt, black pepper, rosemary, Italian seasoning, thyme, basil and lemongrass, and place in refrigerate for one hour. In another bowl, season zucchini with mixture of salt, black pepper, and thyme, and set aside. Stir-fry onion, garlic, and ginger in heated olive oil for a few minutes or until onion turns slightly golden brown. Add seasoned chicken and continue to stir-fry for 2 more minutes as you breaking up ground chicken into smaller pieces. In an oven proof pan place partially cooked noodles. Cover noodles completely with zucchini, onion and chicken mixture, and top with sliced tomatoes. Sprinkle tomatoes with lemon juice.

Bake uncovered in the oven for 25 minutes. Remove from oven, sprinkle with goat cheese and basil, return to oven and continue bake for 2 more minutes or until done. Serve warm.

Pasta baked with chicken, zucchini and tomatoes

Pasta with Mango Sauce

Serves 6

Mango Sauce:

4 tablespoons mango powder*

¼ cup thickened chicken broth

3 tablespoons sugar

2 tablespoons olive oil

½ teaspoon curry powder

½ teaspoon sea salt OR to taste

¼ teaspoon black pepper, freshly ground

Brown Rice Pasta:

1 gallon fresh water (4 quarts)

¼ teaspoon olive oil

1 teaspoon sea salt OR to taste

10 oz. whole grain brown rice spaghetti

Garnish:

½ cup green onion, and red bell pepper, cut 1-inch diagonally

In a small saucepan, mix sauce ingredients (mango powder, chicken broth, sugar, 2 tablespoons olive oil, curry powder, ½ teaspoon salt, and pepper). Simmer for a few minutes until a paste is formed, and set aside.

In a large stock pot, bring water to rolling boil. Add ¼ teaspoon olive oil, 1 teaspoon salt and pasta. Cook pasta for 8-9 minutes or until cooked but still firm, stir gently a few times while pasta is cooking. Drain pasta and rinse with cold water. Toss with mango sauce and garnish with onion and bell pepper.

*Ground, sun-dried, unripe, green mango is called Amchur/Amchor in India.

Rice Spaghetti

(Gluten free pasta)

Serves 6

Pasta:

1 gallon water (4 quarts)

2 tablespoons sea salt OR to taste

¼ teaspoon olive oil

10 oz. brown rice whole grain spaghetti

Prepare Sauce:

2 eggs, lightly beaten

6 tablespoons olive oil OR 2 tablespoons butter

½ cup tomato basil sauce

Garnish: ¼ cup shredded basil leaves and 12-oz. organic shredded mild cheddar cheese

In extra large stockpot, bring water to boil. Add salt and ¼ teaspoon olive oil. Add spaghetti to boiling water, and begin timing for 7 minutes or until desired tenderness. Gently stir occasionally while maintaining a rolling boil so spaghetti does not sticky together. Drain pasta and immediately rinse with a little cold water (pasta will not be completely cooked). In meantime prepare sauce.

In a large saucepan, scramble eggs into 6 tablespoons heated olive oil for 30 seconds and stir in tomato basil sauce. Add drained pasta loosely (without stirring) on top of sauce. Gently mix pasta and sauce. Transfer pasta into individual warmed serving plate and garnish with basil and perimeter of the plate with cheese prior to serve.

Vegetables Pasta with Chicken-Cabbage Lo-mein-style

Serves 4-5

Marinate-sauce and Chicken:

12 oz. (about 2 cups) chicken thighs, skinned, boneless, thinly sliced (¼-inch thick)

1 tablespoon soy sauce/tamari (wheat-free soy sauce)

1 tablespoon rice cooking wine (that has no sugar/synthetic enzyme added)

1 tablespoon toasted sesame oil

1 teaspoon organic cornstarch (dissolve in soy sauce, rice wine and sesame oil mixture)

1 pinch black pepper, freshly ground

Spaghetti and Vegetables:

1 gallon (4 quarts) water

2 teaspoons sea salt (for cooking pasta)

½ cup vegetable oil (divided) plus a few drops olive oil for cooking pasta

10 oz. organic brown rice spaghetti

1 onion, chopped

6 cloves of garlic, chopped

1-inch ginger root, peeled, chopped

2 cups green onions, shredded

8 cups Napa cabbage, thinly sliced

2 cups crimini button mushrooms, cleaned, pat-dried, sliced

Base Sauce to Stir-fry:

1 teaspoon cornstarch

2 tablespoons cold water (to be combined with cornstarch)

¼ cup vegetable oil (olive oil is preferable)

1 tablespoon tamari OR soy-sauce

1 dash sea salt and black pepper OR to taste

Garnish (optional):

¼ cup lightly toasted sesame seeds

½ cup organic bean-sprouts

Marinate-sauce and Chicken: In a small bowl, combine chicken with marinate-sauce (mixture of soy-sauce, rice wine, sesame oil, cornstarch and pepper) and refrigerate in covered bowl for several hours/overnight. When you are ready to stir-fry, drain meat (if any liquid remains).

Spaghetti and Vegetables: In a large pot, bring water to a boil. Add 2 teaspoons salt and a few drops of olive oil. Add spaghetti to boiling water; stir gently for a few seconds. Cook spaghetti about 4-5 minutes (or according to package directions) while maintaining a rolling boil and stirring occasionally until the texture is al-dente; do not overcook. Drain and immediately rinse for a few seconds with cold water, shaking well to remove excess water. Heat a wok over high heat until hot (and a few drops of water vaporizes within 1-2 seconds of contact). Swirl in 2 tablespoons vegetable oil and add pasta. Stir-fry for 30 seconds, with a spatula, until color changes slightly. Remove the pasta from wok and keep warm in a covered container (to prevent evaporation and maintain moisture). Clean the wok if necessary.

Heat 2 tablespoons vegetable oil in wok, and place over medium-high heat; add onion, garlic, ginger. Stir-fry for 1 minute; add marinated chicken and arrange evenly in wok. Brown chicken quickly over medium-high heat to seal juices by cooking undisturbed for 30 seconds and continuing to stir-fry for 1 minute. Remove chicken from wok and keep warm in another covered container.

Heat ¼ cup vegetable oil in wok over medium-high heat; add green onions and cabbage. Stir-fry for 1 minute, add mushrooms, and continue to stir-fry until vegetables color changes slightly. Pile all vegetables on one side of wok or remove to another container.

Base Sauce to Stir-fry: In a small mixing bowl, mix cornstarch and cold water, add ¼ cup vegetable oil, tamari, salt, and black pepper. Add to the wok. Stir-fry quickly for 30 seconds until sauce thickens. Add partially cooked chicken and pasta to sauce and stir for 30 seconds. Add vegetables, stir-fry quickly for 1 minute more or until chicken is cooked, noodles are heated through and vegetables are coated with sauce. Garnish with sesame seeds and sprouts and serve immediately.

Pickles and Relishes

The seasoned brine and/or vinegar used to preserve foods also enhances their flavor.
Pickles and relishes can be very refreshing when served as a condiment with a main dish. A study shows that
fermented vegetables such as sauerkraut and kimchi are good for digestion because during the fermentation
process, chemicals changes occur from enzymes produced by good bacteria.
These changes can encourages better intestinal health.
From a flavor standpoint, pickled fruits and vegetables and fermented foods
(such as yogurt, kimchi, pickles) are the best.

Cucumber, see Glossary, Page 213
and
Cucumber Pickling, page 97

Chutney with Apple, Mango and Pineapple

Chutney originated in India, and is usually made from fruits, vinegar, sugar, and aromatic herbs and spices. Its texture can be smooth or chunky and its flavor can be mild to hot. It is flavorful, can boosts the appetite and aid digestion. Chutney is used as a condiment to various dishes such as roast or tandoori chicken.

Serves 6

> 1 red apple, cored, diced
>
> 1/3 cup bell pepper, peeled, seeded, diced
>
> 1/3 cup red onion, chopped
>
> ½ cup pineapple flesh, diced
>
> ½ cup mango flesh, diced
>
> 1 dash sea salt OR to taste
>
> 1 dash black pepper, freshly ground
>
> ½ dash hot red pepper (optional)

Combine all ingredients, serve and enjoy.

Chutney with Tamarind

(A delicious relish from the East India)

Serves 6+

> 4 ounces Hindi tamarind pulp (purchase in Indian market)
>
> 4 cups distilled hot water
>
> ½-inch ginger root, grated
>
> 1 dash coriander, ground
>
> 1 pinch jalapeno chili pepper
>
> ¼ teaspoon sea salt OR to taste
>
> 2 tablespoons raw honey OR brown sugar

In a non-acidic reactive covered container, soak tamarind pulp with hot water for several hours. Strain through a fine sieve into a bowl, pressing on the tamarind solids with the back of a spoon to extract the liquids then discard the solids. In a saucepan combine tamarind liquid and remaining ingredients (ginger, coriander, chili pepper, salt and honey). Simmer over low-medium heat, stirring often until the mixture is thick. Test for taste, add more water or seasoning if needed. Allow to cool and refrigerate in air-tight sterilized jar for 2 weeks/freezer for 2 month.

Variation: Master Worcestershire Sauce (serves 4):

> 1 tablespoon balsamic vinegar OR malt vinegar (from distilled barley)

1 tablespoon olive oil

1 ½ tablespoons tamarind paste

2 tablespoons brown sugar OR 2 teaspoons molasses

¼ cup distilled water

1½ teaspoons arrowroot powder

¼ teaspoon ginger powder

1 pinch cayenne and 1 pinch peppercorn (freshly ground)

½ teaspoon sea salt OR to taste

¼ teaspoon of each ground spices (turmeric, coriander, fennel, fenugreek, and cinnamon)

In a blender, blend ingredients until smooth. Pour liquid into a saucepan, bring to simmer, reduce the heat, stir continually and simmer for 2-3 minutes until desire consistency sauce is made (about ½ cup). Allow to cool and refrigerate in airtight sterilized jar for several hours. Use "*Master Worcestershire Sauce*" for seasoning meats and as a table condiment.

Cucumber Pickling

Cucumber Pickling:

1-inch cinnamon bark, cut into small pieces

1 teaspoon coriander seeds

½-inch ginger root, cut into small pieces

2 whole cloves

1 teaspoon sea salt OR to taste

1 pinch each of the following spices and herbs: allspice seeds, mustard seeds, black peppercorns, dill seeds, cardamom seeds, hot chili pepper and bay leaf (crushed)

8 small cucumbers, poked a few times with a fork

10-ounce distilled white wine vinegar

6-ounce distilled water

Fold 6-inch of cheesecloth a few times and place all of the spices and herbs in the center (cinnamon, coriander, ginger root, cloves, salt, allspice, mustard seeds, peppercorns, dill seeds, cardamom seeds, chili pepper and bay leaf). Gathering the edges of cheesecloth and tie securely. Place the cheese cloth at the bottom of an airtight sterilized pickling jar. Fill the jar with cucumbers, white wine vinegar and water. Cover the jar and store in a dark, cool place. While pickling occurs over the next 2-3 weeks, shake the jar occasionally. Remove spices after 3 weeks or when cucumbers are ready for use.

Kimchi

(This national Korean dish date back to millennia).

Serves 6

1 Chinese napa cabbage

1 dash sea salt

1 teaspoon vinegar

¼ teaspoon sea salt OR to taste

1 dash hot chili pepper

¼ teaspoon horseradish, peeled, finely chopped

6 cloves of garlic, finely chopped

1-inch ginger, peeled, finely chopped

4 scallion bulbs, cleaned, pat-dried, chopped

2 teaspoons rice vinegar

1 teaspoon sesame oil

1 teaspoon sesame seeds

In a large bowl, soak the Chinese cabbage in fresh water (the water should cover the cabbage), along with 1 dash salt and 1 teaspoon vinegar for 1 minute. Remove cabbage and pat-dry. Place cabbage on cutting board and cut in half vertically. Cut a small V-shape around each cabbage stems and remove. Place each cabbage half, flat side down on cutting board and cut in half length wise (creating 4 sections). Slice each section into thin strips. Place cabbage strips into large bowl and sprinkle with seasonings (¼ teaspoon salt, chili pepper, horseradish, garlic, ginger and scallions) and add remaining ingredients (rice vinegar, sesame oil and sesame seeds). Gently mix with your clean hands.

Store kimchi in sterilized jar in refrigerator. Serve as a condiment after 1 or 2 days.

Note: German sauerkraut "*sour cabbage*" is made from shredded "*green cabbage*" flavored with salt and juniper berries. Korean kimchi and German sauerkraut both are pickled, preserved, tenderized and fermented in brine.

Pickled Onions

Serves 10

    2 pounds miniature onions, remove only the outer layers of the onions bulbs
    1 pinch dried mint
    1 teaspoon sea salt OR to taste
    1 small jalapeno hot pepper (optional)
    2 quarts (8 cups) distilled white vinegar OR enough to cover onions

Place onions, mint, salt and jalapeno in sterilized pickling jar, and add enough vinegar to cover onions. Place lid on jar and tighten. Leave in a cool, dark place for 2 months before serving. Pickled onions add zest to your condiment dish (especially if jalapenos peppers are used).

Variation: Combine 12 oz. pearl onions (peeled), ½ teaspoon turmeric. ½ teaspoon sea salt or to taste. Place in sterilized jar and add 1 cup apple cider to cover onions. Place lid on jar and tighten. Place jar in cool place at least 48 hours, shake periodically. Serve as a condiment with your favorite main dish.

Pickled Cauliflower and Carrots

Serves 10

    1 head cauliflower, cut into florets
    2 large carrots, peeled, cut into chunks
    ½ bay leaf (laurel)
    ½ teaspoon sea salt OR to taste
    ½-inch cinnamon bark
    ¼ teaspoon of the following spices: cardamom seeds, dill seeds,
    black peppercorns (black pepper), allspices, whole cloves, coriander seeds and
    mustard seed
    ¼ teaspoon ginger root, finely chopped
    1½ cups white vinegar
    ½ cup distilled water

In a sterilized pickling jar, place cauliflower, carrots, bay leaf, salt, cinnamon, cardamom and dill seeds, peppercorns, allspices, cloves, coriander and mustard seeds, and ginger. Fill the jar with vinegar and water, close the lid tightly, and leave undisturbed for 2 weeks in a cool and dark place. After 2 weeks, shake the jar and leave for another week before serving.

Pickled Eggplant with Herbs and Spices

Serves 10

  4 Asian eggplants, roasted, peeled, chopped
  ½ cup distilled water
  1½ cups distilled vinegar
  2 carrots, peeled, diced
  ½ cup cabbage, chopped
  2 tablespoons cauliflower, chopped
  1 tablespoon celery, minced
  10 cloves of garlic, crushed
  1 dash hot red pepper, chopped
  ¼ teaspoon sea salt OR to taste
  ½ tablespoon dried parsley
  ½ teaspoon dried onion (optional)
  1 teaspoon dried basil
  1 teaspoon dried mint
  ½ teaspoon Italian salad herbs
  ½ teaspoon of each spice (cardamom seeds, black caraway seeds, black cumin seeds, angelica, dill seeds, and coriander seeds)
  ¼ teaspoon turmeric, ground
  1 teaspoon sugar OR honey OR 1 sweet mango (peeled, seeded, and chopped)

Please see Glossary, eggplant,
page 215

Place eggplants into blender and blend for 30 seconds. In a large saucepan combine and mix blended eggplant with remaining ingredients. Place on stove top over medium heat and let the mixture come to a simmer and simmer for 15 minutes over low heat. Taste and adjust the seasoning if needed. Allow mixture to cool and place in sterilized air-tight pickle-jars and refrigerate overnight before serving as a condiment.

Pizza

Honest Vegetable Pizza

Lightly fry 1 large grated russet potatoes (squeeze the juice out and discard) in 2 tablespoons heated olive oil to make a round *"**potato-pizza-crust**"*. Reduce the heat to low-medium. Add ½ cup olive oil to the pan from corner. Pour vegetables omelet ingredients mixture (From page 161, "A *fabulous omelet with vegetables*" or your favorite omelet) on top of potato crust. Follow the omelet direction on page 161.

Pizza Dessert with Fresh Fruits

(Harvest moon pizza)

Serves 8

Preheat oven to 350   Grease pizza-pan and dust with flour

Pizza Dough:

3 cups unbleached all-purpose flour

2 teaspoons baking powder

1 dash sea salt (sift together flour, baking powder and salt twice)

½ cup granulated sugar

¾ cup sweet butter (1½ sticks), cut into small pieces and chill

2 large eggs at room temperature (slightly whisk eggs and lemon zest together)

Zest of 1 organic lemon, freshly grated (about 1 tablespoon)

Pizza Topping:

½ cup heavy whipping cream

2 tablespoons powdered sugar (confectioners' sugar)

1 cup fresh strawberries, cut in half

8 red grapes cut in half

8 white grapes cut in half

2 kiwis, peeled, sliced thin

1 banana, peeled, sliced thin

1 peach, sliced thin

1 tablespoon powdered sugar (or as desired)

To prepare pizza dough, see Tips, how to make "*pastry dough*", page 177.

Whip ½ cup chilled heavy whipping cream in a large chilled bowl with electrical beater until it begins to thicken, Add 2 tablespoons powdered sugar; continue to beat until it is just about firm enough to hold its shape (stiff but not dry). Spread this mixture on top of baked and cooled crusts. Arrange strawberries, red and white grapes, kiwi, banana, and peach on baked crust. Sprinkle with powdered sugar. Serve pizza while fresh and colorful.

Note: You may use pineapple instead of grapes.

Pizza with Herbs

(Using herbs and spices in this recipes not only to add flavor,
but contribute useful minerals to your diet).

Serves 8

Preheat oven and baking stone to 425 degree F.

Dough ingredients for *two 9 ½-inch* round pizza:

3 cups unbleached all-purpose flour (organic flour is my preference)

2 teaspoons baking powder

1 dash sea salt (sift flour, baking powder and salt together)

½ cup granulated sugar

¾ cup sweet butter (1½ sticks), cut into small pieces and chill

2 large eggs at room temperature (slightly whisk eggs and lemon zest together)

Zest of 1 organic lemon, freshly grated (about 1 tablespoon)

Topping:

1 sweet red onion, chopped

6 cloves of garlic, chopped

4 tablespoons olive oil, divided

4 small red potatoes, thinly sliced

½ teaspoon sea salt OR to taste

1 dash black pepper, freshly ground

6 sprig Italian parsley, chopped

½ sprig rosemary, chopped

½ teaspoon black cumin seeds

1 dash saffron (optional)

6 sprigs basil

To prepare pizza dough (see Tips, how to make "*pastry dough*" and "*pastry crust*" page 177).

Stir-fry onions and garlic in 3 tablespoons heated olive oil for 30 seconds. Add potatoes and stir-fry for 5 minutes. Add salt, pepper, parsley, rosemary, black cumin and saffron. Continue to stir-fry for 1 more minute or until the potatoes are lightly golden brown. Turn off the heat. Add basil, and mix gently. Spread the mixture evenly over <u>unbaked pizza dough.</u> To keep vegetables moist, brush with remaining 1 tablespoon olive oil. Bake in the oven for 10-15 minutes or until done.

Super Chicken Pizza

Serves 2

Preheat oven to 400 degree F.

To Prepare Thin Chicken:

2 chicken breasts, boned, skinned, slice each breast very thin without detaching
(You have two thinner pieces of chicken breasts which are almost twice as large)

3 tablespoons olive oil, divided

1 dash sea salt

1 dash black pepper, freshly ground

1 dash oregano OR marjoram

Tomatillo Mexican Green Sauce:

6 green tomatillos, cleaned and
cut into bite size pieces

1 dash hot chili OR jalapeno pepper

Salt and pepper to taste

4 teaspoons squeezed lime juice, divided

2 tablespoons cilantro, chopped

4 cloves of garlic, chopped

Cheese:

1 cup Mozzarella cheese, shredded

Garnish:

8 rings of red onions

¼ of red bell pepper, thinly sliced

A few cilantro sprigs

To prepare chicken, spread 1 tablespoon of olive oil on chicken and sprinkle with, salt, pepper and oregano, set aside. To prepare sauce add all sauce ingredients (tomatillo, hot chili, salt and black pepper, 2 teaspoons lime juice, cilantro, garlic and 1 tablespoon olive oil) in blender and run for 1 minute or until sauce is formed (if the sauce is too watery, strain the juice and use solid part). Spread sauce on chicken and sprinkle with Mozzarella cheese. Place on middle rack of the oven and cook for 8-10 minutes. Meantime prepare garnish, sauté onion and bell pepper in 1 tablespoon olive oil for 30 seconds, turn off the heat and cover sauté pan for a minute so garnish gets a little soft. In a mixing bowl add sautéed onions, peppers, and 2 teaspoons remaining lime juice and mix together. Garnish pizza with the mixture and add cilantro on the perimeter.

Rice Dishes

Rice is champion-like grain that easily takes on any flavor gracefully.
So you can fill your kitchen with an aroma of delicate and exotic Persian-style rice dishes.

Steamed Basmati Rice
It is decorated with saffron and a variety of vegetables such as
basil and mint leaves, radishes and scallions.
(Magnificent Presentation)

Basic Steamed Basmati Rice

(To prepare rice on stove top, and oven cooking).

Serves 6-8

Preheat oven to 300 degree F.

> 3 cups long grain basmati rice
>
> 10 cups spring water
>
> 2 tablespoons sea salt
>
> 1/8 teaspoon olive oil (about 8-10 drops)
>
> ¼ cup boiling water
>
> ¼ cup olive oil
>
> ¼ teaspoon ground saffron

1. Clean and rinse the rice gently a few times with fresh water or until the water is clear and soak the grains for 10-15 minutes and drain (traditional rinsing and soaking the grains thoroughly is the key for "*Persian rice cooking*" to remove some starch initially so when rice is cooked it does not sticky together but becomes fluffy).

2. In a 4-quart (heavy-based) pot over high heat, bring 10 cups of water to a rolling boil. Add salt, rice, and 1/8 teaspoon olive oil. With a large slotted wooden spatula, gently stir twice from the bottom to the top.

3. Cook the rice over high heat, uncovered, about 10-to 14 minutes. Occasionally, give the rice another gentle stir (the foam floating at the top should be skimmed off with a spoon as it arise). The rice is ready for draining when it is partially cooked (soft yet still firm). Rice must be carefully watched after 10 minutes of boiling and some rice has risen to the top. Do not overcook*.

4. Using a large (fine-mesh) strainer/colander, drain rice completely.

5. Put ¼ cup boiling water into a heavy-bottomed, smaller (3½ quart) ovenproof pot.

6. Place drained rice into smaller pot in the shape of a pyramid. Drizzle ¼ cup olive oil over the rice and sprinkle mound with ground saffron.

7. Cover with a tight fitted lid, and cook rice gently over a low-medium heat on the stovetop until steam is visible and coming out from under the cover. Watch carefully to prevent burning.

8. Once steam forms, place the covered pot into preheated oven for 2½ hours or until rice is done (**a long slow cooking is the secret of making steamed _"aromatic Basmati rice"_**). Serve warm rice in classic serving plate.

   *Perhaps the most difficult step in making rice is assessing the exact moment of **rice boiling time** when it's done and ready to strain.

Aromatic Brown Rice

Serves 5-6

Preheat oven to 300 degree F.   A few layers of 5-inch square cheese-cloth

>   2 cups, long grain basmati brown rice
>   8 cups spring water, divided
>   2 teaspoons sea salt
>   ¼ cup olive oil OR chicken broth
>   1¾ teaspoons mixture of ground aromatic spices, see *"master rice seasoning"**

Presoak brown rice with 4 cups of fresh water overnight and drain. To a 4 quarts ovenproof pot, add rice and 4 cups fresh water. Bring contents to a simmer at slow-medium heat on stove top. Stir a few times with wooden spatula and watch rice to prevent boiling over. After 10-15 minutes, when the rice is slightly soft, but still firm and some liquid remains, add salt, olive oil and stir twice.

Place cheesecloth contain spices into rice pot. Bring to a simmer and transfer the covered pot into oven; cook for 1½ hours or until water has evaporated and rice is done. Remove cheese cloth and discard. Rice is ready to serve warm.

*Master Rice Seasoning: Combine and finely grind ¼ teaspoon of each of the following spices: Cardamom, coriander, cloves, Ceylon cinnamon (bark-chips), fennel, black cumin seeds and black peppercorn. In recipe above, place the ground spices in the center of cheesecloth, gather the corners and tie the top securely.

Variation: Cabbage Rice "*Kalam polo*", in a small bowl, make a mixture of dried and ground seasoning: 2 tablespoons basil, 1 tablespoon tarragon, 1 tablespoon turmeric and 1 tablespoon Persian "*advieh-poloye*", (see Tips, page 185).

In a frying-pan, stir-fry 1 large onion (thinly shredded) in ¼ cup heated olive oil until lightly brown color, add 2 bunch parsley (chopped), 1 bunch Chinese parsley (chopped) 1 bunch green onion (chopped), 1 pound cabbage (thinly shredded) and zest of 1 organic lemon (freshly grated). Stir a few times and set aside. Cook rice according to "*Basic Steamed Basmati Rice*", from page 106, up to step 6. In a large mixing bowl, gently mix drained rice with seasoning and vegetable mixture. Return to heavy- based pot and follow from step 6, 7 and 8. Enjoy this beautiful vegetarian rice "*kalam polo*" with relaxing vegetables and herbs. Serve "*cabbage rice*" with fish and pickle (turshi).

Note 1: It is better to boil brown rice a few minutes longer and cook a shorter time in the oven.

Note 2: You may omit ¼ teaspoon ground saffron or use saffron water the last 5 minutes of cooking (see Tips, "*saffron water*", page 186).

Persian Rice Golden Cake

Serves 8

Preheat oven to 300 degree F.   Grease generously a tart-tatin (9 ½ x 2 ½ inch round) dish OR a non- stick baking dish with a tight fitted lid

Rice Cooking:

3 cups long grain basmati rice

10 cups spring water

2 tablespoons sea salt

1/8 teaspoon olive oil

¼ tablespoons boiling water

¼ cup olive oil

Eggs Mixture:

2 eggs, slightly beaten

1 tablespoon unsalted butter, softened

¼ teaspoon ground saffron (make saffron water by adding 1 tablespoon boiling water)

2 tablespoons strained yogurt

2 cups of strained rice (half cooked)

Garnish: ½ cup "*saffron-zereshk-jam*" (optional, see Tips, page 186), a few radishes and green onions and green lemon leaves and 1 baked sweet potato slices.

Golden cake with a crispy crust

Cook rice according to "*Basic Steamed Basmati Rice*", page 106 up to step number 5.

In a small bowl, add eggs, 1 tablespoon butter, saffron-water, strained yogurt and 2 cups of strained rice, and gently mix together. Spread and pack egg mixture on the bottom and sides of Tart-Tatin dish within ½-inch from the bottom. With a slotted wooden spoon add the remaining strained rice. Drizzle ¼ cup olive oil over the rice and cover with tight fitted lid and follow steps 7-8 on page 106.

When rice is done, leave lid on and place rice dish in shallow (½-inch cold water) water bath for 2 minutes, for easy removal of rice crust. Remove the lid and then with a small turner carefully go around the rice dish to make sure rice is completely detached. Replace the lid with serving plate that is slightly larger than the rice dish. Turn up-side-down, so the bottom of golden cake rice is up on serving plate. Garnish with "*saffron-zereshk-jam*", radishes and green onions in the center and arrange green lemon leaves and sweet potato slices in a circle around the perimeter of "*rice golden cake*". Serve with broiled Cornish games and green salad. Enjoy!

Tomato Rice with Mushrooms

Serves 12

2 onions, cut in half and thinly shredded

¼ cup extra virgin olive oil

1 cup potato, diced

1 pound green string beans, cut into ½-inch lengths

¼ cup chicken broth (see Tips "*chicken broth*", page 178)

2 pounds crimini mushrooms, wipe-dried with a clean cloth, sliced

2 tablespoon olive oil

¼ teaspoon cinnamon

¼ teaspoon sea salt OR to taste

1 dash black pepper, freshly ground

1 cup tomato puree (see Tips "*tomatoes puree*", page 190)

Basmati Rice Ingredients:

10 cups water

3 cups long-grain basmati rice

2 tablespoons salt

¼ teaspoon olive oil

Garnish: 1 tablespoon Italian parsley, finely chopped

In a skillet, sauté onion in ¼ cup heated olive oil for 2 minutes. Add potato and string beans; stir-fry for 5 minutes. Add chicken stock, and simmer for 2 minutes. Transfer to a bowl and set aside. Stir-fry mushrooms in 2 tablespoons heated olive oil for a few minutes until slightly golden brown. Add cinnamon, salt and pepper and stir once, add tomato puree, mix together and set aside.

Basmati Rice Cooking: Cook rice according to "*basic basmati rice*", page 106 up to step 6. Then mix rice with all ingredients (onion-mixture and mushroom-tomatoes mixture), and complete rice cooking to steps 8. Garnish with parsley and serve warm.

Wild and Brown Rice with Almond

Serves 4-5

Preheat oven to 275 degree F.

> ½ cup wild rice, rinsed with spring water, drained
>
> 1½ cup long grain brown rice, rinsed gently with spring water, drained
>
> 2 large onions, chopped
>
> 2 tablespoons olive oil
>
> 1-inch cinnamon bark
>
> 1 teaspoon sea salt OR to taste
>
> ½ teaspoon black cumin seeds, toasted lightly, ground
>
> ¼ teaspoon nutmeg OR cardamom, ground
>
> 3 cups chicken broth
>
> 2 bay (laurel) leaves
>
> 1 dash saffron, ground (optional)
>
> 2/3 cup almond slivers

Mix wild and brown rice and soak overnight in the refrigerator. Next day drain rice.

In a large saucepan stir-fry onion in heated olive oil until golden brown. Add wild and brown rice. Stir-fry over low heat for 2 minutes. Add cinnamon bark, salt, cumin, and nutmeg and continue to stir for a few seconds over low heat. Add chicken broth and bay leaves, bring to a simmer, cover the pot, and simmer for 30 minutes, stirring occasionally to prevent burning.

After 30 minutes of cooking, remove the bay leaves and cinnamon bark. Add saffron and almonds and mix gently. Transfer rice into ovenproof pot and place in the oven for 1½ hours or until done.

Note: You can double ingredients to serve more people.

Salad and Salad Dressing
Delightful Summery Salad with Peaches

Serves 4

2 large ripe peaches, divided
2 cups plain cooked chicken breast, diced
1 small red onion, sliced, diced
4 tablespoons olive oil
1 tablespoon balsamic vinegar
1 tablespoon lemon juice freshly squeezed
1 teaspoon honey
½ teaspoon sea salt OR to taste
¼ teaspoon black pepper, freshly ground
8 cups baby lettuce, cut into bite size pieces
plus lettuce for decoration
¼ cup walnuts, lightly toasted, coarsely chopped
1 tablespoon basil leaves, chopped

The peaches' fresh flavor really shines through.

Slice one peach and cut into small pieces. Combine with cooked chicken and onion in a medium size bowl and set aside. In a small bowl mix olive oil, vinegar, lemon juice, honey, salt and pepper; whisk until blended. Add to chicken mixture and stir to coat. Cover bowl and refrigerate for a few hours.

Prior to serving toss lettuce (bite size pieces), walnuts, and chicken mixture together. Mound salad in serving bowl. Cut remaining peach into thin wedges. Garnish salad perimeter with green lettuce and peach wedges and sprinkle center with basil leaves and serve.

Note: You may use 2 teaspoons brown sugar and 1 pinch cayenne instead of honey and black pepper.

Broccoli Green Salad

Serves 2

½ pound broccoli, blanched*

Salad Dressing:

½ teaspoon brown Dijon mustard

1 teaspoon honey

½ teaspoon sea salt OR to taste

¼ teaspoon black pepper, freshly ground

2 tablespoons shallots, peeled, chopped

2 cloves of garlic, chopped

2 tablespoons olive oil

2 teaspoons raspberry vinegar OR balsamic vinegar

2 tablespoons almonds, slivers, slightly toasted

To the blender add Dijon mustard, honey, salt and pepper, shallot, garlic, olive oil, and vinegar. Blend for 30 seconds or until thoroughly blended. Taste dressing and make adjustments if needed. In serving bowl toss broccoli florets with dressing and slivered almonds.

*In a large pot, bring, 8 cups water to boil. Add broccoli to boiling water, remove from heat and let sit for 2 minutes in covered pot, then strain. Trim and remove stems and separate broccoli florets.
Note: Broccoli not only have fiber, it also promote good health and contains nutrients that gradually repair damage cells; steamed broccoli can be added to many salad. For more information, please see Tips, ways to cook *"broccoli"*, page 191.

Broccoli

Cauliflower Surprise Salad

Last night I planned to make a green salad. I looked into my refrigerator to see what vegetables were available for a nice green salad. Your salad may be different depending on vegetables in your refrigerator.

Serves 2

    1 cup water

    1 cup cauliflower (only floret), cleaned

    2 baby buck choy

    2 cups broccoli (only floret), cleaned

    2 scallions (only head), cleaned, diced

    2 Persian cucumber OR 1 English cucumber, cut thinly lengthwise

    ¼ cup *"dress-sauce dressing"* see page 115

    Garnish:

    ¼ cup Italian parsley, washed pat-dried, chopped

    ¼ cup cherry tomatoes, cut in ½

In a medium pot, Bring water to simmer, add cauliflower, buck choy, and broccoli. Simmer slowly for 5-8 minutes in covered pot, until vegetables are slightly wilted but still firm and bright (watch carefully so they do not burn). Drain and let cool.

Cut steamed vegetables (broccoli, buck choy, and cauliflower) into bite size pieces if necessary.

Add salad dressing to serving salad bowl; add cauliflower, buck choy, broccoli, scallions and cucumbers and gently toss. Garnish with parsley and cherry tomatoes. You may double the ingredients to serve more people.

Cauliflower, see Glossary, page 207

Coleslaw

(A salad of Dutch origin)

Serves 5-6

Salad:

¼ cup sweet red onion, thinly shredded

2 cups white cabbage, thinly shredded

¼ cup red cabbage, thinly shredded

¼ cup fennel bulb, trim off top and bottom, sliced thinly and shredded

¼ cup daikon, thinly shredded

¼ cup olive oil

Salad Dressing:

2 teaspoons balsamic vinegar

½ teaspoon sesame oil

Zest of 1 organic lemon

¼ teaspoon sea salt OR to taste

1 dash black pepper, freshly ground

Garnish: 2 tablespoons golden raisins and 1 tablespoon sesame seeds, lightly toasted

In a heavy-based frying pan, stir-fry salad ingredients (onion, white and red cabbages, fennel, and daikon) in heated olive oil for 1-2 minutes. Remove from the heat and set aside.

In a small mixing bowl, mix salad dressing ingredients (balsamic vinegar, sesame oil, lemon zest, and salt and pepper). Add dressing to cabbage mixture and toss gently. Garnish with raisins and sesame seeds. Chill prior to serving.

Cabbage family, see Glossary, page 206

Dijon Mustard Dressing

Serves 4

    1 cup thickened chicken broth, (see Tips "*chicken broth*", page 178)

    1 tablespoon chopped basil

    1 tablespoon lemon juice, freshly squeezed

    1 teaspoon sugar

    1 teaspoon Dijon mustard

    1 teaspoon arrowroot powder

    2 cloves of garlic, chopped

    ¼ teaspoon sea salt

    1 dash black pepper, freshly ground

Place all ingredients in blender. Blend for a 30 seconds or until thoroughly mixed. Pour into small saucepan. Let the mixture come to a simmer and simmer for 4-5 minutes. This dressing enhance the flavor of fish, or mixed vegetables, such as zucchini, carrots, eggplant, asparagus and bell pepper.

Dress-Sauce Dressing
(This versatile master salad dressing has many uses)

Serves 12

    1 cup extra virgin olive oil

    ¼ cup + 1 teaspoon aged balsamic vinegar

    Juice of 1 lemon, freshly squeezed

    6 cloves of garlic, finely chopped

    ½-inch ginger root, peeled, finely chopped

    ¼ teaspoon sea salt OR to taste

    1 dash black pepper, freshly ground

    1 dash Italian salad herb

    1 tablespoon raw honey

Place all ingredients in a blender and run for 1 minute or until thoroughly blended. Place in air-tight-sterilized jar, and refrigerate for 24 hours prior to using. Best use within one week. A cooled "*dress-sauce-dressing*" has excellent flavor and travels well for picnics or potlucks.

Variation: Divine Salad Dressing (*herb-flavor*)**:** To the blender add ½ cup olive oil, 2 tablespoons balsamic vinegar, 1 tablespoon freshly squeezed lemon juice, ¼ cup sweet basil leaves (chopped), ¼ teaspoon sea salt and 1 dash black pepper (freshly ground), 1 pinch of each fresh herb (rosemary, thyme, oregano), 2 teaspoons mild Anaheim pepper (chopped) and 2 teaspoons honey/turbinado raw sugar. Blend for 30 seconds refrigerate for a few hours. Use with green salad (baby lettuce and/or spinach), garnish with almond slivers.

Elegant Tasty Chicken Salad with Rice

Serves 6

    2 pounds chicken breast, seasoned, baked, and cut into bite size pieces (see "*seasoned chicken green salad*", page 126)

    1 hardboiled egg, diced

    1 carrot, peeled, thinly sliced

    2 slices sprouted rye-caraway seed bread, toasted, cubed

    6 tablespoons salad dressing (see "dress-sauce dressing", page 115)

    1 head Romaine lettuce, cleaned, pat dried, cut into bite size pieces

    4 cups cooked rice

Garnish:

¼ cup sprouted (micro) radish

Toss all salad ingredients except rice (chicken, egg, carrot, bread cubes, dressing and lettuce) together. Place warm rice around perimeter and salad in the center of serving platter; garnish with sprouted radish.

Elegant Tasty Green Salad with Chicken over Rice

Flavorful Spicy Potato Salad

Serves 4

Preheat oven to 325 degree F.

    2 large russet potatoes

    ¼ cup olive oil

    ¼ teaspoon of each whole spices (cardamom, black cumin seeds, coriander seeds, peppercorn, and fennel seeds)

    ¼ teaspoon cinnamon, powder

    ½ teaspoon turmeric, powder

    1 dash clove, powder

    ½ dash red chili pepper, minced (optional)

    ½ teaspoon sea salt OR to taste

    Garnish: 1 tablespoon cilantro, chopped

Bake potatoes in the oven for 18-20 minutes or until nearly fork tender and allow to cool. Peel, and cut each potato into 8 sections. Stir-fry partially cooked potatoes in heated olive oil for 1 minute and set aside in covered pan.

Prepare whole spices by dry roasting (cardamom, cumin, coriander, peppercorn, and fennel) in heated skillet (without oil) for 30 seconds. Let spices cool and grind to powder. Combine spice mixture with cinnamon, turmeric, clove and chili pepper; stir into potatoes and sprinkle with salt. Return potatoes to stove top and continue to stir-fry potatoes mixture for a few minutes or until potatoes are fork tender. Cover the pan, turn off the heat, and let it steam for 1 more minute. Garnish with cilantro. This is similar to an Indian dish which is called "alloo".

See Glossary, chili pepper, page 209

Ju-lian Toh

Green Salad with Kale
(Excellent)

Serves 4

    ½ pound curly green kale leaves, cleaned, stemmed, blanched, strained, cut into bite size pieces

    1 pound Romaine lettuce leaves, cleaned, pat-dried, cut into bite size pieces

    1 hardboiled egg, sliced

    1 carrot, peeled, shredded

    2 avocados, peeled, cut into small pieces

    ¼ teaspoon sea salt OR to taste

    ¼ teaspoon black pepper

    ½ cup cauliflower, thinly sliced

    6 tablespoons salad dressing, (see *"dress-sauce dressing"*, page 115)

    2 tablespoons goat cheese, crumbed

    1 tablespoon green onion, chopped (optional)

    1 tablespoon lemon juice, freshly squeezed

    Garnish: 1 tablespoon red radish OR red bell pepper, thinly sliced

Mix all ingredients together, garnish with radish and serve.

Grape Juice Dressing

This salad dressing is loaded with herbs that gives a fresh and vibrant taste.
It is wonderfully balanced and not over powering.

Serves 20

    ½ cup olive oil

    ½ cup grape juice (freshly squeezed)

    1 ripe tomato, peeled, cut into small pieces

    1 tablespoon honey OR turbinado raw sugar

    1 tablespoon basil leaves, chopped

    1/8 teaspoon of each dried herb (tarragon, mint, thyme, rosemary)

    ¼ teaspoon sea salt OR to taste

    1/8 teaspoon black pepper, freshly ground

Blend all ingredients in blender until smooth. Refrigerate for 24 hours prior to serving.

Irresistible Raspberry Salad Dressing

Serves 20

    ½ cup + 1 tablespoon raspberry wine vinegar

    1 tablespoon Dijon mustard

    4 cloves of garlic, chopped

    2 tablespoons turbinado raw sugar

    1 teaspoon honey

    1 dash of each dried herb (oregano, savory, thyme, and basil)

    ¼ teaspoon black pepper, freshly ground (optional)

    1½ cups olive oil

To blender add raspberry wine, mustard, garlic, sugar, honey, oregano, savory, thyme, basil and pepper. Pulse blender a few times, less than 1 minute. Gradually add olive oil until very well blended. Taste and adjust the sweetness and tartness of dressing if needed. Pour into sterilized jar and refrigerate until chilled before serving.

Lettuce Rolls

Serves 2

    2 butternut lettuce (soft) leaves, cleaned, pat-dried

    2 green basil leaves (Asian basil is preferable)

    2 ounces thin rice noodles, cooked

    2 thinly slices of cucumber, cut lengthwise

    2 slices of carrots, shredded

    2 ounces (¼ cup) sprouted mung beans*

    2 pieces of cooked shrimp, OR fish, OR chicken OR cheese

Arrange each lettuce leaf separately on working wooden board, cup-side up. Pile and layer in order each ingredient in the center; basil, rice noodles, cucumber, carrots, sprouted beans, and shrimp. Fold the sides of each lettuce over the filling. Place seam side down on plate and serve with soy-sauce dip (optional).

*Mung beans are one of the most popular staples in India and are highly regarded in Ayurveda (ancient art of self-healing). Mung beans are easier to sprouts and digest than most beans.

Marinated Cucumber

Serves 2

   1 English cucumber, brush skin under running water, thinly sliced*

   1 teaspoon rice vinegar

   1 teaspoon sesame oil

   1 dash sea salt OR to taste

   1 dash black pepper, freshly ground

   1 dash sugar (optional)

In a small mixing bowl, combine all ingredients and refrigerate before serving.

*You may use mandarin to thinly sliced cucumber, strain off juice if there is any.

Mint Vinegar Dressing

Serves 2

   ¼ cup apple cider vinegar

   ½ cup fresh water

   2 teaspoons turbinado raw sugar

   2 mint sprigs

In a small saucepan add apple cider vinegar and water. Bring to simmer. Stir in sugar and mint. Simmer for 1-2 minutes, adjust the sweetness and mint flavor if needed. Remove mint and allow dressing to cool prior to use. Serve with baby lettuce.

Mustard Salad Dressing

Serves 18-20

   2 teaspoons (brown and white) mustard seeds, ground

   ¼ teaspoon thyme, dried

   ¼ teaspoon all spice, ground

   ½ teaspoon sea salt OR to taste

   ½ teaspoon brown sugar

   1 dash black pepper, freshly ground

   1 small Laurel bay leaf, dried, cut into small pieces

   1 teaspoon organic lemon zest, freshly grated

   1 cup olive oil

   ¼ cup balsamic vinegar

Blend all ingredients together and chill. It can be used with mixed green salad.

Quinoa Tabbouleh Salad

(In this recipe I used quinoa *"gluten free"* instead of *"bulgur wheat"* like a traditional tabbouleh salad)

Serves 4-5

Salad:

1 cup brown quinoa grains

4 cups spring water

1 large red tomato, peeled, diced

4 small Persian cucumber OR 1 English cucumber, diced

1 carrot, peeled, diced

2 scallions (green onion), cleaned, chopped thinly

2 cloves of garlic, finely chopped

½ cup Italian parsley leaves, cleaned, chopped

1 teaspoon dried mint OR 1 tablespoon fresh mint, chopped

¼ cup raisins, rinsed, cleaned

Salad Dressing:

¼ cup extra virgin olive oil

1 tablespoon rice vinegar

2 tablespoons lemon juice, freshly squeezed

½ teaspoon sea salt OR to taste

¼ teaspoon black pepper, freshly ground

Serve on:

5 lettuce leaves, shredded

Place quinoa in a heavy-based saucepan, toast quinoa slowly for 2-3 minutes on stove top over low heat while stirring constantly to prevent burning. Remove quinoa from saucepan and set aside. Add water to saucepan and bring to a boil. Reduce the heat and add quinoa. Simmer for 20 minutes, stir occasionally (the foam floating at the top should be skimmed off) until quinoa is tender and completely cooked. Drain and fluff with wooden spatula. Spread out quinoa on a baking sheet and let it cool. In a salad bowl, combine the following ingredients (tomatoes, cucumber, carrot, scallions, garlic, parsley, mint, and raisins. Add quinoa and salad dressing mixture (olive oil, vinegar, lemon juice, salt and pepper). Toss gently to coat salad. Chill and serve on bed of lettuce.

Royal Rose Salmon Salad

Serves 4

    1 head red radicchio*, cleaned, pat dried, cut into bite size pieces

    1 tablespoon red cabbage, shredded

    1 tablespoon parsley, cleaned, chopped

    1 tablespoon basil, cleaned, chopped

    1 teaspoon culinary rose petals

    1 teaspoon dill weed

    2 baby potatoes, baked, thinly sliced

    4 ounce smoked salmon OR sautéed halibut, cut into bite size pieces

    Garnish: 1 lemon wedges

In a classic salad bowl combine and toss all ingredients. Serve with (*"salad dressing with mustard and honey"*, page 123). Garnish with lemon wedges. This salad has warm luxurious royal taste.

*A variety of red-leaf lettuce native to Italian red chicory. **Radicchio di Verona** is similar to butter-lettuce but it has a small loose-leaf head of burgundy color with white ribs. Radicchio can be used in salads or sautéed or baked.

Roasted Cauliflower Salad

Serves 2-3

Preheat oven to 375 degree F.

    ½ pound cauliflower (only floret), cleaned, pat dried, cut into 1-inch pieces

    2 slice of breads*, cut into small cubes

    1 tablespoon olive oil

    ½ cup plain yogurt

    8 ounces goat cheese, finely crumbled

    2 cloves of garlic, finely chopped

    1 dash sea salt OR to taste

    1 dash black pepper, freshly ground

    1 teaspoon coriander, ground

    ½ teaspoons black cumin seeds, ground

    1 dash anise seeds (optional), ground

    Garnish:

    2 tablespoons Chinese parsley, cleaned, pat-dried and finely chopped

In a mixing bowl add cauliflower and bread cubes; drizzle with olive oil and gently mix together. Arrange mixture in a single layer on a roasting pan and place in oven on lower rack. Roast until the edges of cauliflower** and bread are slightly golden brown (about 6-8 minutes). Let cool slightly.

In meantime, blend remaining ingredients (yogurt, cheese, garlic, salt, and pepper, coriander, cumin, and anise), to make a creamy dressing. Place cauliflower and bread into salad bowl, add dressing and gently toss. Garnish with Chinese parsley.

*Sprouted rye bread made of whole grain and caraway seeds is my preference.
**Cauliflower develops a touch of sweetness when roasted. It pairs well with aged goat cheese and the hint of sweet and sour in creamy yogurt.

Salad Dressing with Mustard and Honey

Serves 16

      1 cup olive oil

      ¼ cup + 2 tablespoons balsamic vinegar

      2 tablespoons lemon juice, freshly squeezed

      1 tablespoon honey

      2 teaspoons Dijon mustard

      ½ teaspoon sea salt

      ¼ teaspoon black pepper, freshly ground

      1 dash mint, dried

      1 dash oregano, dried

Place all ingredients in a blender and run for a minute or until well blended. Taste and adjust the seasoning if needed. Refrigerate salad dressing in sterilized jar. Dressing is best if used within 1-2 days.

Mint is an exceptional soothing
and cooling herb

Salad with Red Cabbage

(A gift of thoughtfulness)

Serves 4

1 small head of red cabbage (about 12 oz.)

4 cups water

¼ teaspoons sea salt, divided

1 large onion, finely chopped

¼ cup olive oil

4 cloves of garlic, finely chopped

2 large red apples, peeled, diced

1 dash pepper, freshly ground

1-2 tablespoons lemon juice, freshly squeezed

1-2 tablespoons sweet and dark grape juice (optional)

Garnish: ¼ cup almond slivers

Separate the cabbage leaves, remove veins and cut leaves in half. Set aside. In medium saucepan bring water and 1 dash salt to a boil. Add cut cabbage leaves and let steam in covered pot for a few minutes or until leaves are slightly wilted but still firm. Drain completely and let cool slightly. Cut the cabbage leaves into bite size pieces.

In meantime stir-fry onion in heated olive, for 2 minutes, add garlic and stir for 2 more minutes until onions are slightly golden brown. Add apples and stir for 2 more minutes. Add cabbage, and remaining 1 dash salt and pepper. Stir and cover the pot and let it steam for 5 minutes; watch carefully so it does not burn. Sprinkle with lemon juice, and stir once. Transfer salad into serving dish and garnish with almonds.

Beautiful dark blue-black color concord grapes originated in
Concord, Massachusetts in 1849 (see Glossary, grape, 223).

Sautéed Swiss Chard Green Salad

Serves 3-4

  1 bunch (rainbow) Swiss chard

  4 cups water

  2 tablespoons extra virgin olive oil

  2 shallots, finely chopped

  2 cloves of garlic, finely chopped

  1 small sweet red chili pepper, seeded, chopped

  ¼ teaspoons sea salt OR to taste

  1 pinch black pepper, freshly ground

  2 tablespoons lemon juice, freshly squeezed

Remove stems and veins from Swiss chard and cut into 2-inch pieces. Bring water to rolling boil in a 4 quart pot, add chard and blanch for one minute or until green leaves wilt slightly.

Transfer chard to a colander, and rinse with cold water. Squeeze the green leaves gently with your hands to remove excess water. In a skillet, heat olive oil over medium-high heat. Add shallot, garlic, stir for 2 minutes, and add chard, chili pepper, salt, and black pepper. Stir for one minute or until chard is done. Sprinkle with lemon juice. Toss and serve.

Note: You can make this salad using kale instead of Swiss chard (rainbow).

Chard as a part of cruciferous vegetables, is valued for its mineral, vitamin content and alkaline salt properties.

Seasoned Chicken Green Salad

(Chicken makes this green salad an enjoyable nutritious meal).

Serves 6

Preheat oven to 400 degree F.   Grease broiler pan

Seasoning for Chicken:

¾ teaspoon sea salt OR to taste

¼ teaspoon black pepper, freshly ground

¼ teaspoon turmeric, ground

¼ teaspoon black cumin, ground

¼ teaspoon cinnamon

¼ teaspoon coriander, ground

¼ teaspoon paprika

2 pounds chicken breast* (about 3 pieces), skinless, boneless, defatted

4 teaspoons olive oil

1 tablespoon lemon zest, freshly grated, mix with 4 teaspoons olive oil

In a small mixing bowl, mix all dried ingredients (salt, pepper, turmeric, cumin, cinnamon, coriander, and paprika) together and set aside. Brush both sides of chicken with mixture of olive oil and lemon zest. Rub chicken generously with spice mixture. Place chicken on a small broiler-tray and cover tray tightly with heavy aluminum foil. Transfer onto middle rack of oven. Bake for 15 minutes, lower the temperature to 350 degree F. and continue to bake for 30 minutes more or until chicken is done. Let chicken cool and cut into bite size pieces to be used in a green salad.

*Spices can penetrate thicker meaty parts of **chicken breast** better if you poke them with a fork in several places, before rubbing with spices.

Note: To have the chicken golden brown, simply remove aluminum from the broiler tray and broil chicken uncover for a few minutes, watch carefully so it does not burn.

Green Salad:

2 romaine lettuce, cut into bite-size pieces

2 avocado, peeled, pitted, cut into bite-size pieces

2 slices of rye breads, toasted, cubed (optional)

4 medjool-soft dates, seeded and diced

Garnish: 1 cup watercress, cleaned, pat dried

To assemble: In a large salad bowl, add green salad, seasonal chicken and ¼ cup flax seeds salad dressing. Toss together gently a few times. Garnish with watercress.

Flax Seeds Salad Dressing:

¼ cup olive oil

2½ teaspoons balsamic vinegar

2 tablespoons flax seeds, ground

1 tablespoon brown mustard seeds, ground

¼ teaspoon coriander, ground

1 tablespoon lemon juice, freshly squeezed

½ teaspoon honey

¼ teaspoon sea salt OR to taste

1 dash black pepper, freshly ground

1 dash oregano, dried

1 dash cayenne pepper

Blend all salad ingredients in blender for a minute to make a salad dressing (it makes about ½ cup salad dressing). Transfer into sterilized jar and cover. Refrigerate for one hour prior to serving.

Herbs and Spices Variation for Seasoning Chicken: Make a mixture of ¼ teaspoon of each of the following seasoning: Cardamom, cinnamon, coriander, allspice, black cumin, and black pepper, 1 dash cayenne, 1 dash lemon peel, and 1 tablespoon rose petals (ground), and ½ teaspoon sea salt. Brush chicken pieces with 4 teaspoons of olive oil followed by rubbing in seasoning mixture. Cook according to recipe on previous page.

Note 1: All vegetables need to be cleaned, and pat-dried

Note 2: You may grind flax seeds, mustard seeds and coriander in coffee grinder at the same time.

Olives are rich in Essential fatty acids
And a variety of vitamins and minerals
(Please see Glossary, page 232)

Superb Mixed Greens with Orange and Mint

Serves 4-5

    ½ pound of mixed greens: Baby romaine (lettuce red and green), baby spinach, butter lettuce, baby chard (red and green), baby arugula, and baby radicchio, cleaned, pat-dried

    2 oranges OR tangerines, sectioned (see Tips, how to section *"orange"*, page 176)

    2 tablespoons olive oil

    8 Kalamata olives, rinsed, pitted, cut in half

    2 tablespoon mint leaves, chopped

    ¼ cup goat cheese, crumbled

    1 dash black pepper, freshly ground

    2 tablespoons pomegranate syrup

    Garnish: 2-3 tablespoons almond slivers, lightly toasted OR chopped walnuts

In a large salad bowl toss all ingredients except pomegranate syrup (mixed greens, oranges, olive oil, olives, mint, cheese, and black pepper). Drizzle the pomegranate syrup and gently toss again. Garnish with almond slivers.

Super Cucumber Ribbon Salad

Serves 2

Honey-lemon Dressing:

½ cup cucumber, peeled, diced

1 large avocado, pitted, peeled, diced

2 tablespoons lemon juice, freshly squeezed

1 teaspoon honey

1 teaspoon olive oil

¼ teaspoon sea salt OR to taste

1 pinch cayenne pepper (optional)

2 tablespoons freshly cut basil, chopped

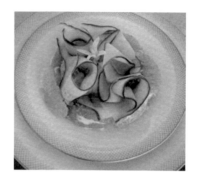

Salad:

2 medium English cucumbers OR 2 Persian cucumbers

2 oranges, sectioned (see Tips, how to section "*orange*", page 176)

Garnish: Orange blossoms OR 2 basil sprigs

To make honey-lemon dressing, place all ingredients (cucumber, avocado, lemon juice, honey, olive oil, salt, cayenne, and basil) in blender, blend for 30 seconds and set aside.

Using vegetable peeler, slice cucumber lengthwise into ribbons. Place honey-lemon dressing on serving plate; arrange orange-sections around dressing. Top with cucumber ribbons. Garnish with orange blossoms.

Basil, please see Glossary, page 203

Ways to Make an Imperial Cucumber Salad

Serves 8

      1 large English cucumber, thinly sliced

      4 small red onions, thinly sliced

      2 salad tomatoes, vertically quartered

      1 sprig tarragon

      A few thin vertically slices of green Anaheim pepper

      Garnish: 1 tablespoon green leaves chives, cut with scissors into ½-inch sections.

On a plate arrange cucumber slices in a circle around the outside of plate. Arrange slices of onion in a circle inside the cucumber slices. Place a small bowl in the center of the cucumber slices. Arrange tomatoes, tarragon sprig and Anaheim pepper in the bowl. Sprinkle the cucumber slices with chives. Offer a salad dressing on the side.

Imperial Cucumber Salad

Sauce and Spread

Tuna is served with *"Vinaigrette Mustard Sauce"*
(Fish variation, *"**spark like tuna**"*, page 59)

Vinaigrette Mustard Sauce

Serves 4-6

      2 tablespoons mustard seeds (soak with 2 tablespoons spring water overnight)

      2 tablespoons Italian parsley, chopped

      2 green onions (bulbs only), chopped

      1 tablespoon balsamic vinegar

      1 teaspoon green leaves oregano, chopped

      1 teaspoon honey

      ½ teaspoon sea salt OR to taste

      ¼ teaspoon black pepper, freshly ground

      ½ cup olive oil

Add all ingredients to blender, blend for 30 seconds until well blended. Chill prior to use.

Afghan-Turshi Sauce

Serves 4

    12 cloves of garlic (about 1 head garlic), peeled, finely chopped

    1½ cup cilantro (about 2 bunches), cleaned, pat-dried, chopped

    1 teaspoon sweet jalapeno pepper, chopped OR 1 pinch cayenne (for hot spicy dish)

    ¼ cup +2 tablespoons aged balsamic vinegar

    ¼ teaspoon sea salt OR to taste

    1 pinch black pepper, freshly ground

To blender, add ingredients (garlic, cilantro, jalapeno, vinegar, salt and pepper), and process for a few seconds (alternative you may use mortar and pestle instead of blender). Taste and adjust ingredients if needed. Serve this sauce with fish.

Apple Chutney

Serves 4

    2 green apples, cored, diced

    1 onion, finely chopped

    ¼ -inch ginger root, finely chopped

    1 tablespoon olive oil

    1 teaspoon honey OR turbinado raw sugar

    ¼ teaspoon balsamic vinegar

    ½ cup plain yogurt, strained

    Garnish: A few mint sprigs

Stir-fry green apples with onion and ginger in heated olive oil for one minute. Stir in honey and vinegar. Cover the pan. Cook over medium heat, until apples become soft. Remove from heat and stir in yogurt. Garnish with mint and serve.

*A spicy chutney that complements curried dishes in East India.

Barbeque Sauce with Worcestershire

Serves 4

    ½ cup Worcestershire sauce (variation *"master Worcestershire sauce"*, page 96)

    ¼ cup pineapple puree

    1 tablespoon tomato paste

    ½ teaspoon Hickory smoke

    1 tablespoon brown sugar and 1 dash dried orange peel

Blend all ingredients until smooth. Brush on chicken drumsticks while barbequing.

Barbeque Sauce

Serves 8

    1 onion, finely chopped

    4 cloves of garlic, minced

    2 tablespoons olive oil

    2 cups tomato puree (see Tips, "*tomato puree*", page 190)

    1 teaspoon natural hickory seasoning

    4 tablespoons sweet white wine

    2 tablespoons Dijon mustard

    2 tablespoons unsulfured molasses

    2 tablespoons red wine vinegar

    1 teaspoon sea salt OR to taste

    ½ teaspoon of each herb and spice (thyme, peppermint, nutmeg and celery seeds)

Sauté onion, and garlic in heated olive oil for a few minutes until golden brown. Add all other ingredients (tomato puree, hickory seasoning, white wine, mustard, molasses, red wine vinegar, salt, thyme, peppermint, nutmeg and celery seeds). Simmer uncover, for 10 minutes over low heat. Allow to cool, and place in blender for a few seconds. Store in refrigerator for 24 hours prior to using as a meat marinate.

Barbeque Sauce with Basil Leaves

Serves 1-2

    1 cup basil green leaves, chopped

    1 lemongrass, minced (see Tips, how to prepare "*lemongrass*", page 180)

    1 clove of garlic, minced

    ¼ cup olive oil

    Juice of 1 lemon, freshly squeezed (about 4 tablespoons)

    ¼ teaspoon sea salt OR to taste

    ¼ teaspoon black pepper, freshly ground

    1 dash sugar

To blender add basil, lemongrass, garlic, olive oil, lemon juice, salt, pepper and sugar. Blend for a few seconds or until creamy. Serve this delicious sauce as a topping for barbeque sea food (such as grilled tuna).

Barbeque Sauce with Laurel Bay Leaf

Serves 8

    ½ cup olive oil

    ¼ cup red wine vinegar + 1 tablespoon tarragon vinegar

    ¼ cup distilled water

    1 tablespoon Worcestershire sauce (optional, variation *"Worcestershire sauce"*, page 96)

    2 cloves of garlic, minced

    1 shallot, chopped

    2 teaspoons brown sugar OR 1 tablespoon honey

    ½ teaspoon sea salt OR to taste

    ¼ teaspoon mustard seeds, ground

    ¼ teaspoon celery seeds, ground

    1 dash clove, ground

    1 dash chili powder

    1 teaspoon oregano

    1 Laurel bay leaf, crushed

Place all ingredients (olive oil, wine and tarragon vinegar, water, Worcestershire sauce, garlic, shallot, sugar, salt, mustard seeds, celery seeds, clove, chili powder, oregano and bay leaf) in power-blender and blend thoroughly. Pour mixture into a saucepan and simmer slowly for 20 minutes, stir occasionally, until sauce is formed. Adjust the thickening and seasoning if needed. Use this sauce to marinate meat/poultry/fish for barbequing or roasting. It works well for a summer back yard party.

Chermoula Sauce

(A North Africa, Moroccan-style sauce)

Serves 6

    1 cup Italian parsley leaves, cleaned, pat-dried, finely chopped

    ¼ cup cilantro leaves, cleaned, pat-dried, finely chopped

    4 cloves of garlic, minced

    ¼ teaspoon of each spice (coriander, cumin and turmeric)

    1 dash black pepper, freshly ground OR 1 pinch cayenne

    1 tablespoon extra-virgin olive oil

    1 teaspoon dried mint, ground

    1 teaspoon lemon juice, freshly squeezed

½ cup strained plain yogurt OR Greek yogurt, divided

1 tablespoon crumbled goat cheese (blend with ¼ cup yogurt until smooth).

To the power-blender add all ingredients except goat cheese-yogurt mixture (parsley, cilantro, garlic, coriander, cumin, turmeric, black pepper, olive oil, mint, lemon juice and ¼ cup remaining yogurt). Blend for a few seconds until sauce is smooth. Pour sauce into serving bowl and stir in goat cheese-yogurt mixture.

Note: Chermoula sauce is used primarily to marinate fish or as a side dish for grilled salmon.

Dahi East Indian Cuisine

Dahi/dal is a common name given to all kinds of pureed vegetables prepared with curry sauce, especially curried puree made from legumes (lentils or peas cooked with water, then seasoned with variety spices).

Serves 4

1 cup dried brown lentils

6 cups fresh water, divided

Curry Sauce:

1 large onion, minced

4 cloves of garlic, minced

¼ cup extra virgin olive oil

1 teaspoon curry powder

½ teaspoon coriander

1 pinch cayenne (about 1/16 teaspoon)

1 teaspoon sea salt OR to taste

¼ teaspoon black pepper, freshly ground

Juice of 1 lemon, freshly squeezed

Garnish: A few cilantro sprigs (optional)

In a bowl, soak lentils with 3 cups fresh water overnight. During soaking change the water twice and strain (If there is any water left). Place strained lentils in heavy-based saucepan, with 3 cups water; bring to simmer and simmer in partially covered saucepan, over low-medium heat, for 1 hour or until partially cooked (but not mushy), stirring occasionally to prevent burning. Meantime prepare curry sauce.

Curry Sauce: In a heavy-based frying-pan, stir-fry onion and garlic in heated olive oil for 3-4 minutes until onions are golden brown. Turn off the heat, add seasoning (curry, coriander, cayenne, salt, and black pepper) into onion mixture and stir. Add curry sauce into lentils and continue simmering, in covered saucepan, for 25 minutes until lentil is completely cooked and fork tender. During last 5 minutes of cooking stir in lemon juice. Garnish with cilantro. You may serve "*dahi sauce*" with chapatti (Indian flat bread). Excellent.

Fennel and Mustard Seed Sauce

Serves 4-5

> 1 cup plain yogurt, strained
> 1 tablespoon olive oil
> ¼ cup shelled sunflower seeds, lightly toasted, ground
> 1 teaspoon Dijon mustard seeds
> 1 clove of garlic, minced
> ½ teaspoon fennel seeds
> 1 dash sea salt OR to taste
> 1 dash black pepper, freshly ground

Blend all ingredients (yogurt, olive oil, sunflower and Dijon mustard seeds, garlic, fennel seeds, salt and pepper) in blender until a smooth sauce forms. Use sauce for oven baked beets for a delightful meal.

Ginger and Tamari Sauce (Korean-style)

Serves 2

> ½ cup tamari soy sauce*
> ¼ cup brown sugar (packed)
> 4 tablespoons garlic (6-8 cloves), grated
> 1 tablespoon (1-inch) ginger root, grated
> 1 tablespoon brown rice vinegar
> 1 teaspoon toasted sesame oil**
> 1 dash of each chili pepper powder and black pepper (freshly ground)
> 2 teaspoons arrowroot powder (to be dissolved in 2 teaspoons cold water)

In a small saucepan, combine all ingredients except arrowroot mixture (tamari soy sauce, sugar, garlic, ginger, brown rice vinegar, sesame oil, chili pepper and black pepper) and bring to boil. Reduce the heat and stir in arrowroot mixture. Simmer for a few minutes or until mixture thickens. Brush sauce on broiled (unseasoned) chicken wings. Barbeque chicken wings, garnish with sesame seeds and scallions and serve.

*Tamari comes from Japan and is similar to "*Chinese soy sauce*" however it is usually aged. Tamari sauce is darker, thicker, and mellower than soy sauce (although both are made from soy beans) and is primarily used as a condiment or for making sauces or basting. **Toasted sesame oil can be purchased at Chinese or specialty market.

Green Pesto Sauce

Serves 10

     2½ bunch green parsley leaves, chopped (about 2 ½ cups)

     2 cloves of garlic, minced

     ½ cup hazelnuts, lightly toasted, OR almond meal

     ¼ cup shelled sunflower seeds, OR pine nuts, lightly toasted

     ¼ cup green basil leaves, chopped (optional)

     ½ cup + 2 tablespoons olive oil

     ½ teaspoon sea salt OR to taste

     ¼ teaspoon black pepper, freshly ground

     ¼ teaspoon, tarragon, freshly cut

     Juice of 1 lemon, freshly squeezed

Place all ingredients (parsley, garlic, hazelnuts, sunflower seeds, basil, olive oil, salt and pepper, tarragon and lemon juice) in food processor or power-blender. Blend for a few seconds or until smooth. Taste, and adjust seasoning if necessary. This sauce can be served over pasta or use as a spread on bread or have with crumble cheese on crackers. Enjoy!

Guacamole Salsa

(A popular Mexican sauce)

Serves 4-5

     4 ripe avocado, peeled, pitted, diced

     3 ripe red tomatoes, diced

     2 cloves of garlic, minced

     2 tablespoons sweet chili pepper (preferred roasted), diced

     ¼ teaspoon sea salt OR to taste

     1 dash black pepper, freshly ground

     1 dash black cumin, freshly ground

     Juice of 1 lime, freshly squeezed

     1 tablespoon extra-virgin olive oil

     1 tablespoon cilantro leaves, chopped

     Garnish: 2 tablespoons scallions (green onions), finely chopped

In a power-blender, place all ingredients (avocado, tomato, garlic, chili pepper, salt, pepper, cumin, lime juice, olive oil and cilantro), until puree. Garnish and use as dip/sauce.

Note: Keep fresh salsa in sterilized tightly covered container and refrigerated to keep avocado from discoloration.

Mango Coconut Sauce

Serves 4-6

> 2 medium ripe mangoes, peeled, pitted, cut into 1-inch pieces
> ¼ cup coconut slivers
> 1 dash white pepper
> 1 pinch cayenne
> 1 dash sea salt OR to taste
> 1 tablespoon organic lemon zest, freshly grated
> 2 teaspoons lemon juice, freshly squeezed
> 1 teaspoon Arabic gum OR cornstarch (needs to be dissolved in lemon juice first)

Place all ingredients (mangoes, coconut, pepper, cayenne, salt, lemon zest, lemon juice and Arabic gum) into blender and run for 30 second or until well blended. Pour into saucepan, place over medium heat and simmer for 5 minutes while stirring continually to make sauce. Chill prior to serving. This sauce can be served on grilled salmon.

Moroccan-style Spicy Tomato Sauce
(Harissa-style sauce)

Serves 6

> 1 heirloom ripe tomato, peeled, chopped
> 1 red bell pepper, roasted, peeled, seeded, chopped
> 1 Anaheim (mild) pepper, roasted, peeled, seeded, chopped
> ½ cup shelled sunflower seeds, toasted, ground to a paste
> ½ teaspoon of each whole spices* (caraway seeds, anise seeds, coriander seeds, and dill seeds), lightly toasted and ground
> 2 cloves of garlic, chopped
> ½-inch ginger root, peeled, chopped
> ½ teaspoon sea salt OR to taste
> ¼ teaspoon black pepper, freshly ground
> 1 tablespoon lemon juice, freshly squeezed
> 1 teaspoon honey
> ¼ cup olive oil

Place all ingredients (tomato, bell pepper, Anaheim pepper, sunflower seed paste, caraway, anise, coriander and dill, and garlic, ginger, salt and pepper, lemon juice, honey and olive oil) in a power-blender and run for 30 seconds or until you have a smooth sauce. Refrigerate overnight to allow flavors to blend for better taste.

*In a small dry cast-iron skillet/frying-pan, lightly toast spices (caraway seeds, anise seeds, coriander seeds, and dill seeds). Stirring frequently until their color changes slightly and you smell their fragrance; cool and grind.

Mushroom Sauce

Serves 6

> 1 pound mini mushrooms, cleaned, pat dried, thinly sliced
> ½ cup olive oil, divided
> 1 cup chicken broth
> 1 cup milk
> ¼ cup flour
> ½ teaspoon paprika and 1 dash cayenne (optional)
> ¼ teaspoon sea salt OR to taste
> 1 teaspoon organic lemon zest, grated

In a large skillet stir-fry mushroom in ¼ cup of heated olive oil for a few minutes until mushrooms color slightly changed. Remove from heat. In a blender add chicken broth, milk, flour, paprika, cayenne, salt and remaining ¼ cup of olive oil. Blend for a minute. Gradually add liquid mixture to mushrooms and simmer over low heat for 6-8 minutes while stirring constantly, add lemon zest until sauce thickened. Use sauce for shrimps.

Romesco Sauce

(A classic Spanish-style sauce)

Serves 8

> 2 tablespoons olive oil
> 2 medium tomatoes, peeled, chopped
> 2 tablespoons scallion, bulbs only, cleaned, chopped
> 4 cloves of garlic, chopped
> ¼ cup slivered almonds
> ¼ teaspoon thyme, dried
> ¼ teaspoon sea salt OR to taste
> 1 tablespoon balsamic vinegar OR red vinegar
> 1 tablespoon red bell pepper, chopped

Place all ingredients (olive oil, tomato, scallions, garlic, almonds, thyme, salt, vinegar, and bell pepper) in blender. Blend until a smooth and creamy sauce forms. Serve sauce with grilled fish or poultry.

Sauce with Butternut Squash

Serves 4-5

     1½ cups butternut squash, cooked, diced

     ¼ cup orange juice, freshly squeezed

     2 tablespoons lemon juice, freshly squeezed

     1 tablespoon organic lemon zest, freshly grated

     2 tablespoons olive oil

     ½ teaspoon black cumin seeds, ground

     1 dash cayenne

     1 dash sea salt OR to taste

     1 dash black pepper, freshly ground

Place all ingredients (squash, orange juice, lemon juice, lemon zest, olive oil, cumin, cayenne, salt and pepper) in blender and run until smooth and creamy. This sauce complements steamed green beans or steamed green vegetables.

Sauce with Fresh Herbs

Serves 4

     1 cup Italian parsley leaves, cleaned, chopped

     ¼ teaspoon oregano

     ½ cup olive oil

     4 cloves of garlic, chopped

     2 tablespoons lemon juice, freshly squeezed

     2 teaspoon organic lemon zest, freshly grated

Blend all ingredients (parsley, oregano, olive oil, garlic, and lemon juice and lemon zest) in blender for a few seconds until creamy. Use over grilled vegetables; especially good with eggplant.

Special Sauce for Brown Rice

Serves 4

     ½ cup tomato paste (see tips, page 189)

     ½ cup plain Greek yogurt, strained

     ¼ teaspoon sea salt OR to taste

     ¼ cup coconut cream, unsweetened (coconut cream is available in Asian markets)

     1 tablespoon olive oil

1 tablespoon brown sugar

1 teaspoon brown rice vinegar

1/8 teaspoon of each dried herb (onion, ginger, garlic and chili powder OR cayenne)

1/8 teaspoon of each dried spice (cumin, coriander and turmeric)

Garnish: A few thyme and rosemary sprigs

Blend all ingredients in blender until smooth and creamy. Simmer sauce for a few minutes until thickens, stir as needed to prevent burning. Use the sauce on hot brown rice and garnish with thyme and rosemary sprigs for a lunch treat.

Sauce with Lentils and Herbs

Serves 4-5

1 cup dried brown lentils, rinsed and drained

1¼ cups chicken broth (see Tips "*chicken broth*", page 178)

1 large onion, finely chopped

4 cloves of garlic, finely chopped

2 medium heirloom tomatoes, peeled, diced

2 tablespoons olive oil

2 tablespoons champagne vinegar OR rice vinegar

½ teaspoon sea salt OR to taste

¼ teaspoon black pepper, freshly ground

2 tablespoons lime juice, freshly squeezed

2 tablespoons Italian parsley, cleaned, chopped (sniped with scissors)

3 tablespoons green basil leaves, cleaned, chopped, divided

In a medium saucepan, combine lentils, chicken broth, onion, and garlic. Let the mixture come to a simmer, reduce the heat to low and simmer in tight covered saucepan for 35-45 minutes or until lentils are cooked but not mushy. Watch carefully to prevent food from burning.

Stir in tomatoes, olive oil, champagne vinegar, salt and pepper, and lime juice. Continue to cook for 5-8 minutes until only a small amount of liquid is left, stir occasionally to prevent burning. Add parsley and 2 tablespoons basil. Mash lentils while still warm with a masher (or you may use mortar and pestle to masher). Garnish with 1 tablespoon remaining basil. One way to serve mashed lentils is to spread on flat bread, or by adding more chicken broth and adjust seasoning to make a lovely soup. Enjoy!

Note: Dried lentils and beans should always be examined, sorted and rinsed well before cooking to assure maximum quality of the natural product.

Sesame and Sunflower Seed Spread

Serves 10-12

  ½ cup sesame seeds, lightly toasted*, ground

  ½ cup shelled sunflower seeds, lightly toasted*, ground

  ¾ teaspoon sea salt OR to taste

  ¼ teaspoon black pepper, freshly ground

  ½ cup rice vinegar

  ¾ cup olive oil

  2 teaspoons honey OR to taste

  ½ teaspoon lemon juice, freshly squeezed

Blend all ingredients (toasted sesame and sunflower seeds, salt, pepper, vinegar, olive oil, honey and lemon juice) in high power-blender until a creamy spread forms. Refrigerate in sterilized jar for a few hours and use for salad with shredded *cabbage and carrots* (see below recipe direction).

Salad with Shredded Cabbage and Carrots:

  1 pound cabbage, shredded

  2 carrots, peeled, julienned

  2 stalks celery, julienned

  2 scallion bulbs, julienned

  1 sweet red bell pepper, seeded, julienned

  ¼ cup olive oil

  Garnish: A few tablespoons of "sesame and sunflower seeds spread" (see above)

Combine cabbage, carrots, celery, scallions, and red bell pepper and add to wok containing heated olive oil, stir for 1 minute. Remove from heat and let it cool. Transfer onto serving platter, cover, and refrigerate for a few hours. Prior to serving sprinkle with a few tablespoons of "*sesame and sunflower seeds spread*" and gently toss.

*On an oven proof tray, spread sesame and sunflower seeds, in single layer, toast in preheated 275 degree F. oven for 4 minutes or until slightly toasted (watch carefully to prevent burning). Let seeds cool and grind in coffee grinder.

Super Tomato Sauce

(Ketch-up for daily use)

Serves 25

      10 pounds ripe (meaty), red tomatoes, peeled, chopped

      4 onions, peeled, chopped

      2 red bell peppers, peeled, seeded, chopped

      2 tablespoons honey

      ¼ cup brown sugar

      1-inch Ceylon cinnamon, cut into small pieces

      ½ inch ginger root

      1 teaspoon allspice (Jamaican pepper)

      1 dash black pepper

      1 dash mustard seeds

      1 teaspoon celery seeds

      1 teaspoon mace

      ½ teaspoon fennel seeds

      ½ teaspoon oregano

      1 Laurel bay leaf, cut into small pieces

      ½ cup cider vinegar

      1½ teaspoons sea salt OR to taste.

In a large heavy-based stock pot, add tomatoes, onions, bell peppers, honey, and sugar. Let the mixture come to a simmer, and reduce the heat to medium-low. Simmer for 45 minutes until tomatoes are cooked. Let cool and puree in high power-blender (or run through a food mill) until creamy and smooth. In a multi-layer cheese cloth (or a small muslin bag designed to holds herbs and spices), combine seasoning (cinnamon, ginger root, allspice, black pepper, mustard seeds, celery seeds, mace, fennel, oregano, and bay leaf). Tie cheese cloth tightly and add with tomato puree to large stock pot. Simmer the contents for 60 minutes, stirring as needed to prevent burning (long simmered ketch-up with seasoning is refreshing). Remove cheese cloth (or muslin bag) and discard. Stir in cider vinegar and salt. Continue simmering until your sauce is reduced to half its original volume (about 1½ hours) stir as needed to prevent burning. Let it cool. Store in sterilized jars with sealed covers. Refrigerate up to a few weeks. This homemade versatile tomato sauce "***ketch-up***" can be used for many dishes like barbeque (chicken/steak), French fries or pizza or dip (mix together 1 cup ketch-up, 1 tablespoon grated horseradish, 1 tablespoon brown sugar and 2 tablespoons lime juice. Serve this as a dip with cooked shrimps).

Superb Mango Sauce

Serves 2

Mango sauce on grilled salmon

       1 ripe mango, peeled, pitted, cut into small pieces

       1 tablespoon olive oil

       1 tablespoon lemon juice, freshly squeezed

       1 tablespoon organic lemon zest, freshly, grated

       ¼ teaspoon ginger root (optional), grated

       ½ teaspoon sea salt OR to taste

       1 pinch cayenne pepper

To the blender, add mango, olive oil, lemon juice, lemon zest, ginger, salt and cayenne pepper. Blend for 30 seconds or until creamy sauce is formed.

Note: This sauce can be served on grilled salmon. Transfer salmon onto a warm serving plate along with shallots and garlic cloves (cut a few shallots and garlic cloves in quarter and stir-fry for 2 minutes), and lime wedges. Garnish with freshly cut green tarragon leaves.

Yogurt Condiment Delight

(This yogurt condiment is bursting with superb flavor)

Serves 8

       4 cups plain yogurt, strained

       1 bunch green onion, finely chopped

       1 teaspoon mint, dried

       ½ teaspoon sea salt OR to taste

       ¼ teaspoon black pepper, freshly ground

       1 pinch cayenne (optional)

       4 medium Persian cucumber, roughly chopped

       2 tablespoons raisins, cleaned

       ¼ cup walnuts, coarsely chopped

Mix all ingredients (yogurt, onion, mint, salt and pepper, cayenne, cucumbers, raisins, and walnuts). Place in covered bowl, and refrigerate overnight prior to serving.

Note: Sauce-Kashk-Style, in blender mix 2 cups sour plain yogurt, with 2 ½ tablespoons kudzu root starch (first kudzu has to be dissolved with 2 tablespoons cold water) and 6-8 tablespoons goat cheese (cut into very small pieces). Run blender for 45 seconds. Transfer this mixture into a small saucepan and simmer while stirring continuously over low-heat until a creamy thick white sauce is formed. Turn off the heat. Cover saucepan and let it cool. This sauce can be used with various food such as *Spread on Bread with Jam*" or "*Kashk-Bademjohn*" etc.

Soups
Bitter Gourd Clear Soup

Serves 2-3

2 large fresh bitter gourds*
2 onions, chopped
¼ cup extra virgin olive oil
½ teaspoon turmeric powder
1 tablespoon fennel seeds
1 teaspoon black cumin seeds
½ teaspoon brown mustard seeds
½ cup fennel bulb, chopped
¼ cup cilantro leaves, chopped
¼ teaspoon sea salt OR to taste
¼ teaspoon black peppercorn, freshly ground
1 teaspoon tamarind paste OR 1 tablespoon freshly squeezed lemon juice
3 cups chicken broth OR vegetable broth (see Tips, "*vegetarian broth*", page 178)
2 tablespoons brown rice flour
Garnish: A few cilantro sprigs and lemon wedges

Wash bitter gourd, trim top and bottom, cut lengthwise in half, scrape out the seeds, peel and discard the skin, and cut into ½-inch slices. Set aside.

In a heavy-based stock pot, stir-fry onion in heated olive oil until translucent (2-3 minutes). Stir in spices (turmeric, fennel seeds, cumin seeds and mustard seeds) for 30 seconds, add bitter gourd and stir for 2-3 more minutes. Add fennel bulbs, cilantro leaves, salt and pepper, and tamarind paste. Stir once and add chicken broth. Bring the contents to a simmer, reduce the heat to medium-low and cover the pot and simmer slowly for 20 minutes (this allows time for vegetables and spices to blend with broth; taste soup and adjust the seasoning if necessary). Strain and return the clear soup back into the pot, stir in rice flour and cook for 5 more minutes or until soup is done. Garnish with cilantro and lemon wedges and serve warm.

*Bitter gourd is a common vegetable in India and it is called "***plant insulin***", moderate consumption may be very beneficial to diabetes in lowering the blood sugar levels. Please be sure the bitter gourd is fresh and firm (see medicinal herbal plants, "bitter gourd", page 258).

Asparagus Soup with Pistachio Cream

Serves 4-5

Preheat oven to 400 degree F.

Pistachio Cream:

¾ cup clear chicken broth OR boiling water

1 teaspoon olive oil

1 cup unsalted pistachios, shelled, lightly roasted, finely chopped

1 tablespoon fresh mint leaves, chopped

1 tablespoon lemon juice, freshly squeezed

1 teaspoon lemon zest

1 dash sea salt OR to taste

Soup:

2 pounds asparagus, snap off tough ends, shaved and cleaned

2 teaspoons olive oil + ¼ cup olive oil (to fry onion and garlic)

1 medium onion, chopped

4 cloves of garlic, finely chopped

1 leek, cleaned, coarsely chopped

1 medium golden potato, peeled, diced

1 small red sweet pepper, seeded, chopped

½ teaspoon sea salt OR to taste

¼ teaspoon black pepper, freshly ground

4 cups chicken broth

Juice of 2 lemons (about 6 tablespoons), freshly squeezed

Garnish: 4 sprigs mint OR 4 asparagus's tips

Pistachio Cream: Blend ingredients (¾ cup chicken broth, olive oil, pistachios, mint leaves, lemon juice, lemon zest and salt) in blender until smooth and creamy, set aside.

Soup: Arrange asparagus on roasting pan in a single layers. Drizzle asparagus with 2 teaspoons olive oil and place in the oven to bake for 6-8 minutes. Remove, cut asparagus into small pieces and set aside. In a large and deep frying-pan, stir-fry onion and garlic with ¼ cup heated olive oil for a few minutes until translucent. Add leek and stir for 1 minute. Add potato, sweet pepper and sprinkle with salt and pepper and continue to stir for 2 more minutes. Add 4 cups chicken broth and bring to a simmer in covered pan over medium heat for 6 minutes or until potatoes are fork tender, stir occasionally to avoid burning. Let cool. Combine onion-potatoes mixture with asparagus and lemon juice. Place in food processor in batches and process until vegetables are pureed and smooth. Adjust the seasoning and thickening if needed. Serve soup warm in individual soup bowl drizzle with pistachio cream and garnish with mint. Excellent.

Asparagus soup with pistachio cream

The vegetable garden gala
Ju-lian Toh

Butternut Squash Barley Soup

Serves 6

      1 pound butternut squash, precooked, peeled, seeded, diced

      1 medium potato, peeled, diced

      1 leek, cleaned, coarsely chopped

      1 bunch Italian parsley, cleaned, chopped (about 1 cup)

      1 bunch green onion, cleaned, chopped

      1 cup whole barley, cooked (see Glossary "*barley*", page 203)

      1 teaspoon ginger root, peeled, chopped

      ½ teaspoon sea salt OR to taste

      ½ teaspoon black cumin seeds, ground

      ¼ teaspoon black pepper, freshly ground

      5 cups chicken broth

      Juice of 1 lemon, freshly squeezed

      Garnish: ½ cup plain yogurt (unflavored yogurt), strained, mixed with 1 tablespoon creamy goat cheese, 1 teaspoon lemon zest and a few basil sprigs

Place all ingredients, except chicken broth and lemon juice in food processor (butternut squash, potato, leek, parsley, green onion, barley, ginger, salt, cumin, and pepper). Process for 30 seconds. Transfer the mixture into a large stock pot, add chicken broth. Bring the mixture to simmer, and simmer for 25-30 minutes or until squash is cooked. Add lemon juice the last 5 minutes of cooking. Taste and adjust the seasoning and thickening if needed. Transfer to serving soup bowl and garnish with mixture of yogurt, goat cheese, lemon zest and basil sprigs. Enjoy this warm and tasty soup.

See Glossary, Italian parsley, page 234

Butternut Squash Soup

(A fabulous flavorful soup)

Serves 8

Preheat oven to 350 degree F.

> 2 pounds butternut squash
>
> 6 tablespoons olive oil
>
> 2 medium onions, chopped
>
> 6 cloves of garlic, chopped
>
> 2 small golden potatoes, peeled, diced
>
> 2 carrots, peeled, sliced
>
> 2 small leeks, cleansed, sliced, diced
>
> 1 small fennel bulb, chopped
>
> 4 cup boiling water
>
> ¾ teaspoon sea salt OR to taste
>
> ¼ teaspoon black pepper, freshly ground
>
> ¼ teaspoon black cumin seeds, ground
>
> 2 zucchini, sliced, diced
>
> 2 tablespoons Italian parsley, cleaned, chopped
>
> 2 cups chicken broth (see Tips "*chicken broth*", page 178)
>
> Juice of 1 lemon, freshly squeezed

Cut butternut squash in halves lengthwise and remove seeds. Place the halves cut side down in baking dish. Bake uncovered in a preheated oven for 20 minutes or until the thin skin can be easily removed with a knife. Remove skin and cut squash into 2-inch pieces.

In a large wok, heat olive oil, add onions and stir-fry until slightly golden brown color. Add garlic, and stir for 30 seconds. Add butternut squash, potatoes, and carrots. Continue to stir-fry for 4 minutes. Add leeks, fennel, water, salt, pepper and cumin seeds. Mix gently. Let the mixture come to a simmer and simmer in covered wok, at medium-low heat for 15 minutes. Place the mixture in food processor and add zucchini and parsley. Pulse 5 times and return to the wok. Add chicken broth and lemon juice to the mixture. Bring to simmer over medium heat, stirring frequently to avoid burning. Simmer for 5 minutes, and serve warm.

My Favorite Vegetable Soup

(Have this soup all day long and all day strong)

Serves 4

Preheat oven to 300 degree F.

> 6 cups homemade chicken broth (see Tips *"chicken broth"*, page 178)
>
> ½ cup steel cut-oats, soaked overnight
>
> 1 carrot, washed, peeled, thinly sliced
>
> 1 stalk celery, cleaned, chopped
>
> 1 cup green onion, cleaned, chopped
>
> 1 medium size leek, cleaned, thinly sliced
>
> 1 cup butter-nut squash, partially cooked, peeled, seeded, cut into small pieces
>
> 1 cup sweet potato OR yam, partially cooked, peeled, cut into small pieces
>
> 1 bunch dandelion greens (about 1 pound), cleaned, chopped
>
> ½ pound chard, cleaned, chopped
>
> 2 tablespoons dried mint
>
> 2 tablespoons dried tarragon
>
> 1 teaspoon dulse (dark brown edible seaweed)
>
> ¼ teaspoon salt OR to taste
>
> 1 dash cayenne
>
> 1 stalk lemongrass*, remove loose outer leaves and trim the bottom of lemongrass bulb, and cut into 3-inch length
>
> Juice of 1 lemon, freshly squeezed

In a 4 quarts ovenproof pot, place all ingredients except lemon juice (chicken broth, oats, carrot, celery, onion, leek, squash, sweet potato, dandelion greens, chard, mint, tarragon, dulse, salt, cayenne, and lemongrass). Bring contents to a simmer, cover the pot, remove from heat and place in the oven and cook for 1½ hours or until the steel-cut oats and vegetables are done. Add lemon juice, let it cool to room temperature and remove and discard lemongrass. Place the soup into blender, and blend for 30 seconds (you may have to do in batches). Return soup to pot and reheat prior to serving.

Soup Variation: Please see Tips, *"vegetarian soup"*, page 178.

*The inner stalk of lemongrass has a ***lemony taste*** that can add a little lemony zest to food (one way to use lemongrass in soups/stews is cut lemongrass in chunks, add chunks to soups/stews while cooking and remove before serving) giving it a wonderful taste and harmonious flavor. When using lemongrass in omelets/meat patties, you have to chop very finely the soft inner stalk of lemongrass and add to omelet/meat patties mixture. Lemongrass is used in Southeast Asian cuisines such as Thai and Vietnamese and to flavor various herbal teas.

Perfect Luncheon Soup

(Tasty chicken barley soup)

Serves 6

Preheated oven to 275 degree F.

- ¾ cup pearl barley, pre-cooked
- ¼ cup brown lentils, pre-cooked
- 5 cups chicken broth, divided (see Tips "*chicken broth*", page 178)
- 1 teaspoon sea salt OR to taste
- ¼ teaspoon black pepper, freshly ground
- 2 onion, chopped
- 10 cloves of garlic, finely chopped
- ¼ cup heated olive oil
- ½ teaspoon turmeric powder
- 2 cups parsley, chopped
- 1 cup cilantro, chopped
- 2 tablespoons Anaheim pepper, chopped
- Juice of 2 lemons, freshly squeezed

Blend pre-cooked barley and lentils in blender and add chicken broth generously to cover it. Blend together and transfer blended mixture into a large, oven-proof-pot. Add remaining chicken broth, salt and black pepper; set aside. Stir-fry onion and garlic in heated olive oil until golden brown. Add turmeric, parsley, cilantro, and Anaheim pepper and stir for 4 more minutes. Add onion mixture to barley-lentil mixture and bring content to simmer. Partially cover the pot and place in oven. Cook for 1½ hours. Taste and adjust seasoning if necessary. Stir in lemon juice, return to the oven and continue cooking for 15 more minutes or until done. This is an excellent soup.

See Glossary, garlic, page 217

Satisfying Pea Soup with Herbs and Spices

(Persian-style pea soup with dried lemon)

Serves 8

Preheat oven to 300 degree F.

½ cup great (northern) beans

1 cup split peas*

4 cups spring water for soaking peas

5 cups chicken broth (see Tips "*chicken broth*", page 178)

1 large onion, chopped

4 cloves of garlic, chopped

½ cup olive oil

1 celery stalk, cleaned, diced

2 carrots, peeled, diced

1 teaspoon turmeric

½ teaspoon black cumin seeds, ground

1 teaspoon paprika

1 teaspoon salt

¼ teaspoon black pepper, freshly ground

1 tablespoon basil, dried

1 tablespoon mint, dried

2 cups chopped parsley, divided (save 2 tablespoons for garnishing)

2 large heirloom red tomatoes, peeled, coarsely chopped

2 dried lime (limu-omani)**

In a mixing bowl, soak mixed beans (great northern beans and split peas) over night with 4 cups spring water overnight, and please be sure there is 1-inch water over the beans. It is best to change the water twice during soaking (for gas reduction). After soaking the volume almost double. Strain beans.

Place strained beans into a large heavy-based oven proof stock pot (about 4½ quarts). Add chicken broth, cover partially and gradually bring to simmer on stove top. Transfer pot into oven. Let it cook for 1½ hours or until beans and peas are cooked. Remove from oven and mash beans roughly with a masher.

In meantime, stir-fry onion and garlic in heated olive oil in a large heavy-based frying-pan for 2-3 minutes or until onion is lightly golden brown. Add celery and carrots and continue stir-frying for 2 more minutes. Turn off the heat. Add turmeric, cumin, paprika, salt and pepper, basil, mint and parsley. Stir a few times.

Add onion mixture along with tomatoes and dried limes to beans mixture. Return back to oven and continue to cook in covered pot for 1 hour or until done (slow cooking is the secret of good soups). Remove the dried lime and discard. Garnish soup with remaining parsley. Excellent.

*You may use garbanzo beans instead of split peas.
**Dried lime (limu-omani): Dried lime provide a nice taste and flavor to various Persian dishes; it not only gives the slight sour taste of lime, but also add a pleasant deep aroma to the food. Dried lime is easy to use; soak in a small covered bowl of hot water for a minute, poke lime a few times with a fork and add to your special soup. Remove dried limes prior to serving.

A Time to Share

Artist unknown

There is an admirably strong
sense of family gathering and sharing among animals as
they enjoy food.

Sorghum Soup

Serves 2

 4 cups milk

 ¼ cup sorghum flour (combined with milk until smooth)

 4 cups chicken broth (see Tips *"chicken broth"*, page 178)

 2 tablespoons olive oil

 1 large onion, chopped

 ½ teaspoon sea salt OR to taste

 ¼ teaspoon black pepper, freshly ground

 ¼ teaspoon cayenne

 ¼ teaspoon nutmeg

 4-inch lemongrass, crushed

 1 cup asparagus tips, finely chopped

 1 cup spinach, chopped

 ½ teaspoon kelp-seaweed (optional)

 Garnish: A few asparagus tips

In a large saucepan, add the mixture of milk and sorghum flour, stir and bring to simmer, add chicken broth, olive oil, onion, salt, pepper, cayenne, nutmeg and lemongrass. Continue simmering in covered saucepan over medium low heat for 6-8 minutes or until a creamy soup is formed; stirring occasionally to prevent burning. Add asparagus, spinach and kelp-seaweed. Simmer soup for 4 more minutes or until done. Taste, and adjust seasoning and liquid if needed. Remove lemongrass. Garnish with asparagus tips and serve warm.

Handsome free range rooster

Super Vegetable Soup

Serves 4

2 lemongrass, finely chopped

1 leek, chopped

2 cups green beans OR asparagus tips, finely chopped

1 onion, chopped

2 cloves of garlic, finely chopped

¼ cup olive oil

¼ cup whole wheat flour

½ teaspoon sea salt OR to taste

½ teaspoon turmeric

¼ teaspoon black cumin seeds, ground

¼ teaspoon black pepper, freshly grounded

¼ teaspoon coriander powder

4 cups chicken broth (see Tips "*chicken broth*", page 178)

Juice of 1 lemon, freshly squeezed

Garnish: 1 tablespoon parsley, chopped

Place lemongrass in food processor. Run for a few minutes or until lemongrass is finely chopped. Add vegetables (leek, green beans, onion and garlic). Run again until vegetables are finely chopped.

In a medium pot, gently heat olive oil and gradually add flour and stir for 30 seconds. Turn off the heat, add seasoning (salt, turmeric, cumin, black pepper, coriander) and chicken broth while continuing to stir. Return the heat, gradually, bring contents to a simmer and simmer for 5 minutes in covered pot until a thin gravy is formed. Add vegetables and continue to simmer for 35-40 minutes. Add lemon juice. Taste, and adjust seasoning and liquid if needed. Garnish with parsley prior to serving.

Note: If you do not like *the texture* of lemongrass in the soup, you may place ground lemongrass into a muslin cloth or cheesecloth, tie securely and place in soup while cooking; remove when soup is done.

Swiss chard Soup

Serves 4

      1 large onion, chopped

      4 cloves of garlic, chopped

      ¼ cup olive oil

      1 pound okra (ladyfinger), trim the ends, cut into small pieces (see Glossary, okra, page 232)

      1 tablespoon brown rice

      2 teaspoons coriander seeds, ground

      ¾ teaspoon sea salt OR to taste

      ½ teaspoon black cumin seeds, ground

      1 dash cayenne pepper

      4 cups red Swiss chard, cleaned, stems removed, green leaves chopped

      5 cups chicken broth (see Tips "*chicken broth*", page 178)

      Juice of 1 lemon, freshly squeezed (about 4 tablespoons)

      Garnish: 2 tablespoons olive oil and 2 tablespoons dried mint (mint-oil*)

In a large skillet stir-fry onion and garlic in heated olive oil until nearly golden brown. Add okra and stir-fry for a few more minutes, add brown rice, coriander, salt, cumin seeds, and cayenne, stir twice and let it cool slightly. Transfer into food processor along with chard. Run processor until all vegetables are finely chopped.

In a stock pot bring chicken broth to boil, reduce the heat and add vegetable mixture. Simmer gently and partially covered until vegetables are tender (about 10-12 minutes). Add lemon juice and cook for 2 more minutes. Serve soup in a classic serving bowl garnished with mint-oil.

*Mint-oil: In a small saucepan heat olive oil until hot but not smoke. Remove saucepan from the heat and stir in dried mint (that is coarsely ground). Spoon some mint-oil on soup as a garnish.

Vegetable Soup with Herbs

Serves 6

½ pound string beans, cut into small pieces

2 slices fresh pineapple, diced

2 red potatoes, cut into small chunks

4 large ripened tomatoes, peeled, cut into small pieces

2 cups chicken broth (see Tips "*chicken broth*", page 178)

½ teaspoon sea salt OR to taste

1 dash black pepper, freshly ground

1 bouquet garni (2 sprigs of each herbs: oregano, tarragon, thyme, and rosemary) ties together (see Tips, bouquet garni, page 173)

1 medium red onion, chopped

2 cloves of garlic, finely chopped

2 teaspoons olive oil

Garnish: 2 tablespoons parsley, finely chopped

2 tablespoons mozzarella cheese, shredded

In a large stock pot, combine string beans, pineapple, potatoes, tomatoes, chicken broth, salt, pepper, and herb bouquet. Let the mixture come to a simmer over medium heat. Cook for 10 minutes and set aside.

In a frying-pan, stir-fry onion and garlic in heated olive oil until onion is slightly golden brown. Add to stock pot and combine with soup ingredients. Let the mixture come to a simmer and simmer in covered pot for 30 minutes or until done, stir occasionally to prevent burning. Remove the herbs bouquet and discard. Transfer soup into individual soup bowl; garnish with parsley and cheese and serve.

Variation: Vegetable Soup with Zucchini, in a large stock pot, stir-fry 1 large white onion (chopped), and 4 cloves of garlic (chopped) in ½ cup heated olive oil until onion is translucent. Add 3½ pounds organic zucchini (trim top and the bottom and diced). Continue stir-fry about 8 minutes. Add 1 dash of each spices: nutmeg, all-spices and black pepper, and 1 mild jalapeno (chopped). Stir two times. Add 5 cups chicken broth, 1 cup of white drinking wine, 1 cup Italian parsley (chopped), ½ cup basil (chopped) and 2 teaspoons sea salt. Bring content to simmer and simmer slowly uncovered for 20 minutes or until zucchini completely cooked. Blend soup with hand masher. Stir in 6 ounce shredded mozzarella cheese. Reheat soup gently and pour into serving soup bowl. Garnish with 1 cup plain yogurt and 1 basil sprig. Enjoy!

Vegetable Soup with Turnip

(This superb soup may help you to cleanse your body)

Serves 5-6

> 3 bunch Italian parsley, chopped
> 1 bunch dill, chopped
> 1 leek, chopped
> 1 fennel bulb, chopped
> 2 small young turnips, peeled, cubed
> 2 small golden potatoes, peeled, cubed
> 2 cups butternut squash, partially cooked, cubed
> 1 small bell pepper, peeled, seeded, diced
> 1-inch ginger root, peeled, chopped
> ½ cup olive oil
> ½ teaspoon of each spice (turmeric, black cumin, and coriander seeds)
> 1¼ teaspoon sea salt OR to taste
> ¼ teaspoon black pepper, freshly ground
> 1 extra-large heirloom red tomato, peeled, diced
> 4 cups spring water
> 2 pounds chicken breast with bones, skinned, defatted
> 2 tablespoons honey
> Juice of 3 lemons, freshly squeezed

Carefully wash, clean, pat-dry, and chop all vegetables. In a large heavy-based stock pot (about 5 quarts) stir-fry vegetables (parsley, dill, leek, fennel, turnip, potatoes, butternut squash, bell pepper and ginger) in heated olive oil for 8 minutes until the color of vegetables changes slightly. Stir occasionally to prevent burning. In a small mixing bowl, mix seasoning (turmeric, cumin, coriander, salt, pepper) and stir into vegetables mixture. Continue to stir-fry for 2 more minutes. Reduce the heat, add tomatoes, water, and chicken (with bone side down). Let the mixture come to a simmer in covered pot and simmer over medium-low heat for about 1 hour 15 minutes or until soup is done. Stirring occasionally to prevent burning. Remove chicken (use for another occasion). Stir in honey and lemon juice. Simmer slowly for 5 more minutes. Serve warm. Enjoy!

Note: You may use 300 degree F. oven, instead of stove top, and cook soup in oven proof pot for 1½ hours or until done.

Vegetables and Vegetarian Dishes
Green Peas-Pesto with Soft Cooked Eggs

Serves 4

½ pound young green peas

4 tablespoons olive oil, divided

¼ cup goat cheese, crumbled

¼ cup basil green leaves, chopped

¼ teaspoon salt OR to taste

¼ teaspoon black pepper, freshly ground

Juice of 1 small lemon, freshly squeezed

4 sliced French bread, toasted (see note 1)

Topping:

4 eggs, soft cooked, sunny side up

2 tablespoons olive oil for frying eggs

Alexandra Ambwani

To the blender add blanched and stir-fried green peas (see note 2), 2 tablespoons olive oil, goat cheese, basil, salt, pepper and lemon juice. Blend for 30 seconds until creamy. Spread *"green peas-pesto"* evenly on toasted bread and top with soft cooked egg. Use for lunch or dinner or cut into smaller pieces as appetizer.

Variation: You can use *basil-pesto* (freshly made from basil, garlic, olive oil, pine nuts and cheese), instead of *peas-pesto* in recipe above.

Note 1: Toast sliced French bread in 375 degree oven for 2 minutes. Rub with bruised garlic and lightly brush with olive oil.

Note 2: Blanch young green peas for 1-2 minutes and strain well. Lightly stir-fry green peas in 2 tablespoons heated olive oil for just 30 seconds.

Ju-lian Toh

A Lovely Mediterranean-style Vegetable Stew

Serves 4

     1 onion, finely chopped

     ½-inch ginger root, peeled, finely chopped

     4 cloves of garlic, finely chopped

     ½ cup olive oil

     1 bay leaf (Laurel)

     1 large eggplant, top and the bottom trimmed, peeled, coarsely chopped

     ½ teaspoon of basil

     ½ teaspoon thyme

     ¼ teaspoon rosemary

     ¼ teaspoon marjoram

     ½ teaspoon sea salt OR to taste

     1 dash black pepper, freshly ground

     1 red bell pepper, seeded, diced

     4 medium ripe tomatoes, peeled, cut into chunks

     2 zucchinis, cubed

In a medium size stock pot (French-oven casserole dish is my preference), stir-fry onion, ginger and garlic in heated olive oil until golden brown. Add bay leaf, eggplant and continue to stir-fry about 4 minutes. Stir in dried herbs (basil, thyme, rosemary and marjoram) and salt and pepper. Stir for 1 minute. Add bell pepper and tomatoes. Let the mixture come to a simmer and simmer in covered pot for 20 minutes or until eggplant is tender and completely cooked. Add zucchinis and continue to cook for 3-4 more minutes. Remove bay leaf and serve.

Note: Light steaming of vegetables softens them without depleting much of their nutrients.

Most nutritious stew, Ju-lian Toh

A Fabulous Omelet with Vegetables

A Persian national dish which is called "***kuku-sabzi***".
The omelet vegetables add to its digestibility and nutrition.

Serves 8

2 cups parsley, green leaves, finely chopped

½ cup cilantro, finely chopped

¼ cup dill weeds, finely chopped

¼ cup chives or green onion, finely chopped

2 tablespoons fenugreek green leaves, chopped OR 1 teaspoon dried fenugreek

1 teaspoon mint, dried

1 onion, chopped

1½ tablespoons olive oil

1 teaspoon zereshk (Persian small cranberries)

1 teaspoon flour (to coat zereshk)

½ teaspoon turmeric

¾ teaspoon sea salt OR to taste

¼ teaspoon black pepper, freshly ground

6 eggs, slightly beaten

½ cup extra virgin olive oil

Garnish: A few basil sprigs OR a few tablespoons shredded mild cheddar cheese

All fresh herbs (parsley, cilantro, dill weeds, chives, and fenugreek) need to be rinsed, pat dried and finely chopped.

In a large heavy-based (8½-inch) frying-pan lightly sauté onion in 1½ tablespoons heated olive oil, transfer onion into bowl and let cool. In a mixing bowl combine and mix parsley, cilantro, dill, chives, fenugreek, mint, zereshk-flour mixture, turmeric, salt and pepper along with eggs and sautéed onion; stir and mix thoroughly (you may use blender to mix ingredients in batches, each time for 30 seconds).

Heat ½ cup olive oil in frying-pan until hot but not to smoke. Carefully pour all the vegetable mixture into center of pan (all at once) and make level. Cover the pan and cook for 6-8 minutes or until the bottom of "*kuku-sabzi*" is slightly golden brown. Cut omelet in wedges, and turn each wedge over and cook for 5 more minutes or until both sides of omelet are golden brown, watch carefully so it does not burn. Garnish with basil, and serve with plain yogurt or make into a sandwich or pizza (page 101). Enjoy a nutritious and delicious vegetable omelet.

Brussel Sprouts and Butternut Squash

Serves 4

Preheat oven to 350 degree F.

> Juice of 2 oranges, freshly squeezed
> 1½ pounds Brussel sprouts, end trimmed, cleaned, halved
> 1½ pounds butternut squash, peeled, seeded, cut into bite size pieces
> 1 tablespoon organic orange zest, freshly grated
> 1 tablespoon brown sugar
> ½ teaspoon sea salt OR to taste
> 1 dash black pepper, freshly ground
> 1 dash nutmeg
> 2 tablespoons olive oil
> **Garnish:** A few pecans, halved

In a heavy-based oven-proof pot, add orange juice, Brussel sprouts and butternut squash. Let the mixture come to a simmer, over low-heat. Mix together orange zest, sugar, salt and pepper and nutmeg. Sprinkle over vegetables and gently stir a few times. Drizzle with olive oil. Cover the pot and transfer the pot into oven. Cook for 25 minutes or until cooked. Garnish with pecans.

Crispy Onion with Golden Raisins

Serves 6

> 1 large onion, shredded
> ¼ cup olive oil
> ¼ cup raisins, cleaned
> ¼ cup pine nuts
> 1 pound baby spinach leaves, cleaned, pat-dried
> ¼ pound baby sorrel leaves, cleaned, pat-dried, chopped
> ¼ teaspoon sea salt OR to taste
> 1 dash black pepper, freshly ground

In a wok, stir-fry onion in heated olive oil until crispy and golden brown. Turn off the heat. Add raisins and pine nuts, stir twice and toss with spinach and sorrel. Sprinkle with salt and pepper, gently toss again and serve as a warm green salad.

Indian-style Spicy Vegetarian Dish

Serves 4

2 onions, chopped

6 cloves of garlic, minced

1-inch ginger root, peeled, minced

¼ cup extra virgin olive oil

¼ teaspoon black cumin seeds, ground

¼ teaspoon gram-masala

½ teaspoon turmeric

½ teaspoon sea salt OR to taste

1 pinch black pepper, freshly ground

1 pinch jalapeno pepper, chopped

1 cup red lentils, washed, soaked overnight and drained completely

1½ cups water, OR as needed

Garnish: 2 teaspoons Chinese parsley (cilantro), chopped

In a wok stir-fry onions, garlic, and ginger in heated olive oil until onions are golden brown. Add spices (cumin, gram-masala, turmeric) and seasoning (salt, black pepper, and jalapeno pepper. Stir-fry for a few seconds.

Add lentils to onion-spices mixture and continue to stir-fry for 2-3 minutes. Add water, cover the wok and bring to simmer. Simmer slowly for 25 minutes or until lentils are cooked.

Remove wok from heat and allow to cool slightly. Place the mixture in power-blender and blend at low speed for 30 seconds or until completely pureed. Serve warm on chapatti Indian flat bread. Garnish with Chinese parsley.

Note: Roasted ginger, garlic, onion, tomatoes and mushrooms seasoned with fragrant spices is one of my favorite vegetarian dish.

Lightly Steamed Spinach

Serves 3-4

    4 large shallots, chopped

    1-inch ginger root, peeled, grated

    4 cloves of garlic, grated

    ¼ cup extra virgin olive oil

    1 pound spinach, cleaned, chopped, pat-dried

    1 tablespoon sherry wine

    ¼ teaspoon sea salt OR to taste and 1 dash black pepper, freshly ground

    Garnish: 1 tablespoon lightly toasted sesame seeds and 1 lemon, thinly sliced

In a wok or skillet stir-fry shallot, ginger, and garlic in heated olive oil for 2 minutes or until golden brown. Add spinach, sherry wine (from the corner of pan), salt and pepper. Stir for 1 minute, cover the pan and let steam for 2 minutes. Watch carefully to prevent burning.

Garnish with sesame seeds and lemons; serve as a side dish or make spinach-cheese sandwich.

Mixed Assorted Fresh Herbs Platter

(An aromatic and flavorful Persian herb platter with feta cheese called "*sabzi khordan*")

Serves 12 +

1 bunch of each assorted fresh herbs:

    Scallions,

    Chives,

    Tarragon,

    Mint and basil,

    Savory,

    Watercress,

    Radish (or sprouted young radish),

    Parsley (young leaves)

    8 ounces goat feta cheese, cut in small squares

    2 sheets of Lavash, cut into 4-inch squares

Arrange these herbs with small pieces of feta cheese on a platter along with (lavash) flat bread. You can fill the bread with herbs and wrapped/fold to make a sandwich or you may place herb filling on soft flat bread, roll it up and enjoy. Sandwiches can be served with steamed Persian rice and/or meat dishes.

Note: A freshly made lavash sprinkled with black sesame seeds and nigella seeds is one of my favorite bread.

Omelet with Yam/Sweet Potato

Serves 4

       1 cup yam OR sweet potato, precooked, peeled, grated

       4 eggs, slightly beaten

       1 medium onion, grated, squeeze, discard juice (see note)

       1 teaspoon arrowroot powder OR cornstarch

       ½ teaspoon sea salt OR to taste

       ¼ teaspoon black pepper, freshly ground

       2 teaspoons dried cranberries

       2 teaspoons ginger root, peeled, grated

       Zest of 1 organic lemon, freshly grated

       ¼ teaspoon savory herb

       ¼ cup + 2 tablespoons extra virgin olive oil

       Garnish: 4 green onions (optional)

In a mixing bowl combine and mix all ingredients except olive oil (yam, eggs, onion, arrowroot, salt, pepper, cranberries, ginger, lemon zest and savory herb). Heat olive oil in skillet or frying pan. Add omelet mixture, level, and cover pan with lid. Reduce the heat to medium heat. Cook for 4-5 minutes, uncover the pan and continue to cook until the edge is slightly golden brown. Cut omelet into four sections, flip each section and cook for a few more minutes or until done. Garnish with green onion and serve with steamed rice, bread and yogurt.

Note: Place a cheesecloth on top of small bowl. Add grated onion into center of cheesecloth and gather four corners. Twist it hard to remove juice. Onion adds a nice texture and moisture to the omelet.

Sweet potatoes and cranberries

Roasted Tomatoes with Garlic

Serves 4

Preheat oven to 350 degree F.

        2 large heirloom red tomatoes, peeled, cut horizontally in half

        2 small heirloom tomatoes, peeled, cut horizontally in half

        4 teaspoons olive oil

        2 cloves of garlic, minced

        ¼ teaspoons sea salt OR to taste

        ¼ teaspoons black pepper, freshly ground

        ¼ teaspoon basil, dried

        8 ounces feta cheese, crumbled

        Garnish: 4 green onions, cleaned, pat-dried, and 2 basil sprigs

Brush each tomato half, with mixture of olive oil and garlic; sprinkle with salt and pepper and basil. Arrange tomatoes halves, cut side up, in rimmed baking dish. Transfer dish to oven and bake uncovered for 35-45 minutes.

Transfer tomatoes to rimmed serving platter and arrange so larger tomato halves are topped by the smaller ones. Sprinkle tomatoes with feta cheese and decorate the perimeter of platter with green onion and top with basil sprigs.

Note: Roasting tomatoes at 350 degree F. caramelizes sugar, concentrates sweetness and the tomatoes remain moist so they are not chewy like sun-dried tomatoes.

Green onion, see Glossary, page 233

Spinach Quiche

Serves 8

Preheat oven to 375 degree F.

Ingredients for Making One Pastry Shell:

1½ cups unbleached all-purpose flour (organic flour is my preference)

1 teaspoon baking powder (aluminum-free)

1 dash sea salt

4 tablespoons sugar, powdered (turbinado raw sugar is my preference)

6 tablespoons sweet butter, cut into small pieces and chill

2 teaspoons lemon zest, freshly grated

1 large egg at room temperature (slightly beaten and mix with lemon zest)

Filling:

1 large white OR red onion, chopped

¼ cup extra virgin olive oil

4 cloves of garlic, chopped

1 mini sweet red pepper, seeded, chopped

1 pound fresh baby spinach leaves, stemmed, washed, pat-dried

3 eggs, (slightly beaten with salt and black pepper)

¼ teaspoon sea salt

1 dash black pepper, freshly ground

¼ teaspoon fresh thyme leaves, chopped

¼ cup milk

8 ounces semi-hard Mozzarella cheese*, grated, divided

Pastry Shell: The above ingredients are for one 9-inch pastry shell. For preparation instructions see Tips "*pastry dough*", page 177.

To Make Filling:

In a large fry pan, stir-fry onion in heated olive oil for 4 minutes over medium-high heat; add garlic and red pepper, continue to stir-fry until onion is nearly translucent (about 2 minutes). Gradually add spinach (a small amount at a time). Stir-fry spinach and onion for 3 minutes until spinach leaves become wilted.

In separate mixing bowl combine eggs, salt, pepper, thyme, milk and 6 ounces cheese and add onion-spinach mixture. Pour into *unbaked pastry shell*, sprinkle remaining 2 ounces cheese on the top. Bake on middle rack of oven for 25-30 minutes or until the center is almost set. Cool and transfer the quiche to a warm platter, slice and serve.

*Semi-hard mozzarella cheese is good for grating; since most hard cheeses contain salt, use less salt in recipe.

Note: When you are making quiches, put the filling (such as finely sliced leeks, sliced mushrooms, chopped scallions, and grated ginger etc.) into the basic quiche filling (eggs, milk and cheese), to give the quiche its distinct flavor. Place the fillings into an _unbaked pastry shell_ and bake.

Stir-fry Broccoli and Carrot

Serves 3-4

> 1 tablespoon ginger root, peeled, grated
> 2 cloves of garlic, chopped
> ¼ cup extra virgin olive oil
> 1 extra-large red heirloom tomato, peeled, cut into small pieces
> 2 carrots, peeled, thinly sliced OR cut into julienne strips
> 1 pound broccoli florets cleaned, pat dried
> 1 dash sea salt OR to taste
> 1 dash black pepper, freshly ground
> **Garnish:** 3 sliced red onion rings (optional)

In a heavy-bottomed frying-pan, stir-fry ginger and garlic in heated olive oil for a few seconds, add tomato, stir once and cover the pan and let it simmer for 2 minutes. Add carrots and broccoli, sprinkle with salt and pepper. Reduce heat to medium, and cook in covered pan for about 5-6 minutes or until carrots are fork tender. Stir gently and watch carefully to avoid burning. Place in serving dish and garnish with onion rings. Enjoy the taste of this beautiful and nutritious vegetable dish.

Variation: Steamed Broccoli and carrot. In a saucepan add the following ingredients: 1 cup chicken broth, 1 cup broccoli, 1 carrot (peeled, thinly sliced), 1 celery (thinly sliced), and add 1 pound small crimini mushrooms (cleaned and pat dried). Cover the saucepan; bring the contents to a simmer and simmer for 6-8 minutes or until broccoli and carrot are cooked (watch carefully to avoid burning). Meantime in a small bowl make dressing from the mixture of 2 tablespoons olive oil, 2 tablespoons freshly squeezed lime juice, ½ teaspoon sea salt and ¼ teaspoon black pepper (freshly ground), 1 tablespoon sweet basil and 1 teaspoon European rosemary (chopped with scissors). In a serving bowl, toss vegetables and dressing together and serve. This is excellent vegetarian dish for people who prefer steamed-vegetables to stir-fried vegetables.

Note: You may serve steamed broccoli with dressing (olive oil, vinegar, salt and pepper) and serve with boiled eggs.

Sweet Potatoes/Yams with Spices

Serves 6

      1 teaspoon brown mustard seeds

      2 bay leaves (Laurel)

      ¼ cup extra virgin olive oil

      1 onion, chopped

      ½-inch ginger root, peeled, minced

      4 cloves of garlic, chopped

      ½ teaspoon turmeric

      ½ teaspoon paprika

      1 pound sweet potato OR yam, precooked, cut into 1-inch cubes

      (Please see Tips, how to bake *"sweet potato/yam"*, page 174)

      1 large heirloom tomatoes, cut into small pieces

      ½ teaspoon salt OR to taste

      ¼ teaspoon black pepper, freshly ground

      1 teaspoon lemon juice, freshly squeezed

Garnish: 1 tablespoon cilantro (Chinese parsley/coriander), chopped

In a wok, add mustard seeds and bay leaves to heated olive oil; stir over medium-low heat for a few seconds or until seeds start jumping around. Add onion, ginger, and garlic and stir until onion is slightly golden brown. Add turmeric, paprika, and sweet potatoes. Stir for 1 minute, add tomato, salt and pepper. Simmer mixture in covered wok for 10-15 minutes or until sweet potatoes are cooked. Watch carefully and stir occasionally to prevent burning. Stir in lemon juice. Garnish with cilantro and serve as a side dish.

See Glossary, coriander, page 212

Vegetarian Dish with Eggplant and Zucchini

Serves 3 +

Preheat oven to 400 degree   Line a rimmed baking sheet with parchment paper

    1 extra-large Asian eggplant, trim top, bottom, cut in half lengthwise and slice diagonally 1-inch thick

    1 large zucchini, trim top and bottom, cut in half lengthwise and slice diagonally 1-inch thick

    2-3 tablespoons olive oil

    ½ teaspoon sea salt OR to taste

    ¼ teaspoon black pepper, freshly ground

Dressing:

    ¼ cup strained yogurt OR Greek yogurt

    4 cloves of garlic, smashed

    ¼ cup sesame seeds, finely ground OR tahini*

    ½ teaspoon black cumin seeds, ground

    1 pinch jalapeno pepper, seeded, chopped

Garnish:

    2 tablespoons feta cheese, crumbled

    1 tablespoon of each basil leaves and red onion, chopped

    A few grapes leaves for decoration (optional)

Arrange vegetables (eggplants, zucchini) in single layer, cut side up, on baking sheet. Sprinkle with olive oil and salt and pepper, transfer to middle rack of oven and bake for 15 minutes. Remove baking sheet from the oven, turn over vegetables and return to oven. Continue to cook for 10 minutes or until vegetables are tender and slightly browned. Meanwhile, make dressing by combining yogurt, garlic, sesame seeds, cumin and jalapeno in blender until smooth. Decorate serving plate with grape leaves and place baked vegetables in the center, sprinkle with dressing. Garnish with feta cheese, basil and onion.

Variation: Eggplant with Tomatoes, use "*roasted eggplant slices*", see Tips, page, 174 except cut eggplant thinner lengthwise. Place 1 teaspoon of sour cream at the end of each slice and roll carefully like a cylinder. In a heavy bottom saucepan, add 3 cups of "*tomato-garlic-basil sauce*", ¼ cup chicken broth, 1 teaspoon ginger (grated) and a thyme sprig. Bring the content to simmer. Place eggplant rolls carefully into tomato sauce. Simmer in covered pot for 8 minutes; spoon some of juice on eggplant until done. Garnish with chives; serve with parmesan cheese. Enjoy!

*Tahini: a thick oily paste made of lightly toasted and finely ground sesame seeds.

Vietnamese-style Cabbage Roll

Serves 6

      12 asparagus tips (3-inch long)

      6 Chinese napa cabbage leaves (5-inch long from the top)

      1 carrot, peeled, cut in 2½-inch sections, julienned each section

      1 red bell pepper, seeded, julienned

      1 tablespoon olive oil OR vegetable oil

      1 bunch scallions, cut in 2½ inch long from the bulbs

      ½ teaspoon of each tabasco sauce and sushi sauce (mix together with a dash of honey)

      2 sushi nori seaweed sheet, cut in thirds, make six (2½" x 5") sections

Simmer asparagus with water in covered pot for 6 minutes, drain and set aside. Add cabbage leaves, simmer for 1-2 minutes and drain. Sauté vegetables (carrots, bell pepper), in heated olive oil for 2 minutes, remove pan from heat, add scallions, season with sauce-mixture and cover the pan. On a wooden board, lay out sushi sheets, top each sheet with one cabbage leaf (cup side up), seasoned vegetables and asparagus (lay asparagus with heads out). Roll sushi sheet and cabbage tightly like a cylinder. Cut in half and serve with extra condiment sushi hot sauce.

Zucchini Vegetarian Sandwich

Serves 2+

Preheat oven to 350 degree F.

      2 zucchini, peeled, slice into ½-inch strips lengthwise

      2 tablespoons olive oil, divided

      1 dash sea salt OR to taste

      ¼ cup mozzarella cheese, grated

      2 tablespoons walnuts, coarsely chopped

      4 slices rye bread, slightly toasted

      1 red heirloom tomato, thinly sliced

      ½ cup baby green lettuce, shredded

Arrange zucchini in single layer on cookie sheet lined with parchment paper. Drizzle top with 1 tablespoon olive oil and salt. Place on lower rack in the oven. Bake for 10-12 minutes or until zucchini is fork tender. Remove from oven, sprinkle with mozzarella cheese and walnuts while still warm. Place zucchini-cheese on two slices of bread. Cover with tomato and lettuce, drizzle with remaining olive oil. Top with a second slice of bread, cut in half and enjoy this wonderful sandwich.

Asparagus (Asparagus officinalis)

CHAPTER 3

TIPS

ALMOND: See Glossary, almond, page 200.

Almond blanching: Plunge raw almonds into boiling water briefly (for a few minutes or until it becomes easy to remove their skins); then plunge into cold water. Remove skins, drain, and allow 10 hours to dry.

Almond meal/almond flour: Place dried almonds in food processor, run until ground to flour (do not over-process or you will get almond butter) and sieve. Almond meal/almond flour (fine ground almonds) can be used in dessert, etc.

Almond paste, place blanched almonds with a few tablespoons of water into the food processor. Run processor for a few minutes until a paste is formed. Almond paste has a moist texture and rich buttery taste.

Almond milk: Add more water to almond paste and blend again. Place several layers of cheese cloth into a strainer and pour almond mixture into cloth. Pull the edges of the cheesecloth up around the almonds and tie it together to allow liquid to drain off. Keep the almond milk and throw the solids away.

Almond toasting: You may dry-toast raw almonds in a 275 degree F. oven for 5-6 minutes or until slightly golden brown, stir almonds once during toasting. Toasted almonds make a tastier almond butter. The same method of toasting can be used for raw walnuts (at shorter time).

AROMATIC HERBS: Including basil, burnet*, bay leaves, chives, chervil, garlic, lavender, mustard, onion, oregano, parsley, rosemary, sage, savory, saffron, tarragon and thyme.

*Burnet is a European herb; its leaves when bruised have a fragrance similar to cucumber. The young leaves are used in green salad and also flavored drinks.

Note: Crushing or mincing fresh herbs before using brings out the volatile oils and true flavors.

BAIN-MARIE/WATER BATH: To form a Bain-Marie water bath in the oven, first add batter, custard, chocolate, etc. to ovenproof pan you wish to Bain-Marie bath. Place pan into a larger (***ovenproof***) baking pan. Place both in pre-heated oven on lower rack. Using a teakettle carefully pour boiling water from the corner into the outer baking pan to ½-inch deep and bake as directed. This method is designed to distribute heat evenly from all sides of the baking pan when making delicate dishes such as chocolate, custard and sauces which might curdle.

BEANS/SEEDS SPROUTING (new born plants are nutritious and delicious; sprouting creates live enzymes that convert complex carbohydrate starch into sugar and help with digestion): ***Purchase organically grown fenugreek seeds/soy beans/adzuki beans/wheat berries.*** Wash 2-3 tablespoons whole (not hulled) dried beans thoroughly in fresh water. Soak them for several hours/overnight, change the soaking water twice. Rinse and drain beans. Place them in sprouting strainer with a suitable pot underneath (for ventilation and collecting dripping water) and cover with wet cheesecloth. Let beans germinate at room temperature (such as the top of the refrigerator) for a few days. While they are sprouting, the seeds must be kept moist and need to be rinsed with water at least twice a day. Thoroughly drain after each rinsing, to prevent mold. The length of sprouting time depends on the type and size of seeds, and your personal preference for the size of the sprouting roots and shoots. Young sprouts are the most nourishing and have the highest protein and nutrient contents. Sprouted beans are great when added to sandwiches, salads or stir-fried with vegetables.

Note: For mix sprouting seeds, use 1 tablespoon of both fenugreek seeds and mung beans, and several garbanzo beans; mix together and sprout as directed above.

BOUQUET GARNI WITH FRESH HERBS: You may make a bouquet garni by using fresh sprig of herbs such as oregano, tarragon, thyme, and rosemary or English lavender. Securely tie herbs together in a bunch. Cook with vegetables in gourmet/soup dishes. Remove before blending soup or prior to serving.

Note: Rinse all fresh herbs just before using (see French-style cooking, page 183).

BOUQUET GARNI WITH DRIED HERBS: Instead of fresh herbs, you may use dried herbs. To a small bowl, add 1 teaspoon of each dried herbs (parsley, thyme, marjoram, crushed laurel bay leaf), and ¼ teaspoon dried sage. Mix and tie herbs in a small muslin cloth (about 5-inch square). Add this to your soup during cooking, remove before serving.

EGGPLANT: Roasting Eggplant: Choose a firm and glossy skin eggplant without any blemishes or scars (the peak season from August-September). Asian narrow, purple eggplant is preferable in some cooking, because they have thinner skin, softer flesh, and smaller seeds than regular eggplant. Eggplant is low in fat and has a nice fragrance after cooking. To roast a whole eggplant, poke several times with a fork (so it won't burst) and place on roasting pan uncovered in preheated 400 degree F. oven for 45-60 minute; when done let eggplant cool on a wire-rack, and then remove the skin with your fingers. Trim off the stem and top and discard. Slice or chop eggplant flesh depending on use.

Baked Slices: Trim off both ends of the eggplant and use a vegetable peeler to remove skin as thinly as possible. Cut eggplant widthwise into slices ½-inch thick. Grease generously, a baking pan/broiling tray (you may also use a greased baking parchment paper-lined pan). Arrange slices of eggplant in a single layer on baking pan/broiling tray. Brush eggplant slices lightly with a few teaspoons of olive oil and a dash of sea salt. Cover with foil and bake in a pre-heated 350 degree F. oven for 45 minutes, or until done. You may also "*roast eggplant slices*" in an uncovered broiling tray at 375 degree F. for (30-35 minutes) a shorter period of time.

GRATIN: The term "*gratin*" is French, refers to the golden brown bits on top of rich-delicious foods flavored with herbs. Food is cooked in a shallow, oven proof pan (the increased of surface helps to produce a higher quality and crispy dish), topped with cheese/bread crumbs and baked in the oven or under a broiler until golden brown and crispy.

HOW TO BAKE "*BUTTERNUT SQUASH*": Wrap whole butternut squash in heavy duty aluminum foil, place in oven proof dish and bake in 300 degree F. oven for 1 ½ hours or until squash is cooked. Cool squash, cut in half. Use a serrated spoon for scraping out the seeds and stringy material from the butternut squash. Remove skin and cut/slice as your recipe call for.

HOW TO BAKE "*SWEET POTATO/YAM*": Wash sweet potatoes and pat-dry with paper towels. Place each potato on a sheet of heavy aluminum foil. Fold foil over the potatoes and sealed at the ends so the foil is air-tight (this will retain the moisture in the potatoes). Bake sweet potatoes in pre-heated 350 degree F. oven for 30 minutes for pre-cooked or 45 minutes for completely cooked but still firm and not mushy. Cooking time may vary depending on the size of potatoes. Dry-baked sweet potatoes can be garnished with tangerine or orange.

HOW TO CHOP AND CRUSHED *"GARLIC"*:

Crush each clove of garlic with flat end of your chef knife to remove the skins easily. Chop finely or use a garlic presser to crush garlic (brings out the volatile oil and true flavor of garlic). **Note:** *How to use "**garlic on toasted bread**"*: First toast or slightly grill a slice of French bread, then rub it with 1 clove of garlic and brush with olive oil.

HOW TO COOK *"BARLEY"*: See Glossary, Barley, page 203.

Whole/Grit Barley Cooking: Wash and presoak (to 1 cup barley add 4 cups fresh water and refrigerate for 24 hours, change the water twice); and drain. To a large ovenproof saucepan add 4 cups fresh water and presoaked barley; bring to simmer, and transfer pot to a 275 degree F. oven and cook for 2½ hours or until barley is done. To make soup transfer cooked barley into blender and blend for 30 seconds, add seasoning, vegetables and chicken/lamb broth. Blend again, remove from blender and cook for 8-10 minutes to make a delightful soup.

HOW TO CUT AND SECTION *"POMEGRANATE"*:

1. Choose a fresh and ripe pomegranate; you need a sharp cutting knife (a paring knife or a knife you are comfortable with).
2. On a flat work surface, remove the top and bottom of the pomegranate. This gives you a flat surface on which to set the pomegranate. Cut pomegranate in half horizontally.
3. With a sharp knife and slightly curved motion, go around the pomegranate twice between the skin and white flesh of the pomegranate, making sure skin is completely separated from rest of fruit.
4. Remove the fruits from the skin and cut into section. Now you can easily remove membranes and pomegranate seeds.
5. Do the same for the other half of the pomegranate (see picture, pomegranate, page 61).

HOW TO CRACK *"CHESTNUTS"*: Cover dried chestnuts with warm water and

soak overnight. Next day, place chestnuts in a pot, bring to a simmer (with its soaking water) and place pot in preheated 325 degree F. oven for 2 hours or until chestnuts are tender but not mushy. Drain water, cool, peel, and chop chestnuts as you desire.

HOW TO CUT *"WATERMELON WITH DESIGN BORDER"*:

1. Try to cut one side of watermelon ½-inch larger than the other half.
2. With a bread knife slice a ½-inch round from the larger half and set aside (now both cut watermelon looks the same size).
3. Separate the flesh from the rind on both large watermelon pieces and cut into smaller bitesize chunks.

4. Fill serving bowl with watermelon pieces.
5. The slice which you set aside, cut into 8 pie shape pieces and decorate the perimeter of the serving bowl. Garnish with cut pineapple.

Note: Choose you're serving bowl so that the top of the bowl is almost the same diameter as the center of the watermelon that you cut for design purpose.

HOW TO PREPARE *"BUCKWHEAT GROATS"*: Seeds may be purchase raw or lightly roasted (roasting enhances their flavor). Wash one cup buckwheat in cold water, rinse, and place in medium size saucepan and add 2 cups of boiling water. Cover and simmer for 20-25 minutes; stir a few times to prevent burning. Fluff when cool and use in salad.

HOW TO PREPARE *"CAROB INSTEAD OF MELTED CHOCOLATE"*: Start with double boiler with boiling water in the bottom. To the double boiler top combine 1 cup carob powder with ¼ cup milk and ¼ cup sugar. Heat the mixture over low heat for no longer than 5 minutes stirring vigorously until it's all melted and mixed. After that, it is best to keep it covered in a cool dry place, otherwise it can lose its flavor.

Note: a) If mint carob is desired, add a few fresh green peppermint leaves to milk; cook for a few minutes and strain. Then add this peppermint-flavored milk to the melted carob in the double boiler. b) A wonderful hot carob drink can be made with mixture of 2 cups milk, ¼ cup carob, 1 tablespoon sugar, ½ teaspoon cornstarch flower (or arrowroot powder) flour, and ½ teaspoon vanilla extract in a double boiler. c) Again, the best way to prepare carob is in the double boiler. d) When mixing carob or chocolate with other ingredients for cooking, please follow the instructions carefully so it does not overcook.

HOW TO SCRAPE *"VANILLA BEANS"*: Choose a vanilla beans that has a little flexibility (not completely dry); then with small knife cut it open lengthwise and carefully scrape out its small seeds. The seeds are excellent for cooking.

HOW TO SECTION *"ORANGE PERFECTLY / SUPREME"*:

1. Choose a fresh, firm, and seedless orange.
2. You need a sharp cutting knife and/or paring knife or a knife you are comfortable with.
3. On a flat work surface, place an orange, remove the top and bottom of the orange with a cutting knife. This gives a flat surface on which to set the orange.
4. Remove the orange skin along with outer most membrane of each orange section with a slightly downward motion using a sharp paring knife (see note below).
5. With a sharp paring knife make a cut to the right and left of each orange section to remove the flesh from the membrane. Continue with each orange section.
6. Add removed orange sections to fruit salads or use as a garnish/presentation.

Note: If you do not remove all the white part on your first cut when removing skin don't worry, you can go around the orange a second (or third) time and remove any remaining membrane. It takes practice to master this technique.

HOW TO SIMMER *"ARTICHOKE"*: Remove loose outer leaves from artichoke and wash. Remove thick stem near base of artichoke with a small sharp knife. Using kitchen scissors, cut off the thorny edge from each leaf about ½-inch down from the tip. Place artichoke in steamer (vegetable basket) cover about 3½-inch of water, and 1 teaspoon vinegar. Simmer for 45-60 minutes or until the leaves can be easily removed; drain artichoke by placing upside down on a rack. Cut artichoke in half vertically and serve with your favorite dip. Cooked artichoke can be served either cold or warm.

HOW TO MAKE *"PASTRY-DOUGH"*:

Ingredients for making dough:

> 3 cups unbleached all-purpose flour
> 2 teaspoons baking powder
> 1 dash sea salt (sift together flour, baking powder and salt twice)
> ½ cup sugar, powdered (turbinado raw sugar is my preference)
> ¾ cup sweet butter (1½ sticks), cut into small pieces and chill
> 2 large eggs at room temperature (slightly whisk eggs and lemon zest together)
> Zest of one lemon, freshly grated (about 1 tablespoon).

Processing ingredients to make dough: To food processor, add sifted ingredients (flour, baking powder and salt), and sugar. Pulse a few times to mix well. Add butter pieces one by one through feed tube, as you pulse each time. Then add egg-lemon mixture into feed tube while food processor is running. Pulse a few more times until all the flour is mixed thoroughly and the dough cleans the bowl and becomes one lump. Please see note.

Note: Once dough is ready, remove dough from food processor, ***divide in half*** and wrap each half in thin plastic wrap; place in sealed plastic zip bag, and refrigerate for several hours or overnight. When you are ready to use the dough for cookies/quiche/pizza/pie-shell/tart-shell, ***remove one-half of dough from refrigerator***, and leave out for 2 hours until it reaches room temperature before rolling. Cover a wooden board with thin plastic wrap; place pastry dough on the plastic wrap and cover with another plastic wrap. To make a ***pastry shell or pastry crust*** use your hands and press gently on top of dough to create a smooth flat surface and roll the pastry dough gently about ¼ -inch thick and remove top plastic wrap. Transfer onto greased pastry-pan and chill. Gently prick the surface with a fork and bake in preheated 325 degree F. oven for 8-10 minutes or top of "***pastry shell***" is slightly golden brown.

HOW TO MAKE *"APPLE SAUCE"*: In a medium saucepan, add 3 tablespoons spring water to the bottom of a pan and add 4 apples (peeled, cored and diced). Cover the pan and bring the contents to simmer and simmer gradually about 10-12 minutes or until apples are cooked and soft; stirring occasionally to prevent burning. Mash apple with fork or potato masher. Honey-crisp apple is my preference; adding a pinch of sugar, lemon and cinnamon is optional.

HOW TO MAKE "*CARAMEL TOPPED CUSTARD*": First add sugar into a heavy based saucepan over high-medium heat until sugar melts and caramelized (it is also called "*burnt sugar*"). Quickly pour into soufflé dish, tilting to coat the bottom evenly; let stand for a few minutes. Add custard mixture such as (eggs, milk, sugar and flavoring). Then place mold into a larger oven-proof pan and place both in the oven. Carefully add hot water (by a teakettle) into larger pan from the corner (see "Bain-Marie/water bath", page 173), and follow recipe direction or bake at 350 degree F. oven for 55 minutes or until done. Remove from oven and let cool. Please see recipe "*Caramel Topped Custard*", page 43.

HOW TO MAKE "*CHICKEN BROTH*": Chicken broth/stock is the foundation for many soup, sauces, and other dishes. The technique for preparing a good homemade chicken broth is simmering for an extended period of time. Start by washing a whole chicken, removing skin and visible fat and cutting the chicken into quarters. Place chicken quarters into a large stock pot and add 8 cups of boiling water. Simmer for 1½-2 hours (if you desire cut a piece of fresh ginger root about the size of a garlic and add to the pot). Strain off broth (liquid) and use solids for another use. This stock/broth can be placed in covered, sterilized jars and refrigerated for up to 1 week in the refrigerator. Please be sure to remove solid fat from surface before using broth.

Note: There are two different ways that this broth /stock can be made into richer and more flavorful broth: a) **Thicker/richer chicken broth**, by simmering broth for an extra ½ hour or more to evaporate liquid and concentrate. It can be used in most recipes that require thickening chicken broth. b) **Flavor chicken broth** by adding fresh herbs such as thyme, rosemary, and parsley tied together with string during simmering of chicken broth. Remove herbs before using broth. Do not use powder dried herbs as this may cloud your clear broth.

HOW TO MAKE "*VEGETARIAN SOUP/CLEAR BROTH*":
1-inch ginger root, peeled, chopped (1 tablespoon)
2 lemongrasses, cut in pieces
2 bay leaves, bruised
4 dried (black) limes, bruised and cut into small pieces OR juice of 1 lime
6 thyme sprigs (European thyme is preferable)
2 large onions, chopped
½ cup olive oil
2 pounds shitake fresh mushrooms, washed, thinly sliced and discard stems

2 potatoes, peeled, diced (see note 1)

2 carrots, peeled, sliced

2 parsnips, peeled, sliced

2 leeks, cleaned, thinly sliced

1 sweet bell pepper, peeled, seeded, sliced

3 bunches parsley, cleaned, chopped

2 bunches dill, cleaned, chopped

1 bunch cilantro, cleaned, chopped

1 teaspoon sea salt OR to taste

In a large stock pot (about 6 qt.) add 8 cups of spring boiling water. Place ginger root, lemongrass, bay leaves, dried limes and thyme in a cheesecloth. Securely tie and set aside. In a frying pan, stir-fry onion in heated olive oil for 2-3 minutes or until translucent; add onion to boiling water in stock pot, along with tied cheesecloth and remaining ingredients (shitake mushrooms, potatoes, carrots, parsnips, leeks, bell pepper, parsley, dill, cilantro and salt). Reduce the heat, cover the pan and bring the contents to simmer and simmer gradually for 45 minutes or until potatoes and vegetables are fork tender and are cooked. Stir occasionally, check for consistency and taste, and add a little seasoning or water, if needed. Remove cheesecloth and let it cool. There are several ways to serve this soup; *you may serve as it is with cooked vegetables or strain and serve clear soup as a vegetarian base broth for various soup.* Either way (it is one of the best vegetarian dish) the soup is great especially when refrigerated overnight and reheated the next day.

Note 1: Cut vegetables (potatoes, carrots, parsnips, leeks, and bell pepper) into 1-inch slices/dices.

Note 2: When purchasing shitake mushrooms make sure the underside of the mushroom is light cream colored (darkening indicates mushrooms are not fresh).

HOW TO MAKE "*STARTER FOR RYE BREAD*": It takes almost one week to make a starter but worth it to be able to make a moist, tasty, and nutritious bread.

Day 1: In a non-reaction jar or small bowl, mix 1/3 cup whole rye flour, 1/3 cup whole grain wheat flour, and 1/3 cup spring water. Cover with a cheese cloth and set aside at room temperature.

Day 2: Add 2 tablespoons rye flour and 2 tablespoons wheat flour and ¼ cup spring water and lightly mix.

Day 3: Add 2 tablespoons rye flour and 2 tablespoons wheat flour and ¼ cup spring water and lightly mix.

Day 4: Add 2 tablespoons rye flour and 2 tablespoons wheat flour and ¼ cup spring water and lightly mix.

Day 5: Add 2 tablespoons rye flour and 2 tablespoons wheat flour and ¼ cup spring water and lightly mix.

Day 6: Add 2 tablespoons rye flour and 2 tablespoons wheat flour and ¼ cup spring water and lightly mix

Day 7: Feed lightly with the same ingredients (rye and wheat flours and water), and let it set for 1 hour. Then add starter into stand mixer-bowl and add 2 cups of rye flour. Start kneading on #2 speed for 5 minutes then add 1 teaspoon salt (or to taste), and continue kneading at the same speed for 5 more minutes. You may adjust the flour/water by sprinkling a few tablespoons flour/water into dough while it is kneading. When dough is ready, transfer to prepared loaf-pan (brush pan with oil and dust with flour) and cover with cheese cloth for several hours to allow dough to raise in loaf-pan. Bake at 350 degree F. oven for 45 minutes or until done. Makes a wonderful bread.

HOW TO PREPARE *"LEMONGRASS"*: The lemongrass stem does not have a noticeable lemon aroma until the stem is cut. Trim thinly the root end of lemongrass and discard. Cut stem 4-5 inch long (from white base up to where leaves begin to branch and stem becomes woody), bruise, slice vertically, chop and mince very finely; it is ready to use. Fresh lemongrass can be wrapped in plastic bag and stored in refrigerator for one to two weeks.
Note: Alternatively, the stem end can be bruised at one end to make a brush, and used to baste meat with oil etc.

INSTANT SOUP:
2 cups chicken broth
1 carrot, peeled, diced (½ cup)
1 stalk celery, diced (½ cup)
1 small potato, peeled, diced (½ cup)
1-inch rosemary sprig
¼ teaspoon cumin seeds, ground
¼ teaspoon sea salt and 1 dash black pepper
Juice of 1 lime, freshly squeezed

In a saucepan, add all ingredients except lime juice (chicken broth, carrot, celery, potato, rosemary, cumin, salt and pepper). Simmer for 12 minutes or until carrot is fork tender. Remove rosemary sprig and stir in lime juice and simmer 2 more minutes to make a delightful soup.

MACRONI/SPAGHETTI: Is an Italian name for solid and dried long pasta which is made from wheat "*Semolina flour*" and a liquid. Sometimes herbs and spices are added to pasta for flavoring or vegetables like tomatoes or spinach for coloring. Pasta can also come in a variety of shapes and sizes.

Noodles, the main difference between noodles and spaghetti (dried pasta) is that noodles contains eggs in addition to flour and water (generally known as egg noodles). Most "*Asian noodles*" are made with eggs and flour such as rice, soy, wheat flour, etc. There are many varieties of noodles; they can be fresh or dried in various shapes; they can be cooked in various ways including steaming and/or frying.

*Semolina flour, is made from "Durum wheat", a type of wheat that has a high gluten content, and is used mostly for pasta; it does not absorb much water when cooked so it remains beautifully firm.

MUSSELS (a dark blue sea shells): Mussels season is November-April. Choose mussels with tightly closed shells to insure they are alive and fresh (smaller mussels are more tender than larger ones). Refrigerate mussel soon after purchase and use within 2 days. Place mussels in a bowl of salted cold water. Let stand for a few minutes, strain, discard the water and rinse again under cold water and thoroughly drain. Mussels can be cooked in a variety of ways, including steaming, light frying or baking.

Note: Europeans (especially Italian) love mussels, which are usually cultivated on especial mussel's farms to meet the high demand.

MUSTARD COOKING TIPS: a) If you plan to add mustard powder to hot dishes such as stew/sauce, stir in at the very last minutes of cooking and gently heat on the lowest heat to retain its aroma and flavor. **b)** For toasting mustard seeds to bring out its aroma, have a pan-lid ready so as soon as they start to pop, you can cover the pan and remove from heat. **c)** You can sprout mustard seeds; sprouted mustard seeds have a milder hot spicy flavor and can be used in green salad. **d)** For salad dressing always mix mustard seeds with cold water/liquid prior to blending.

OAT-CRUMBS: Place dry ingredients (2¼ cups rolled oats, ½ teaspoon baking powder, ½ teaspoon sea salt and ½ teaspoon cinnamon) into food processor and run for a few seconds or until thoroughly mixed. Gradually add liquid ingredients (2 tablespoons chilled sweet butter, cut into small pieces, 2 tablespoons olive oil, ¼ cup water), as you pulse until mixture resemble course flour (about 30 seconds). On a rimed and pre-greased cookie sheet spread oat-crumbs evenly (about ¼-inch thick). Bake in preheated 350 degree F. on lower rack oven for 10 minutes or until top is slightly golden brown. Add ¼ cup slivered almonds to "baked oat-crumbs" and mix together. Oat-crumbs can be used instead of bread crumbs in some recipes or you may use to top smoothies. **Example:** Place 1 banana (peeled, sliced), 1 apple (peeled, diced), 1 tablespoon rosewater, and 1 teaspoon pomegranate syrup in blender, blend for 30 seconds or until smooth. Fill glass 2/3 full with this mixture, top with 2 tablespoons oat-crumbs, drizzle top with 1 teaspoon of pomegranate syrup and serve.

ROASTING BABY BEETS: Roasting bring out the natural sweetness of beets. Choose ½ pound red-baby beets, trim off top and the bottom and clean thoroughly. In a mixing bowl, toss beets with 1 tablespoon olive oil and salt and pepper. Arrange beets in a single layer in a small shallow baking dish and cover with heavy aluminum foil and place in preheated 425 degree F. oven. Bake beets for 25 minutes, uncover and roast for 10 more minutes or until fork-tender. Cool, peel, cut into quarters. Cut each quarters in half to be used for salad.

SEASONING: *Try mastering the blending of your own exotic herbs and spices for ethnic cooking:*
Chinese-style Five-Spice Powder (a blend of five spices for **slow cooking**):
    2 cloves
    4 star anises
    1 teaspoon fennel seeds
    ¼-inch cinnamon bark
    ¼ teaspoon peppercorn (black pepper).
Grind to powder. Use this sparingly in slow cooking Chinese cuisine.
Chinese-style Stir-fry Seasoning Sauce:
    2 tablespoons rice vinegar
    1 teaspoon organic cornstarch (dissolve cornstarch in rice vinegar)
    1 tablespoon soy sauce
    1 dash black pepper/cayenne
    1 tablespoon packed brown sugar
Mix ingredients (cornstarch mixture, soy sauce, black pepper and brown sugar) during last few minutes of **stir-frying**, compile all the food on one side of pan and pour the seasoning mixture at the bottom of pan and stir constantly until thickened. Mix sauce with food (vegetables and chicken) cover the pan for a few seconds and serve. Stir-fried Chinese food is tasty.
English-style Sweet Baking Spices:
    ½ teaspoon cardamom
    ½ teaspoon nutmeg

¼ teaspoon mace,

¼ teaspoon cloves,

1 teaspoon Ceylon cinnamon.

Grind to powder, use for sweet baking cuisine (like cakes, cookies and fruit cakes).

French-style Cooking: In most French classic gourmet slow cooking, a bouquet-garni (a little *"fresh herb bundle"* tied with culinary string and wrapped in cheese cloth or tied inside of a tube made of two short cut celery stalks or sandwiched in a split leek) is used to flavor stock. Discarded prior to serving. The standard bouquet-garni consists of French laurel bay leaves, tarragon, thyme, and parsley; the flavor and the amount of herbs can be varied according to type of dish being prepared, for examples:

For *lamb* use bay laurel leaf, parsley and thyme OR marjoram, green garlic and a few strips orange peel OR savory, thyme, parsley and sage. For *fish* use dill, fennel, green onion and a few strips of lemon peel. For *poultry* use bay laurel leaf, parsley, bruised lemongrass and tarragon OR savory, marjoram, and rosemary. For *vegetables* use parsley, thyme, oregano and bay laurel (see bouquet-garni, page 173).

French-style Dried Seasoning Mix: Combine 3 tablespoons of each dried herbs (rosemary leaves, savory leaves, sweet marjoram leaves and thyme leaves), add 1 tablespoon lavender flowers, and 1 tablespoon sage leaves. Save in sterilized and airtight spice jar along with other spices. Use small amount of this classic French seasoning in vegetables and chicken dishes.

Indian-style Cuisine: Combine ¼ teaspoon of each spice (cardamom, cumin, peppercorn and fennel), and 1 tablespoon coriander, ½ teaspoon cinnamon and 1 clove. Grind and keep in sterilized jar along with other spices. This mixed spices is ready to use in many dishes such as cooking rice, soups, vegetable-chicken stew (particularly if white wine is used with chicken).

Note: **Biryani**, Indians use exotic flavors from blending herbs and spices (such as bay leaf, cardamom, cinnamon, clove, coriander, cumin, ginger and saffron) mixed with yogurt to marinate meat used to prepare **biryani masala dish and serve with rice.**

Indian-style Curry Powder Mixture: Typical Indian spices used to flavor meats such as lamb and chicken include blends of the following:

2 tablespoons ground turmeric

1½ tablespoon coriander seeds (it is called dried cilantro seeds)

1 teaspoon ground ginger root

1 teaspoon mustard seeds

1 teaspoon fennel seeds

1 clove

¼ teaspoon ground cinnamon

¼ teaspoon black cumin seeds

¼ teaspoon cardamom seeds

¼ teaspoon peppercorn (black pepper)

¼ teaspoon dried red chili pepper (optional)

The whole seeds are lightly toasted prior to grinding to improve the flavor of the curry powder. To do this, heat a small pan. Add a small amount of seeds. Swirl the pan, allowing the seeds to move freely in the pan while heating for just a few seconds. Remove the spices from the heat (this releases their volatile oils and essences for better taste and aroma). Grind seeds, combine all ingredients and save in sterilized and airtight spice jar for future use.

Gram-masala*, one form of blended curry powder mixture in India:

1 tablespoon cardamom

½ tablespoon coriander

1 teaspoon Ceylon cinnamon

1 teaspoon fenugreek seeds

1 teaspoon black cumin seeds

2 cloves

½ teaspoon ground nutmeg

¼ teaspoon dried chili peppers, ranging from mild to hot

*Masala, spice blend (like garam-masala is the principal masala) is used in Indian cuisine. It comes in various varieties depends on the cook and the dish being preparing. One form of masala is prepared with green mint leaves, coriander leaves, green pepper and a little coconut milk and form a mild masala paste called "***green-masala***" which is a wonderful addition to your spices and is best used with prawns and vegetable dishes.

Mint-masala/Green-masala (Hindi word for blended spices with various seasoning):

1 tablespoon fenugreek seeds, soak with ¼ cup spring water overnight, drain

¼ teaspoon cardamom, powder

1 clove

½ teaspoon turmeric, ground

¼ teaspoon sea salt OR to taste

1 dash black pepper, freshly ground

2 cloves of garlic, peeled, finely grated (1 tablespoon)

½-inch ginger root, peeled finely grated (1 teaspoon)

¼ cup green mint leaves, chopped + 1 teaspoon chocolate mint leaves

¼ cup coriander leaves (Chinese parsley), chopped

1 teaspoon dried curry leaves (optional)

2 tablespoons green bell pepper, seeded, finely chopped

¼ cup coconut milk

¼ cup sunflower seeds oil OR toasted sesame seeds oil

2 tablespoons apple cider vinegar

Place drained fenugreek seeds in power-blender along with other ingredients (cardamom, clove, turmeric, salt, black pepper, garlic, ginger root, mint leaves, chocolate mint leaves, coriander leaves, dried curry leaves, green bell pepper, coconut milk, sunflower seeds oil and apple cider vinegar). Blend the mixture for a minute. Taste for consistency and adjust the seasoning, if necessary. Refrigerate "*mint-masala*" for several hours prior to use for grilled prawns/vegetable.

Note: Dry-toasting seeds such as cardamom and clove prior to grinding will enrich the aroma and flavor.

Italian-style Pizza Herbs Seasoning: Combine herbs together and add to pizza.

2½ tablespoon oregano

1 tablespoon basil

1 teaspoon marjoram plus 1 dash chili pepper

Italian-style Salad Herbs Seasoning:

¼ cup of each dried herbs (basil, marjoram, savory, and thyme).

2 tablespoons dried oregano

1 tablespoon each dried herbs (rosemary and sage)

Combine herbs together and keep in a covered sterilized jar to be used in small amount for green salad/salad dressing.

Persian-style Cuisine: The Persian love for various herb blends was developed over many centuries; fresh herbs are used during the summer when available and dried herbs are used during the winter.

Persian-style Herbs Mixture (for amazing flavor and aroma, use the following seasoning herbs):

For "*sabzi-polo*", use fresh herbs such as parsley, cilantro, fenugreek, chive, and mint.

For soup "*sabzi-ash*", use fresh herbs such as parsley, cilantro, spinach, fenugreek, dill and mint and plenty of crisp-fried onions.

For rice mixture "*advieh-poloye*", finely grind ¼ teaspoon each of the following spices: Ceylon cinnamon, cardamom, coriander, black cumin seeds and saffron with 1/8 teaspoon ground nutmeg, 1 clove and 1 tablespoon rose petals.

For stew "*advieh-khoreshtie*", use the same spices as "*advieh-poloye*" except instead of saffron use 1 teaspoon turmeric and add 1 teaspoon sour dried powder such as grapes or amchur-mango powder or lime and 1 dash of ground peppercorn or chili powder. Both advieh-poloye and advieh-khoreshti are "*Master seasoning*" in Persian cuisine.

Saffron-Water: To make saffron water use ½ teaspoon ground saffron dissolved in ¼ cup boiling water. It can be sprinkled over steamed rice to add flavor and color.

Safron-Zereshk-Jam: In a small saucepan, heat ¼ cup (clarified) sweet butter (do not overheat). To the butter add 1 cup zereshk (cleaned, presoaked and drained), 1 cup granulated sugar, and ¼ cup ground rose petals and ¼ cup of saffron-water mixture. Stir and simmer on low heat for 1-2 minutes. Turn off the heat, cover saucepan, and let saffron-zereshk steam for a few minutes. It is ready to be mixed with "*Basic Steamed Basmati Rice*", page 106 to make a "***saffron-zereshk-polo***" or let it cool, place in sterilized covered jar and refrigerate.

Note: Grind saffron in a coffee/spice grinder or with a mortar and pestle: Use 1 ounce saffron with ¼ teaspoon sugar. You may grind saffron ahead of time. Save in a sterilized spice jar and store with other spices in a spice rack; sprinkle saffron over rice toward the end of your cooking process to preserve its aromatic flavor.

Persian Green Herbs Mixed (Delal):

> 2 cups snipped peppermint leaves OR ½ cup Penny royal (*Menthe pulegium*), that is called "*Ponneh*" in Persian
>
> ½ cup green parsley leaves
>
> ¼ cup snipped sweet basil leaves
>
> 1 teaspoon thyme leaves and ½ teaspoon oregano leaves
>
> 1 teaspoon sea salt and ¼ teaspoon peppercorn, freshly ground

Place cleaned herbs including salt and pepper in pestle and mortar; grind to a puree. Use a small amount as a spread or mix with grape juice to be used as a dressing. Store in sterilized jar and refrigerate for later use.

Barbeque/Grill Seasoning: It is similar to seasoning used in Southern France, where the people used to flavor their barbeque/grill much as we use salt in our food.

> 2 teaspoons each dried herb marjoram, savory, tarragon, and thyme,
>
> 1 teaspoon each dried herb (laurel bay leaves, lavender, rosemary, sage and mint),
>
> 2 tablespoons basil
>
> 2 tablespoons oregano
>
> 1 teaspoon fennel seeds (optional)

Mix together in coffee/spice grinder. Store in sterilized spice jars and use in small amounts for **dry rubbing** on chicken prior to barbequing.

Barbeque/Grill Seasoning (Starlight Barbeque):

> 1 lemongrass (minced)
>
> Juice of 1 lemon
>
> 1 cup unsweetened coconut milk to be mixed with 1 tablespoon brown sugar
>
> 4 tablespoons sesame seeds

2 tablespoons tamari sauce

1 tablespoon ginger root, grated

2 tablespoons garlic, chopped

1 teaspoon turmeric powder

1 teaspoon coriander powder

1 teaspoon black cumin seeds, ground

¼ teaspoon sea salt OR to taste

To the power-blender add all the marinate seasoning. Blend until smooth. Place 2 ½ pounds chicken breast (skinned, boned, cut into bite size cubs) in a plastic bag. Pour marinade sauce over chicken in bag and shake until all pieces are covered. Refrigerate for several hours. Skewer chicken (with presoaked wooden skewers) and barbeque 2-3 minutes each side or until done. Serve with shredded lettuce and *"Divine Salad Dressing"*, see variation, page 115.

Garbanzo Beans Seasoning:

2 cups cooked garbanzos beans

6 tablespoons olive oil

6 cloves of garlic, grated

2 teaspoons ginger root, grated

4 tablespoons balsamic vinegar

2 tablespoons lemon juice, freshly squeezed

½ teaspoon sea salt or to taste

¼ teaspoon black pepper, freshly ground

4 heads of scallions, chopped

1 teaspoon mint, dried

Combine all ingredients, adjust seasoning if needed and refrigerate in sterilized jar for 24 hours before using. Toss with salad greens or serve as a side dish.

Grilled Chicken Seasoning: Combine all seasoning and use to season chicken when grilling.

1 teaspoon curry powder OR lemon zest

½ teaspoon cumin, ground

½ teaspoon turmeric, ground

½ teaspoon coriander, ground

¼ teaspoon cinnamon, ground

1/8 teaspoon red pepper (flakes are preferable}

Ground Fish Seasoning: In a small bowl, mix together:

¼ teaspoons of each of the following (parsley, garlic powder, oregano, rosemary and lemon zest)

1 pinch of black and chili pepper

¼ teaspoon sea salt or to taste

Use a small amount of this mixture for ground fish.

Mexican-style Mixed Spices:

½ tablespoon paprika, ½ teaspoon cumin seeds, ½ teaspoon sea salt, ¼ teaspoon peppercorn, ¼ teaspoon thyme and 1 dash chili pepper.

In a grinder, grind the herbs and spices and mix with 1 teaspoon garlic (crushed), 1 tablespoon olive oil and 2 tablespoons lime juice. Blend together and use to marinate meat for **fajitas** (a Mexican dish consisting of ½ pound chicken strips thinly cut). Refrigerate overnight before grilling.

Moroccan-style Mixed Spices, Using *"Tagine cookware"***:**

1½ tablespoons paprika (mild paprika is preferable)

1 tablespoon coriander seeds, ground

1 teaspoon cinnamon

½ teaspoon allspice, ground

¼ teaspoon clove, ground

¼ teaspoon cardamom, ground

1 dash chili powder

Blend all together and use for lamb shanks casserole.

Seasoned Walnuts:

1 pounds shelled walnuts

½ cup maple syrup

1 tablespoon lemon zest, freshly grated

1 teaspoon turbinado raw sugar (optional)

1/8 teaspoon each of the following: Salt, cinnamon, and chili powder

Mix thoroughly. Spread mixture on parchment lined rimmed cookie sheet in single layer, and bake in preheated 275 degree F. oven, lower rack, for 12-14 minutes or until slightly golden brown. Stir once to prevent burning. Store in sterilized jar in the refrigerator for several weeks.

THE SECRET OF A GOOD CASSEROLE DISH:

a) Use casserole dish with tight fitting lid. b) Add lightly sautéed vegetables and chicken/meat. c) Be imaginative in flavoring your casserole dish with lemon/black lime powder/bitter orange/sour grape powder/mango powder/sour-pitted cherries.

d) Do not use too much liquid. e) Lightly combine ingredients; do not over stir. f) Cook slowly with low heat.

TOASTING NUTS/SEEDS FOR SNACKS: In a mixing bowl, add about 1¼ cup of each unseasoned raw nuts/seeds (sunflower seeds, Chinese pumpkins seeds, and pine nuts) and 2 tablespoons of tamari/soy sauce. Mix together. Line a cookie sheet with aluminum foil and place mixture on it in a single layer. Transfer cookie sheet to preheated 275 degree F. oven on lower rack, and toast uncover for a few minutes (about 5-6 minutes). It is good for snacking.

TOASTING WHOLE SPICES: Toasting whole spices prior to grinding releases their volatile oils and essence for better taste and aroma. Heat a small pan, add spices to the pan and swirl; allowing the spices to move freely in the pan while gently heating for a few seconds. Remove spices from the pan, cool and grind. Keep ground spices in a sterilized jar. Label and store along with other spices for convenient use.

TOMATOES AND TOMATOES SAUCE: In general, when making tomato sauce choose a large deep skillet, so moisture evaporates more quickly, reducing cooking time and preserving the fresh taste and bright color of the tomatoes.

Roasting Tomatoes in the Oven: Puncture 8 plump tomatoes on all sides with a fork (or use three extra-large sliced heirloom tomatoes). Arrange tomatoes in a single layer, on a large baking pan lined with parchment paper. Bake tomatoes in 350 degree F. oven for 35 minutes until the skin removes easily and tomatoes are slightly dried out. You may use these tomatoes for pizza topping or peel, cut into chunks, and puree while still warm to make "*tomato puree*".

Tomato Basil Sauce: In a large saucepan, fry 1 large onion (finely chopped) and 4 cloves of garlic (chopped) in 4 tablespoons heated olive oil for 3-4 minutes or until golden brown, stirring constantly. Add 4 cups ripe red meaty tomatoes (peeled and chopped), ½ teaspoon sugar, and ½ teaspoon sea salt and 1 dash of each dried herb (marjoram, thyme, basil and black pepper). Simmer slowly in an uncovered saucepan until mixture thickens, stirring occasionally to prevent burning. Let cool and puree in blender. Sauce can be used for green beans, vegetables and pasta dishes.

Tomato Paste: Continue cooking "*tomato basil sauce*" until the desired thickness is reached. Stir occasionally to prevent burning. Cool tomato paste, place in sterilized jars and store in refrigerator until you are ready to use. Spread on a pizza crust, add pizza topping like meat, vegetables (you may sauté sliced mushrooms in heated olive oil flavored with garlic, and herbs) and cheese. Bake pizza according to your recipe instruction.

Tomato Sauce with Roasted Garlic (for chicken, soups, beans, or pasta): Peel, seed and juice 8-10 large ripe meaty red tomatoes. Chop the tomato flesh and set aside. In a large heavy pot, add tomato juice and bring to a boil. Cook uncovered for 30 minutes or until juice is reduced to half its original volume. In the meantime, combine and blend the following spices and herbs: ¼ teaspoon black pepper, ¼ teaspoon coriander, 1 pinch each of dried herbs (parsley, tarragon, basil, thyme, and mint), and ½ teaspoon oregano, and ½ teaspoon cinnamon. Add mixed spices to simmered tomatoes along with 1 garlic head (roasted and crushed), 4 tablespoons granulated sugar, 1½ teaspoon sea salt, and 4 teaspoons apple cider vinegar and 2 tablespoons olive oil. Combine the mixture with chopped tomatoes flesh. Simmer sauce for 10 minutes or until it reaches the desired thickness. To make a "*tomato puree*", place sauce in blender until smooth and simmer to concentrate. The thickest intense version of tomato puree is "*tomato paste*". Continue simmering and stirring puree until very thick.

Tomato Puree (simple and spicy): Peel 8 ripe meaty red tomatoes. Chop tomato pulp. Cook slowly in an uncovered saucepan until the mixture is reduced to half of its original volume. Add 6 cloves of garlic (roasted and crushed), a dash of jalapeno powder, and 2 red bell peppers (baked, peeled and chopped). Place in blender and blend mixture until pure and smooth.

Tomatillo (*means little tomato in Spanish),* has lemony, tangy taste and has paper-like husks and glossy skins. They need to be husked and washed prior to use. Tomatillo are mainly used in **salsas** and **sauces**. Look for hard-fleshed and glossy tomatillos; you can keep them dry in a paper bag in the refrigerator for up to two weeks.

Salsa is a Spanish word for sauce, it is either cooked or made of fresh ingredients. Traditionally, the main ingredients are tomatillo/tomatoes, onion, chili and cilantro.

Tomatillo Sauce (*a fabulous Mexican vegetable green sauce*):

> 1 onion, chopped
> 2 cloves of garlic, chopped
> ½ teaspoon jalapeno pepper, seeded, chopped OR 1 dash hot chili
> 2 tablespoons olive oil
> 6 fresh tomatillos, husked, washed, cut each tomatillo into 8 pieces
> Salt and pepper to taste
> ¼ teaspoons black cumin seeds, freshly ground
> ¼ cup cilantro, finely chopped

In a large frying pan, sauté onion, garlic and jalapeno pepper in heated olive oil for a few minutes until onions are translucent. Add tomatillos and continue to sauté for 3-4 minutes. Let it cool completely. Add this to food processor and run for one minute or until pureed. Place salsa in a bowl. Sprinkle with salt and pepper and cumin seeds and stir in cilantro.

Note: For oven roasting tomatoes with other vegetables, it is better to use cherry tomatoes (cut in ½) since cherry tomatoes have less juice.

Pesto (*pasta sauce*): A fresh Italian sauce made with basil, garlic, olive oil, pine nuts and parmesan/pecorino cheese. Ingredients are pounded and crushed in mortar and pestle and served over pasta.

TOPPING FOR PORRIDGE/PUDDING: Thoroughly mix 1 cup coconut flakes, 1 pinch salt, ¼ cup brown sugar, 2 teaspoons softened butter, 2 teaspoons rosewater. Spread evenly on parchment paper-lined cookie sheet and place in preheated 350 degree F. oven. Bake about 5-6 minutes or until coconut-mixture becomes slightly golden brown.

VARIOUS MUFFIN TOPPING: Three of the most popular topping ones are:

1) Mixture of ¼ cup brown sugar, ¼ cup ground pecans and 1 tablespoon ground cinnamon.
2) Mixture of ¼ cup brown sugar, ¼ cup rolled oats and 1 tablespoon ground cinnamon.
3) Mixture of ¼ cup brown sugar, 2 tablespoons flour, 1 tablespoon ground cinnamon and 1 tablespoon butter.

After filling muffin tins 2/3 full with batter, sprinkle your favorite coarse crumb topping on each muffin prior to baking. Bake according to muffin recipe directions.

VARIOUS CUPCAKE FROSTING: To the blender add 2/3 cup almond butter, 1½ tablespoons maple syrup, ¼ teaspoon honey, ¼ teaspoon vanilla extract ¼ teaspoon cinnamon, and ¼ teaspoon ginger root (finely chopped). Blend ingredients until creamy. Use as a cupcake frosting.

Note: It is easy to make almond butter; to high power-blender, add organic, raw and thinly *sliced* almonds (*not ground*) and very little almond oil, and blend until creamy.

WAYS TO COOK "*ASPARAGUS*": Asparagus shines when it is lightly cooked. First break off the bottom of each stalk at the place where it breaks most easily and discard. Scrape off the scales from asparagus tops. Wash completely and gather asparagus stems into a bundle. . In a medium size stock pot (with an expandable steamer basket), add 2 cups of boiling water with a dash of salt, a few drops of lemon juice and olive oil if desired. Add bundled asparagus to steamer basket, reduce the heat to simmer and cook asparagus for 6-8 minutes or until tender. Remove steamer basket and immediately plunge cooked asparagus into ice water, drain and flavored with a few drops of lemon juice. You can also roast asparagus in a preheated 375 degree F. oven for a short time (6-8 minutes) and then top with crumbled goat cheese.

WAYS TO COOK "*BROCCOLI*":

1) In a medium size stock pot (with an expandable steamer basket), bring 2 cups water to boil, add 2 pounds broccoli florets to steamer basket and reduce the heat to medium. Simmer for 6-8 minutes, or until tender. Slice 1 orange (or 2 tangerines) in half and remove the

fruit sections with a grapefruit spoon and cut each section into smaller pieces. In a serving bowl, toss cooked broccoli with 2 tablespoons olive oil, orange sections, and ½ cup "*seasoned walnut*" (see Tips, page 188). Serve warm as a side dish.

2) In a medium bowl, add 2 pounds broccoli florets (with 1-inch of trimmed stem), 2 tablespoons olive oil, 2 cloves of garlic (grated), ¼ teaspoon sea salt and ¼ teaspoon peppercorn (freshly ground) and 1 lemon zest (freshly grated); toss until broccoli is evenly coated. Spread broccoli mixture evenly on a cookie sheet and place on middle rack of 400 degree F. oven; cook uncovered for 5 minutes. Turn the heat down to 350 degree F. and continue to cook for 12 more minutes or until the edges of broccoli are slightly golden brown. Toss roasted broccoli with ¼ cup crumbled goat cheese, 2 tablespoons basil leaves (chopped), and 2 tablespoons freshly squeezed lemon juice.

WAYS TO COOK "*QUINCE*": Quince fruit is high in natural pectin making it perfect for use in jellies and jams.

> 2 quinces, peeled cored, cut into 1-inch thick wedges
> 2 cups fresh water
> 1 cup (turbinado raw) sugar
> 2-inch vanilla beans, split the pod and scrape out the seeds and discard
> 1 tablespoon culinary rose petals, dried
> 1 dash cardamom, ground
> Zest of 1 organic lemon, freshly grated

Add quince in a medium saucepan, along with 2 cups water, sugar, vanilla beans, rose petals and cardamom. Bring to boil and partially cover saucepan over medium heat and simmer until 1 cup of syrup remains and flavor intensifies, stir occasionally to prevent burning. Remove vanilla beans, and add lemon zest and continue to simmer until quince softens (but not mushy) and turned to pinkish-red color. Remove saucepan from the heat and let it cool. Place quince in sterilized jar and refrigerate to keep its freshness.

Quince/Strawberries Clear Fruit Glaze: In a small saucepan, over medium heat, melt quince or strawberries jelly/jam with a few tablespoons water, over medium heat, stirring frequently to prevent food from burning. Remove from the heat and whisk until smooth; strain immediately into small bowl. While still warm apply strained clear quince or strawberries glaze on top of cold fresh fruits with a pastry brush.

Note 1: If glaze becomes too thick to spread, add additional water about 1 tablespoon at a time, until glaze is the right consistency to spread.

Note 2: By blending cooked quince with a little of its syrup you have a *clear bright jelly* to garnish cheesecake or use as a filling for various dessert, cakes and cookies. Please see Glossary, quince, page 237.

WAYS TO MAKE "*VANILLA PASTRY CREAM*": This basic and smooth "*vanilla pastry cream*" is a versatile custard filling for tarts and puff pastries.

    2 cups milk
    3 large egg yolks, slightly beaten
    6 tablespoons brown sugar
    Zest of 1 organic lemon, freshly grated
    1 teaspoon vanilla extract
    1 tablespoon of both wheat flour and cornstarch, sifted together
    ¼ cup + 1 tablespoon sweet butter, softened

In heavy-bottomed saucepan, bring the milk gradually to simmer, over medium-heat remove saucepan from the heat, remove milk-skin, cover saucepan and set aside. In mixing bowl, whip the egg yolks and sugar until fluffy. Add the lemon zest, vanilla and flours. Add some of the simmered milk into egg yolk mixture and stir until no lumps remain, and gradually add remaining milk. Cook over medium-low heat while stirring constantly until mixture thickens (about 10 minutes). Remove from the heat and stir in butter until blended and smooth.

Note 1: To make "*almond pastry cream*", simply stir in ½ cup finely ground almond meal/almond flour and 2 tablespoons "*Disaronno amaretto*" liqueur into pastry cream the last minutes of cooking.

Note 2: Pastry cream can be made ahead of time and refrigerate up to one day.

WAYS TO MAKE "*OATMEAL*" FOR BREAKFAST: In a 3 qt. pot soak 1 cup **steel-cut oats** in a 4 cups of boiling spring water and 1 dash sea salt. Let it cool to room temperature and refrigerate overnight. Next day bring the contents to a simmer, add 2 apples (peeled, cored, grated) and 1 cup milk and continue to simmer over low-medium heat in partially covered pot (a heavy-based pot with fitting lid such as "*Le Creuset*" is preferable) for 15-20 minutes or until oats are completely cooked; stir occasionally to prevent food from burning. Remove from heat and let it cool a little so you can handle it. Blend cooked oats in food processor for 30 seconds or until creamy. Stir in 1 tablespoon turbinado raw sugar and ½ cup more milk and bring back to a simmer for a few minutes. Garnish with cinnamon powder and ¼ cup walnuts (coarsely ground).

WAYS TO MAKE "*OLIVE SAUCE*": Blend 1 teaspoon lemon zest (freshly grated), 1-2 cloves of garlic (chopped), 1 tablespoon basil leaves (chopped) using a mortar-pestle, then mix in 8 black **calamari olives** (pitted and chopped). Brush this mixture on toasted French bread and top with goat cheese (optional). Excellent for a treat.

Radish (Raphanus sativus)

CHAPTER 4
Glossary
(Introduction)

Herbal remedies have grown out of their health benefits passed on by generations of knowledgeable and experienced herbalists, and now often backed by scientific research. Still, much of the herbal lore is not based on scientific evidence from nature's oldest **"*Herbal Green Pharmacy*"** as related to preventing illness, providing soothing care and improving longevity. Diet with a focus on essential fresh fruits and vegetables is now recognized as a key preventive factor for many diseases. The right lifestyle can protect our health and even minimize our familial and genetic tendencies for diseases such as heart problems, cancer, and diabetes. This if from an exciting and expanding field of *Epigenetics*, the affects of lifestyle on gene expression.

Throughout history, our ancient ancestors were mainly "*hunters and gatherers.*" They hunted when they could for animal proteins, but primarily built their diets around fruits, vegetables, nuts, seeds, legumes, and grains that naturally grew in their fields or at home. They harvested them when they were at their peak so they could have the benefit of freshness, taste, optimum color, and nutritional value. Most mature fruits and vegetables, like our life, depend on the sunshine to become beautifully full-flavored and beneficial, because the sunlight matures fruits and vegetables as no artificial light can.

As new vegetables and fruits were introduced throughout the world during the past millennia, each civilization added their own spices and herbs, and unique method of food preparation.

These changes resulted in distinct ethnic cuisines. To become seasoning experts, we must learn more about our herbs and spices from leaves, seeds, bulbs, roots, and flowers. Herbs from leafy part of plant like (basil, bay leaf, chives, mint, oregano, parsley, and rosemary) and spices from the bark, buds, berries, roots and seeds either whole or ground like (anise, cloves, cumin, coriander, cardamom, fennel, ginger, mustard, peppercorn and turmeric) not only add a magical flavor touch to our food but complement our foods' natural flavors. They also contain nutrients, namely phytonutrients that include many carotenoids and bioflavonoids, which can protect our health; in this way, herbs are healing. We are aware for many centuries that herbal remedies can improve and naturally help maintain our health. ***However, herbs and spices need to be used sparingly and carefully because some of them or excessive amounts of some can have adverse medicinal effect on our body.*** Certain herbs and spices may cause irritation and other problems, and this is often an individual reaction. Most people can handle garlic or cayenne pepper easily, yet some cannot. The best method of assessing the value of a new herb or spice in your diet is to learn about it, and to use one at a time, so you can evaluate them individually.

The Dance of Herbs and Spices in the Kitchen:
Throughout the world, the cooking of every country is recognized by the way in which herbs and spices are used to give their special foods and dishes a unique character. With so many herbs and spices now readily available in the marketplace, cooking can be a great experience that will transport you to any part of the world through its cultural cuisine.
The glossary presents the name and benefits of popular traditional herbal plants and some important fruits, vegetables and foods (such as honey which is not an herbal plant) that also have great nutritional benefits. Please read, carefully, ***Chapter one, page vi,*** for safe use.

DISCLAIMER

The information in this book reflects the author's personal opinion and experience. It is not intended to replace individualized professional advice. All recipes (including philosophy, introduction, heading and footnotes, tips, glossary, herbs, spices, fruits, vegetables and medicinal herbal plants) are used at the risk of the consumer. We cannot be responsible for any hazards, loss or damage that may occur as a result of any use of this information without proper consultation with a health care provider. It is not intended as a substitute for any treatment that may have been prescribed by your doctor. For all matters pertaining to your health, a qualified health professional must be consulted.

INDEX OF GLOSSARIES
(THE LIST OF FRUITS AND VEGETABLES)

- CELERY (*Apium graveolens*), 208
- CHARD (*Beta vulgaris*), 209
- CHICKPEA/GARBANZO BEANS (*Cicer arietinum*), 209
- CHILI PEPPER, 209
- CHERVIL (*Chervil*), 210
- CHIVES (*Allium schoenorasum*), 210
- CINNAMON (*Cinnamomum zeylanicum*), 210
- CITRUS FRUITS (*Citrus sinensis*), 210
- CLOVE (*Caryophyllus aromaticus*), 211
- COCOA (*Theoloroma cocoa*), 211
- COCONUTS (*Cocos nucifera*), 212
- CORIANDER/CHINESE PARSLEY/CILANTRO (*Coriangrum sativum*), 212
- CORN (*Zea mays*), 212
- CRANBERRIES (*Vaccinium vitis idaea*), 213
- CUCUMBER (*Cucumis sativus*), 213
- CUMIN SEEDS (*Cuminum cyminum*), 213
- CURRY LEAVES (Murraya koenigii), 213
- DANDELION (*Taraxacum officinale*), 214
- DATE (*Phoenix dactylitera*), 214
- DILL (*Aniethum graveolens*), 214
- DULSE (*Palmaria palmate*), 215
- EDIBLE FLOWERS (to garnish food), 215
- EGGPLANT (*Solanum melongena*), 215
- ELDERBERRY (*Sambucus nigra*), 216
- FENNEL (*Foeniculum vulgare officinale*), 216
- FIG (*Ficus carica*), 216
- FLAXSEEDS (*Linum usitatissimum*), 217
- GARLIC (*Allium sativum*), 217
- GINGER ROOT (*Zingiber officinale*), 218
- GOJI BERRY (*Wolfberry*), 218
- GOOSEBERRY/GOLDEN BERRY, 218
- GRAINS (*including gluten free*), 218
- GLUTEN FREE (GF) GRAINS, 219-222
- GRAPE (*Vitus labrusca*), 223
- HAZELNUTS (*Corylus avellana*), 223
- HERBAL-SAP, 223
- HONEY (*Herbal sap*), 223
- JUJUBE FRUITS (*Zizyyphus jujube mill*), 224
- KAFFIR LIME LEAVES (*Citrus hystrix*), 224

- KALE (*Brassica oleracea var. sabellica*), 225
- KELP (*Focus vesiculosus*), 225
- KIWI (*Actinidia deliciosa*), 225
- KUDZU ROOT (*Pueraria spp.*), 225
- LAVENDER (*Lavandula officinalis, langusti-folia*), 226
- LEEK (*Allium porrum*), 226
- LEGUMES, 226
- LEMON (*Citrus limon*), 227
- LEMONGRASS (*Cymbbopogon citratug*), 227
- LENTIL (*Lens culinaris medic*), 227
- LETTUCE (*Lactuca sativa*), 227
- MANGO (*Mangifera indica*), 227
- MARJORAM, 227
- MARSHMALLOW (*Althaea officinalis*), 228
- MELONS, 228
- MINT (*Mentha piperita*), 228
- MOLASSES, 229
- MULBERRIES (*Morus alba*), 229
- MUSHROOMS, 229
- MUSTARD, 230
- NIGHTSHADE VEGETABLE FAMILY, 230
- NORI, 230
- NUTMEG (*Myristica fragrans*), 230
- NUTS, 231
- OATS (*Avena sativa*), 231
- OILY SEEDS, 232
- OKRA (*Hibiscus esculentus*), 232
- OLIVE (*Olea Europaea*), 232
- ONION (*Allium cepa*), 233
- ORGANO/WILD MARJORAM (*Origanum vulgare*), 234
- PAPAYA (*Carica papaya*), 234
- PARSLEY (*Petroselinum sativum*), 234
- PARSNIP (*Pastinaca sativa*), 234
- PEACH (*Amygdalus persica*), 235
- PEAR (*Pirus communis*), 235
- PEAS, 235
- PERSIMON (*Diospyros kaki*), 235
- PEPPERCORN (*Piper nigrum*), 235
- PEPPERMINT (*Mentha piperita*), 235

ACAI BERRY, a dark purple colored berry from the acai palm tree, is native to South America and grown wild in the depth of the Amazon rainforest. Acai is called a wonder or super food, because it is extremely rich in nutrients and antioxidants (so, it needs to be refrigerated and please check the expiration date on package prior to use). This nutrient-dense fruit, in a small amount, can be ideal for any blended smoothies.

AGAR-AGAR (Seaweed gel): The flakes (kanten) are extracted from a type of seaweed and have a natural jelling substance that has the benefit of being free of animal products, and so is used by people who do not want to consume animal-derived gelatin. The flakes dissolve in hot liquids, and form a gel as they cool; it is often used for its thickening properties in desserts, pudding, sauces, and baked good fillings. You can find agar-agar at health food stores.

ALLSPICES /JAMAICAN PEPPER (*Imenta officinalis*): The fruits (small berries) of an evergreen, native to Central America, South America and Mexico, are also called "***pimientos.***" Allspice berries have a distinct flavor that appears to be a combination of cinnamon, cloves, juniper and pepper.

ALMOND (*Amygdalus*): All nuts are a good source of protein and essential fatty acids (healthy oils). ***Almonds are a good vegetarian protein sources and are also rich in calcium*** (the whole almonds are even better source than almond butter or almond flour). Almonds help both physical and mental health. They are rich in many essential minerals needed by the body, however, almonds do not contain as much phosphorous as other nuts and seeds. According to new study, almonds can help support the cardiovascular* system. Almond butter makes a rich protein substitute for peanut butter.
*Cardiovascular disease is arterial plaque (a fine layer of fatty material that forms within the arteries and blocks blood flow).

ANISE SEEDS (*Pimpinella anisum*): Anise plant resembles fennel and anise seeds are tiny and gray-green. They are botanically related to the parsley family. The herb is cultivated mostly for its mild sweet licorice flavor and is used to make Anisette liqueur. Anise seeds are also used as a flavoring in cooking and salad dressings. In ancient Egypt, India and Greece, anise seeds were used as a spice in dessert such as cake. ***Chewing anise seeds or using them to make tea improves digestion (anise is one of the best known digestive herbs). In ancient India, anise seeds were chewed after a meal to assist digestion, enhance ones breath and ease coughs, colds and sore throats.*** The seeds taste slightly sweet when chewed.

APPLE (*Pyrus malus*): *Apples contain a good balance of calcium, phosphorus and iron along with vitamins A, B1, B2, B3, and C, and thus, it may be helpful in developing a strong immune system.* An organic whole apple is one of the best blood purifiers. A peeled, grated and cooked apple can be an excellent remedy for illnesses involving diarrhea. The famous German herbalist *Hildegard* prescribed raw and ripe apples as a tonic for healthy people and cooked apples as the first treatment for any sickness. Apple production peaks during autumn and their flavor is best when freshly harvested.

APRICOT (*Armeniaca bulgar*): Apricots are nutritious and have a pleasant sweet yet a slightly sour taste. They are high in B vitamins, C, beta-carotene (beta carotene is converted to vitamin A in the body), phosphorus, potassium, calcium, and iron with trace minerals such as copper, manganese and zinc.
Note: Apricots are used more often in Hunzas's diet. Hunzas live in the Himalaya Mountains in the Kashmir region, and are well known for longevity of over 100 years old.

ARABIC GUM/GUM ARABIC: It is highly soluble in water, and is a complex mixture of calcium, magnesium, and potassium salts of gum Arabic acid. It is a natural food additive from the Acacia tree, used as a thickener, stabilizer (*it keeps baked goods from crumbling*), and emulsifier (*consistency/uniformity*) agent in foods. The pods and seeds of the Acacia tree are dried and ground into flour; an ideal substitute for gluten in gluten-free baking and bread making. The gum is also used in making candy, ice cream, jellies, chewing gum and beverages. It is usually safe, however people sensitive to acacia may have a mild allergic reactions. Please read *Chapter one, page vi,* for safe use.

ARROWROOT: A flour made from the root of a tropical tuber that is used as a thickener in sauces and desserts. *It is more easily digested than wheat flour and contains no gluten. Arrowroot has twice the thickening properties of regular flour and almost no taste.* One teaspoon of arrowroot starch (powder) can be dissolved in 1 tablespoon fresh water prior to use.
Note: Arrowroot starch makes an excellent addition to pancake recipes as it gives the finished product an excellent texture, soft inside and crispy outside. Another alternative starch is kudzu root starch, made from the wild kudzu plant; it is rich in minerals (see Glossary, kudzu page 225).

ARTICHOKE (*Cynara scolymus*): The name of globe artichoke comes from Articiocco, Italy and means fruit of pine; in fact it is similar to the fruit of a pine tree. In ancient Greece the artichoke was prized as a food of the noble class. The green leaves and heart of artichoke are useful after cooking. *The "flower-heads" are commonly eaten as a vegetable and have some vitamin C, calcium, potassium, and are a good source of dietary fiber.* The artichoke plant needs a lot of water to grow; artichokes are not herbs, but have been used for their medicinal value. *Eating moderate amounts of artichokes is known for many things including helping irritable bowel syndrome (IBS) and improving gall bladder and liver function in some people.* Artichoke juice may aid digestion. Artichoke may reduce cholesterol, blood sugar, ear buzzing sound and help lose weight. Eating artichokes frequently may cause mild allergic reactions. Artichoke peak season is from March through May. For cooking instruction, see Tips, artichoke, page 177.

Note: Please do not confuse regular (green) globe artichoke with Jerusalem artichoke.

ARUGULA: Resembles radish leaves. They are rich in iron, vitamin C and A. and can help with body detoxification. The plant has tender dark green leaves that have a spicy mustard flavor. Arugula leaves hold a lot of dust and need to be thoroughly washed before using. Italians use a lot of young, tender arugula leaves in their mixed green salad (with olive oil and balsamic vinegar salad dressing and parmesan cheese), as well as in soups and pasta to add a spicy flavor.

ASPARAGUS (*Asparagus officinalis*)**:** A vegetable with edible plant tips and stalks and a unique flavor. This vegetable is best served after light steaming, and many people serve it chilled. It may be served plain or with a glaze. *Asparagus is a good source of vitamin B1 and B2 (which boost mood and energy levels), C, beta carotene (a vitamin A precursor), and iron.* The peak season is from early spring-to June. In fact, spring is the most fruitful part of the year for most plants and gives us an opportunity to enjoy the early stage of their life cycle.

AVOCADO (*Persea americana*): Avocados contain healthy unsaturated fats, and have a lush buttery texture and mild nutlike flavor. They are like a nut in some ways and the oily fruit of a large tropical tree, ripening in hot summer. Research suggests that the avocado fruit helps to lower cholesterol levels and new research shows that the *avocado is a good source of fiber, some protein, good quality oils, and high in vitamins B complex (B-3 Niacin)*. Avocado also has some vitamin A, C, and E.* It is rich in minerals such as potassium, magnesium, iron and manganese. Avocado flesh darkens quickly when exposed to air. Therefore, once an avocado is cut, serve immediately or wrap and refrigerate to prevent discoloration. Avocados are great in salads, blended into a dressing or a dip, or served as guacamole. The Hass avocado is my favorite as it has excellent flavor and rich buttery flesh.

*B3 Niacin is one of the water-soluble B-complex vitamins and has been shown to lower blood cholesterol, but it is wise to take these supplements under the supervision of your medical doctor.

BANANAS (*Musa Paradisiaca*): This tropical fruit is one of the world's most popular fruit and children's favorite. It is sweet and satisfying with a good amount of carbohydrate, potassium and many vitamins and minerals including some iron. Plantains are larger and contain more starch than regular bananas and are used only for cooking.

BARLEY (*Hordeum vulgare*): Barley is one of the oldest known grains; this hardy grass goes back many millennia. Barley is used in cereals, breads, and soups. Hulled/husked/shelled barley is whole-grain barley (minus the outer husk), and it can be cut into barley grits (coarsely ground barley with the bran intact). Whole barley takes longer to cook than pearl barley, which has its bran removed and is steamed and polished; pearl barley has less nutritional value than the whole barley kernel. Organic whole barley kernel can have healing property when properly cooked and may aid stomach digestion. **Barley malt** is basically a sugar extract from barley and normally is made of sprouted whole grain barley. You may use barley malt to replace sugar or honey or molasses in your diet.

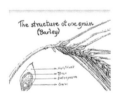  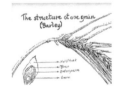

Barley

BASIL (*Ocimum basilicum*): Basil is a member of the mint family and one of the world's most loved herbs. The basil leaves are regarded as an anti-stress herb. Leaves of sweet basil have an enduring sweet fragrance and were called "*Royal herb*" by ancient Greeks. Basil comes in many varieties (most basils have soft green leaves, however **opal basil** has a beautiful purple color and milder flavor). Most basils complement fishes and tomato dishes. **The Italian large basil leaf** is the star of Italian cuisine and is used mostly for pesto and sauces. **French basil** has a characteristic flavor that blends well with most other herbs. **Thai basil** has reddish stems, its leaves have a distinctive anise and sweet licorice flavor and it is used mostly in Thai cooking (stir-fry, curries and chutneys). **Lemon basil** leaves have a deliciously sweet lemon scented that is good for lemony pesto. Basil leaves are a nice addition to tomato sauces, green salads, or vegetable soups. Treat fresh leaves carefully as they bruise and blacken easily. Basil tea may help reduce stomach cramps and relieve gas. The peak season for fresh basil starts in midsummer.

Note: Basil is a stimulant and digestive tonic herb. Adding basil and olive oil into pesto/guacamole gives a great taste; basil imparts a sweet fragrant and flavor to cheese, and spaghetti sauces.

BAY LEAF/LAUREL (*Laurus nobilis*): It is a European French type ***bay, noble laurel leaf*** (from mountain Laurel) and a basic flavor of French cuisine. The green leaves from the bay tree are strongly aromatic and can be used fresh or dried. Bay leaves are used whole to flavor stews, soups and sauces and must be removed before serving.

Note: Usually the Laurel European bay leaf is not toxic, however some varieties of California bay leaves can be toxic, so purchase from reputable dealer only.

BEANS (*Pisum sativum*): soybeans (*Soja hispida moench*), garbanzo beans/chickpea (*Cicer arietinum*), fava beans (*Fava vulgaris*), and kidney beans (*Phasaeolous vulgaris*). Regular dried beans need to be soaked in water for several hours or overnight prior to slow cooking (see Glossary, legumes, page 226).

BEETS (*Beta vulgaris*): The beet plant has a deep red (or orange) color, with a round, sweet-tasting root. *Their leaves resemble **chard**, have a characteristically salty taste and are more nutritious than the roots.* The beet roots like carrots, contains a large amount of natural sugar but have a stronger taste. ***Beets are a good source of vitamin C, manganese, potassium, iron, and dietary fiber.*** Look for small beets as they are tenderer; larger beets become a little woody. The beautiful and colorful beet with its earthy natural sweetness can be baked and added with seasonal fruits and nuts to salads. Try adding a little shredded beet to fresh vegetables juice or cooking beets with other root vegetables in a casserole dish.

BELL PEPPER: A wonderful combination of mild sweet taste and crunchy texture. Bell pepper comes in a variety of colors ranging from green, red, orange, and yellow. Bell peppers provide us with good levels of vitamins A and C. The peak season is in early fall.

BERRY FRUITS: Bilberry (*Voccinium myrtillus*), blackberry (*Rubus fruticosus, R. villosus*), blueberry (*Vaccinium corymbosum*), cranberry/tart berry (*Vaccinium macrocarpon*), elderberry (*Sambucus nigra*), raspberry (*Rubus idaeus*) and strawberries (*Fragaria vesca*) in recent studies show moderate berry consumption has been linked to maintaining normal brain function. This may be due to their anti-oxidant properties. They also contain some vitamins such as vitamin C. Normally berries are harvested when they are just ripe in the early fall before they become too soft.

BILBERRY (*Vaccinium myrtillus*): In the family of blueberries and cranberries, bilberries are *one of the most popular fruit in Great Britain. Bilberry has anti-oxidant properties and a powerful effects on the eyes, promoting clear vision.* The fruits are smaller and tarter than their cousin, the American blueberries. You can make tasty jam/syrup with them. *Bilberry leaves contain a vegetable insulin and using them for tea may reduce blood sugar.*
Note: People using the computer for long period of time, may drink bilberry tea to reduce eye fatigue and preserve vision.
Caution: Bilberry may cause allergic reactions or other unexpected side effects in some people; if any symptoms develop, please stop taking it immediately, contact your physician.

BLACKBERRY (*Rubus villosus*): **A tea made from the leaves of the blackberry plant are a long-standing home remedy for diarrhea.** Leaves contain a large amount of astringent tannins that play a role in helping control bowel movements. The blackberry itself may help prevent cancer. The astringent property of blackberry leaf tea (a few dried leaves) may also be used for soothing a sore throat and reducing hemorrhoids, but check with your practitioner or herbal doctor prior to use.
Note: In large amounts, tannins may cause upset stomach. Do not give blackberry leaf tea to a child or pregnant woman/breast feeding woman.

BLACK SEEDS (*Nigella sativa*): This mild tasting spice is also known as "*seeds of blessing.*" They are very small and black in color and they have been used for millennia for their medicinal benefits and fragrance. It is a traditional remedy used by Indian herbalist doctor to improve the immune system, as an effective antibiotic (antibiotic will kill bacteria in our intestinal tract), and as a stimulant in treating indigestion and flatulence. Black seeds are used principally on flat bread, in pickling and chutneys in Indian, Afghanistan, and Persia and all the way to Turkey. It is best to sprinkle very small amounts on flat bread during the last minutes of cooking to preserve its taste and nutritional value.

BLACK PEPPER: Please see Glossary, peppercorn, page235.

BLUEBERRIES (*Vaccinum corymbosum*): Blueberries consumption may improve memory and this may be related to their high level of anti-oxidants, which can promote a balanced metabolism that enhances nerve communication, linking blueberries to better mental functioning. Blueberries are a low glycemic fruit, meaning they do not cause much a blood sugar increase that many other fruits do.

BROCCOLI (*Brassica oleracea*): *Is nutritious, low in calories and are know to have numerous strong anti-oxidants, anti-cancer, anti-inflammatory and immune supportive properties. Broccoli contains a good source of calcium, B vitamins and vitamin A and vitamin C.* According to a new study cruciferous vegetables (such as broccoli and asparagus) not only contain dietary fiber, they also promote good health by gradually repairing damaged cells. The peak season for broccoli is from October-April.

BUCKWHEAT GROATS (GF): Buckwheat has a strong robust flavor. Despite its name, biologically speaking it is not wheat and a totally different grain. Buckwheat groats have a little pyramid shaped seeds. Like most whole seeds, they are rich in protein, minerals, B vitamins, vitamin E and are a good source of dietary fiber. When buckwheat is ground, it forms a gelatinous, sticky flour. Buckwheat can be used as a main dish, hot porridge (cereal), soup, salads and as a stuffing in vegetable dishes.

CABBAGE FAMILY (*Cruciferous vegetables*), *Cabbage, broccoli, and Brussels sprouts along with the others are foods that possess anti-bacterial, anti-oxidant, and anti-cancer properties. These vegetables are likely are most important to consume, as they are valued for their anti-oxidant and anti-cancer properties, as well as their high mineral and vitamin content and alkaline salt properties.* Cabbage and all seventeen members of the cabbage family are low in fat, high in dietary fiber, and *contain many vitamins and minerals, including vitamin C, calcium and iron.*

Cabbage family include: Brussels sprouts, broccoli, cauliflower, kale, buck choy, arugula, wasabi, watercress, rutabaga (*also known as Swedish turnip*), radish, daikon, mustard green, turnip, horseradish, chard (*also known as Swiss chard*), collard greens, and kohlrabi.

Note: Since high temperatures can destroy anti-oxidants, cabbage and all members of cabbage family (cruciferous vegetables) should be lightly cooked to maintain their nutrients. They can also be eaten raw, although this causes gas for some people.

CARAWAY SEED (*Carum curvi*): Is a member of the carrot family (its roots may be cooked and eaten like carrots) and one of the world's oldest medicinal spices. Caraway seeds are strongly aromatic and produce a sense of warming when eaten. They have been used since millennia to help soothe an upset stomach and prevent flatulence (intestinal gas). Studies in Germany and other countries show that *caraway seeds produce similar relief from indigestion symptoms as herbs like peppermint, fennel* *and fenugreek.* Caraway seeds are best known for their use in rye bread. In India the people chew a few caraway seeds after their meal or grind them and add to cheese, soup and pickles.

CARDAMOM SEED (*Elettaria cardamomum*): is a member of the ginger family. It is native to Southern India, but also cultivated in other tropical areas. The small fruit of the cardamom tree has a three-celled capsule holding up to 16 seeds. It is one of the best and safest digestive stimulants. *Medicinally, cardamom is used to treat a cold, cough, fever, sore throat, stomach upset and flatulence. Like cinnamon, it can increase the appetite.* Cardamom seeds are a very pleasant aromatic spice with a warm soothing flavor that lift the spirit and calms the mind. Ground cardamom is delicious in pastries (please be sure to remove cardamom seeds from the pods before grinding). Cardamom is a key ingredient in a traditional herbal remedy used in India and is a favorite spice in Scandinavian countries.

CAROB also known as Locust Beans (*Ceratonia silique*): A caffeine free plant extract; carob comes from the bean pod of the carob tree. By nature this dark brown powder is mildly sweet with a slight chocolate flavor, and can be used as a chocolate substitute. *It is a carbohydrate that contains most of the B vitamins, calcium and phosphorus.*
Note: In nondairy "*carob chips*" products contain ingredients that include whole grains, malted barley and corn, carob powder, fractional palm kernel oil, and lecithin. These chips may also contain refined sugars and additives. Since manufactures may change their formulations, please read ingredients labels carefully.

CARROT (*Daucus carota*): Carrots are rich in beta-carotene (the carotene is converted into vitamin A in the body). Carrot is a strong anti-oxidant and a powerful cleansing food, especially when juiced with other vegetables. In addition to color and flavor, these edible roots of the carrot are rich in alkaline elements, which purify and revitalize the blood, and nourish the entire system and helps maintain acid-alkaline balance in the body. *Carrot contains starch, sugar, iron, calcium, phosphorous, appreciable amounts of vitamins A, B, and C and dietary fiber.* Vitamin A is important for proper vision, especially night vision. Carrots contain some natural "*vegetable insulin,*" but can safely be eaten in moderation by diabetecs. In general drinking freshly made carrot juice may help prevent infections of the eyes, throat, and sinuses as well as of the respiratory organs. According to a new study, root vegetables such as carrots, beets and ginger can help people improve brain function. The peak season for carrots is early spring.

CAULIFLOWER (*Brassica oleracea var. botrytis*): Is a member of the cabbage family and has been cultivated since millennia. Cauliflower quality peaks in cool weather. Use cauliflower raw in salads or steam briefly with a small amount of water to maintain its nutrition value, flourish bright color and texture. When buying cauliflower, choose one that feels heavy and has fresh leaves.

CAYENNE PEPPER (*Capsicum anuum*): Cayenne pepper is a hot pepper, and may be sold as *a blend of various ground red chili peppers.* Cayenne originated in South America, and it is related to a family of bell peppers, jalapenos, and paprika. According to Ayurveda (traditional India medicine), cayenne is a very valuable medicine; it is a strong stimulant that aids both the circulatory and digestive systems. It has almost the same properties as black pepper but is more potent. Fruit of the cayenne pepper has been used for many centuries as both a medicine and spicy seasoning in food. It was considered helpful for ailments such as abdominal pain, cramping, and gas (by stimulating the digestive system), arthritis joint pain (topically) as well as for increasing overall vitality and energy. Cayenne is one of nature's best stimulants for increasing mental and physical energy usually with no adverse side effects other than the feeling of heat from enhanced circulation. According to some scientific studies cayenne may help improve migraine headaches. Cayenne and hot red chili pepper (jalapeno) is often used in African, Indian, and Mexican cooking; it stimulates the flow of saliva and stomach juices. You can achieve optimum results by using sparingly.

Caution: Please be careful when using any irritating products such as cayenne and read *Chapter one,* page vi for safe use.

CELERY (*Apium graveolens*): Prior to the 16th century, celery was used primary as a medicinal herb. *Celery is a source of vitamin C and dietary fiber, low in calories, and contains a substance with a similar effect to vegetable insulin. Its healing property may help people with diabetes and blood pressure* and its aromatic oil gives flavor to numerous dishes. Celery is related to the parsley family. A stalk of the celery has a high-water content. It has a cooling effect similar to that of the cucumber; celery may also help calm the nervous system by allowing blood vessels to relax. The celery stalk contains some sodium and calcium, a little iron, and a small amount of beta carotene. Celery is a great addition to vegetable salads, and cooked veggies. *Celery seeds* have anti-inflammatory properties and helps to improve symptoms of arthritis and is carminative (relieves flatulence, and expelling gas from the body). Celery is used to flavor dishes like potato salad, sauce, soup, fish and meat.

Celery like cabbage, Brussels sprouts, and turnip are winter vegetables. Celery is a filling crunchy snack for people wanting to keep their calorie count low. Celery mixes well with carrots and apple in a blender to make a fresh juice drink.

Note: Due to its healing properties, celery is one food that I eat faithfully, in moderate amount, almost every day.

CHARD (*Beta vulgaris*): Chard's stalks resemble beet's stalks with a variety of colors—red, yellow and green. Their leaves are much larger than spinach's leaves and have a stronger flavor. Chard season is during the summer, but they can be available all year. *Chard is part of cruciferous vegetables and is a good source of vitamin A, fibers, fair amount of vitamin C and alkaline minerals: sodium, magnesium, calcium and potassium.*

CHICKPEA/GARBANZO BEANS (*Cicer arietinum*): See Glossary, beans, 204.

CHILI PEPPER: *is a powerful anti-coagulant food. Chili peppers are very effective in preventing blood clots.* They are native to Mexico and Central America, but are now cultivated in tropical regions of other countries. They are warming and stimulating, and can be taken to improve blood flow and circulation in the body. Chili peppers come in many different colors, shapes and sizes, from mildly warm to very hot (*red cayenne*) or fruity or licorice flavors. Three of my favorite peppers include: *Anaheim,* a bright-green pepper with a sweet, mild flavor; it can be used for stuffing and can be roasted, peeled and chopped, then used in dips like guacamole and salsa. *Jalapeno* is a dark green pepper with smooth thick flesh, medium-hot and tasty; when fully ripe it turns to scarlet red and is often used for pickling and dipping (it needs to be de-seeded since the seeds and veins are very hot). *Serrano* is a light-green pepper with serrated edge that ripens to a bright red and hot savory flavor. It can be used fresh or cooked in a variety of dishes, especially sauces.

Note 1: Chili powder is a blend of various Mexican hot peppers, and often may include oregano, cumin, garlic, paprika and salt.

Note 2: Please do not consume chili seeds as they may be toxic. Remove all seeds and membranes from chili pepper. Avoid touching your eyes after cutting, because some chili peppers contain volatile oils that can irritate your eyes. See previous page on "*Cayenne pepper*".

Note 3: Paprika is a blend of skins from dried red chilies. Hungarian paprika typically has a sweet mild taste. I love sweet paprika as it provides the great flavor of chili pepper without all the heat.

Note 4: Red hot pepper (*Capsicum amnwm*), also known as "*cayenne pepper.*" It improves digestion as it stimulates secretion of saliva, and stomach acids to aid the digestion process. Please read **Chapter one**, page vi for safe use herbs and spices.

CHERVIL (*Cher-vi?? namel*): An herb of the parsley family, chervil has a mild flavor and is native to Russia. Chervil with its dark green curly leaves has digestive, diuretic and stimulant properties; it is the best when used fresh (like parsley) to save its delicate aromatic flavor. The juice pressed out of this fresh herb, and tea infusion has more popularity in Europe than the United States.

CHIVES (*Allium schoenoprasum*)**:** Chives (leaves) are the tops of a small plant in the onion and leek family. Fresh chives have long slender, hollow green stems; the flavor of chives is similar to onions but milder. The leaves are thinner than those of green onions. The leaves and their purple flowers in spring are edible food, but customary that only the leaves of chives are used. Both chives and their beautiful purple edible lavender-like flowers can be used in small amount in cream cheese, potato salad, and various soups to add flavor and color. *Fresh chive leaves help to stimulate appetite and promote the digestive processes, and are a good source of vitamin A.*
Note: Chives can be snipped and used as a garnish for a last-minute flavor enhancer, particularly good when added to goat cheese, boiled eggs and mashed potatoes.

CINNAMON (*Cinnamomum zeylanicum*): Cinnamon comes from the light yellowish-brown bark of an ancient evergreen tree. This slightly spicy herb/seasoning is highly aromatic and is warming digestive remedy. It provides a sweet taste without putting harmful sugar into our body, and also has a tonic effect on the kidney's and helps stimulate circulation*. Ancient Ayurveda practitioners use cinnamon bark as a treatment for fever and diarrhea. Cinnamon has some antibiotic property (called a natural antibiotic) and may help lower blood sugar; cinnamon tea helps one relax and relieves symptoms of the flu or colds.* Cinnamon is used to flavor many dishes such as breads, pastries, stews, and soups. A little cinnamon goes a long way in many delectable dishes; sprinkle a little cinnamon on apples or fruit salads or add a few sticks of cinnamon bark to the sugar jar to impart flavor to the sugar. Ceylon cinnamon (light, yellowish-brown and mild flavor) is my preference.

CITRUS FRUITS: Sweet orange (*Citrus sinensis*), Seville orange (*Citrus aurantium*) tangerine/mandarin (*Citrus nobilis*), grapefruit (*Citrus paradise*)*, lemon, and lime all contain large quantities of vitamin C (vitamin C increase the body's iron absorption) and some calcium. Citrus fruits also contain naturally occurring anti-oxidants, called bioflavonoids. At present these are considered very beneficial. The body requires daily vitamin C to strengthen capillaries, support connective tissue, *assist the immune system, and possibly to protect against cancer*. Vitamin C has a short half-life and is destroyed by exposure to air and sunlight. Seasonal fresh citrus fruits are best when eaten immediately after peeling or cutting, and drink it soon after squeezing. All *citrus fruits* are low in sodium, have vitamins A, B1, B2, B3 and minerals (the minerals are presented in the rind and the white part of citrus; pulp has more minerals which help fat metabolism). They may help to prevent cancer by supporting the body's immune system. Moderate use of *citrus fruits especially lemon is good for weight loss and strengthening hair growth.* Citrus fruits are available year round but are generally harvested in late summer to early fall. See Glossary, lemon (page, 227) and Seville orange (page 240).

*Grapefruit, because of its flavor popularity and anti-diabetic properties grapefruit has great value among citrus fruits according to expert.

Note: To make lemon-water drink, just mix freshly squeezed lemon juice with water (2 tablespoons of lemon juice with 2 cups fresh water and a little natural honey) and serve. Lemon blossom, **lemon peel and lemon zest** are good way to make tea; lemon tea with a small amount of honey is a time-honored treatment for coughs and colds. For making lemon zest and lemon peel, it is best to use lemons that are organically grown with skin free from pesticide.

CLOVE (*Caryophyllus aromaticus*): *This popular spice is a powerful anti-inflammatory and anti-coagulant. According to scientists, clove may help keep blood free of dangerous clots, almost the same way as garlic and onion do.* An ancient world's famous spice grows in tropical area whose dried flower buds were used in cooking and as an antiseptic. Its strong warm aroma and flavor contributes to most gram-masalas and curry powders in India.

COCOA (*Theoloroma cocoa*): Cocoa gives dark chocolate its addictive flavor and quick memory-boosting quality. The history of the cocoa tree and its fabulous beans is called "*Heavenly God Food*" and goes back to the Aztecs from Mexico. They sipped enormous amounts of pure dark chocolate as a hot bitter drink. When Henri Nestle started to combine milk and cocoa powder to make chocolate candies, its popularity increased and it became one of most loved and favorite foods for people around the world. Chocolate is a product of the cacao tree. Chocolate and cocoa powder both come from cocoa beans. The beans are removed from their pod, fermented, dried, roasted, cracked and the nibs are separated from the shells; the clean nibs are dried and ground into a thick paste which is called "*chocolate liquor or mass*". Chocolate can be refined further by remove cocoa butter, leaving a dry "*cocoa powder.*" White chocolate is made from the white part of cocoa butter and has much more fat than dark chocolate. Most chocolate is a blend of chocolate liquor, cocoa butter, sugar and vanilla or other sweeteners. Chocolate is high in fat, it may contain anti-oxidant compounds. Cocoa has much less caffeine than coffee, so it causes less gastric stimulation and irritability. However, both the caffeine in chocolate and coffee are powerfully addictive and are linked to anxiety and elevated blood pressure, blood cholesterol and blood sugar levels. It is best to limit the intake of these stimulants. Some naturopathic doctors recommend a moderate drink of hot chocolate instead of regular coffee for treating a person convalescing from acute illness.

Caution: Please look for high quality dark chocolate made from natural ingredients and containing less fat and sweeteners. You can find chocolate without milk and its fats as well. Check with your health provider before having chocolate on a regular basis.

COCONUTS (*Cocos nucifera*): This fruit of the large tropical palm trees contains a shell, flesh, and watery liquid. Coconut water, the liquid inside of coconut has no fat. The coconut flesh is edible food and contains saturated fats (coconut oil is solid at room temperature). Coconut milk comes from grinding the soft flesh of young coconuts. Coconut milk and oil are common ingredients in curries and soups in Thailand. *Coconut has traces of B vitamins and C, some minerals (potassium, phosphorus and iron) and a small amount of protein and carbohydrate.* Coconut palm sugar is a sweetener.

CORIANDER/CHINESE PARSLEY/CILANTRO (*Coriangrum sativum*): Coriander originated in India about two thousand years ago, and then it was imported to China. Coriander is a member of the parsley family and its leaves are similar in color to parsley with a strong and unique flavor able to enhance many dishes. *This aromatic plant is valued in Ayurveda medicines (in India) for its digestive and carminative (relieving flatulence) property.* The dried cilantro seeds have aromatic flavor reminiscent of lemon, caraway and sage and is a popular ingredient in curry spice blends and in pickling. Ground seeds are used in cooking and baking especially in India and Asian cuisine. Cilantro green leaves are often used in salad, salsa, fish dishes and savory omelets and it is best to use in moderation. Coriander, cumin and fennel seeds are related plants with similar properties; these three seeds can be ground and used together when preparing foods and are a good indigestion remedy when used in moderation.

CORN (*Zea mays*): Corn was an important food crop for the Aztec Indian; it is also known as Indian corn or maize. *It is a rich source of carbohydrate (sugar and starches), fiber and several minerals including potassium, phosphorus and magnesium. Corn has various vitamins, such as vitamin B3 (niacin).* You may barbeque or steam corn in boiling water for short time.

Note: Corn syrup results from processing corn starch and is *composed of dextroglucose.* Since most corn syrup is man-made and not part of our body systems, it does not break down in our body the same as natural sugars found in fruits or vegetables. The biggest concern is with the highly processed high corn syrup sweeteners, which are low in nutritional value and can overstimulate the pancreas to secrete *insulin*. This initially signal into action the nervous system and can cause problem with energy and emotion. Corn syrup is used extensively in sweetened foods, such as sodas, fruit drinks, baked goods and candies that may increase obesity and diabetes. One corn syrup byproduct is "***xanthan gum,***" which is used as a thickener, stabilizer and emulsifier in foods including gluten-free baking. Please study carefully and limit the use of processed sugar and especially corn syrups.

CRANBERRIES (*Vaccinium vitis idaea*): This tart berry contains anti-oxidant property. ***Cranberries are rich in nutrients including vitamin A (as beta-carotene), B-complex, vitamin C, calcium and iron.*** Cranberry juice is often recommended to prevent or lessen urinary tract infections. Cranberry tea (leaves infusion) is good for the kidneys, bladder, and urinary tract. The berries are sour, flavorful, refreshing, and enhance the appetite.

CUCUMBER (*Cucumis sativus*): The cucumber originated in India, and now almost every country cultivates this cooling and refreshing vegetable. Florida grows most of the cucumber in the United States. Cucumber seeds provide the best source of vitamin E. Cucumber is one of the most important diuretic foods. Its juice has been very effective in treating urinary problems like bladder infection. ***Consuming moderate amounts of cucumber (including seeds) can aid the digestive system and help cleans the blood.*** People with a weak digestive system may see benefit when they consume cucumbers daily. Today cucumbers are often waxed to make them shiny and beautiful; this wax may contain harmful chemical residues and they should be peeled prior to consuming. Best to buy unwaxed and ideally organic cucumbers.

CUMIN SEEDS (*Cuminum cyminum*): These seeds can be used with most grains and are often used with beans. Cumin seeds and fenugreek are important ingredients in Chinese, Indian (making curry powder and mango chutney), and Persian cuisine. True black cumin seeds (***jeera***), grown in Kashmir, Pakistan are dark and small and good to use, especially with beans/lentils ***to aid digestion, reduce gas problems and sharpen memory. Black cumin seeds have been found beneficial in the treatment of cloudy memory.***

CURRY LEAVES (*Murraya koenigii*): Curry trees are native to India and Sri Lanka (formerly called Ceylon). The curry tree is a member of the citrus family; their leaves are used widely in Southern Indian and Thai cuisine. A bright green curry leaf looks like a shiny fresh lemon leaf and has a slightly spicy, citrus-like fragrant. Curry leaves do not taste like curry and are completely different than curry powder. They get their name from being used in curry dishes, such as pickles, marinade seafood and chicken. Please see Tips, Indian-style curry powder mixture, page 183.

DANDELION (*Taraxacum officinale*): Dandelion has been a treasured herb for millennia. Dandelion's irregularly dentate green leaves are one of the richest sources of vitamin A in the green vegetable kingdom. The dandelion plant is highly nutritious, and its roots have medicinal properties *as a diuretic and a liver cleanser, helping to digest fats by stimulating and increasing the flow of "bile"* (*a yellowish liquid excreted by the liver to help the absorption and digestion of fats*). Their bright green leaves have a slightly bitter tangy taste; the young leaves can be used for salad and the larger ones can be used for cooking (trim the tough stems ends from dandelion greens and discard). Freshly cut edible sweet *dandelion flowers,* available in spring, can be used for garnishing. Dandelion roots are usually harvested in early spring when the plant is sleepy and has stored energy in its roots; but the leaves are harvested late spring through summer. *Moderate eating of dandelion greens is good for detoxification from a meat diet and after overeating of fatty and/or fried foods.*

DATE (*Phoenix dactylitera*): Date palms are one of the world's oldest trees. The date tree or "*Tree of Life*" has saved a lot of travelers from starvation in desert regions. Dates contain a large amount of fructose, the primary fruit sugar. *Dates are fairly rich in niacin (vitamin B3), calcium, potassium, magnesium and iron. They can provide a nutritious sweetening substitute in many recipes that require white sugar.* A healthy dessert is a fresh apple and one to two dates (*medjool, a soft, sweet date* is my preference). People with sugar sensitivities should eat with caution or talk with a health care provider.

DILL (*Aniethum graveolens*): This aromatic annual plant is originally from the Mediterranean. Their feathery, dark blue-green leaves are similar to fennel (they bloom from July to September) and their stems bear luxurious clusters of numerous yellow flowers Dill and dill seeds have potential healing power for the digestive system with calming action and been used for thousands of years for culinary and medicinal purposes. Dill traditionally has been used to improve digestion; it may reduce abdominal pain and relieve tension in digestive tract muscles. *Dill water made from a distillate of dill seeds has a reputation for helping muscles relax and inducing restful sleep*. Dill seeds are similar to caraway, anise, and fennel seeds with subtle action. Traditional Chinese physicians have used dill seeds for treatment of infant colic. Dill stimulates women's milk and menstrual flow. Beside its soothing effect on digestion and reducing intestinal gas, dill may lessen urinary tract infections as well as aid in treatment of high blood pressure, gallstones, and congestive heart disease. Dill is used in a wide variety of dishes. As a green leaf herb it adds a pleasing flavor to potato salad, fish, and some rice dishes. Dill in ancient Greece meant a sign of wealth and in ancient Rome it was a sign of good luck.

Caution: Please do not use dill seed oil, unless it is recommended by herbal doctor practitioner.

DULSE (*Palmaria palmate*)**, Dulse is one of the best source of natural iodine*, an essential nutrient for normal thyroid function** (*thyroid hormones regulate metabolism of every cell of our body*)**.** Dulse is a mild tasting, dark brown edible seaweed (sea vegetable leaf), rich in protein, natural iodine, iron and other minerals; it is better not to cook, otherwise it becomes chewy. Dried dulse and kelp seaweed, both have a pungent strong salty fishy flavor. Very small amount are used primarily in salad, soups, and condiments.

*The "*Thyroid gland*" produces hormones, which require **iodine** and **proteins (amino acids),** and helps to regulate metabolism, our body's energy level and temperature, as well as mental and physical growth. This important, endocrine gland plays an essential role in our mental, emotional, and spiritual health. When the thyroid hormones are low, we will typically feel sluggish, fatigued, cold, experience dry skin, and even hair lost. Enjoy the wealth of iodine in seaweeds from deep oceans.

Note: Popular ocean vegetable seaweeds are: ***Agar-agar, dulse, kelp and nori***. Nori is a dark sheet seaweed that is popular in Japan and is used to wrap raw/cooked fish, rice, and vegetable in small rolls that can be eaten with the hands.

EDIBLE FLOWERS FOR GARNISHING FOOD: The most popular culinary flower is **Pansies** which add an edible flowers and natural color when used in salads, made into tea or used to decorate food. **Violet** (*Viola Sororia*)**:** The genus viola flowers are cultivated in many garden. The flowers such as **violet/pansies/nasturtium/sweet roses** etc. must be purchased from reputable specialty markets that carry gourmet produce. A flower that has been sprayed with pesticides (from florists/other sources) *should not be used for eating/garnishing food.* To be safe plant an edible flower that adds color and beauty to our home kitchen garden and use it to garnish foods.

EGGPLANT (*Solanum Melongena*)**:** Eggplant is a member of the nightshade family and is related to the potato and tomato. They come in different shapes and colors and their skin is smooth and glossy. *Eggplant contains some vitamins and minerals including vitamin B1, B2, and B3, and iron.* Eggplant is very low in calories unless stir-fried or sautéed. To avoid calories from fat, the best way to cook eggplant is to oven roast or bake the slices, often lightly coated with olive oil. Overall, eating this delicious food in moderate amount can increase energy. See Tips, eggplant, page 174.

ELDERBERRY (*Sambucus nigra*): *Black elderberries are a good source of vitamin C and can be helpful in treating urinary and kidney issues as well as constipation problems. Elder flower blossom tea has a long history as a cold remedy especially during wintery weather. Elderberry fruit is one of the most effective and delicious of the anti-virus, anti-mucus, anti-inflammatory and respiratory strengthening herbs.* Elderberry syrup is often used as herbal medicine to prevent colds and flu and for treatment of mucus congestion and coughs. It has been a European staple herbal medicine for many centuries. The elder blossoms (herb tea) suggest the end of spring while the berry-fruits are ready for maturity the end of summer.

Important note: The elderberries should not be eaten raw or used to make fresh juice as it may cause diarrhea and/or vomiting. Always cook lightly before using. Black elderberries can be made into an excellent jam, which acts as a mild laxative.   Please read ***Chapter One,*** page vi for safe use.

FENNEL (*Foeniculum vulgare officinale*): Florence fennel, aromatic green feathery foliage with celery-like stems was used for centuries to treat digestive problems. Fennel has edible broad bulbous base, stalks, and seeds that have licorice-like aromatic flavor (similar to anise but a milder licorice-taste). *Fennel, like dill, is a reputable ancient and modern digestive remedy for abdominal cramps, and flatulence and has an anti-inflammatory properties. It is rich in vitamin A, calcium, phosphorus and potassium.* Fennel seeds have a licorice-like flavor and chewing those aids digestion and is one of the best herbs for mild digestive problems in children and adult. The seeds are calming to the nerves and their aroma acts upon the mind to promote mental alertness. Ground fennel seeds can be added to sausages, tomato sauce, and pickles. Shave the bulb and use in salads with a citrus dressing, or slice and add with other vegetables when stir-frying. Fennel is available year round and its yellow flowers appear from July to October.

FIG (*Ficus carica*): Like grapes, figs have been cultivated around the Mediterranean Sea for many centuries, especially in Syria, and are often mentioned in the Bible. Figs have a beautiful fragrance and an interesting texture produced by hundreds of tiny edible seeds contained within each fruit. *Figs are rich in natural fruit sugar, minerals (calcium, iron, phosphorus and potassium), and vitamins A, B1 and B3.* Figs need to ripen on the tree during the hot summer to have the best taste and nutrients value.

Note 1: All fruits rich in phosphorus are valuable food to sharpen memory. Such fruits strengthen brain cells and tissues. Phosphorus rich fruits include grapes and dates; these fruits need to be eaten in moderation because consuming large quantities of phosphorus can cause the body to lose calcium.

Note 2: In olden times the fig was used to marinate meat to make it tenderer.

FLAXSEEDS (*Linum usitatissimum*): *Flaxseeds have a nutty flavor and many nutrients. They have similar properties as sesame seeds, particularly for strengthening bones. Golden colored flaxseeds are cultivated for their healthy seeds, fiber, and oils.* The fiber of this plant is used to make linen yarn for thread or woven fabrics. The seeds of flax are used to make linseed (flaxseed) oil that is a rich source of omega-3 essential fatty acids. Omega-3 fatty acids seem to play a role in preventing inflammation and blood clotting in a healthy diet; the omega-3 fatty acid needs to be present in the right balance with other polyunsaturated oils. If there is a higher proportion of polyunsaturated oils, we may suffer from inflammatory disorders and tendency toward blood clotting may occur. Unfortunately, Omega-3 fatty acids go rancid more rapidly than other polyunsaturated fats. Avoid excessive amounts of heat when cooking with omega-3 fatty acid and or other polyunsaturated fats. Flaxseed is best if organic and fresh (keep it refrigerated to ensure its freshness) and not go rancid. Flaxseeds are indigestible unless milled or sprouted. You may use a very small amount (¼ teaspoon) of **uncooked** freshly ground flaxseeds to sprinkle on green salad, morning cereal or yogurt and/or added to smoothies. Flaxseed meal/flour can be used in bread, muffins and pancake, cookies and pudding. Flaxseeds can be sprouted (the germination process causes the starch to change into natural sugars and protein). Adding freshly ground flaxseeds to your diet, in moderate amounts as recommended by your doctor can enhance good health (please be careful with **flaxseed oil,** consult with your health care doctor prior to use) read **Chapter One**, page vi, for safe use. Freshly sprouted flaxseeds contain extra enzyme benefits, see Tips, beans/seeds sprouting, page 173.

Note: You may grind flax seeds into flour and mix with liquid in blender to produce a blended flax-mixture with texture similar to egg whites and use as a replacement for eggs in cake, cookies, and muffins. Soak ¼ cup flaxseeds meal in ½ cup spring water over night in refrigerator. Use this gelatinous mixture to replace 2 whole eggs in your home recipe. Flaxseeds can be stored in sterilized jar and refrigerated for a month or more.

GARLIC (*Allium sativum*): There's so much to say about this important herb. *Garlic is one of the nature's strongest, anti-bacterial foods. Garlic is also a powerful anti-coagulant when eaten in moderate amounts, as it will help thin the blood, reducing its tendency to form blood clots. It is also an immunity booster and heart helper that is safe and effective for many things. Garlic has been treasured for more than 4,000 years for its medicinal and culinary value. Garlic is well-known and found in scientific trials to lower blood sugar in diabetes and help heal sinus and respiratory infections, relieve throat problems, kill bacteria (a natural antibiotic), lower blood cholesterol and blood pressure (possibility it prevents heart attacks similar to aspirin by having anti-coagulant action) in addition to its distinct powerful flavor. Both garlic and onion have been used to strengthen the body immune system and preventing diseases* according to an ancient Egypt belief and supported by modern science.

Note: You may chop four fresh heads of garlic and mix with a few tablespoons of olive oil (cold-pressed, extra virgin olive oil is preferable) and store in sterilized jar in the refrigerator up to one week for convenient regular use.

GINGER ROOT (*Zingiber officinale*): *Ginger possesses natural strong anti-coagulant, anti-inflammatory and anti-flatulence properties. Scientists believe the active agent in ginger (gingerol) chemically resembles aspirin (called the universal medicine). Ginger also helps with nausea, motion sickness, as well as improved blood circulation.* The ginger plant has irregularly shaped roots and is a spicy stimulating and warming herb. Fresh aromatic ginger has played a big role in cooking and healing (it stimulating the appetite and helping indigestion). Ginger root may be peeled and grated or chopped, and cooked with a variety of foods, or used to make tea. **Ginger tea** *soothes a cough, sore throat, flu and indigestion and leads to a feeling of wellbeing.* Ginger is popular in Asian and Indian cuisine.

GOJI BERRY (*wolfberry*): A bright purple color, also known as wolfberry, goji is a popular fruit in China, used in traditional Asian medicine for centuries. It is rich in nutrients, anti-oxidants and a known source of beta-carotene. *It is often called "super power berry" as it is thought to boost the immune system, increase longevity and support healthy hormones balance.* Dried goji berries resemble raisins with a slightly sweet and sour taste. I would like to soak goji in a little water to rehydrate and use for smoothies.

GOOSEBERRIES/GOLDEN BERRIES: A berry from South America, it has been used for many centuries for its healthful properties. *Gooseberries contain carotene, bioflavonoids, and are a good source of dietary fibers.* My preference is to have sun-dried gooseberries that are raw, and non GMO (Genetically Modified Organism).

GRAINS: The grains are the seeds of various grasses and often known as the *"cereal grains." Whole grains naturally contain important nutrients and fiber and all the essential amino acids but do not contain complete proteins. Whole grains are associated with a lower risk of chronic illness, including heart diseases, diabetes, and cancer.* Each grain kernel has three parts: bran, germ and endosperm; when you strip away the bran and germ from grains, you are removing most of the nutritional value and what remains is mostly carbohydrate. There are many types of grains; the most popular grains are: *Wheat, rye, oats, barley, rice and polenta (corn-meal). All can be ground into flour. Barley and rye flour are lower in gluten than wheat flour; oats, rice and corn do not contain wheat gluten and are gluten free.* Among all grains barley is one of the oldest and most flavorful cereal grains.

Wheat (*Triticum aestivum, Triticum durum*): It is one of the most important and most used cereal grains around the world. *Whole wheat is rich in B vitamins complex (except B12), vitamin E and fair amount of minerals such as potassium, magnesium, iron, zinc, copper, phosphorus, and calcium.* Each wheat berry "*kernel*" has three parts:

a) The wheat berry's rough outer covering is called "*bran*". The bran contains some minerals and a few vitamins, yet is mostly dietary fiber. b) The largest part is called the "*endosperm,*" which contains some protein, iron, carbohydrates and gluten, and is used to make white flour. c) The smallest part is the "*germ*" which contains the wheat seeds that sprouts and is rich in vitamins (especially vitamin E), some minerals, and oils. The high fat content of wheat germ limits its shelf life and it should be kept in an airtight container in the refrigerator or even in the freezer to prevent it from becoming rancid. Toasted wheat germ improves its flavor but some of its nutrients will be lost.

Note 1: Many health benefits have been claimed from eating whole wheat. Wheat bran provides important roughage to keep *one regular, and lower blood cholesterol* (oat bran is better for this than wheat bran). When refined white flour is used, the germ or bran has been removed so it lacks many important nutrients and fibers; therefore, whole-wheat flour, stone ground from the entire wheat "*kernel,*" is preferred.

Note 2: Whole wheat is the ideal grain for bread making because of its carbohydrate, nutrients, and gluten content.

GLUTEN-FREE (GF) GRAINS: Ancient gluten-free grains/flours are Amaranth, Quinoa, Mesquite, Millet, Sorghum, Teff, Rice and Oat (please see Glossary, oat, page 231).

- **Amaranth** grain is high in dietary fiber, iron, and protein, and easy to digest. Amaranth seeds can be sprouted or roasted. Since amaranth flour does not contain gluten it does not rise properly in most baked goods; but can be leavened with baking powder for cookies, pancakes etc. You may cook amaranth in milk and stir in honey/maple syrup, walnuts, raisins and cinnamon to make a delightful sweet and soft pudding.

- **Quinoa** grain (*pronounced "keen-wah" grain*) was used by the Aztec Indians for many centuries, and it has been called "the mother of all grains." *Quinoa is* *richer in protein, calcium, phosphorus, potassium, copper, zinc, and iron than other grains.* Since quinoa is gluten free it has to be combined with a high gluten flour to make bread rise properly. Quinoa is prepared the same way as rice; except for a shorter cooking time. It is important to rinse several times until the water is clear (slightly toasting quinoa grains in a heated skillet before preparing gives a better taste). You can use quinoa grains as a hot cereal for breakfast, add to your soup (as a thickener) or use cooked quinoa along with steamed vegetables like carrots, celery, and zucchini along with some herbs (like chopped parsley) to enhance its delicate flavor and nutrition value.

- **Mesquite** grain comes from the seed pods of the mesquite tree that grows wild by the seaside of northern Peru. When ground this versatile flour enhances the flavor of cinnamon and chocolate, and is used in baked goods, soups, and beverages.

- **Millet** (*Panicum milaiceum*): This cereal grain is known as *"the queen of the grains."* **Millet has a good amount of dietary fiber, some protein, B-complex vitamins, and essential minerals.** Millet grains are small and yellowish with a mild flavor (often used for birdseeds). Miller cooks like rice, and flavored with either fruits, or savory ingredients such as onions and pepper or it can be prepared as cereal or ground to use for pudding, bread, and cake.

- **Sorghum** grain was cultivated over 6,000 years ago in Africa and China and is a relative of millet and a powerhouse of nutrition. Its natural sweetness works well in cookies and cakes along with other (GF) flour.

  Note: Organic sorghum syrup spoils quickly (like molasses) and should be stored in a refrigerator after opening and its expiration date checked.

- **Teff:** Is a tiny Ethiopian (North African) grain. ***This whole cereal grain is high in protein, carbohydrate and a good source of iron.*** It has a mild sweet nutty-flavor with grainy texture that makes it a delicious breakfast cereal.

- **Rice** (*Oryza*): In Asia rice is traditionally used as a symbol of fertility and prosperity for health giving, and the word for rice, "fan," is the same as that for 'food.' This member of the grass family, from ancient times, has been known to more people than any other crop. Rice is considered the grain of life and has been a staple grain in Asia and many other parts of the world for centuries. It can be eaten on a daily basis because it combines well with most foods. It started in China, then was cultivated throughout India, Persia, Greece, Europe, and Africa and then expanded to Spain and the America. *Whole grain rice is nutritious and contains good dietary fiber, carbohydrates, some protein, B complex vitamins, and vitamin E, especially in the germ covering.* Rice is sometimes used to help relieve diarrhea. Rice grains can be different colors (white, black, brown, and red), and can be short, long, or round. White and brown rice are versatile, especially brown rice, which is suitable for stuffing, pilafs and salads. Since rice flour is almost pure starch and gluten free, it is used mainly for infant formulas. Various types of rice are suitable for different uses.

- **Arborio Rice** works well to make Italian Risotto since it absorbs a lot of moisture without becoming soggy.

- **Basmati Rice** is imported from India and has been aged for a full year giving the rice its aromatic flavor. It is often used for pilafs.

- **Long Grain Basmati White Rice** is aromatic but the husk, bran and germ have been removed in the refinery process making it white rice that is less nutritious than brown rice. Therefore white rice is enriched, meaning nutrients are added back.

- **Long Grain Basmati Brown Rice** is more nutritious, because it is a whole grain with only the husk removed. *Whole brown rice is a good source of B vitamins, which are necessary for a healthy nervous system and mental state. Whole brown rice provides more nutrients than white rice because the important vitamins and minerals found in the germ and bran have not been removed.*

- **Jasmine Rice,** is a long grain white or brown rice from Thailand with flowerlike aroma and a delicate sweet flavor.

- **Wild Rice,** is not genetically related to rice. The nutritious wild rice can be mixed with brown rice and combines particularly well with chicken broth and mushrooms.

Note 1: Some grains such as barley, rye, and oats, even though they are labeled as gluten-free, still may contain a very small amount of gluten but they are not considered as allergenic to some people like wheat grain is. You may choose gluten-free grain/flour that is certified 100% organic and not manufactured in a facility that also uses tree nuts, soy, wheat, and milk. There won't be cross-contamination (for example: oats are often grown in the field that is rotated with other grains, the oats can be contaminated during the harvest even before arrive at the mill; the same way wheat, barley and rye also can be contaminated).

Note 2: The Basic Ingredients for "*gluten free flour mix*" In a mixing bowl, combine and mix 1½ cup brown rice flour, 1½ cups potato flour, and ½ cup corn flour. Store in sterilized, air-tight container and keep in the refrigerator. This gluten free mix is ready to use for muffins, cookies and pancake as a replacement for wheat flour. You may double ingredients if desired.

Ancient Grains Rise Again

Growing interest in traditional grains such as variety rice,
millet, oat, amaranth, teff, quinoa and sorghum,
goes far beyond their gluten-free credentials.

GRAPE (*Vitus labrusca*): Grapes (vine fruits) are one of the most valuable gifts of nature. This fruit possesses anti-coagulant properties to help prevent the formation of blood clots, particularly when grapes are eaten with their skin. They come in many varieties and colors. Grapes have a good amount of dietary fiber, are high in natural fruit sugar (also known as *fructose*), and contain lots of nutrients, such as vitamins A, C, B1, B2, B3, along with minerals potassium, calcium, phosphorous, and magnesium, and trace of iron. The grape has an exceptional diuretic value due to its high water contents of water and potassium salts. *Eating fresh organic grapes, harvested in late summer and autumn, may be a good way to cleanse our body and improve memory. When the seeds are also eaten, they contain some protein and good oils that may help lower cholesterol levels. Unripe (sour grapes) may be very useful to help loose excess fat.* Young tender grape leaves are edible food and used for stuffing. Fermented grape juice for making wine goes back millennia. The earliest evidence of wine making is grape residue found at the bottom of a clay pot in Western Persia near Hamedan dated around 4000 B.C. when Persians were fermenting grape juice in airtight containers. **Raisins** (*dried grapes*) are one of the most convenient and healthy sweet snacks, and have a fair amount of vitamins and minerals including some iron. A special variety of grape, called "*Muscat,*" **has a** sweet aroma and pleasant flavor and is my favorite.

HAZELNUTS (*Corylus avellana*)**:** Also called "*Filberts,*" hazelnuts are usually ripe by late September/October and ready to be picked. When ripe, their skins are easy to remove. Hazelnuts have a very favorable fat-protein ratio and important mineral content (as do almonds). They can be used in a vegetarian diet as an important protein source.

HERBAL SAP: *Organic maple syrup comes from maple trees that have not been sprayed.* The trees are tapped and their sap is collected and processed through boiling until it is concentrated to the desired thickness. By continuing to concentrate the sap it becomes thicker and is called *maple honey*. *Maple sugar* (natural fruit sugar from maple syrup*) is the result of removing all the liquid from the sap by boiling under controlled conditions; maple sugar is almost twice as sweet as granulated white sugar and is used on pancakes, in baking cakes, on cereals, and in tea.

*Natural fruit sugar is also known as *fructose*. Canada does not allow formaldehyde spray on their maple trees used for syrup production, but the United States does (Canada is known for superior maple syrup). True organic maple syrup grade B, dark amber color, is better than grade A (because the latter has been filtered and has less nutrients value). Maple syrup needs to be refrigerated after opening.

HONEY (*herbal sap*)**:** Organic raw honey, one of nature's gifts, has been used as a nutritive sweetener and for its healing power for millennia. Primitive man not only used honey as food, but also used honey from nature's pharmacy as medicine to heal wounds. It is so important to choose honey from floral sources where nature is abundant with wild flowers that flourish in undisturbed frontier wilderness areas. The flowers' nectars are gathered by honeybees and is converted into honey by the bees in their hives. It is stored in beehive cells (wax combs) to feed and stimulate the growth and development of the queen bee. *Honey has a strong antibiotic property. It is very beneficial in treating some infections, such as throat sore or open wounds. Honey is primarily carbohydrate/sugar and the sweetness is almost twice that of regular table sugar. In addition, honey contains trace amounts of vitamins, minerals, anti-oxidants, and some live enzymes.* As honeybees go about their precious mission of pollinating plants, they dance from flower to flower collecting nectar to produce honey while supporting and sustaining our natural environmental health by spreading pollen and helping propagate plants. Honey's delightful taste benefits our culinary world. My preference is tiny (very small amount) of orange blossom honey (with its light delicate fragrance and taste) in my morning mint tea.

Caution: Pregnant and breast feeding women, children under 2 years old, and people with diabetes should be careful in their use of honey; please check with your doctor prior to use. Please read *Chapter one, page vi* for safe use of honey, and be sure to obtain this precious food from a pesticide-free environment.

Note: Raw honey contains some **bee pollen**, which is one of the nature's most complete and sustaining *"Power foods."* Bee pollen is a rich source of protein and B vitamins. It may improve digestion, and help prevent pollen allergies. According to Chinese medicine, bee pollen can *"restore and stimulate"* the immune system. Please consult with your health practitioner prior to using bee pollen as some people can be allergic to the flower pollens.

JUJUBE FRUITS (*Zizyyphus jujube mill*): An ancient fruit, originally from China (Chinese date), is seeded and eaten fresh, dried as a snack in some countries, including Persia, or it can be used in desserts. *Jujube contains high amounts of minerals like potassium, phosphorus, manganese, calcium, sodium, zinc, iron, and copper; and vitamin C, vitamin B1 (thiamine) and vitamin B2 (riboflavin).* These minerals and vitamins from jujube fruit enhance the metabolism and may help to clean blood vessels in our body. Street vendors in China sell fresh jujube fruits on a stick.

KAFFIR LIME LEAVES (*Citrus hystrix*): Originally from Southeast Asia, their fresh glossy, dark double green leaves (two leaves are joined together base to tip); the leaves release an intense balsam lime scent when torn. Leaves may be rolled into cylinders, sliced, and chopped to use in salads, curries, and soups. The kaffir lime tree has small citrus fruits. Their fruit's rind and leaves are used in *Thai, Indonesian and*

Malaysian cuisines (it mixes well with basil, chili, cilantro, coconut milk, ginger and star-anise).

Note: A torn Kaffier lime leaf with a few celery sticks steeps in boiling water is one of my favorite teas.

KALE (*Brassica oleracea var.sabellica*): Is a strong-tasting green leafy vegetable. *Kale is an excellent source of beta carotene (a vitamin A precursor), vitamin C, and a good source of calcium and iron.* There are several varieties of kale, some with curly leaves and some with flat leaves; all are very rich in calcium and iron plus vitamins A and C. Kale can be cooked in many different ways and young leaves can be used in green salad.

KELP (*Focus vesiculosus*): *Kelp may help to regulate energy level in our body by supporting the thyroid gland. Kelp and dulse are rich in iodine, folic acid/folate, and the four major alkaline organic minerals: sodium, magnesium, calcium, and potassium.* They are popular in Asian cuisine, especially Japanese. Kelp and dulse are both sea vegetables with a salty flavor when sun-dried. You may use ¼ teaspoon "*crispy kelp*" each day. They are primary used as a low-sodium, salt alternative seasoning in salad, soup and condiment.

Note: I add kelp salts (powder) into my table salt shaker by mixing ¼ cup kelp salt with 1 cup finely ground sea salt and place it on my table for convenient use when I need extra salt.

KIWI (*Actinidia deliciosa*): These fruits have green juicy flesh with many tiny seeds in the middle, and a fuzzy brown outer skin that is edible if fruit is organic. They are sweet, a bit tart as times, and are a rich source of vitamin C. Like most fruits, they contain potassium. Kiwis also contain enzymes that may help circulation and reduce cholesterol. Kiwis have an interesting history; they were first called "Chinese gooseberries" growing naturally in the Far East. Then about 45 years ago, the New Zealand government financed the development of this fruit in New Zealand and with worldwide publicity named them "*Kiwi*" after the New Zealand national bird.

KUDZU ROOT STARCH (*Pueraria spp.*): Kudzu **root starch** has been popular in Japanese and Chinese cuisine for millennia. This starch is an excellent thickening agent for dressings, gravies, puddings, pie fillings, and soups. Mix two tablespoons of cold liquid to one tablespoon kudzu root starch until dissolved. While stirring, add dissolved kudzu to your food, and heat until clear and slightly thick. It thickens more as it cools. *Kudzu is considered good for intestinal disorders as it is high in fibers and soothing to the gut lining.*

LAVENDER (*Lavandula officinalis, L. angusti-folia*): Lavender culinary flower is one of the most loved herbs for beauty and relaxation. *Lavender's relaxing effect can also help digestion problems related to stress. It is knbown to be helpful for treating headaches and migraines.* Lavender is a Western Mediterranean herb now found all over the world. It is prized for its delightful scent in herb gardens and its aromatic purple flowers (flowering time is July to September). *French lavender is a small plant with beautiful deep purplish flowers and a mild fragrance* (French lavender flower is historically known as the "*herb of love*"). Sipping a cup of tea from lavender flowers is an aromatherapy treatment for the digestive and nervous system (I call it a relaxing lavender evening tea). Use ½ teaspoon dried lavender flowers in 1 cup boiling spring water, steep for 4-5 minutes, strain and serve. Please read *Chapter one*, page vi, for safe use.

LEEK (*Allium porrum*): The handsome leek looks like giant "scallions" and is related to the onion and garlic family, but has a more subtle flavor than scallions and garlic, is cylindrical, with a thick white stalk and dark green leaves. It is a great addition to gourmet and soup cooking (there is an ancient belief that moderate eating of leeks can improve one's digestion and singing voice). Slit the leek from top to the bottom and wash thoroughly, to remove any dirt.

LEGUMES: All peas, beans, lentils, and alfalfa are members of this plant family (even the peanut is a legume). As plants, they have bacteria in their root nodules, which helps add *nitrogen* to the soil. Thus, it is beneficial for farmers to grow them to enrich their soil. *Most legumes have a good amount of lysine* therefore when we eat legumes and whole grains together, they complement each other and provide us with good amount of protein and all essential amino acids to maintain good balance in our diet.* The edible seeds of legumes (inside the pod) contain more protein than any other vegetable and they are the major protein source in most vegetarian (vegan especially) diets (legumes with lower calorie, lower fat and lower sodium can be one of the best meat substitute). Ofcourse, diary and eggs are protein sources for those eating a lacto-ovo vegetarian diet. *Legumes make a healthful addition to most diets because they are also high in carbohydrate, rich in minerals and B vitamins, and contain plenty of soluble dietary fiber, which may help stabilize blood sugar levels in the normal person and may help prevent heart disease.*

*Lysine is found in most protein food sources such as (legumes, fish, meats, dairy products and some vegetables and fruits). Lysine is concentrated in muscle tissue, which helps in absorption of calcium from the intestinal tract and *to build up collagen for connecting tissues and bone growth.*

LEMON (*Citrus lemon*)**:** Originally from India, lemons are king of the fruit kingdom with many benefits to limit illness; they are high in vitamin C and potassium. *Lemons are a great cleanser and are the basic part of the Master Cleanser fasting program (along with water, cayenne pepper and maple syrup). Lemons are also a good immunity booster, fight infection, help with fat digestion and utilization, aid in preventing the thickening of the arterial walls, and strengthen blood vessels. Lemon can reduce cholesterol and support gallbladder and liver function.* See Glossary, citrus fruits, page 210.

LEMONGRASS (*Cymbbopogon citratus*)**:** **Lemongrass** is a tall, aromatic grass that has an essential oil, similar to what is found in lemon peel; it has a sour lemon-like flavor and fragrance. *Lemongrass tea was traditionally used to treat digestive upsets and alleviate stomach aches and cramping. Fresh lemongrass is used in Thai and Vietnamese cuisine such as in soups, in meat marinades, and it is a perfect partner for coconut milk.*
Note: If lemongrass is not available use zest from an organic lemon.

LENTIL (*Lens culinaris medic*)**:** See Glossary, legumes, page 226.

LETTUCE (*Lactuca sativa*)**:** *Lettuce is the most popular of all the salad vegetables and is regarded as the king of vegetable for salad. It is rich in vitamins and minerals, especially the anti-oxidant vitamin C. It also has mineral salts providing alkaline elements to the diet.* There are many varieties of lettuce, the most popular one is romaine lettuce, head (round) and butternut lettuce. Romaine lettuce has a long, wide slightly crisp and crunchy leaf and is my favorite. Eating moderate amounts of lettuce daily in salads can ease digestive problem by increasing roughage, help cleanse our blood, keep our mind alert and our body in good health.

MANGO (*Mangifera indica*)**:** The flesh of mango has a sweet taste when ripe. *The ripe mango is a diuretic, laxative and astringent. Mango has been found to be effective in fighting common infections such as the cold; this is attributable to high concentration of vitamin A (beta carotene) in mangoes.* *Mango is a good addition to any fruit salad. The ground, sundried, unripe green mango is called *amchur* in India. Mango powder is added to curries, chutneys, soups and marinades.
***Mangoes** are a rich source of beta-carotene (which the body converts into vitamin A), fiber, and easily digested carbohydrate.

MARJORAM: Is part of the parsley family and there are two types: 1. Sweet marjoram **is an ancient herb** with green-gray leaves. It has a mild sweet aroma, and pleasant flavor reminiscent of thyme. It complements fish, beans and poultry dishes, is especially good in slow-cooked lamb and some stuffing dishes. When fresh, it can be used as a garnish. 2. **Wild marjoram** is called oregano and has a pungent taste. See Glossary, oregano/wild marjoram, page 234.

MARSHMALLOW (*Althaea officinalis*): The marshmallow root has been used for thousands of years. It needs to mature enough (2 years) prior to harvest; wash and peel the root bark to expose the white pulp, and slice. It has a slightly sweet flavor, and can be boiled or cooked like vegetables. *The root of marshmallow contains large quantities of high quality gelatinous fiber (called "mucilage"). When mucilage comes in contact with cold water it absorbs the water and swells.* It is used to make a spongy sweet known as marshmallows (now mostly made with artificial ingredients and lots of sugar). The sweet extract of the roots of the marshmallow plant and flowers are used for culinary and medicinal purposes (pregnant/breastfeeding women need to check with their doctor prior to use). *The real ancient marshmallow candy made by Egyptians many centuries ago is different from those commercially-made marshmallows today that use egg-whites, corn syrup/cane sugar, gelatin/Arabic gum, and food flavoring.* **Note:** Marshmallow flowers are used to make tea in France. Since its taste is plain, orange/lemon zest or rose petals are added to give a charm to its taste when making a soothing tea.

MELONS: Sweet fruit with flesh that have a very high water content. Melons have a tough inedible skin and often multiple seeds in the center (these can be roasted in the oven for a crunchy protein/oil snack). There are many varieties of melons, such as cantaloupe (*Cucumis melo var. cantalupensis*), honeydew (*Cucumis melo var. inodorus*), watermelon (*Citrullus lanatus*), and many others. *Melons are rich in beta-carotene that our bodies can convert into vitamin A and they are a good source of potassium.* Their peak season is mid to late summer.

MINT (*Mentha piperita*): *Mints are an exceptionally soothing and cooling herb. Through their delicate aromatic nature they help relieve mental and emotional tension and calm digestive problems.* Their widespread popularity in culinary and medicinal usage around the world has increased since ancient times. Some of the many varieties include **apple mint, peppermint, spearmint, ginger mint, orange mint, pineapple mint, lemon balm mint and chocolate mint** (*mostly used as a garnish in salads and cold drinks*). ***Peppermint*** (*Menthe piperita*) with its bright green color and peppery flavor and ***spearmint*** (*Menthe spicata*) are the most popular mints. Mint can be used with vegetables, meat, and beans. Most mints are available all year round and are especially plentiful in the summer. They can easily be grown in your garden or in pots.

Mint leaves can be used to make a delightful, refreshing and calming tea. Mint is also often used in toothpaste for its refreshing flavor.

Caution: Please do not use "***mint oil***" unless prescribed by your health care practitioner or naturopathic doctor. "***Pennyroyal mint oil/Mentha pulegium oil***" ***has a very bad reputation because*** even when consumed in small amounts, it can be toxic and fatal. According to a new study, plain spearmint and/or peppermint tea or a blended mint tea (such as mint leaves with fennel and caraway seeds) is good for indigestion, abdominal cramps, irritable bowel syndrome, bloating, flatulence, and constipation. Vapor from mint leaves can helps clear sinuses, and chest congestion. If you are pregnant or breast-feeding or have a child who experiences any unexplained side effects when using mint, stop and consult your health care provider. For commercial preparation please follow the package direction carefully and read ***Chapter One,*** page vi for more information and safe use.

MOLASSES: Blackstrap molasses has a strong distinct flavor that comes from sugar cane refining and is rich in iron and B vitamins. *Dark molasses from sugar cane and sugar beets have superior nutritional value (iron, calcium, and phosphorus) as compared to pure white sugar (that had most of its minerals and nutritional value removed during the refining process).* Since sugar has a tendency to activate pleasure receptors in the brain, we all seem biologically engineered to be addictive and crave more sugar. Although, it's wise to be able to take a sugar break occasionally so that we keep our use under control and not add weight to our body.

Note: The nutrient-rich thick syrup produced from sugar refining (cane or beet) is used in bread, cookies, pastries, etc.

MULBERRIES (*Morus alba*): The white mulberry tree is native to Northern China, and is now cultivated in India, Afghanistan, Persia and all the way to Europe. Its bright green, wide leaves were widely cultivated for thousands of years to feed the silk worm in the production of silk. The white mulberry fruit is delightfully fragrant and sweet and can be eaten fresh or dried. ***In traditional Chinese medicine, the fruit is used for blood cleansing and to relieve coughing and constipation.*** According to experts the mulberry fruit is not harmful to people with diabetes if used in moderate amount. Please check with your health provider prior to use.

Note: My preference is to have white mulberries that are naturally sweet, sundried, and no preservatives.

MUSHROOMS: *A powerhouse of B vitamins with low calories that need be a regular part of our healthy diet. Mushrooms also contain a fair amount of protein along with some vitamin C and potassium.* There are many varieties of mushrooms with medicinal qualities, such as "***Shiitake mushrooms,***" which have a meaty taste due to glutamic acid (a natural flavor enhancer to intensify the taste of food). Shiitake has medicinal value, more protein, and helps strengthen and support the immune system; it is good to use in soups or in stir-fried vegetables. A small light brown mushroom called

"*Crimini mushroom*," has a slightly firmer and fuller flavor than white button mushrooms. The "*Portobello mushroom*" in its fully matured form is larger than its relative, the crimini mushroom. You can add sliced mushrooms to soups, pasta dishes, omelets, and rice for immune enhancement (it is best cooked lightly to avoid destroying vitamins).

Caution: Please do not eat mushrooms that you have picked in the wild, unless you are very familiar with the different species, because some are highly toxic and can cause neurological problems or result in death. In addition you want to be very careful with medicinal mushrooms such as **oyster mushrooms** (*pleurotus ostreatus*) and **shiitakes mushroom** (*lentinus edodes*). Please check with your health provider prior to use.

MUSTARD: The seeds of the mustard plant come in a variety of colors: white mustard (*Brassica alba*), brown mustard (*Brassica juncea*) and black mustard (*Brassica nigra*). *The mustard plant is a member of the cabbage family and is a source of vitamins A, B1, B2 and C. According to researches, mustard seeds have medicinal properties that relieve respiratory complaints and contribute to colon and lung health.* The green young mustard leaves are often good in salad mix and add a spicy taste. Gargling with mustard seeds in hot water may be helpful in relieving a sore throat.

Note: Brown mustard seeds are slightly hotter and more pungent than white mustard seeds. French "*Dijon Mustard*" is traditionally prepared from black mustard seeds blended with wine or sour grape juice (unripe grapes), salt and spices; it is more popular than any other blended mustard.

NIGHTSHADE VEGETABLE FAMILY: The fruits (flowering vegetables) of these vine-like plants are fairly nutritious, however, some people should avoid them if they have an adverse reactions such as joint pains when consuming them. Nightshades include tomato, eggplant, bell peppers, hot peppers such as jalapeno, and cayenne (cayenne spice is made by grinding the seeds of hot pepper). Potatoes also come from tubers, a member of this family. The potatoes are a traditional staple of the Irish diet, and are the most highly consumed vegetable in the world (see Glossary, potato, page, page 236).

Note 1: These vegetable fruits have strong, characteristic tastes that go well with cheese and basil.
Note 2: White and black peppers (peppercorns) are not members of this family.

NORI (*Porphyra tenera*): A crispy thin sheet of pressed seaweed vegetables, coming mostly from Japan, is used primarily for making sushi by wrapping fish, vegetables, and/or rice into the nori.

NUTMEG (*Myristica fragrans*), and **Mace:** The tropical nutmeg tree is an evergreen native to East Indies. The egg-shaped seed is called nutmeg, but the outer

shell covering the nutmeg seed is ground and called mace; the orange-yellow color of ground mace has a deeper flavor than nutmeg. The large seeds of nutmeg are ground and have a slightly sweet flavor. Freshly grated nutmeg can be sprinkled in small amounts, over cakes, cookies, meats, vegetables and seafood to enhance their flavor.
Note: Nutmeg is less spicy than mace; it is often used in combination with cinnamon, allspice, and ginger. In addition nutmeg adds a spicy taste to applesauce and apple pie that owe their flavor to nutmeg.

NUTS: All nuts (including almonds, Brazil nuts, cashews, chestnuts, hazelnuts, macadamia nuts, pecans, pine nuts, pistachios, and walnuts) are rich in protein and essential fatty acids. *They contain more protein than grains, and more natural oils than legumes. They are also rich in minerals, as well as some B vitamins and dietary fibers.* Some *nuts and seeds are like mini-vitamin/mineral supplements.*
Note: It is important not to let nuts become rancid (the oils spoil with oxidation), especially walnuts that are more susceptible to rancidity than other nuts. Rancidity can be prevented by consuming nuts fresh out of their shells, storing them in the refrigerator (even safer in the freezer), and by not roasting or cooking them at high temperatures; please do not eat nuts if they become rancid or have a bitter taste. When buying nuts during the summer months, be aware that they may be left over from the previous year and are more likely to be or become rancid.

OATS (*Avena sativa*): This is a most nutritious grain that also has the label "*does not contain gluten.*" For millennia, oats have been a staple in the Scottish and European diet, and was traditionally prepared for breakfast as oatmeal or porridge during cold weather to provide warmth and energy. *Whole oats are a wonderful tonic food to the nervous system, supplying many nutrients and a high amount of complex carbohydrate and dietary fiber, as well as B vitamins and minerals that enhance our body's ability to cope with stress. Scottish Oats/Irish Oats/Steel-cut Oats* are whole grain "*groats*" that have been cleaned, lightly toasted, hulled, and cleaned again. They become whole oat groats when kernels are cut into small pieces by high-speed steel roller or a stone grinder (stone ground oats, the method used for centuries by our grandparents is superior to steel-cut oats made with the roller). *Hulled Whole Oats*, means that only the outer covering or husk is removed (hulled) from the oat kernel, but the bran, endosperm and germ, which contain higher amounts of B vitamins, a variety of minerals, some vitamin E. and dietary fibers (which help colon function), remains intact. *According to recent research, having whole oats daily helps: a) regulate and balance blood sugar levels, b) reduce and lower blood cholesterol, c) support weight loss, d) reduce cancer risk and e) enhance nervous system ability to cope with stress.* *Oat Flour* (from oat groats that have been ground into flour) does not contain gluten. In order to make yeast breads or baked goods that need to rise, we must mix oat flour with a flour that contains gluten (like wheat flour). *Oatmeal* is coarsely ground oats that can be cooked as a hot cereal or used in baked goods and is also known as "*Old-fashioned Oat Groats.*" Oatmeal is as essential to the Irish diet as rice is to the Japanese and Chinese diet. There are many ways to make oatmeal, and consistency can range from thick to thin. *Porridge* is a thick, pudding-like oatmeal made with water or milk, sugar and spices like cinnamon, and serve as a hearty hot breakfast cereal. *Rolled Oats or Oat Flakes*, are steamed, dried and rolled into flat flakes (most of the bran and germ is removed during processing); therefore, they have less nutritional value than whole oat groats. Rolling (flattening) oats enables them to be cooked in just a few minutes. " or whole oats, retain more nutrients than rolled oats. *Baby/Instant Rolled Oats* are a smaller version of rolled oats. The smaller size allows for even quicker cooking. *Oat Bran* comes from whole oats, which is steamed, and then the bran is removed and rolled into flakes. These flakes are ground, sifted, and separated into coarser fraction known as "*Oat Bran.* The whole oat plant (*Avena sativa*) is called "*Oatstraw*".

Note: Studies in children show that oatmeal (whole meal) is one of the best breakfast foods if you are looking for a mentally productive morning. Consuming excessive amounts of oats should be avoided as it may cause gas, abdominal bloating, pain, and weight gain, especially when added sugars, butter, fruit, and other sweeteners are added.

OILY SEEDS: Oily seeds are similar to nuts, but are smaller. Like nuts, they are rich in protein and essential fatty acids. Also like nuts, they must be eaten fresh in order to prevent rancidity (see Glossary, *Nuts*, page 231). Because seeds contain the nutrient reserves for plant germination, they are rich in B vitamins and minerals. Common seeds include: **Flax seeds** (exceptionally rich in Omega-3 essential fatty acid), **melon seeds, pumpkin seeds** (contain a natural anti-oxidant and good levels of zinc, especially good for men and very tasty after light toasting), and **sunflower seeds** (it is best to shell and lightly toast them just before eating as shelled seeds go rancid more quickly).

OKRA (*Hibiscus esculentus*): A green vegetable; okra is called "*ladyfingers*" because of its shape and size. *It contains a large amount of mucilage*. It tastes something like eggplant, but has a stickier texture. It is delicious in stews, soups and stir-fried vegetable dishes. Once cooked, okra has a gelatinous texture and slippery consistency that is not to everyone's liking.

OLIVE (*Olea Europaea*): The olive is a symbol of unity and peace in Greece. Most olives are picked by hand and were originally cultivated in Italy and Spain. *Olives are rich in essential fatty acids and have a variety of vitamins, such as vitamins A, E, and Bs, plus the minerals copper, iron, calcium, magnesium, phosphorus, and* *sodium. Olive oil is one of the richest sources of monounsaturated fat*; this makes olive oil one of the healthiest dietary fats and an important part of a healthy diet, and a vital part of the Mediterranean diet.* Extra virgin olive oil is the cold, first pressed part and considered the finest and the type that has undergone the least processing, so it is good for cooking. This superb olive oil can be beautifully used in baking (for bread) instead of butter, which contains saturated fats. In general, olive oil should be kept in dark bottle and place away from the light. Too much heat can destroy beneficial enzymes while fundamentally altering the oil's color and taste, so use only with mild heat when cooking. *Overall consuming moderate quantities of olive oil (according to expert) can have many health benefits such as reducing blood pressure, lowering cholesterol, and preventing cancer.* **Kalamata black olives** are dark purple in color and originated in Greece. It has a rich and fruity flavor and normally is marinated in wine vinegar. It is one of my favorite olives. **Olive leaves** are for sale as a supplement in health food store, and olive leaf extract may have natural antibiotic and anti-viral properties.

*Monounsaturated fats do not raise blood cholesterol, nor are they as likely to go rancid as quickly as the polyunsaturated fat found in most vegetable oils.

Note: **Canola oil** contains both polyunsaturated fats and monounsaturated fats. I prefer olive oil as a salad oil and for cooking (yet, avoid extreme temperature).

ONION (*Allium cepa*): *Onion is one of civilization's oldest medicines and it is one of the richest anti-oxidant and anti-coagulant foods (eating it in moderate amounts, either raw or cooked, helps to prevent blood clots). Onions contain many nutrients including vitamin C and potassium, and may have some blood cholesterol lowering properties; onion like garlic has vegetable insulin, which may help control blood sugar (therefore people consuming onion including raw onion in their daily diet may have better blood sugar control).* Onion is one of the most versatile and greatest seasonings in the culinary world. It's a member of the same family as garlic and leek but has a stronger, unique (both sweet and spicy) flavor. It is used both in its *green stage as a scallion or green onion* (it can be eaten raw) and its mature stage as a bulb that imparts a unique flavor to many different savory dishes. Green onion is one of my favorites and I use it frequently in my diet, however, excessive use of onions should be avoided.

Note: In general when buying fresh vegetables like green onions remove the top greens as soon as possible to prevent leaves leaching out moisture and nutrients from the bulbs.

OREGANO/WILD MARJORAM (*Origanum vulgare*): Is an herb that is used mainly in Italian dishes, such as pasta sauce and pizza. Oregano goes with almost anything that contains tomatoes. It has a flavor that is similar to that of marjoram. One dash of dried green leaves of oregano adds depth to pizza crust, roasted potato, tomatoes, and omelets.

PAPAYA (*Carica papaya*): A tropical fruit with black seeds, papaya has a soft, inedible skin. *Papaya flesh contains some digestive enzymes (often isolated and referred to as "papain").* New research says: Papaya has rejuvenating properties and may help control the aging process, cleanses the body and acts as an excellent tonic and energy booster.

PARSLEY (*Petroselinum sativum*): Parsley is a well-known herb that goes back thousands of years. Parsley leaves are the super cleanser in the vegetable kingdom and helpful in reducing most toxic conditions of the blood system. *Green parsley leaves are a good food and herb, and are very mineral rich, including iron, calcium, potassium, magnesium as well as vitamins A, Bs, and C. Parsley is thought to protect against heart disease and cancer. Traditionally, parsley leaf is specifically known as a "blood purifier" and the reason may be that it provides the cells of the body with needed nutrients that can assist the normal functions of the body to eliminate toxins from cells and tissues. Its benefits are numerous; parsley can be good for digestion, relieve flatulence and accelerates the excretion of toxins. There are several different varieties of parsley; in addition to the curly-leaf variety, there is <u>Chinese parsley (or cilantro)</u>, and Italian parsley. Each has a characteristic flavor.*

Parsley-Drink: Place a small amount of beet and carrot juice in a power blender, and at the last minute, add green parsley leaves to preserve their vibrant green color and taste. The aroma and taste of fresh parsley leaves are mild and subtle so they can complement most dishes and make pleasant and delightful food-like omelets, scrambled eggs, sauces, salads and soups very special. They are also agreeable to the stomach. The peak season for parsley starts in mid-spring.

Caution: Before consuming a large quantity of parsley leaves and/or seeds, especially for pregnant or breast feeding woman or young children, one needs to consult with their practitioner health doctor.

PARSNIP (*Pastinaca sativa*): A winter root vegetable, parsnips have a carrot shape with light creamy color and delightfully sweet flavor. *Parsnips have a small amount of vitamin C and iron.* The young and smaller parsnips have better flavor and taste; remove the skins with a vegetable peeler, trim the root and stem ends, remove the woody central core (if there is any) and slice thinly lengthwise. Sauté parsnips in cooking oil for use in soups or simmer in light syrup, add a teaspoon of rosewater and cook for several minutes or until tender. Serve as a side dish.

PEACH (*Amygdalus persica*): See Glossary, stone fruits, page 242.

PEAR (*Pirus communis*): Pears are similar to apples, have moderate amounts of nutrients and a good amount of fiber (see Glossary, Apple, page 201).

PEAS: They are an annual and productive vine and a member of the bean or legume family. Their seeds are edible food and rich in protein. There are many varieties of peas, either green or yellow. Some peas are called field-peas; they are usually dried for use in soups. *Split peas* are peas split into two parts for faster and easier cooking. Some peas are only grown to be eaten fresh, like *snow peas* and *sugar peas*. See Glossary, legumes, page 226.

PERSIMMON (*Diospyros kaki*): Persimmon fruits should stay on the tree until a frosty day comes; it then falls off and is ready to eat. Japanese persimmon can be eaten slightly under ripe; otherwise, the fruit is eaten soft and sweet with its unique flavor. *Persimmon has a good amount of vitamin A as beta-carotene, some vitamin C, a tiny potassium, iron and calcium.* They are available from late October through December.

PEPPERCORN: The plant, commonly called black pepper (*Piper nigrum*), is native to India and Indonesia and one of the most popular spices in the world. *The berries have a hot flavor that enhance the taste of many dishes, and helps improve digestion.* Peppercorn is not a member of the "nightshade family"; it has spherical seeds, while the nightshades have flattened seeds. *Peppercorns are best when freshly ground in a pepper mill at the table to provide optimum flavored black pepper.* Peppercorn comes in different colors, ranging from white through red, and brown to black.

PEPPERMINT (*Mentha piperita*): *Contains natural anti-oxidants that can help protect against heart disease and cancer as well as have a beneficial effects on the digestive system and the lungs. Peppermint is often used to relieve gas and calm the stomach; it has many other applications including treating nausea and headache.* Peppermint is mostly used as a tea or flavoring in such things as chewing gum, toothpaste, and mouth wash.

PINEAPPLES (*Ananas comosus*): A sweet golden-yellow tropical fruit known as a symbol of generous hospitality. It has a tough brown inedible skin, and a sour taste if not completely ripe. *Fresh pineapple is rich in vitamin C and contains a naturally* occurring digestive enzyme *"bromelain" that has anti-inflammatory properties.* Pineapple is available almost year round.

Note: Freezing or canning pineapple can destroy the *"bromelain"* enzyme that has been used for treatment of inflammatory chronic respiratory problems such as bronchitis. Look for certified organic pineapple to ensure that growers have not used heavy chemicals or ripening agents to force a golden color in the pineapple.

PISTACHIOS (*Pistacia vera*): See Glossary, nuts, page 231.

PRUNES/DRIED PLUMPS: See Glossary, Stone Fruits, page 242.

POMEGRANATE (*Punica*): Pomegranate is one of the super fruits that has been eaten for thousands of years, beginning with the ancient Persians. *A ripe pomegranate has a large numbers of edible seeds, is high in vitamin C, and is one of the richest sources of anti-oxidant* and anti-tumor properties (it may help control prostate cancer). Even modern healers recognize it as helping prevent and heal cell damage. Several laboratory studies on humans and animals show that drinking moderate amounts of fresh pomegranate juice may help prevent inflammatory diseases, heart disease, and reduced blood pressure, improve the quality of blood, control diabetes and cancer.* Pomegranates with their sweet-tart ruby seeds are in season during fall, October-December. See Tips, how to cut pomegranate, page 175.

*Anti-oxidants are also found in dark-colored fruits, including raspberries, blackberries, blueberries, cherries, and dark-red grapes.

Note: Pomegranate is one of my favorite foods, particularly pomegranate juice/syrup, which I use when cooking duck as the pomegranate acidity helps balance well with fatty duck's natural flavor.

POPPY SEEDS (*genus Papaver*): Dark bluish poppy seeds have a pleasant nutty flavor (especially noticeable after light toasting); they are often used in conjunction with nutmeg in cakes and pastries. If you soak poppy seeds in boiling water, the seeds swell up and when ground turns into a paste that may be used in baking as a substitute for ground almonds. These very tiny seeds should be stored in an airtight container in the refrigerator and used within a few months. *Poppy seeds are antidotal to the gas producing properties of legumes (they help reduce intestinal gas).*

POTATO (*Solanum tuberosum*): **There are literally thousands of varieties of potato in the world. Peru has many, as do many countries.** Please avoid eating unripe green potatoes as they might be poisonous because they were harvested too early, stored for a while and became slightly green in color. Diabetics should limit the quantity of potatoes eaten since potatoes are high in starch that is converted to sugar in the body. Please consult with your health practitioner doctor for more information.

PUMPKIN (*Curcubita pepo, Curcubita maxima*) and **BUTTERNUT SQUASH** (*Caryoka nuciferum*): Pumpkin and butternut squash with their inedible hard shell need longer to cook than the softer summer squashes. Select a pumpkin that is firm and has a nice orange color. Fresh pumpkin is available in autumn.

Pumpkin seeds (*Curcubita pepo*): Edible hulled/husked pumpkin seeds in Mexico are called "*pepitas.*" **Pumpkin seeds have good oils and mineral, especially zinc.** It is traditional for the people in Russia, Turkey, Persia (Iran) and Bulgaria to eat a handful of toasted pumpkin seeds almost every day as a snack. Sometimes people enjoy using pumpkin seeds with their husk on, breaking the husk with their teeth, eating the kernel and discarding the hard shell. When you are preparing fresh pumpkin, save the seeds and then clean, dry and lightly toast them with a little Tamari sauce for a tasty treat.
Note: Mix a few cups of pumpkin seeds with a small amount of tamari sauce (about 1 teaspoon), and crisp toast at low temperature in the oven for a short time.

QUINCE (*Cydonia*): Quince originates in Persia and Turkey. Currently the quince tree is grown in most countries. *Quince is a member of the apple family, and like apple, it is a source of minerals (calcium, potassium, phosphors and iron), vitamins B1, B2, B3 and C, and is rich in a natural water soluble dietary fiber called pectin, a substance used for thickening gelatinous products.* Pectin is used for making perfect jams and jellies; pectin only works when combined with the right proportion of sugar and acid. You can find pectin in quince, apple pulp and the rinds of citrus fruits. A ripe quince has a wonderful fragrance, and is somewhat hard and dry. After slicing quince and simmering in water for a while, the pectin allows the flesh to become soft and a lovely deep rose-pink color with a floral fragrance and pleasant taste. Quince is available mostly during fall.
Note: Blending cooked quince with a little of its syrup in a blender can make a clear bright jelly to garnish cheesecake or as a filling for a various desserts. Please refrigerate to keep its freshness.

RADICCHIO (rah-DEE-kee-oh): Is a variety of red-leaf chicory native to Italy. Two popular varieties are **Radicchio di Verona** and **Radicchio di Treviso**. Radicchio di Verona is similar to butter lettuce and has a small burgundy color, a loose-leaf head with white ribs. The Radicchio di Treviso has a tighter head and narrow pointed leaves. Radicchio can be used in salads or may be sautéed or baked.

RADISH (*Raphanus sativus*): *Radish contains sources of iron, calcium and sodium and assists in body detoxification.* Radish is a member of the cabbage family, which includes kale and mustard. The radish root is eaten and has a hot, spicy flavor that can stimulate appetite and digestion. *Radish juice is traditionally thought to* *bring relief from gallstones and help the gall bladder function properly.* Please consult with your naturopathic doctor about gallstones if you want a natural herbal treatment program.

RHUBARB (*Rheum hybridum*): Rhubarb looks like red celery and has a delightfully bitter flavor; it helps prevent constipation. *Rhubarb is one of the best purgative (strong laxatives) herbs and it is milder than the herbs Cascara sagrada or senna leaf, (see "Medicinal Herbal Tea Plants", Senna, page 278). Rhubarb is a good source of calcium and very low in calories.* However, rhubarb stems are naturally very bitter and require stewing and sweetening with sugar, so obviously calories increase. Choose stalks that are fresh, firm and crisp. Do not eat rhubarb leaves as they are poisonous.

ROSE (*Rosa species*): The queen of the flowers is a symbol for love, vibrant beauty, relaxation and long life. Roses are usually very fragrant, come in a variety of colors and are joy for most people, other than the thorns. They bring out the emotional pleasure of romance. Roses are cultivated not only for their ornamental beauty, but for a variety of uses in the culinary world as they are thought to *help fight against infection in the digestive tract.* Parts of the plants used in food preparation are rose buds, rose hips and rose petals.

Rose buds, a small flower that has not opened or bloomed yet.

Rose hips are the fruit of the roses after blooming and the *petals* have fallen. Rose hips have a very high concentration of vitamin C and are used to make vitamin C supplements as well as rose hips tea. You can make a delightful, fruity, and nutritious tea from rose hips. *An infusion of rose hips may help relieve cold and flu symptoms.*

Rosewater: Freshly made rosewater, with its beautiful aroma is often used in pastry or beverage. It is made by boiling fresh *rose petals* in water and condensing the steam into another vessel.

Note 1: Rosewater should be made from "*culinary roses*" and purchased from a reliable market that certifies organically grown, without any pesticide or coloring added.

Note 2: The highly perfumed "*Damask rose*" is used for making rosewater (a distillation of rose petals) and is cultivated and consumed widely in most of Middle East countries such as Turkey and Persia.

Note 3: The delicate, scented fresh rose petals can be dried in the shade to make "*pot-pourri*". I also use rose petals for a facial steam; drop a cup of petals into a pot of water just boiled and place a towel over my head and breath.

ROSEMARY (*Rosmarinus officinalis*): Evergreen leaves of the rosemary plant are best known as a culinary herb that is aromatic and pleasant tasting. It has been highly regarded for centuries as a symbol of love and fidelity. It is **valued in traditional medicine for enhancing concentration and memory as well as improving circulation of blood to the head (stimulating the brain), reducing headache, relieving stress, relaxing the nervous system, stimulating hair growth and acting as an anti-oxidant; it also has a restorative effect on both the body and mind.** Rosemary is available year round, especially in mid-winter. Look for tiny blue flower on savory stems. Rosemary blooms June through late summer.

Note 1: Rosemary is a delicious and powerful herb; it can dominate a dish, so please use only a little to add fragrance to your food.

Note 2: Adding rosemary green leaves to stews, barbeque, soups, stir-fry along with onion and mushrooms contributes a delightful taste and flavor. For more on herb safety, please read **Chapter One**, page vi, for safe use.

SAGE LEAVES (*Salvia officinalis*): Sage is the herb of wisdom as you age and a symbol of infinite spirit. Sage has beautiful fragrant leaves, is from the mint family and has been historically used as a healing herb. There are many varieties of sage like gold, purple and tricolor sage. **Sage is high in nutrients to tone the body, and has a unique ability to clear the mind, fight off respiratory infection and act as an anti-oxidant. Sage may reduce high blood pressure and lower blood sugar level.** Culinary dried sage can be substituted for summer savory and thyme in some recipes. Sage tea may be helpful for digestion (reduces stomach gas), and relaxation. It may help people with chronic fatigue to restore their energy, prevent hands and feet from going to sleep and from hair falling out. In ancient times sage tea was used as a scalp massage; it was left on the hair for 25 minutes and then rinsed out. Sage is used to complement the flavor of stuffing, stews, beans, and sausage dishes.

Note: Adding a little chopped sage leaves to poultry, sautéed onion with beans, chopped garlic and cheese or stews help bring out a unique flavor. Warm sage tea makes a good gargle for sore throat.

SAVORY (*Satureja hortensis*): An herb of the mint family, its aroma and delicate spicy sweet flavor and is a cross between mint and thyme. **Summer savory** (*Satureja nortensis*) has a milder flavor than **winter savory** (*Satureja montana*), and is more suitable for bean dishes. Savory herb is an annual so herb plant must be replaced each year.

SEEDS: There are many different types of seeds, which are ***the most nutritious part of the plant, the part that sprouts and carries on life.*** They are all rich in B vitamins and minerals, and they ideally form an important part of most diets. Seeds fall into four broad categories:

- **Grains** are rich in starch and fiber, with some protein, with rice and quinoa as examples (see Glossary, gluten-free (GF) grains, page 218).
- **Legumes** are rich in protein and fiber, and high in carbohydrate, as with black beans, garbanzos, lentils, and peanuts (see Glossary, legumes, page 226).
- **Nuts** are rich in protein and natural oil, and include almonds and walnuts (see Glossary, nuts, page 231).
- **Oily seeds** are similar to nuts, seed examples include sunflower, and sesame and pumpkin seeds (see Glossary, oily seeds, page 232).

Sesame seeds (*Sesamus indicum*)**:** *The tiny small seeds are a treasure trove of key minerals. They are a rejuvenated tonic for the bones, teeth and a good source of minerals such as calcium, zinc (may help improve memory and prevent depression) and magnesium (can help sleep).* All sesame can be toasted and ground and used as a seasoning with sea salt. Also, tahini (a thick oily paste made of lightly toasted and finely ground sesame seeds) is a nutritious protein, oil, and nutrient-rich spread can be used in salad dressings and sauces. Unhulled brown sesame seeds are my favorite.

SEVILLE ORANGE/BITTER ORANGE (*Citrus aurantium*)**:** An ancient form of sour (bitter) orange, it is grown in many countries around the Mediterranean, Mexico, and Southern Arizona, not only for its fruit but also for its beautiful fragrant blossoms. *Bitter orange is carminative (relieves gas) and improve digestion.* The Bergamot orange rind yields a fragment oil that can be used in several dishes including orange marmalade due to its bounty of color, fragrance and taste. The tart "*Seville orange*" in French is called "***bigarade.***" Please see Glossary, Citrus fruits, page 210.
Note: The petals from orange flowers were traditionally used by Europeans as a mild soothing herbal blended tea.

SHALLOT (*Allium cepa var aggregatum*)**:** Is a member of onion family**,** has a mild onion flavor, and is formed like a head of garlic. Shallots can be used the same way as onion in soups, sauces and pickles. Dried shallot is often served with plain yogurt in Asian dishes.

SORREL (*Rumex acetosa*)**:** A native of Europe and member of the buckwheat family. A green sorrel leaf, resembles a spinach like leaf. *Sorrel is packed with carotenoids, bioflavonoids, and citric acids*; these nutrients enhance the oxygen uptake in tissues, help repair body tissues, cleanses the kidneys, bladder and liver, aids in removing harmful deposits from blood vessels, and can improve the body's immune system. *Sorrel contains a large amount of vitamin A plus some calcium, potassium,* *phosphorus and magnesium.* It comes in several varieties and the mildest variety is known as a *"spinach dock."* The leaves have a slightly acidic sour taste; young and tender leaves can be added raw to a salad or cooked with vegetables.

SOYBEANS (*Glycine max*): There is so much to say about soybeans. *Soybean products are a rich source of an "estrogen like hormone" that may be helpful during menopause. The soybeans* (or soya beans or soy peas) *are considered one of the four sacred grains in China, along with rice, barley, and millet. Whole soybeans have good nutritive value with a fair amount of protein yet low in carbohydrates, and contain B complex vitamins, along with some vitamins K, D, E, and C and is part of a healthy Asian diet. The Chinese believe eating moderate amounts of soybeans (instead of large amounts of meat protein) can lower blood cholesterol, lower blood sugar and help balance insulin levels for people who are diabetic.* There are so many soybeans products in the market today, and these include: soybean oil, tempeh*, soy milk, tofu, sprouted soybeans, soy sauce, tamari, and miso paste (used to make a Japanese favorite soup).

Note: Soybean oil is extracted from the soybean and is low in saturated fats and high in monounsaturated and polyunsaturated fats. It has a high smoke point and has anti-oxidant properties. *Tempeh is one of soybeans fermented product that quickly picks up the flavors from the food it is cooked with (as doe's tofu) and it holds its shape during cooking. Please be sure soybeans and its fermented soy products are organically grown. See "Tips, beans/seeds sprouting", page 173 and Glossary, legumes, page 226.

SPINACH (*Spinacia oleracea*): Spinach is on a list as one of my top green leafy vegetables. *Spinach is very rich source of anti-oxidants and anti-cancer compounds. This vegetable leaf contains calcium, iron, beta-carotene (vitamin A) and vitamin C.* Young green spinach leaves can be eaten alone as a separate dish (a good substitute for lettuce in a salad) or incorporated into a variety of dishes. Spinach is available year-around and the peak season begins in mid spring.

SQUASH (*Lagenaria vulgaris and others*): Squash can be winter squash or summer squash. *Winter Squashes are members of the gourd family and are high in fiber and carbohydrate (primarily starch), contain beta-carotene, vitamin C and some mineral such as potassium and calcium.* Winter squashes have a tough skin and some of the varieties include acorn, buttercup, butternut and spaghetti squash. **Zucchini** is a popular summer squash and it does not require long cooking like winter squash. There are also many varieties of summer squahes. (See Glossary, pumpkin and butternut squash page 237).

STAR ANISE (*Illicium verum*): Is one of the important ingredients in Chinese five-spice-powder. Star anise is used as ***a digestive aid in traditional Chinese medicine***. The dark brown, star shape fruit/seed of Chinese magnolia tree has a powerful, licorice-like flavor and provides a unique touch in the preparation of some Chinese dishes. Star anise is used in Chinese cuisine almost the same way as Americans use cinnamon, cooking it slowly in meat, poultry, and soup dishes.

STONE FRUITS: These fruit have a "*stone*" or "*pit*" in the center and include cherries, plums, peaches, apricots, and nectarines. Like all fruits, they are a good source of potassium. ***These fruits have almost as much vitamin C as citrus fruits. They are also a source of natural bioflavonoids (it is known as vitamin P that is helpful in the absorption of vitamin C and anti-oxidants); nutrients that strengthen the immune system and help protect the body against cancer.*** They also contain dietary fiber, some iron, and many of them contain beta-carotene that the body can convert to vitamin A.

SUGARS: There are two types of carbohydrate sugars—simple and complex (carbohydrates are a broad category of sugars, starches, fibers and starchy vegetables). Sugars occur naturally in plants and milk, and are used by the body principally for energy. They are converted to glucose, which is used for energy by most cells. **Simple carbohydrate sugar**s include glucose and fructose, which is found naturally in fruits (such as grapes), vegetables (cane sugar and beets) and lactose (from milk). **Complex carbohydrate sugars** (maltose from cereal and grains) are most commonly found in whole grains and legumes; these take longer to break down for digestion, but they provide more nutrients than simple sugars do in our body. *Glucose* is the primary metabolized form of sugar that is found naturally in fruits such as grapes, carried by cells in our blood stream to create energy. *Fructose* is the sweetest natural sugar and is found mostly in fruits, honey and maple syrup. *Lactose* comes from milk products (some people have an intolerance to this sugar with a deficiency of the enzyme *lactase* and should avoid milk products). *Sucrose* is composed of glucose and fructose and this is found in fruits, sugar cane and sugar beets and maple syrup. **Important Note: Blackstrap molasses** from refining sugar cane /beets has a strong, distinct flavor and contains calcium, potassium, phosphorous, iron and B vitamins. By further refining this, we get regular **molasses,** which has a milder flavor. Still further refining results in **brown/old fashioned sugar,** or **turbinado/raw sugar,** which has a delicate molasses taste, and finally, **granulated/white sugar** (a simple sugar that contains none of the nutrients from molasses, except the calories). White sugar may be refined further to make **powdered or confectionary sugar**. It is important to know that simple white sugars (glucose, fructose, sucrose and lactose) contain no nutrients except calories. Simple sugars are quickly absorbed into the blood stream and cause '*spikes*' in blood sugar that the body converts into fat if not used for energy (by exercise), with weight gain and obesity as a result. Excessive consumption of sweets contribute to obesity, diabetes and tooth decay. It is best to keep the use of sugar in the diet to a minimum.

Note 1: Stevia, called *sweet-leaf*, a sweet-scented annual plant stevia, has green leaves and white blossoms in the summer. Its sweet leaves can be chopped, dried, ground and used as a low-calorie sweetening agent, nowadays used in some cold drinks, cakes, candy, gum sauce, syrup, or as a tabletop sweetener. The extract from stevia's sweet leaves is a hundred times sweeter than regular table sugar and appears to have minimal calories. Please carefully do your own research and check with your doctor whether stevia is good for you!

SUMAC (*Rhus corraria*): A dried fruit (barberries) of this wild plant grows in warm climates, such as the Middle East, Mediterranean areas, and Persia. It has an astringent quality with a pleasing tart and lemony flavor and is used with cooked rice and barbecued chicken or shish-kebab. Sumac can be found in most Middle East groceries store. Please check the package label carefully to make sure it is culinary sumac. Use only dried culinary sumac since some varieties of sumac can be poisonous.

SUNFLOWER SEEDS (*Helianthus annuus*): Sunflowers (the flowers resembles a sunburst) are native to North and South America and were cultivated by the American Indians; the seeds have been used as a medicine to ***increase energy***** for millennia. (**Sports figures** are often seen munching on sunflower seeds during games.) Sunflower seeds, among all shelled seeds, are one of the most mineral rich and contain ***copper, iron, manganese, phosphorus, potassium and vitamins B and E plus good fiber along with low sodium. The polyunsaturated fats in sunflower seeds include the essential linoleic acid and vitamin E which both healthy body tissues.*** Cold-pressed sunflower oil has a lower rancidity level compared with other seeds oils and can be used some for cooking as well as a base for salad dressing.

*Sunflowers twist their stems and their flowers follow the sun throughout the day. When the plants are tall and in full bloom, monarch butterflies love sucking nectar from them during their fall migration, and the birds and bees love them too.

Note: Herb experts say: Sunflower tea from the *"inner stem"* is good for ***ringing ears.*** Please read ***Chapter One***, page vi for safe use.

TAMARIND also is called *"Date palm of India."* The pulp has acidic substances that are considered to have several medicinal properties including: a carminative (relieves gas), a digestive aid, and a laxative. Tamarind has a dark brown and sweet-sour pulp that is the chief flavoring agent in chutneys, curries and sauces in India as well as in **Worcestershire** *"fermented barbeque sauce"* (a mixture of tamarind paste, distilled water, fermented wine vinegar/barley malt vinegar, brown sugar or molasses, and natural flavoring (powder) like onion, garlic, clove, coriander, chili pepper, salt and peppercorn) in Europe (please see *"Master Worcestershire Sauce"*, page 96).

TARRAGON (*Artemisia dracuculus*): Tarragon, with its narrow pointed and delicate dark green leaves, has an aromatic anise-like flavor and is best used to flavor tomatoes, chicken, and sea food. French tarragon (*Artemisia dracuculus sativa*) has small shiny green leaves that have a wonderful aromatic licorice scent. **Tarragon is a common herb in French cooking and is thought to prevent fatigue on long journeys and aid digestion due to its lovely fragrant and medicinal benefits (it may help treat diabetes).**

THYME (*Thymus Vulgaris*): With many varieties, one of the most aromatic thymes is "*Thymus vulgaris*" that is like marjoram. Thyme is a member of the mint family and its benefits have been known for millennia. Thyme in ancient Greek meant "*courage.*" **The leaves are a stimulating tonic for the digestive system and helps with muscle relaxation.** Thyme has powerful aromatic leaves with a sweet warming smell. You can dry bunches of this herb in your kitchen away from the sun and it will retain thyme's beautiful flavor for later use. Dried thyme can be used as a part of bouquet-garnish to flavor fish, especially sardines, meats, poultry, stews, and soups. Fresh thyme is especially good with green salads, soups, potatoes and green vegetable dishes. Thyme contains B vitamins. C and D, iodine*, sulfur, and a trace of sodium. Thyme tea is a tonic tea used to treat anemia.

*The "*thyroid gland*" produces hormones that contain *iodine* and that regulate metabolism and our body's energy level, temperature, and mental and physical growth. These important hormones are secreted directly into the blood system and play an essential role in our mental, emotional and spiritual health. Low thyroid levels cause sluggishness, fatigue, feeling cold, dry skin and hair loss.

Note: Wild thyme (*Thymos serpyllum*): This beautiful plant grows wild in sunny Southern Europe on stony hillsides with well-drained soil. It has white-purple flowers that bloom in midsummer. The plant makes a nice well-kept clipped hedge.

TOMATO (*Lycopersicum esculentum*): The quality and flavor of tomatoes depends on the variety, freshness, and how they were grown, which means how fertile the soil is, the quality and quantity of water, the amount of sunshine they receive and the sugar content. Select red ripe tomatoes that are firm with meaty flesh, and robust sweet flavor that are locally grown and freshly harvested; their peak season is from June-September (see Tips, Tomatoes and tomato sauce, page 189 and Glossary, nightshade vegetable family, 230).

TURMERIC (*Curcuma longa*): **Turmeric is an excellent anti-inflammatory with natural antibiotic properties as well, and can be used as a digestive aid and to treat colds.** Chinese medicine uses turmeric for treating mild liver problems and gallstones (turmeric stimulates gallbladder function). Turmeric root is an important anti-inflammatory herb from the ginger family; it has a deep yellow color with a sharp woody taste and is an important ingredient in **curry powder,** popular in Indian and Asian cooking. The turmeric plant is native to South Asia and has a long orange root that is ground to make the spice.

TURNIP (*Brassica napus*) is called a **natural antibiotic** (kills microbes) and is rich in carbohydrate. It was first used in the Middle East over 4000 years ago. **Turnip is a good source of vitamin C and was used to treat stomach infections and to improve vision in olden times.** This vegetable root is a member of the cabbage family and has a rounded shape and varies in color from white, black, yellow, or green. Turnip is a winter root vegetable that as it increases in size its texture becomes woodier. Turnips can be boiled or baked, and then peeled, sliced thinly (Julienne-style) and steamed, stir-fried or used in stews or soups.

Note: Rutabaga (*Swedish turnip*): Resembles turnips but is sweeter; both root vegetables are member of the cabbage family. Rutabaga contains a small amount of vitamin A and C. It is often cooked and added to soups and stews.

VANILLA: The long thin vanilla pod is the fruit of an orchard plant (*Vanilla planifolia*), both the pod and the seeds are used for flavoring. Vanilla is a tropical plant native to South America; originally it was cultivated, processed and used by the Aztecs in Central Mexico as a food flavoring for chocolate, sweet dishes such as custard, vanilla yogurt, cocoa-based beverages and vanilla orange juice. They slit the vanilla pod lengthwise down from the center, scrape out the seeds and add them directly into food dishes. Today vanilla is cultivated in many tropical countries and is gaining in popularity. The aromatic natural flavor of vanilla powder or pure vanilla extract (the latter needs to be used in small amounts in selective sweet dishes) is a great addition to the food industry. Vanilla powder (from whole dried and ground seeds) is preferable to be used in baked goods since its flavor stays longer than vanilla extract.

Note: It is important to buy your vanilla pod, vanilla powder and vanilla extract organically grown and processed from reliable sources to ensure quality of your products. Vanilla beans should be wrapped tightly in a plastic wrapper, placed in airtight jar, refrigerated and used within a few months. You may add dried vanilla beans to sugar and store in an airtight container for a few months to enhance the fragrance of sugar, which can be used for sweet dishes or baked goods. Pure vanilla extract should also be refrigerated after opening.

WALNUTS (*Juglans regia*): The handsome walnut tree is native to Persia. A Persian walnut is called "**Titmouse walnuts**" because the titmouse bird can break the thin shell and eat it. **Walnuts are rich in omega-3 essential fatty acids and as a part of a healthy diet may reduce harmful cholesterol and lower blood sugar.** Shelled walnuts should be stored in a sterilized sealed container in the refrigerator or freezer for a few months to prevent them from becoming rancid (see Glossary, Nuts, page 231).

WATERCRESS (*Rorippa nasturtium-aquaticum*): Is a member of the mustard family and its green leaves have a slightly spicy (peppery) taste. It grows in fresh-running water by the creek-side in most mild climates. *Watercress leaves are packed with anti-oxidants, and have high levels of carotenes and vitamins C; plus, vitamin E makes watercress a valuable nutritional food. The peppery taste of oil in watercress leaves is a powerful, natural antibiotic that isn't harmful to our body's intestinal flora, especially if eaten raw in green salad.* To make a beautiful salad, wash the watercress leaves, pat dry, tear into bite-sized pieces, add sprouted beans, green onions (cleaned and chopped) and salad dressing (from olive oil, vinegar, salt, pepper, cayenne, garlic, honey and lemon). Yum!

WATERMELON (*Citrullus vulgaris*): These bright pink, giant melons originated in Southern Africa where they grow wild. Watermelon has very thick skin and the center pulp is sweet, juicy and deliciously refreshing, especially during hot summer. *The seeds of watermelon are edible and commonly eaten in China and Middle East. Experts suggest that freshly watermelon juice made from watermelon flesh and the kernel of watermelon seeds are high in beta-carotene, vitamin C, and potassium; and it is a good diuretic and kidney cleanser.*

WILD YAM (*Dioscorea villosa*): Wild yam originated in Africa about 10,000 years ago. *It is a good source of vitamins (A, B-complex) and minerals (calcium, magnesium, zinc and potassium).* The Aztecs regarded wild yam as a relaxing digestive remedy especially *helpful for treating irritable bowel syndrome (IBS) and menstrual pain. Wild Yams contain a natural plant progesterone that can be converted to other hormones in the body. This corticosteroid hormone has an important impact on the balance of female hormones that regulate levels of estrogen and relieve mood swings in PMS and menopause. Wild yam is used for easing menstrual cramps, uterine pains and to reduce stress and tension.* They are tubers that are similar in appearance to *sweet potatoes* (although not related). True yams contain more natural moisture than sweet potatoes. Yams can be baked, boiled, fried, and substituted for pureed pumpkin in baked muffins, pies, etc. Yams should be stored in a cool, dark dry place (not in the refrigerator) and the peak season is autumn to early winter.

Caution: Pregnant, breast feeding women and children should avoid wild yam; please check with your professional health practitioner or naturopathic doctor prior to use.

Note: Wild yam tea is recommended by naturopathic doctors and may be a good treatment for arthritis and irritable bowel syndrome (IBS).

Saffron (*Crocus sativus*)
Page 278

Fenugreek (*Trigonella foenum-graecum*)
Page 264

Chives (*Allium schoenoprasum*)
Page 210

Mint (*Mentha piperita*)
Page 228

Ju-Lian Toh

Quince (Cydonia)

You can peel, cut up and simmer quince until it gets soft. Strain off liquid to make a delightful tea or continue to cook and make a sweet jelly or jam. You may also bake or poach quince (see Glossary, quince, page 237)

CAPTER 5

MEDICINAL HERBAL TEA PLANTS

(**Green Pharmacy Introduction:** Rejuvenate and heal with an inspiring collection of aromatic tea plants as seen in this educational glossary, which reviews many herbs' essential benefits).

Herbs have a great variety of biochemical and physiological effects on the body, ranging the whole spectrum of body functions. That's why they have been used for millennia throughout the world and are still very popular today as part of medical care by both practitioners and the public.

Herbal teas may help reduce blood pressure by their relaxing and vasodilating effects, or some may fight obesity by acting as metabolic stimulants, and may also provide numerous essential vitamins and minerals as a natural supplements.

Natural Foods as Miracle Medicine

God Promises a Fruitful Life, by giving us treasure from nature-immunity boosters. Plants are our natural wonders of our living, breathing Earth and we can benefit from exploring and using these valuable gifts. Some commonly used herbs include: bay leaf, black pepper, cayenne pepper, cardamom, cinnamon, coriander seeds, cloves, cumin seeds, dill seeds, fennel seeds, garlic, ginger, mustard seeds, nutmeg, oregano, star anise and turmeric. Some of these herbs and spices act as gentle immunity boosters that help our body adapt to support and protect our health.

Herbal teas, without any artificial colors, flavors, and additives can help us relax, reduce tensions, lower blood pressure and improve our quality of life, especially when we include them along with meditation, quiet times, rest, and quality sleep.

Ancient herbal wisdom will bring us all the richness, benefits and goodness of herbal teas. We need to be passionate in encouraging the use of herbal teas as the first line of treatment for most illness, in consultation with health care and/or naturopathic doctor.

Most teas come in several different forms in the market, such as dried loose tea leaves or tea bags, both as individual herbs and as a wide variety of formulas for general health or specific health issues. Tea is often blended during processing to give additional flavor. For example, green tea may be blended with jasmine, or black tea sprayed with orange blossom oil to make "*Earl Gray,*" or spearmint tea is blended with peppermint and lemon balm. Refreshing, a cup of suitable tea can pick you up or calm you down at any time of day and night. While making tea you are inhaling its aromatic benefits through the steam; drinking and after-taste, your body is open for receiving the healing process and experiencing the pleasure and benefit of herbal tea.

Enjoying a medicinal tea that is recommended by your healthcare provider knowledgeable about herbs can lift your spirit and replace body fluids, boost the immune system, and protect the body from toxins and microbes. **Herbal tea wisdom** can guide us in how to soothe symptoms of a cold or flu, lower cholesterol and blood pressure, help control diabetes, lessen depression and enhance memory.

Some different teas have varying amounts of caffeine. When their leaves dry and oxidize, their caffeine becomes more concentrated.

Overall, it is extremely important to buy your tea from a reliable market and to choose reputable brands in order to avoid any hidden chemicals or additives. Use organic tea and unbleached tea bags whenever possible, and take precautions when using any herbal plant for making tea, short term or long term use. It is important to ask your qualified health practitioner or naturopathic doctor before implementing any ideas or procedures suggested in this book that may affect your health. Be aware of some teas stimulating effects so they don't interfere with sleep.

Caution: The medicinal uses of herbal plants (such as ginkgo and ginseng) are considerable, and as with all medicinal herbs, these could cause reactions and problems in some people, including young children. These herbal plants are not recommended for use with children under age 13 years old, breast feeding and pregnant women. The standard medical warning is pregnant women should not take any medicinal herbal tea during pregnancy because of the possibility of harming the fetus. These herbal teas are not intended to diagnose, treat, cure or prevent any disease. **All readers are strongly encouraged to consult and work with an experienced health-care practitioner.**

If you have kidney failure, heart failure, diabetes, or are pregnant/breast feeding women, and those with allergies or who may be on a variety of medicines and/or have serious medical problems, please do not use any unfamiliar plants until you check with your health care practitioner and/or naturopathic doctor. Study carefully the health benefits and safe uses before you choose any kind of herbal plants for recipes or teas and/or any dietary supplements, as a part of your medical care. Please read *Chapter one,* page vi, for safe use.

DISCLAIMER

The information in this book reflects the author's personal knowledge, opinion and experience. It is not intended to replace individualized professional advice. The teas discussed here are not intended to treat, cure or prevent any diseases. All recipes (including the philosophy, introduction, heading and footnotes, tips, glossary, herbs, spices, fruits, vegetables, medicinal herbal plants and medicinal herbal tea plants) are used at the risk of the consumer. We cannot be responsible for any hazards, loss, or damage that may occur as a result of any use of this information without proper consultation with a healthcare provider. Ideas here are not intended as a substitute for any treatment that may have been prescribed by your doctor. For all matters pertaining to your health, a qualified health professional must be consulted. Please read *Chapter One*, page vi, for safe use.

Please see Glossary, Annise seeds, page 200

Traditional and Medicinal Herbal Teas:

 As already stated, herbal plants have proven themselves useful for human health for millennia. Herbal tea plants have been valued both as a medicine and for pleasure around the world for more than 5000 years. Tea was born accidentally by the play of wind and nature, with its history beginning in China. Ancient Chinese emperor **Shen Nung**, a scholar and herbalist from 2737 BC, was one of the pioneers who developed his knowledge of plants and passed it orally to future generations. His experience with medicinal plants led to more than 200 uses of these herbs for medical treatment. As one story goes: *"One day Shen Nung, seated by a tree, was boiling water when a leaf from the tree fell into the open kettle. It began infusing the water with the sweet aroma of tea. After tasting it, the Emperor became impressed and that tree's leaves became a famous herbal tea."* These are well-known historic writing about Chinese medicine. Over time, tea became popular and part of daily consumption in many other countries. *Russia and Persia developed excellent samovars (large metal pots used to boil water for convenient use for brewing teas). The samovar then became a desirable item (self-heating boiler) in Russia, Persia and other countries. Japanese have elaborate ceremonies for making magnificent tea parties into a beautiful ritual and art form. Samovars and tea ceremonies have gained popularity around the world as they seed our soul and bless our health with herbal teas.*

Today, there is much interest in self-care to save time and money and prevent diseases and illness. Diseases can have natural and lifestyle causes such as environment, climate, and poor diet (high-fat diets and a sedentary lifestyle living can increase the risk of heart disease and stroke and create other diseases). Many researchers believe that **too much stress** is harmful to the body and can cause chronic ailments that lead to anxiety and other emotional issues. Therefore, it is important for us to learn ways to minimize or avoid stress and to focus on healthy eating and moderate physical exercise in order to gain our optimal state of health.

Herbal plants (including leaves and seeds) are a treasure trove for making a mild-tasting, herbal aromatic tea. Teas are a popular beverage (even more than coffee in some parts of the world), and consuming mild green tea (one or two cups daily) can promote good health. *According to researchers, some green tea has anti-oxidant properties that can reduce chances of getting serious disease such as cancer, heart disease and lowered bone mineral density.* The strength of herbs depends on their plant genetics, growing conditions, maturity, and safety at harvest, as well as their storage time and condition, preparation method and other facts.

Natural Fermentation Aged Teas:

Most of teas in the world are primarily grown and harvested in *China, India and Sri Lanka*.

The best tea leaves come are grown and harvested during months of the year when the weather is nearly perfect, and this produces the finest tea that is ready for natural fermentation (aged tea). The benefit of slow and careful aging over a period of year's fermentation with positive energy, mostly from sun, and proper storing is crucial to make a good tea. Tea leaves gradually lose their moisture by (nature's sun-dried) and become dry and a richer aromatic flavor develops for the tea lover. This process of drying, oxidizing and chemical changes is called *fermentation*. As their leaves dry and oxidize, their caffeine (when contained in the plant) becomes more concentrated. Therefore, the less fermented green teas have less caffeine. The length of time for fermentation and process of oxidization is different for black tea and green tea. **Black tea leaves are wilted and fully oxidized and green tea leaves are wilted and partially/not fully oxidized.** Perhaps one or two cups of mild green tea consumed daily can be the best. My preference is *loose green tea*, which has a rich flavor and less caffeine after brewing.

Sri Lanka (formerly called Ceylon) is a small and vibrant island nation famed for its high-quality teas. It produces the world's finest garden by using traditional methods.

Note 1: In general, g*reen tea (refer to green tea that is not aged) green tea* has lesser caffeine than black tea, which is fully fermented.

Note 2: One of the most famous black teas is called **Darjeeling**, and this is nature's gift from the Himalayan region of Northeast India. The cool temperatures and high altitudes of this region produce these leaves with aromatic flavors that are highly praised.

Note 3: As with tea leaves, most mature fruits and vegetables depend on the sun to become beautifully full-flavored and beneficial.

Herbs Versus Spices (both herbs and spices are used for culinary flavoring and medicinal purpose):

Herb refers to the leafy parts of a plant (either fresh or dried), which have been used by humans from ancient times, and some examples are leaves of mint, basil, chamomile, lavender, nettle, rose hips/petals, rosemary, oregano, thyme, and sage plants. Some flowers, and herbal saps (like maple syrup and honey) can also be referred to as herbs.

Spice refers to dried seeds (such as clove, cardamom, fennel, and pepper), roots (ginger), berries, and barks (like cinnamon barks) of aromatic plants or trees.

Note: **Seasoning**, traditionally, an item added to food to intensify or improve its flavor. The most common seasoning are used include, **herbs** (such as basil, parsley and sage) and **spices** (such as ground turmeric, clove, and cinnamon); salt and black pepper are the most common seasoning. Savory accompaniments for food, such as prepared relish, soy sauce, mustard and ketchup enhance flavor and are the most popular **condiments.**

Cleaning, Drying and Storing Tea at Home:

After cleaning leaves, herbs need to dry to preserve their own natural colors. The simplest way is tie the herbs in small bunches (4-5 stems), depending on their size; hang them upside down in a warm and shady place (about 80-85 degree F), out of direct sun so the air can circulate around the leaves and gradually dry them. Be sure to take them down as soon as they have dried completely (if you are using basket to dry herbs, place herbs in single layers so there is plenty of air circulation). Storing dried herbs needs to be done carefully so their aromatic flavor and color is maintained. Store dried herbs in sterilized glass jars or ceramic containers made from porcelain or stoneware and place them in a cool, dry and dark place to protect them from light and heat.

Brewing Herbal Teas: It is better to use the herb plants in their natural state for infusions rather than use extracts/essences. *Herbal tea infusions tend to be milder in effect than prescription drugs and they are generally safer (prescription drugs, particularly when taken over a long period may cause interference with the balance of vitamins and minerals and alter the body's natural hormone production and cause other imbalances in our body).*

In general, herbal tea is an infusion made by steeping leaves in boiling water (not boiling the herbs). Ideally, pure mountain spring water is best for our body and for efficient metabolic processes that fuel our cells). Steep your tea in sterilized earthenware or porcelain teapot (ideally wrapped with tea-cozy) for 4 to 5 minutes with the cover on. Strain and enjoy. This method brings out the richness of black tea and subtle flavor of green tea. You can make tea by infusing various herbs (single or blended herbs) from the leaves, flowers, berries, seeds, roots and bark from herbal tea plants, and brew in boiled water for a few minutes (roots, barks, and seeds may be placed in boiling water for a few minutes as well to bring out their flavors and healing properties). Please make sure the herbs are not contaminated or moldy before using to make a tea.

To Make a Single Aromatic Herbal Tea from Flowers/Leaves: First place 1 teaspoon of tea leaves into teapot, add 1 to 2 cups freshly boiled water (spring water in herbal teas plays a vital role to increase the effectiveness of tea you are preparing) into a covered teapot, *steep* for a 4 to 5 minutes, strain, and enjoy the taste of exhilarating tea that is freshly made.

To Make a Single Aromatic Herbal Tea from Barks/Seeds/Roots: Cut ½-inch herbal tea plant into small pieces and place (about 1 teaspoon) into saucepan; add 2 cups water to cover pieces and *simmer* for 6-8 minutes in a covered pot and strain off the liquid and enjoy.

To make a single cup of tea using herbal teabags: To make homemade herbal teabags is very simple and useful; place 1 teaspoon of single herb/mixture on a muslin square and tie it into a small bundle with string. Infuse for 4 to 5 minutes in a covered teacup of freshly boiled spring water or place 1 teaspoon of single/mixture herb tea into tea cup, and add 1 to 2 cups boiling water and let it steep for 4 to 5 minutes. Squeeze tea bags to ensure maximum goodness or strain and discard tea leaves after brewing; serve in your favorite cup and enjoy. Freshly made teas can give a remarkably fresh and innovative taste. Please read *Chapter one, page vi,* for safe use.

Note 1: **Hot Infusion or Decoction:** Herb teas are usually prepared in the form of *hot infusion or decoction.* The difference is that *a hot **infusion** involves steeping herbs (leaves/flowers) in boiled water for about 4 to 5 minutes and strain, while a **decoction** involves simmering and boiling down the herbs for 6 to 8 minutes in a covered saucepan over low heat and strain off the liquid (it is one of the best methods for the extraction of hard roots, dried berries, barks, and seeds).*

Note 2: The infusion of blended aromatic herbal teas that are flavored with various floral, herbs and spices such as lemon balm and chamomile for their calming and rejuvenating qualities is called "***tisane***" in French.

Note 3: Herbal tea bags made of natural fiber and unbleached are a convenient option for travelling or for use at work and can be purchased at most food stores. Teas can play an important part of our life and health throughout our years.

Traditional Herbal Tea ... Singles or Blends

The beauty in single and blended herb teas is that we can choose what we like and create a unique flavor and energy that benefits our healing. With a little study and knowledge on various herbs we can easily design an inspirational tea to meet our taste and desires, and personal health needs. Experiment with herbs by combining an herb you know you like with other herbs that support your health and wellbeing. The standard singular or blended teas can be made with **one teaspoon dried herbs in 1 to 2 cups boiling water.** You may drink tea plain or sweeten with a little natural sugar like honey to charm the brew. Sipped slowly, your cup of tea can nourish you and give you relief from what ails you. Ideally, you are using herbal *teas that were also recommended by your healthcare practitioner or traditional naturopathic doctor.* Please always check with your healthcare practitioner to be sure the teas you are using are the best healers and appropriate for your good health.

Brewing Herbal Tea

(Please be sure your teas are free of synthetic pesticides and additives.
This is true if you buy organically grown herbs.)

1. Fill teakettle with spring water and heat to a rolling boil.
2. Measure out 1 level teaspoon of green leaves per cup and place into teapot.
3. Pour boiling spring water over the leaves, cover teapot, and infuse (steep) for 4 to 5 minutes.
4. Pour strained tea into teacup and enjoy sip by sip.

A good cup of tea, naturally brewed, clears our mind, boosts our spirits, and is a good way of fostering
fellowship and nurturing friendship. Share a hot cup of tea with your friend
and have a nice visit.

Samovar, a large metal pot to boil water for convenient use
When brewing teas, along with an elegant tea set
adds a touch of class

.

INDEX OF TEA PLANTS
(THE LIST OF MEDICINAL HERBAL TEA PLANTS)

SPECIAL TEAS:

ALFALFA (*Medicago sativa*): Alfalfa is a member of the legume family, native to Arabian countries and it is called the "*Father of all Foods.*" Alfalfa leaves contain vitamins and minerals, including vitamins K, C, E, A, and iron (twice as much iron as spinach). Moderate use of alfalfa and mint tea (with its unique flavor) is a super body cleanser and mild laxative to keep the intestinal tract in fairly good condition as well as boost energy and sustain power and strength. Please see "*vita-blend nettle and alfalfa leaves tea*", page 275.

ANISE SEEDS (*Pimpinella anisum*): Please see Glossary, Anise seeds on page 200.

Anise and Rose hips Tea: A blended tea using ¼ teaspoon anise seeds along with ½ teaspoon *rose hips* (which are naturally rich in vitamin C) gives you a spicy, aromatic sweet treat that can ease a dry cough.

ASTRAGALUS (*Astragalus membranacous*): Also known as "*Huang quai,*" astragalus herb is native to China and one of the most famous Chinese tonic herbs where it has been used for thousands of years as an energizer for active people and as a young person's tonic. *Its fibrous roots are a natural and wonderful tonic to the immune system where it acts as a natural defense against disease. It is used to help people recover from illness, radiation exposure, surgery and diseases. Astragalus increases the production of white blood cells, restores adrenal glands to proper function, stimulates blood circulation, lowers blood pressure, strengthens the cardiovascular system and helps balance fluids in the body.*
Astragalus and Dong Quai Tea: Place 3 cups of spring water in a saucepan and bring to a boil. Add ½ teaspoon of each herb (astragalus root, dong quai root and orange zest). Reduce heat, cover the saucepan and simmer 6 to 8 minutes and strain to make a delightful and flavorful tea and use only as recommended by traditional naturopathic doctor. (Please see Dang quai, page 262).

BITTER GOURD (*Momordica charantia*): Bitter gourd, also known as *bitter melon/karela/kerila*, resembles a cucumber with rough green skin and pointy ends. It is rich in many of the essential vitamins and mineral, particularly vitamins A, B1, B2, and C, and iron; it has great nutritional value. *It is a common vegetable cultivated in India and it is called "plant-insulin;" the fruit and juice of this vegetable has been found to be very beneficial for people with diabetes in lowering blood sugar and urine sugar levels. Bitter gourd is a great blood purifier and metabolism booster.* It is available in Indian specialty food stores. See recipe, page 145.
Bitter Gourd Light Tea: Place 3 cups spring water in a medium size saucepan and bring to a boil. Add 3-inch bitter gourd (cut bitter gourd lengthwise in half, scrape out the seeds and peel the skin and discard; cut flesh into small pieces), 1 teaspoon dried peppermint and 1 teaspoon anise seeds. Reduce the heat, cover the saucepan and simmer 6 to 8 minutes. Strain and this serves 3 people. Enjoy nutritional bitter gourd/bitter melon with the pleasant harmony of mixed herbal tea.
Caution: Pregnant, breastfeeding women and children should avoid bitter gourd. Please read *Chapter One*, page vi for safe use.

BLACK TEAS *include* (*Camellia sinensis*): Black tea (*fully fermented*), **Oolong tea** (*partially fermented*) **and Green** tea (*young leaves unfermented*) in China. Fresh green tea leaves if partially dried and semi fermented (semi-oxidized) and become **Oolong tea**. When Oolong tea leaves are more fully fermented the leaves become darken and their rich flavors and aroma develops and they become black tea. *Herbal black tea is the most popular tea in the world, most of it is cultivated in China, India (Indian "Assam black tea" has awesome fragrant), Ceylon, Japan and Persia.* Black teas comes in a variety of choices (one type of black tea is called *Darjeeling tea*) and the best quality is usually more costly. Plain black tea may be flavored with essence of bergamot (a small orange like citrus fruit).

Blended Classic Black Tea (Chai) in India: An Indian-style blended black tea that includes cardamom, cinnamon, clove, and milk. In a medium size saucepan combine 4 cups regular milk, 4 teaspoons raw sugar, 4 cardamom pods (opened), 4 culinary rose hips, and ½ teaspoon black tea. Bring contents to a boil, lower heat, and simmer while stirring for a few minutes. Remove from heat, cover and let stand for about one minute to allow flavors to blend. Strain off the liquid and serve as a warm soothing drink, especially in cold weather. This tea in India is prized for its flavor, aroma and rich amber color (please see "*Indian tea*", page 283).

BORAGE (*Borage officinalis*): It is known as the herb of joyousness and relaxation. It may also help relieve flu symptoms and coughs. *Leaves and flowers of borage contain a gelatinous substance that has an historic reputation of stimulating the adrenal-gland. The joy of borage tea that is recommended by traditional naturopathic doctor may be helpful during menopause especially when the adrenal glands take over "estrogen" production. Borage tea should be avoided by pregnant women and children.*

Borage Tea: Select newly opened (purplish star-shaped) borage flowers and pick as soon as the dew has dried from them. Infuse 1 teaspoon borage flower in 2 cups boiling spring water for 4-5 minutes, strain and serve.

Borage Flowers with Raspberry Leaves Tea: In a pot bring 6 cups spring water to a boil. Add 1 teaspoon borage flowers, 1 teaspoon raspberry leaves, 1 teaspoon nettle leaves, and 1 teaspoon spearmint. Cover the pot and let it steep for 4 to 5 minutes, strain and stir in a small amount of honey (if desire). Serve 6 people. Please read *Chapter One, page vi,* for safe use.

Bitter Gourd, page 258

BURDOCK ROOT (*Arctium lappa*), belongs to the family of dandelions (*Taraxacum officinal*), and marigolds (*Calendula officinalis*). ***Burdock root contains elements that can control yeast infections; detoxify blood (a purifying agent), improves liver function, and control bacteria (anti-bacterial). It can also act as a mild laxative.*** Burdock and nettle can both help eliminate toxins from the body. Burdock blended very well with stinging "*nettle leaf*" and "*myrtle leaf*" to give a lemony-citrus taste that promote healthy kidneys and smooth skin.

Burdock, Nettle and Myrtle Tea: Mix 1/3 teaspoon of each dried herb (burdock, stinging nettle and myrtle) in 3 cups of boiling water. Simmer for 6-8 minutes. Strain and enjoy.

Caution: Please avoid use during pregnancy and breast feeding, and do not give to young children. It may interfere with medicine being taken so it should be monitored by a qualified health care practitioner.

CELERY and ARTICHOKE (see Glossary, Celery, page 208 and artichoke, page202).

Celery and Artichoke Tea: Add 4-5 cups water to a medium size saucepan, bring to simmer. Place one small artichoke and 4 stalks of celery, cut into smaller pieces, cover the saucepan and simmer over low-medium heat for 20 minutes or until artichoke is cooked, watch closely so water does not evaporate. Strain and add a few teaspoons of lime juice and serve.

Note: The artichoke can be eaten separately.

CHAMOMILE FLOWER (*Chamaemelum nobile*): Tea from this flower is good as a calming and relaxing tea, supportive of digestive function. *Chamomile also has anti-bacterial* (it helps the body fight off harmful bacterial), *anti-inflammatory* (reduces swelling of tissues), and *antispasmodic* (relaxes muscle tension) effects. **European** chamomile flower tea has been used for centuries around the world. ***This aromatic tea is thought to help reduce gastritis, prevent indigestion and diarrhea, and relieve headaches and calm nerves.*** Chamomile is a popular beverage around the world and has many therapeutic properties and is popular as a calmer.

Caution: Individuals with allergies or women who are pregnant or breastfeeding should consult with a healthcare practitioner before using chamomile on a regular basis. Please read ***Chapter One,*** page vi, for safe use.

Chamomile Flower and Lavender (Lavendula) **Ice Tea:** Steep 1 tea bag of chamomile with lavender in 1 cup of boiling water; infuse for 4 to 5 minutes, cool and discard tea bag. Combine this with 7 to 8 glasses spring water, 1-inch mint sprig, 1 thinly sliced lemon (juiced) and 1 teaspoon honey. Cool in refrigerator; pour into glasses and serve. Adding a few ice cubes if desired. It is a delightful tea.

Chamomile Flower, Lavender Flower and Lemon Balm Tea: Use ¼ teaspoon of both chamomile flower and European lavender flower and ½ teaspoon lemon balm mint. Steep in 2 cups boiling water for 4 or 5 minutes, strain and serve.

Chamomile Flower, Lavender and Passionflower Tea: Use ¼ teaspoon of each chamomile flower and European lavender flower and ½ teaspoon passionflower. Steep in 2 cups boiling water for 4 to 5 minutes, strain and serve. This tea has a nice fresh flavor, and pleasant aroma that helps with relaxation and good sleep.

Chamomile Flower and Floral Herbs Tea (an aromatic joyful tea that calms nerves) Use 1 teaspoon mixture of the following herbs: chamomile flower, hibiscus flower, and linden blossom or culinary rose flower; steep in 4 cups spring boiling water for 4 to 5 minutes, strain and serve 4 people.

Note: Please check with your healthcare doctor prior to use any of chamomile tea.

CHIA: Chia seeds, from the "*Salvia hispanica*" plant, a member of the mint family, have a mild pleasant nutty flavor. It is a nutrient-rich vegetable source with omega-3 fatty acids and dietary fibers. Seeds can be used in beverage, sauces and soups in very small amount. Please see recipe "*A Cold Beverage with Chia Seeds*", page 17. Read *Chapter One,* page vi for safe use.

CINNAMON (*Cinnamomum zeylanicum*): Please see Glossary, Cinnamon, page 210.

Cinnamon Tea: Steep ½-inch cinnamon bark in 1 cup boiling water for 4 to 5 minutes, strain and drink. Cinnamon tea appears to increase energy and happiness.

Cinnamon Mixed Spicy Tea: Mix together 1-inch cinnamon bark, 1 clove, 1 dash nutmeg, 2 cardamom pods (opened), 2-inch organic orange rind and 2 teaspoons dried culinary rose hips. In a saucepan combine this mixture with 4 cups spring water. Slowly simmer for 6 to 8 minutes to extract the flavor, strain, and add a little sweetener/honey (if desired) and serve warm.

COFFEE (*Coffea arabica*): Ethiopia is where coffee was first discovered. The Arabian countries started roasting the coffee beans, then ground and mixed them with boiling water to make freshly brewed coffee. Now after many centuries most coffee is planted in countries near the equator and is gaining in popularity due to coffee houses where people gather to enjoy coffee, reading or talking, or now working on their laptops or phones. Drinking coffee regularly can be addictive because of the caffeine it contains; caffeine will give you a short-lived energy boost. However, coffee gives some relief from stress and headache, provides pleasure and its regular use is a hard habit to break. *A high consumption of caffeine in coffee, acts as a stimulant and over time increases the risk of heart disease by increasing blood pressure and cholesterol, reduces sleep, stimulates the central nervous system, and interferes with absorption of some vitamins and mineral such as iron, zinc and calcium (low levels can lead to osteoporosis) and affects hormonal balance*. There is also concern about *decaffeinating coffee* because the natural coffee beans may go through a chemical process to remove caffeine, which leaves a harmful residue that may create problems in later years.

Chemical processing is much less common nowadays and look for water-processed and organic decaf coffee. Overall, if you are going to use coffee regularly, it is wise to buy organically grown coffee beans and store properly in closed containers, so they keep their flavor and fragrance longer.

Coffee and Chocolate-Milk Drink: Use 2 cups whole milk (your choice of what kind—cow, almond, rice, soy, etc.), ¼ cup granulated sugar, 4 to 5 ounce semi-sweet dark chocolate (shaved), ½ teaspoon ground coffee and ½ teaspoon vanilla extract. Blend all ingredients in a blender for 30 seconds. Pour into saucepan and simmer for a few minutes over low heat until chocolate is melted. You will have a warm winter drink.

Caution: Pregnant and breastfeeding women as well as children should avoid coffee. Please check with your health provider before drinking coffee on a regular basis and read ***Chapter One***, page vi, for safe use.

CURRY LEAVES (*Murraya koenigii*)**:** Please see Glossary, page 213.
The leaves can be juiced with other food to make a drink in India as well as used commonly in cooking.
Note: Curry leaves are also called "*sweet neem leaves*" and are completely different from "*neem tree leaves.*"

DANDELION (*Taraxacum officinale*)**:** See Glossary, Dandelion, page 214. Dandelion blends well with licorice, fennel, and peppermint to make a delightful, slightly sweet tea.
Dandelion Tea: Blend 1 teaspoon dandelion leaves and/or root with a dash of each lemon mint leaves and licorice root for making tea. Steep in 2 cups of boiled spring water for 4 to 5 minutes, strain and serve. This tea can help your body's natural detoxification process by helping the liver break down fats and support the kidney's ability to remove toxins from the blood. Please read ***Chapter One,*** page vi for safe use.

DILL (*Aniethum graveolens*)**:** Please see Glossary, Dill, page 214.
Dill Seeds Tea: Steep in ½ teaspoon crushed dill seeds in 2 cups boiling spring water for 4 to 5 minutes, and strain; add a small amount of honey if desired, and serve. Sipping this tea after meals (in moderate amounts) can produce a restful sleep and improved digestion. Please read ***Chapter one, page*** vi for safe use.

DONG QUAI/CHINESE ANGELICA (*Angelica sinensis*)**:** This enduring herb with a slight fruity-sweet and bitter taste is found in the mountain forests of China. In China, d*ang quai or dong quai* is called the "*herb of the angels.*" It is from the *Umbelliferae* family (other members include carrot, celery, fennel, dill and parsley). It is cultivated in Europe for its aromatic flavor and is used in liqueurs, foods and medicines. ***Dong quai root "tincture tea" may help to maintain normal blood sugar levels for non-diabetics,*** and is particularly beneficial for women as it promotes balance in a woman's hormonal reproductive system by acting to increase blood circulation in the uterus area and relaxing the uterus. This tonic herb should be avoided during pregnancy, breastfeeding, during period of illness, and while taking medicines unless suggested by your physician.
Note: A blended tea from dong quai root, astragalus root, licorice root, ginseng root along with red clover flower and dandelion leaves were used to help strengthen of the endocrine system and build up resistance for physical

and emotional stress due to menstrual and menopause problems but care must be taken when using it. Please consult with healthcare provider prior to use; also read **Chapter One**, page vi for safe use.

ECHINACEA (*Echinacea angustifolia*): Rootstock from Echinacea is well known as an herbal immune stimulant that is prescribed to prevent and treat colds and other respiratory infections including clearing congestion. It is one of the best "*blood-purifying*" herb plants used for conditions such as eczema. It also promotes proper digestion. ***Echinacea is a natural herbal antibiotic and one of the better detoxifying agents.*** Its usage is somewhat similar to goldenseal root, but echinacea has a milder effect on the body (see Goldenseal root, page 267), and is preferable for long term usage. ***Echinacea root is good to take when one has a cold as it support a healthy immune response and has some anti-bacterial properties, and thus*** ideal for almost any sort of infection according to some experts.

Echinacea Light Tea: Use ¼-inch of each herb echinacea root, ¼-inch cinnamon bark, 1 lemon myrtle leaf and 1-inch orange peel in 2 cups of boiling spring water. Let steep for 4 to 5 minutes, strain and serve.

Echinacea Blend Tea: Make a decoction from ½ teaspoon of each following roots: echinacea root, marshmallow root, licorice root, and ginger root), along with ½-inch cinnamon bark (chips), ½ teaspoon fennel seeds, ½ clove and 1-inch organic orange peels. Add 5 cups spring water, simmer for 6 to 8 minutes, strain, and this tea serves 5 people. This nutritional and soothing tea may help ease a sore throat. Please check with your healthcare practitioner and read **Chapter One**, page vi for safe use.

ELDERBERRY (*Sambucus nigra*): (Please See Glossary on *Elderberry*, page 216).
Elderberry Flower Tea (an ancient superb herbal tea): Add 1 teaspoon spring blossoms of elderberry flower in 1 cup of boiling water, let it steep for 4 to 5 minutes and strain. If desired, add a little honey to make a gentle sweet flavored aromatic and relaxing tea. This uplifting floral tea may help mild cold and hay fever symptoms and clear mucus from sinuses and the respiratory system, especially helpful during cold season. Enjoy its delicate honey-floral fragrance. Please check with health practitioner/naturopathic doctor and read **Chapter One**, page vi for safe use.

FENNEL (*Foeniculum vulgare officinale*): Please see Glossary, Fennel, page 216.
Fennel Seed Tea: Make a decoction from 1 teaspoon fennel seeds and 1 to 2 cups spring water; simmer for 6 to 8 minutes, strain. Add a little honey if desired.

Fennel Seed and Rose Petal Tea: Make a decoction from 1 teaspoon fennel seeds, 1 teaspoon rose petals, ½ teaspoon poppy seeds, 1 clove, 1 opened cardamom pod and 3 cups spring water; simmer for 4 to 5 minutes, strain. This tea appears to be helpful in supporting relaxation.

Fennel Seed and Cardamom tea: Make a decoction from 1 teaspoon fennel seeds, 1 opened cardamom pod, 1 tablespoon organic orange peel pieces, ¼ teaspoon freshly grated ginger and 4 cups of spring water. Bring to a boil, reduce the heat and simmer for 6 to 8 minutes in covered saucepan. Strain. Adding a little honey to make a gentle sweet flavor, if desire.

Note: Fennel Seed decoction for externally use: A light tea decoction of fennel seeds, if approved by your eye doctor or another healthcare provider, may be used as an anti-inflammatory eyewash to treat sore eyes or as a gargle for sore throats.

Caution: Use fennel seed tea only as recommended by your naturopathic doctor; otherwise one can over stimulate the nervous system, avoid during pregnancy.

FENUGREEK (*Trigonella foenum-graecum*): Fenugreek is a healing herb whose qualities were brought to the attention of humans by observing animals. Farmers noticed that sick cattle would eat fenugreek plants and recover even when they would not eat anything else. Fenugreek is an annual plant widely cultivated for both culinary and medicinal uses (its regular use, mainly the seeds, will help keep the body healthy). This leguminous herb with a unique aromatic flavor is primarily from ancient Egypt, Greece and Persia and is one of the oldest medicinal plants, used for many centuries. *Fenugreek seeds contain vitamins A, B1, C. and B3 (niacin is important for energy production and maintaining healthy skin). Fenugreek may help control arthritis, improve digestion and vision as well as help lower cholesterol and regulate blood sugar. Fenugreek seeds contain mucilage fiber, which when mixed with boiling water, becomes gelatinous and helps ease sluggish bowels.* Some nutritional doctors believe that people with diabetes should consume *fenugreek seeds* as part of their regular diets (in some people, it may produce some flatulence). Drinking fenugreek seed tea regularly may help prevent plaque build-up in the arteries. **Fenugreek sprouts** are not only easy to grow, they are delicious and nutritious; you can add them to sandwiches, salads, vegetable juice. They are a medicinal vegetable having high anti-oxidant properties that may be used to treat indigestion (see Tips, "*beans/seeds sprouting*" page 173). Fenugreek young tender leaves can be chopped and added to green salad just before serving, or used to flavor a variety of foods.

Fenugreek Tea: Steep ½ teaspoon fenugreek seeds in 4 cups of boiling spring water for 4 to 5 minutes, strain and serve. To detoxify body with fenugreek tea may improve coughs, sore throat and gall bladder and diabetes problems.

Caution: Please consult with your health practitioner prior to using fenugreek leaves/seeds, especially if you are a pregnant or breast feeding woman, or a child under age 13 years old.

FLAXSEEDS (*Linum usitatissimum*): Please see Glossary, Flaxseeds, page 217.

Flaxseeds Tea: Use ½ teaspoon flaxseeds in 1 cup of boiling water, let steep for 4 to 5 minutes, strain and serve.

GINGER ROOT (*Zingiber officinale*)**:** Please see Glossary, Ginger root, page 218.

Ginger Tea: In a covered saucepan simmer 1-inch ginger root (cut in ½) and 4 cups spring water for a few minutes, strain and serve as a tea.

Ginger Lemonade Tea: In a medium saucepan, bring 4 cups spring water to boil, add 1 tablespoon honey, 1 tablespoon turbinado raw sugar and 1-inch ginger root (peeled and sliced). Simmer in covered saucepan for 6-8 minutes until sugar is dissolved. Add juice of 1 lemon and 1 teaspoon rosewater. Simmer for 2 more minutes. Strain and serve warm in cold weather.

Ginger, Orange Slices and Apple Cider Tea: Place ½-inch ginger root (peeled and cut into small pieces), 1-inch Ceylon cinnamon bark (cut into small pieces), and 4 whole cloves of allspice in a tea infuser and set aside. In a large saucepan, bring 8 cups apple cider, 1½ tablespoons honey, and 1 small organic orange slices to a boil (rinse off the skin, slice thinly horizontally into 4-5 slices and remove the seeds). Place tea infuser (containing spices) into apple cider pot. Cover partially and simmer over medium-low heat about 8 to 10 minutes to infuse flavors. Stir occasionally, strain and serve this blended tea as a fruity treat.

Ginger and Scallions Tea: In a covered saucepan, simmer 1 teaspoon ginger (peeled and grated), ¼ cup scallion bulbs (chopped) and 2 cups spring water for 8 to 10 minutes, strain and serve. Watch to prevent burning.

Ginger and Lemongrass Tea: Make a zesty blend of the following herbs: 2 tablespoons lemongrass, 2 tablespoons culinary dried rose petals, 2-inch strips organic lemon peel (cut in ½), 1-inch ginger root (cut in ½), 1 teaspoon licorice root, 1 lemon balm sprig or 1 teaspoon lemon verbena fresh leaves, and ½-inch Ceylon cinnamon bark. Add this mixture to 4 cups boiling spring water and simmer in covered saucepan for 6 to 8 minutes, strain and serve.

Ginger and Pear Tea (one of my favorite drinks for a cold day)**:** In a saucepan bring 4 cups of spring water to a boil. Add 1 Bosc pear (peeled, cored and sliced) and 1-inch ginger root (peeled, sliced). Simmer in covered saucepan for 6 to 8 minutes, strain and serve. Please read **Chapter One**, page vi, for safe use.

GINKGO (*Ginkgo biloba*)**:** *Native to China, one of the most popular and oldest trees/herbs on earth with a reputation for improving memory and hearing loss. Considered "tea of life" ginkgo helps us to feel young and slows the aging process.* The graceful fan-shaped leaves of the ginkgo tree can help improve circulation in the body and brain, increase oxygen absorption and energize all body cells as well as having anti-oxidant and anti-inflammatory properties. Dried leaves can be used in a medicinal herbal tea, with property of an astringent. Ginkgo is seen to be good for improving short-term memory and concentration in elders, and in treating early stage Alzheimer's disease. It also can work to relax blood vessels that may reduce the symptoms of cardiovascular diseases, headaches, hemorrhoids and depression.

Ginkgo helps prevent high blood pressure and strokes, improves vision (protecting the eye by reducing free-radical damage to the retina and repaired retinal blood flow), reduces ears ringing (tinnitus), and helps keep blood sugar in a normal range. The joy and benefit of ginkgo tea as recommended by traditional naturopathic doctor can provide good health value. Please read **Chapter One**, page vi for safe use.

Ginkgo Tea: Place a mixture of ½ teaspoon of each dried ginkgo and mint leaves into a large cup of boiling spring water. Let it steep for 4 to 5 minutes, strain and serve.

GINSENG (*Panax ginseng*): *The root has many uses in strengthening all body systems; this strong energy tonic is used mostly to make tea and is popular among elderly Chinese people.* Traditional Chinese medicine supports the belief that ginseng is a mild aphrodisiac. The "*king of all herbs*" has a history that goes back thousands of years. *It contains many vitamins including A, E, B1, B2, B3 and B12, along with some minerals. Ginseng can stimulate and improve memory and counter physical stress and fatigue. It may support adrenal gland function and has some estrogenic activity.* There are many types of ginseng, such as American ginseng and red varieties from the Orient (Korean* and Chinese ginseng). Siberian ginseng (*Eleutherococcus senticosus*) belongs to a different class of herbs and has more powerful tonic, anti-stress, restorative and energy-boosting properties. *With all its strengths, ginseng root should not be used regularly;* one also has to be very careful as to the amount, variety and source of ginseng being used. Ginseng should not be used by pregnant or breastfeeding women or in children. It should only be used as directed by a knowledgeable healthcare practitioner.

Caution: Please read carefully **Chapter One,** page vi, for safe use.

Natural ginseng root tea contains traces of many vitamins and minerals and has been used by many cultures to assist memory, to maintain vitality, and relieve stress. In the past, some cultures have also used ginseng tea to control blood sugar levels and prevent diabetes. Be cautious when using ginsengs; it can be too stimulating and result in raising blood pressure in certain individuals. Please follow the package instruction carefully and use in moderation when preparing ginseng tea, otherwise this powerful herb can be harmful to your body.

***To make ginseng tea,** stir only a tiny amount (about 1/16 teaspoon) in 1 large cup of boiling spring water and steep for 3 to 4 minutes and serve (certified Korean ginseng extract is my preference).

Caution: Please read and follow instruction on ginseng packaging carefully and ask for guidance from your healthcare practitioner prior to consuming this tea. Pregnant, breastfeeding women and children should avoid drinking ginseng tea. If you are taking ginseng regularly, it is the best to take short breaks from this powerful herb every month or so, and limit other herbal stimulant and caffeine teas. Please read **Chapter One**, page vi, for safe use.

Note: Most ginseng roots today are commercially cultivated; wild ginseng plants used in the past are rare.

GOLDEN SEAL (*Hydrastis canadensis*): This bright yellow *(golden) root has natural antibiotic properties and can help control bacteria and strengthen the body.* Golden seal is from the buttercup family and grows in warm climates. *Golden seal root is a traditional healing herb that was used medicinally by Native Americans to improve poor circulation, as a laxative and tonic to treat stomach upsets, yeast infections, chronic colds, sore throats, chest congestion (upper respiratory infections), gum infection (by gargling a tea made from the root) as well as a wash to cure skin diseases.*

Golden Seal Light Tea: Steep 1 teaspoon dried golden seal root powder in 2 cups boiling water for 4 to 5 minutes; strain and use for gargling. <u>Do not drink unless approved by your healthcare provider.</u>

Caution: Pregnant or breastfeeding woman, as well as people with high blood pressure, and glaucoma.* Those using medicines or having a history of stroke or other serious medical conditions should avoid using golden seal until they check with their health practitioner and/or naturopathic doctor. Experts say, be very careful when using blended golden seal root and licorice root tea.

*Glaucoma, is an eye disease associated with elevated eye pressure in which a person's field of vision gradually becomes smaller and smaller.

GOTU KOLA (*Centella asiatica*): A slender creeping plant with tiny flowers and rounded (fan-shaped) leaves, gotu kola is native to Ceylon (Sri Lanka) and grows in marshy areas. This herb helps one feel younger by its effects on the brain and hormone stimulation and balance. ***Researchers in India believe that gotu kola improves memory, intellectual performance and behavior of mentally-challenged children by inspiring thinking, better focus and concentration.*** Traditional Ayurveda medicine in India used "*gotu kola*" like "ginseng" as a tonic for longevity.

Gotu Kola Tea: Place 1 teaspoon of gotu kola herb into a cup, and add 1 cup boiling spring water and let it steep for 4 to 5 minutes. Strain and serve.

Caution: Pregnant and breastfeeding woman and children should not consume gotu kola. In general if you see any side effects from using this herb, get in touch with your healthcare provider immediately and please read *Chapter One*, page vi, for safe use.

GUAVA (*Psidium guajava*): This tropical fruit tree comes in several varieties, from pale yellow to bright red, depending on the region. Ripe guava has a soft rosy flesh, a spherical seed and tasty sweet and sour flavor similar to plum. *Guava is a good source of vitamin A and C. Its vitamin C makes it excellent for treating colds and coughs. Guava contains a good amount of potassium, iron and high amounts of pectin (a soluble dietary fiber).* You can make jams, sauces or fruit drinks from guava. You can also eat guava fresh, just peel and pit before eating.

HAWTHORN (*Crataegus oxyacantha*): Hawthorn is a rich source of nutrients; hawthorn is best known for its long-term record of preventing and reducing cardiovascular disease. *The leaves, flowers and fruits/berries are used as part of this medicinal herb. The berry is the most commonly used part of the plant. Hawthorn is also called "May Blossom White Thorn," and it has a reputation for controlling high blood pressure and improving and strengthening the cardiovascular system and heart function.* A number of studies show that using hawthorn improves blood flow to the heart by lowering blood pressure and preventing blood clots associated with hardening of the arteries, thus improving blood flow to all tissues in our body. Traditional Chinese medicine believes that hawthorn strengthens cardiovascular function and it has been used as a remedy for regulating heart activity and weakness of the heart muscle. It also has a relaxation effect on the nervous system, helps people unable to sleep (*insomnia*), and acts as an **astringent and anti-oxidant.** *Hawthorn tea (from leaves/flowers/berries) may improve circulation and supply nutrients to the brain, which improve one's memory and ability to concentrate.*

Hawthorn Tea: To one teaspoon hawthorn leaves/flowers/berries, add 2 cups boiling spring water and let steep for 4 to 5 minutes. Strain and serve. This can be a daily tonic if recommended by your health practitioner prior to using hawthorn and read *Chapter One,* page vi **for** safe use.

Caution: Experts suggest that using basic hawthorn herb in mild to modest amounts may be safe for normal people who are not using prescription drugs. Hawthorn can interact with a number of drugs (including some heart medications) and produce undesirable side effects. Hawthorn tea made from leaves or flowers or berries might be effective when used in treatment of mild-moderately irregular heartbeat. Pregnant and breastfeeding women and children should not use hawthorn. Having large amounts of hawthorn can cause a serious drop in blood pressure and/or other unexpected side effects such as faintness. Please consult with health practitioner and/or experience naturopathic doctor prior to using hawthorn.

HIBISCUS FLOWERS (*Hibiscus sabdariffa*): Native to India, Malaysia and China, <u>it is a flavor enhancer and supportive herb in blended teas.</u> The beauty of tropical hibiscus flowers and its vibrant bright rose color has gained popularity in the heart of many people around the world. *Hibiscus flowers are a source of vitamin C and also contain calcium, riboflavin (vitamin B2), niacin (vitamin B3) and iron.* It has a unique delicate tropical flavor, and in its natural state has a mildly-fruity and lemony-tart taste. *Hibiscus flowers help purify the blood, aid the heart physically and spiritually and are thought to promote hair growth.* A blended tea from beautiful hibiscus flowers can be refreshing and delightful. A Persian research study has shown that consuming hibiscus flower tea can lower blood pressure after a few weeks, and this study was confirmed by Mexican scientists. You can make a delightful blended tea from hibiscus flowers with its bright rose color and delicate flavor combined with anise seeds to balance naturally sweet and sour flavors, and/or hibiscus flower with blended blackberry leaves, lemongrass, and a little sweetener; use this teas with consultation of a healthcare doctor.

Hibiscus Tea: Place 3 cups spring water in a medium saucepan and bring to a boil. Add ½-inch cinnamon bark (break into small pieces/chips) and ½ teaspoon ginger root (grated); reduce the heat, cover the saucepan and simmer about 6 to 8 minutes. Add 1 teaspoon hibiscus flower the last minute. Strain off the liquid and add ¼ teaspoon honey (optional) or to taste. Serve hot as a winter drink or chilled as a summer drink. A rich fruity flavor of hibiscus gives wonderful taste.

Caution: Please consult with your health practitioner prior to use hibiscus tea and read *Chapter One, page vi* for safe use.

HOPS (*Humulus lupulus*): A trailing plant that grows in Europe, its leaves are similar to grapes leaves. Hops have traditionally been used for brewing beer; but today modern science in Germany and France supports the use of the fruit and leaves of hops medicinally as *a digestive aid to reduce women's symptoms (PMS) and for treatment of anxiety and sleep disturbance (insomnia) because of the calming effect on the nervous system. Hops herb contains "natural estrogens" and the estrogenic action of hops makes it an excellent remedy for problems around menopause and painful periods (called dysmenorrhea). Hops have also been used to treat irritable bowel syndrome (IBS), digestive stress, ulcers, nervous disorders and as a liver stimulant and blood cleanser.* The buds and new leaves of hops can be blanched to remove some of their bitterness prior to use in making tea.

Hops Tea: To one teaspoon hop leaves, add 2 cups boiling spring water and let steep for 4 to 5 minutes. Strain and serve. It helps relaxation.

Caution: Pregnant and breastfeeding women, breast cancer patients and especially young children should avoid consuming hops tea. Others should drink **hops tea or a blended tea** that includes hops as recommended by their healthcare provider to produce a restful sleep. Please read *Chapter One,* page vi for safe use and follow the package safety instructions.

INDIAN GOOSEBERRY or **GOLDEN BERRY** (*Emblica officinalis-Amla*): *It is grown in India and is one of the richest known natural sources of the anti-oxidant vitamin C. Indian gooseberry is thought to be an ideal medicinal food for diabetes particularly if it is mixed with bitter gourd juice as prescribed by a naturopathic doctor. The use of Indian gooseberry may also help improve eyesight and prevent eye complications in diabetes.* You may use Indian gooseberry fresh or as a powder; add a small amount of powder to water to make a juice or add to a smoothie.

JAMBUL FRUIT (*Jamun*): The jambul fruit is also known as Java plum. It is a well-known and popular fruit in India due to its unique flavor, dark purple outer skin and rose-colored flesh. I found jambul fruit plentiful in the market when I visited India. *In India this fruit is regarded as antidiabetic.* The fruit and/or juice are recommended by naturopathic doctors for use in the treatment of diabetes and to reduce the amount of sugar in urine (see picture of Jambul fruit, page 309).

JASMINE BLOSSOM (*Jasminum grandiflorum*): Many people today as well as ancient herbalists agree that the sensual floral aroma of jasmine's white and star-shaped flowers act as a delicate sweet natural air freshener smell and has calmative properties. Jasmine flower is used to make a fragrant *tisane tea* from blossoms (flowers carefully being hand-picked early in the morning and mixed with semi-processed dried green leaves). Jasmine essential oil is also used in aromatherapy for relaxation (during pregnancy and breast feeding it should be avoided).

Jasmine Blossom Tea: The most popular scented jasmine tea is a blend of ¼ teaspoon dried jasmine blossoms with ½ teaspoon tea leaves to 2 cups boiling spring water. To create ideal floral aroma and flavor, steep for 4 to 5 minutes, strain and serve.

Jasmine Blossom and Rosemary tea: See Glossary, Rosemary, page 238. Steep ½ teaspoon of both jasmine blossom and green rosemary leaves in 2 cups boiling spring water, cover and steep for 4 to 5 minutes, strain and enjoy a robust floral taste.

Jasmine Blossoms and Raspberry Leaves Tea: Infuse ½ teaspoon of both jasmine blossom and raspberry leaves in 2 cups boiling spring water, cover and steep for 4 to 5 minutes, strain and serve. This has a subtle floral aroma and delightfully flavored blended tea. Please read *Chapter One,* page vi for safe use.

LAVENDER FLOWERS: See Glossary, Lavender and lavender tea, page 226.

LEMON (*Citrus lemon*), see Glossary, Lemon, page 227.

Lemon Iced Tea: Drinking freshly squeezed lemon juice with spring water and a hint of natural honey is one of the most refreshing beverages in the world. Serve over ice for an enjoyable summer drink.

Lemon Tea: Use 1 teaspoon lemon juice (freshly squeezed), a tiny bit of honey, 1 cup boiling spring water, a pinch of cayenne pepper, and 1 mint sprig (optional), steep for 4 to 5 minutes, strain and serve. Drinking lemon tea daily may help detoxify the body.

Note: After drinking tea you may rinse your mouth with a plain water to protect your teeth enamel from lemon acidity.

LEMON BALM (*Melissa officinalis*): Is from the mint family and when its leaves are bruised it has an irresistible fragrance like lemon blossom. Lemon balm has been used as a traditional tonic as it is thought to promote the functions of the whole body, as well as support brain function and strengthen memory. Drinking moderate amounts of lemon balm tea has a wonderful nourishing effect on the body and mind. It may help the nervous system to relax (it has a calming "*tranquilizer*" effect without inducing sleep) when under stress or feeling anxious. *Lemon balm herbal tea may be just the right thing for soothing nerves, lifting one's spirit, acting as a superb immunity booster and healing cold sores. The herb contains chemicals called "polyphenols" that help fight some bacterial infections, reduce headache and buzzing in the ears and ease an over-active thyroid gland.* Lemon balm is a great medicinal plant that is easy to grow in any garden.

It is used mostly in sweet and savory dishes and for *tisane* teas (a French word for aromatic herbal tea that is flavored with lemon verbena, lemon balm and various herbs or spices).

Lemon Balm Tea: In a covered teapot, use 1 sprig of freshly cut lemon-balm, a few dried rose petals, a hint of honey with 2 cups of boiling spring water. Steep for 4 to 5 minutes, strain and serve.

Lemon Balm and Burdock Root Tea: Add ½ teaspoon lemon balm and ½ teaspoon burdock root to 2 cups boiling spring water. Steep for 4 to 5 minutes, strain and serve. It may help with body detoxification.

Lemon Balm Iced Tea: Use 1 sprig of freshly cut lemon balm with 2 cups of boiling spring water. Steep for 4 to 5 minutes and strain. Adding a hint of honey and lemon juice and 2 ice cubes will enhance this tea to a superb summer drink for relieving tension.

Caution: Lemon balm may interfere with thyroid hormone activity, especially in pregnant and nursing women and children so they should avoid this herb. Please consult with your health practitioner prior to use, and read *Chapter One* for safe use.

Note : The lemon balm plant not only brings a pleasurable fragrance to the home, its dried leaves blends very well with dried rose petals and lavender flowers to make a beautiful potpourri.

LEMON VERBENA (*Lippia citriodora*) is also known as verbena. Lemon verbena is a rapidly growing elegant shrub that has long slender light green pointed leaves and is native to South America. The leaves are anti-inflammatory, astringent and carminative (eases gas) and are used as a digestive aid for symptoms of flatulence. Verbena is delightfully fragrant and the young leaves have a strong lemony taste; for this reason a light touch is necessary when adding to salads or consuming as a tea. Lemon verbena leaves are used to flavor sweet and tisane teas. You can find fresh or dried verbena leaves in specialty store.

Lemon Verbena Tea: Make a decoction from 4 cups spring water, 1 tablespoon lemon verbena fresh leaves, 1 tablespoon culinary dried rose petals, 1 tablespoon organic orange peel pieces and 1 teaspoon fennel seeds. Bring the content to simmer and simmer for 6 to 8 minutes in covered saucepan, strain off the liquid. Serve with a little honey if desired. This tea will help reduce stress and help one put on a happy face.

Lemon Verbena Ginger Tea Blend: Make a decoction from 4 cups spring water, 1 tablespoon lemon verbena fresh leaves (torn), 1 tablespoon lemongrass (minced), 1 tablespoon organic lemon peel, 1 tablespoon culinary dried rose petals, 1 tablespoon ginger root (minced), 1 teaspoon lemon blossom (optional), ½ teaspoon licorice root (minced), ½ teaspoon anise seeds and ¼-inch cinnamon bark. Bring the content to a low simmer and simmer for 6 to 8 minutes in a covered saucepan, strain and serve. This tea may help with digestion problems.

Note: Iced lemon verbena tea is a wonderfully refreshing and popular summer drink for its cooling effect.

Caution: Please do not use this herb during pregnancy and breastfeeding and for children. Always consult with your health practitioner prior to use and read *Chapter One*, page vi, for safe use.

LICORICE ROOT (*Glycyrrhiza globra*): Licorice is native to Europe, Asia and North and South America. It is a digestive regulator and affects the whole body as "*a great detoxifier and peace maker*". Licorice has been used medicinally for millennia (Chinese call it "*the grandfather of herbs*"). Laboratory studies have found that *licorice root can ease allergy symptoms, act as a relaxing digestive remedy to calm an upset stomach, reduce inflammation and fight fungus infections responsible for common vaginal yeast infections. It also acts to balance (as a tonic) the adrenal glands, which produce the hormones to cope with stress (weak adrenals are associated with constant fatigue, lack of concentration and inadequate nutrients in the body).* Licorice root may improve the voice and vision and strengthen hair. Rinsing the mouth with licorice tea may help to prevent cavities. You can find licorice root in natural foods or herb stores and you need to ask or read labels to see if any licorice candies or products are made from real licorice root. Please read caution below.

Licorice Root Tea: Use a small slices of grated licorice root (½-inch) with 4 cups spring water in a saucepan, and simmer for 4 to 5 minutes, strain and serve.

Licorice Root, Peppermint and Raspberry leaves Tea: Steep ½ teaspoon grated licorice root, 1 teaspoon peppermint and 1 teaspoon raspberry leaves in 4 cups boiling spring water for 4 to 5 minutes. Strain and serve. It can be good for the digestive tract as it eases stomach discomfort.

Licorice Root and Anise Seeds Tea: Steep ½ teaspoon grated licorice root with ½ teaspoon anise seeds in 4 cups boiling spring water for 4 to 5 minutes, strain and serve.

Licorice Root, Fennel Seeds, Spearmint and Dandelion Tea (a super power digestive and cleanser tea): Steep ½ teaspoon of both licorice root and dandelion root, and ½ teaspoon of fennel seeds and ½ teaspoon spearmint leaves in 4 cups boiling spring water for 4 to 5 minutes, strain and serve.

Caution: Consuming licorice tea daily or in large amount can cause some people problems as it can raise blood pressure. Pregnant and breastfeeding woman, children and anyone with a history of diabetes, glaucoma, high blood pressure, and stroke/heart disease should avoid this herb unless recommended by their practitioner. If any symptoms develop like headache/increasing blood pressure, stop using and immediately consult healthcare practitioner and read *Chapter One*, page vi, for safe use.

LINDEN BLOSSOMS/FLOWERS (*Tilia cordata*): Its unique and sweet-nectar flavor makes a soothing and relaxing tea that can reduce internal stress (muscle tension), relieve anxiety and lower blood pressure. You'll often find linden blossoms blended with other herbs because of its harmonizing benefits and taste. Linden blossoms are picked by hand from linden trees and it takes many blossoms to yield a pound. Because of its high labor costs, the tea becomes more expensive. Linden tea is more popular in Europe where it is often served after dinner, or it is used as part of relaxing tea formulas.

Linden Blossom and Lemon Balm Tea: Use ½ teaspoon linden blossom and ½ teaspoon lemon balm in 2 cups boiling spring water. Steep for 4 to 5 minutes, strain and serve.

Linden Blossom Blended Tea (It has outstanding aroma and goodness in every cup of tea you take): Make a decoction (hot infusion) from 2 cups spring water and ¼ teaspoon of each herb (linden blossom, lemon balm, rose hip, licorice root, hibiscus and peppermint). Simmer for 6-8 minutes in covered saucepan, strain and serve.

Caution: Please consult with health practitioner prior to using linden teas.

LYCHEE FRUIT (*Litchi chinensis*): Is a beautiful fruiting tropical tree native to India. The fruits are the size of large cherries with a rough red-pink skin, edible translucent white color flesh and a large oval seed inside each fruit. ***The flesh is very high in dietary fibers, anti-oxidants and is also an excellent source of vitamin C, B complex and minerals including potassium and copper.*** Fresh lychee is available during late summer (August). For eating, carefully peel away the skin without squeezing the fruit and eat the flesh and discard the seed.

Important Note: Diabetics can consume these fruits in moderation as they are low in sugar, yet only after consultation with their health practitioner (see picture of Lychee fruit, page 309).

MINT (*Mentha piperita*): See Glossary, Mint, page 228.

Mint Tea (*Chai*) is served at North African (Morocco, Algeria and Tunisia) tea ceremonies. They use 8 spearmint sprigs (reserve 4 leaves for serving time) and 1 teaspoon green tea. Add this to a teapot and fill with boiling spring water. Cover the teapot and steep for 4 to 5 minutes and strain. Pour out a cup of tea then return to pot to further steep and complete infusion. To serve tea, place reserved mint sprig into each teacup and then pour tea from a little height to make the surface frothy. Sugar cones (the broken pieces from a large sugar cone) are often served with mint tea. It is cooling and aromatic tea.

Spearmint Leaf and Fennel Seed Tea: Use 1 teaspoon spearmint leaves along with ¼ teaspoon of each fennel seeds and caraway seeds in 2 cups boiling spring water, cover and steep for 4 to 5 minutes, strain and enjoy.

Mint Tea, Blend: Use ¼ teaspoon each of the following: Spearmint, peppermint, lavender flower and lemongrass/lemon zest in 2 cups of spring boiling water, cover and steep for 4-5 minutes, and then strain. Add a small amount of honey/sugar if desire and serve. Refresh yourself with the calming, pleasant aroma that will elevate sense of wellbeing (read ***Chapter One***, page vi for safe use).

Note 1: This spearmint tea is complemented by the deep cooling effect of peppermint and the calming, pleasant flavor of lavender for lifting the spirit and inspiring the mind. I enjoy this friendly tea almost every day.

Note 2: By adding a few ice cubes to "*blended mint tea*," it becomes a refreshing ice tea on a hot day. Peppermint ice tea may relieve stress and helps the body to relax.

Caution: Please check with your healthcare provider prior to using mint teas.

MYRRH (*Commiphora abyssinica*): This tree is native to Northeastern Africa and Southwestern Asia. When the myrrh tree bark is scored it releases a yellow oil that hardens in air into a gum or oleoresin. This resin is used medicinally as a purifier and anti-microbial herb, to help clear toxins from the digestive tract, acts as an anti-inflammatory agent, and helps to improve digestion.

Myrrh-gum is useful in treating gout and intestinal parasites. It helps reduce inflammation and destroys bacteria. *Myrrh is one of the most famous and ancient gums/resins substances used for reversing the aging process, rejuvenating the body and mind along with its detoxifying effects and ability to prevent tooth decay (traditional antiseptic for gums).* In Europe, myrrh is commonly added to tooth paste as it fight bacteria that cause decay.

Myrrh-gum Tea: Place ¼ teaspoon of myrrh herb into a tea pot, add 2 cups boiling spring water, and let it steep for 4 to 5 minutes, strain and serve.

Caution: Please check with your healthcare provider prior to use and avoid myrrh tea during pregnancy, breast feeding and/or if there is excessive uterine bleeding or kidney problems. Read **Chapter one**, page vi, for safe use.

MYRTLE LEAVES (*Myrtus communis*): This small flowering plant is native to Southern Europe and Northern Africa. In ancient Greek the myrtle flowers, leaves and fruits were known as a sign of noble love and were thought to bring luck to the home because of their enormous fragrance and beauty (the sweet and spicy essential myrtle oil is used for perfumes and medicinal purposes). *Myrtle tea can help reduce cold symptoms, coughing, headache, and dizziness, and improves night vision. It can also be used as a hair rinse when massaged into the scalp for a few minutes.* (See "*Burdock, Nettle and Myrtle Tea*", page 260).

Caution: Please check with your health practitioner prior to use and avoid myrtle tea during pregnancy and breastfeeding, plus do not give to young children and read **Chapter One,** page vi for safe use.

NEEM TREE (*Azadirachta indica also known as Margosa*)**:** I discovered this *superb natural medicinal* herb on my recent visit in India. An Ayurvedic herb from an evergreen tree of wonder possesses multiple curative properties from ancient times, and the ancestors believed in the spiritual and healing properties of this herbal tree. According to ancient Indian traditions, neem has been called the "*Village Green Pharmacy*" for thousands of years. Neem leaves are one of the best and *most powerful blood purifiers, detoxifiers and antidiabetic herbs used in Ayurveda (Ancient Indian Medicine)* therapy. Today, modern research confirms the healing properties assigned in ancient times. It helps remove the toxins involved in most inflammatory skin diseases, clears away foreign matter and acts as a supplementary astringent that promotes healing. However, in using neem products in adults, short-term basically may be is safe, while long-term use may harm the kidneys and/or liver. Because of the leaves powerful benefits it should be used with caution*.

NEEM
Tree

According to Experts Neem Leaves Benefits are:

- Anti-bacterial,
- Anti-diabetic,
- Anti-fungal (abnormal growth from fungus),
- Anti-inflammatory agent,
- Reduces swelling of joins tissues and muscles pain,
- Blood purifying,
- Detoxifying,
- Enhances the digestive system
- Benefits the circulatory and respiratory systems,
- Improves the urinary tract, and
- Neem leaves have been used to treat dry skin, plus neem oil may help hair growth.

Neem Tea: Use a very small amount of neem herbal leaves (½ teaspoon per cup of boiling water) with infusion or decoction, strain and drink the tea as directed by your healthcare practitioner.

*Caution: Pregnant and nursing women and children should not use neem. Use neem products only in consultation with a professional practitioner or naturopathic doctor. Read **Chapter One,** page vi, for safe use.

Note: Neem leaves are beneficial but the neem oil can be toxic; it is often used as an insecticide.

NETTLE LEAF/ STINGING NETTLE (*Urtica dioica*): This enduring nutritional plant grows in many places throughout Europe, Asia, North Africa and North America. As an astringent leaf it contains a wealth of vitamins and minerals, especially iron and potassium. *The young leaves can be used in soups, green vegetable omelets and as a health-tonifying tea that benefits the circulatory system, and is good for detoxification and in people with diabetes or with high blood pressure. Nettles may also support hair growth.*

Nettle Leaves Tea: To make 1 cup of tea, simmer 1 teaspoon of nettle leaf in 1½ cup spring water and let it simmer for 4 to 5 minutes or until it becomes 1 cup, then strain and serve. As an alternative, simply steep 1 tea bag of nettle leaves in one cup of boiling water for 3 to 4 minutes, press and remove tea bag and serve.

Vita-Blend Nettles and Alfalfa Leaf Tea: Combine ½ teaspoon of each of the following herbs: nettle leaves, alfalfa leaves, oat straw, hibiscus flowers, peppermint leaves, lemongrass chips and red clover blossoms. Add 4 cups of boiling spring water, steep for 4 to 5 minutes, strain and serve up to 4 people. This tea supports general good health.

Caution: Nettle plant has stinging hairs and must be handled with care to prevent nettle rash; remember, it's called "stinging nettle." Pregnant, breastfeeding women and children, and for people using medicines should check with a healthcare practitioner prior to use nettle.

PASSION FLOWER (*Passiflora incarnate*): Its beautiful, colorful flower with sensational purple blossoms has three fingered light green leaves. Passion flower is an effective herb for calming anxiety, relaxing tense muscles and promoting sleep as approved and prescribed by healthcare practitioners.

Passion Flower Tea: It is one of the best herbal teas for aiding relaxation (*it has similar effects as chamomile, linden flower and hops, and is sometimes used in combination with these other herbs*) for those people who cannot sleep due to their inability to relax. It has a minty, mildly acidic and sweet taste that can relieve stress, and reduce tension to bring about joyful sleep.

Caution: Pregnant and breastfeeding women and especially young children should avoid passion flower. It may cause allergic reactions or some side effects. Please check with your healthcare provider and read ***Chapter one,*** page vi for safe use.

PSYLLIUM SEEDS (*Plantago psyllium*): Psyllium is cultivated in North Africa, South Asia, Persia and India. This plant comes from the plantain family and its Latin name is *Plantago psyllium* (plant of healing). Psyllium seed husks are known for their use in making intestinal fiber supplements. Low fiber diets are associated with constipation, gastrointestinal disorders, and colon cancer. Among other fibers, such as ***agar-agar seaweed and Irish moss,*** * psyllium is the most commonly used fiber supplement and has been utilized for centuries in Asia. ***Research has shown that psyllium fiber can help in a gentle way as a mild laxative for relieving constipation caused by a sedentary lifestyle or lack of fiber in the diet. It may help with Irritable Bowel Syndrome (IBS), in lowering cholesterol, blood sugar, and blood pressure, and may reduce the risk of heart disease. Some people are sensitive to psyllium as it may also cause gas and bloating, so they should avoid using it.***

Psyllium Drink: Each teaspoon of whole, ground psyllium seeds is mixed with one or two large glasses of lukewarm pure water. The fiber in psyllium seed husks is highly soluble, absorbs a lot of water, swells in volume within a minute and becomes gelatinous when wet. Make sure you take psyllium with plenty of water so it doesn't cause choking or blockage and drink immediately after mixing it with water. Because psyllium absorbs a lot of water in the intestinal tract, it helps to restore a soft, regular bowel movement.

Please buy the psyllium products from a reputable source to be sure they are organic, fresh, unprocessed, and of proper potency. Safely use with instructions from your healthcare practitioner and/or the product label.

Caution: Please consult with your health practitioner prior to using psyllium seeds/husk or any psyllium dietary supplement to make sure it's right for you. This is especially important for children, pregnant and breastfeeding women and anyone on medication as it can have some interference or adverse effects. Also, it can cause bloating and gas. Some people may prefer Chia seeds, which contain more Omega-3 oils to psyllium seeds.

*****Irish moss plant:** It is a seaweed that grows mostly along the coast of Ireland.

RED CLOVER BLOSSOMS (*Trifolium pratence*): Red clover is native to Europe, North America and Western Asia. It is from the family of legumes. The small round, red clover flowers of the plant have 3 leaves similar to the shamrock (symbol of Ireland). *The flowering tops contain compounds similar to estrogen and historically were used mostly for menopause and hot flash treatment.* Red clover contains some vitamin E, which acts as an anti-oxidant and may help prevent breast cancer and cardiovascular diseases. It is especially useful during convalescence and healing.

Red Clover Tea: Combine 1 teaspoon of each of the following: Dried red clover blossoms, burdock and dandelion and add 4 cups of boiling spring water, steep for 4 to 5 minutes, strain and serve 4. This tea may support liver detoxification.

Caution: Please consult a healthcare practitioner prior to use, especially if one has a bleeding disorder, is pregnant, breastfeeding or on medication, and these people likely would avoid using red clover. Please read *Chapter one*, page vi, for safe use.

RED RASPBERRY LEAVES (*Rubus idaeus*): Leaves from red raspberry bushes have historically been used as both a relaxing and toning astringent* to support the uterus. They are known as a "friend" of female reproductive organs, a reliever of menstrual discomfort, a toner and strengthener of pelvic tissues. *The leaves are rich in nutrients, including minerals calcium, iron, magnesium, potassium, sodium and zinc, plus vitamin A, B-complex (with niacin), and C.*

Red Raspberry Tea: Raspberry leaves with their delicate taste and gentle nurturing properties make a delicious tea. Steep 1 teaspoon leaves in 1 to 2 cups of boiling spring water for 4 to 5 minutes, strain and serve. The warm tea with its deep amber color tends to soothe mucous membranes throughout the body and its mild astringency eases a sore throat and diarrhea. Please read *Chapter One*, page vi, for safe use.

*Raspberry leaves contain *"tannins,"* which are astringent (meaning a substance that constricts/binds tissues together).

ROSE (*Rosa species*): Please read Glossary, Rose, page 238.

Rose Hips (vibrant amber) Tea: Place 1 teaspoon rose hips in 1 to 2 cups of boiling spring water. Allow to steep for 4 to 5 minutes. Strain and serve. Add a small amount of honey to sweeten if desired. If you are using a tea bag, press the bag before removing to enhance the flavor. Rose tea with its considerable nutrients can help fight fatigue and raise energy. Please read *Chapter one*, page vi, for safe use.

ROSEMARY (*Rosmarinus officinalis*)**,** please read Glossary on Rosemary, page 239.

Rosemary and Chamomile Tea: Infuse ½ teaspoon of each herb, rosemary and chamomile leaves, in 2 cups boiling spring water, for 4 to 5 minutes, strain and serve.

Rosemary and Ginger Tea: In a medium size saucepan, add 2 cups spring water, ½ teaspoon rosemary, 1 teaspoon ginger root (chopped), ½ teaspoon black cumin seeds, and 1-inch lemon peel strip. Bring the content to slow simmer. Simmer for 6 to 8 minute and strain. Stir in 1½ teaspoons lemon juice (freshly squeezed), ½ teaspoon honey and enjoy. Please read *Chapter One*, page vi, for safe use.

SAFFRON (*Crocus sativus*): Saffron is from the Iris family. From ancient times, saffron threads were highly valued for their flavor and food coloring properties as well as their medicinal value, which *includes improving blood circulation, reducing cholesterol, helping with digestion and regulating menstruation, female reproduction and supporting overall rejuvenation.* Saffron was cultivated originally in the Middle East (Persia's city of Khorasan) where largely traditional farming practices were used to produce some of the best quality saffron in the world; later it was introduced to Spain. Saffron, particularly the subtle aromatic Persian (Iranian) saffron enhances the richness, color and flavor of many dishes including rice. Saffron is one of the most expensive herbs in the world, and is actually worth more than its weight in gold because each thread must be harvested by hand and dried (farmers must harvest more than a thousand flowers to make one ounce of saffron). The color of saffron changes to a vibrant orange-red color as it dries. Saffron is not only a tonic itself but even in small amounts it catalyzes the tonifying action of other herbs to promote tissue growth in the body. Its distinctive qualities appear to gives energy to love, devotion and compassion.

Saffron Blended Tea: In a medium size saucepan, add 5 cups of spring water. Bring to boil, add 5 saffron threads, 5 cardamom seeds (opened), 5 teaspoons organic culinary rose hips and 1 teaspoon organic rosewater. Simmer for 6 to 8 minutes, strain off the liquid. Stir in ½ teaspoon organic honey, and ½ teaspoon lemon juice (freshly squeezed) into the tea and this serves 5 people.

Caution: Saffron must always be used sparingly and with caution as excessive amounts can have an adverse effect on the nervous system and be harmful to your body. Please read *Chapter one*, page vi, for safe use.

SENNA (*Gassia senna*): *One of the most popular laxative herbs, senna leaf comes from a small 3 feet tall woody shrub, grown mostly in Southern India. Its branched stems have pointed leaves. Senna is used mainly for more challenging levels of constipation due to its strong purgative action and should be taken with care and considered near the last resort for relief of constipation.* It is best to first try increasing dietary fiber (by eating more fiber-containing foods), drinking more fluid, and exercising more often to treat constipation. If this still does not work, try a little senna in consultation with a naturopathic doctor experienced in gastrointestinal health issues.

Senna Plain Tea: Use a very small amount of senna's herbal leaves (½ teaspoon) in 2 cups of boiling spring water), and steep for 4 to 5 minutes, strain and serve. Adding a few drops of honey and lemon juice for taste is optional.

Senna Blended Tea: To improve senna's bitter taste, combine a very small amount of senna's herbal leaves (about ½ teaspoon) with aromatic herbs such as ginger root, licorice root, mint leaves and fennel seeds and follow direction for plain senna tea.

Caution: Pregnant, nursing women, children and people having diarrhea, hemorrhoids, and inflammatory conditions should not use senna. Senna may cause allergic reactions, aggravate constipation, and cause abdominal cramping, as well as weaken the tone of the colon and have other unexpected side effects. Rhubarb is preferable over senna to treat constipation and has fewer harmful side effects (see Glossary, Rhubarb, page 238). Please read *Chapter one*, page vi, for safe use.

Note: The best variety of senna is obtained from the holy city of Medina and in Arabic is called the *"glory of medicine."* Senna has been popular in the Arab world for many centuries and is now famous throughout the world as a powerful and dependable laxative medicine.

SEVILLE ORANGE (*Citrus aurantium*), see Glossary, Seville orange, page 240.
Seville orange/orange/lemon blossom tea: Use one teaspoon of fresh Seville orange/lemon blossom in 1 cup of boiling spring water. Steep for 4 to 5 minutes, strain and serve. According to ancient customs this herb promote peaceful sleep. See, Glossary, Citrus fruit, page 210.

Lemon blossom (the flower of this plant producing an edible fruit)

SLIPPERY ELM (*Ulmus rubra* and *Ulmus fulva*), is also known as American Indian elm. Slippery elm is a tall tree (about 50 feet high) that grows in the forests of Florida and Texas; its branches are covered with a dark brown rough outer bark; the inner bark is whitish and aromatic. The inner bark of the elm tree is rich in soluble fiber (mucilage) that swells and becomes gelatinous when mixed with water, and is used to make a blended tea with licorice and marshmallow root that according to experts is good for a sore throat. ***Slippery elm has a long history as a soothing remedy for not only a sore throat, but dry irritable coughs and digestive and respiratory problems. The soothing herb may calm inflamed tissues. Slippery Elm is often used for recovering from chronic lung ailments.***
Slippery Elm Bark Powdered Tea: For each teaspoon of slippery elm powder use 2 cups of spring water (blend slippery elm powder with a small amount of fresh water in a saucepan to prevent lumps; while stirring add the remaining water) and bring the mixture to a boil over low-medium heat, simmer for 6 to 8 minutes, strain off the liquid and serve or follow package directions. This tea has a mild flavor reminiscent of maple syrup (slightly spicy and sweet).
Caution: Slippery elm is hard to digest and may cause stomach upset; therefore it is wise to use very small amounts and combine with spices such as cinnamon, clove or ginger to improve the flavor. A person should consult with a health practitioner prior to using slippery elm.
Note: Slippery elm (*Ulmus rubra*), psyllium seeds (*Plantago psyllium*) and marshmallow (*Althaea officinalis*) have a large amount of soluble fibers and mucilaginous content.

ST. JOHN'S WORT (*Hypericum perforatum*): The *key uses of this flowering top of an old-world plant are as a diuretic, premier herbal antidepressant, and helpful to treat sleeplessness. St. John's wort is rich in anti-oxidants that counteract free radicals* and it may help the immune system resist viral infections.*

St. John's Wort Tea: Place ½ teaspoon St. John's wort dried leaves in 2 cups boiling spring water, simmer for 4 to 5 minutes. Strain off the liquid and serve.

Caution: Even though St. John's wort has medicinal properties, it also may cause mild stomach upset, rashes or restlessness. Use this tea only when recommended by a healthcare practitioner. Pregnant and breastfeeding women and children should avoid this herb.

*Free radicals (unattached charged particles) occur naturally in the body where they can damage body cells and tissues. These damaging particles increase in numbers as we age due to environmental toxins including radiation, smoking, air pollution, some medicines, etc. Free radicals contribute to health problems such as heart diseases and cancer, by damaging body cells integrity and causing cell death.

Note 1: St. John's wort flowers are used mostly for external inflammations such as burns and wounds.

Note 2: A very small amount of St. John's dried flower is used to make a fragrant bread in Europe.

TURMERIC (*Curcuma longa*)**,** please see glossary, Turmeric, page 244.

Turmeric Root Tea: Place ½-inch turmeric root in a small saucepan, add 4 cups spring water; bring to a simmer for 6 to 8 minutes. Strain off the liquid, add a few drops of freshly squeezed lemon juice and serve.

TURNIP (*Brassica napus*): Please see Glossary, Turnip, page 245.

Turnip Root Tea: To make turnip root tea, grate one young turnip (trim top and bottom and peel), add ¼ cup grated turnip to 4 cups boiling spring water, let steep for 4 to 5 minutes strain and serve (adding a dash of honey and/or freshly squeezed lemon juice is optional). Please read **Chapter one**, page vi, for safe use.

VALERIAN ROOT (*Valeriana officinalis*):   Comes from wild plant with pretty pink flowers, native to Europe, Asia and North America. *The yellow-brown, tuberous rootstock has properties, acting as a calming agent, a carminative (relieves gas), nervine and mood balancing (the root is useful for all sorts of nervous conditions).* Valerian root is used as a tranquilizer to treat conditions such as an insomnia*, nervousness, seizure disorders, and headaches, especially migraine. One should avoid prolonged and excessive use of valerian (please see caution below).

Valerian Borage Tea, in a small saucepan add 4 cups of spring water, bring to boil; add 1-inch valerian root, 2 teaspoons borage flowers and a small amount organic honey or fruit sugar to taste. Simmer slowly in covered pan for 6 to 8 minutes, strain off the liquid; stir in 2 teaspoons lime juice, and this serves 4 people.

***Insomnia** (sleeplessness) means inability to sleep well. The cause maybe excessive fatigue, too much caffeine, some medication, stress or illness.

Note: The following may help one go to sleep: Lie on your back, relax your mental activity, do 10 to 12 deep breaths and with each breath say *"Thank God for my many blessings"* and then lie on your side. A cup of warm milk can also help you to go to sleep.

Caution: Please be careful when using valerian and avoid prolonged use; excessive overuse can create problems such as restlessness, agitation, nausea, and visual illusion (blurred vision). Consult with your health practitioner to see if valerian root is good for you and follow label direction carefully. Do not give valerian to children under age 13 years. Read *Chapter one, page vi,* for safe use.

VERVAIN (*Verbena officinalis*): Is a member of the same family as lemon verbena. It is native to South America ***and is known as a mild natural aspirin.*** Their bruised leaves have a pleasant aroma with a lemon-like bitter taste. A benefit of vervain tea leaves, as recommended by traditional naturopathic doctor, is its use as a substitute for aspirin for mild pain and inflammation such as headache, subtle tooth aches, and slight constipation and for sleeplessness.

Vervain Mint Tea: In a small saucepan add 4 cups of spring water, bring to boil; add 1 pinch of the following herbs: vervain leaves, borage leaves and mint leaves. Simmer slowly in covered pan for 6 to 8 minutes, strain off the liquid; stir in a small amount of lemon juice and honey or fruit sugar to taste. Serve 4 people.

Vervain Lemon Ginger Root Tea: In a small saucepan add 4 cups of spring water, bring to boil, add 1 pinch of the following herbs: vervain leaves, lemongrass chips, lemon peel, cinnamon, ginger root, and rosehips. Simmer slowly in covered pan for 6 to 8 minutes, strain off the liquid; stir in a small amount of lemon juice and honey or fruit sugar to taste. Serve 4 people.

Vervain, Ginger and Peppermint Tea: In a small saucepan add 4 cups of spring waters, bring to a boil, and add 1 pinch of the following herbs: vervain leaves, ginger root and peppermint, and a little sweetener such as honey. Simmer slowly in covered pan for 6 to 8 minutes, strain off the liquid and serve 4 people. The warming heat of ginger will balance the cooling effect of peppermint in this superb tea.

Caution: Vervain stimulates the intestines and uterus. Pregnant and breastfeeding women, children under 13 years old and people with heart problems need to be cautious. Please check with a traditional naturopathic doctor prior to use vervain and read *Chapter one, page vi,* for safe use.

YARROW (*Achillea millefolium*): The name yarrow means thousand leaves, and this plant has a very strong aroma and flavor. Yarrow herb is native to Europe and Asia. This *"wound healer"* has a noble history during World War II; after cleaning a soldier's wound carefully, cooled yarrow was apply to stop bleeding. ***Yarrow may help suppress bacterial infections (and viruses in the early stages of cold /flu), reduce blood toxins, stop bleeding, improve healing and repair damaged tissue.*** Yarrow tea (an herbal aromatic tea) is helpful to regulate menstrual cycles, reduce heavy bleeding during periods and relieve uterine pain. It has even been suggested that it may help prevent baldness when yarrow light tea is used as a scalp wash, as recommended by traditional naturopathic doctor.

Note: Yarrow fresh leaves have a pleasant flavor; a small amount may be added to salads and sandwiches for extra flavor.

Caution: Pregnant, breastfeeding women and children should avoid yarrow as it may interfere with medicine they are taking. Consult with a health practitioner prior to using yarrow and read *Chapter one,* page vi, for safe use.

YELLOW DOCK ROOT (*Rumex crispus*) *is helpful in reducing most toxic conditions of the circulatory blood system; it has a powerful cleansing effect on blood, liver and skin (detox in gentle way), and it also acts as a mild laxative on the digestive tract.*

Yellow Dock Root Drink: One way to cleanse (detox) your gut is to use a mixture of ½ teaspoon of each of the following ground dried herbs: yellow dock root, parsley leaf, mustard green, licorice root, echinacea, garlic, golden seal root, along with a small amount of cayenne. Add mixture to 4 glasses of boiling water, steep for 4 to 5 minutes, strain and serve 4 people.

Caution: This simple detoxification formula needs to first be checked with your natural healthcare practitioner (a doctor experienced in using herbs as a natural healing process for treating diseases). It is especially important that breastfeeding and pregnant women and young children consult with a healthcare provider. Excessive use of this herb may lead to diarrhea.

Important Note: a) Our liver is an important organ of our body; it plays a huge role in immunity and removing toxic elements from our blood. It helps to regulate protein and recycle hormones. A slow and poor functioning liver can create problems such as chronic fatigue, indigestion, depression, poor circulation, mood swing, lack of concentration etc. and threaten the health of whole body. b) Everyone needs to keep their intestine naturally clean by consuming fruits and vegetables high in fiber. People who eat a highly congesting diet such as with large amounts of meat, dairy products and refined foods, need even more detoxification to repair damaged tissues.

Basil is a key herb of Mediterranean cooking
(see Glossary, basil, page 203)

MASTER TEA THAT HEALS

(Herbal tea that may relieve cold and cough symptoms).

Serves 4

    4 cups spring water

    1 bay leaf, dried, bruised

    1-inch cinnamon bark

    2 teaspoons fennel seeds OR 1-inch licorice root

    1 tablespoon ginger root (about 1-inch), cut in small pieces

    2 teaspoons coriander seeds

    1 teaspoon (black) cumin seeds

    1 clove

    4 black peppercorns

    4 cardamom pods, opened

    4 sweet basil leaves, torn

    4 strips organic lemon peels

In a medium saucepan, bring water to boil. Add all ingredients (bay leaf, cinnamon bark, fennel seeds, ginger root, coriander seeds, cumin seeds, clove, peppercorns, cardamom pods, basil and lemon peels). Bring the contents to simmer; simmer slowly in covered saucepan for 12 to 14 minutes. Strain off the liquid, add a little honey (if desire) and serve.

Caution: Use this tea only when recommended by a healthcare practitioner and read **Chapter One**, page vi, for safe use.

INDIAN TEA KNOWN AS "*BOMBAY CHAI*"

(A cup of tea that gives cheers and may help digestion)

Serves 4

    4 cups spring water

    1 tablespoon ginger root, cut in pieces

    1 teaspoon "*Indian Assam*" black tea

    1 black peppercorn

    1 cardamom pod, opened

    1-inch vanilla beans and ½-inch of each spices (cinnamon bark, clove and star anise)

In a medium saucepan, bring water to boil. Add all ingredients (ginger root, black tea, black peppercorn, cardamom, vanilla beans cinnamon, clove and star anise). Simmer slowly in covered saucepan for 6 to 8 minutes, strain off the liquid. This tea has a light sweet flavor and by adding a few iced cubes you can make an awesome summery iced tea.

Caution: Please consult with your health practitioner and read **Chapter One**, page vi, for safe use.

Pomegranate (Punica)

CHAPTER 6

MEDICINAL HERBAL FOOD PLANTS THAT MAY HELP

There are many "***Healing Herbs***" and these comprise of roots, stems, leaves, flowers, berries, and seeds. As a group, these medicines have been used through centuries and can help remedy various common illnesses to reduce problems and optimize health. The following pages talk about various body functions, health conditions, as well as offer insights into some of the effects of herbs and also noting which ones are used for specific health issues.

ANTI-BACTERIAL: It helps the body fight off harmful bacterial and prevent minor infections.

Infections that do not heal or get worse require professional care from a physician or other appropriate healthcare provider. Herbs can also have other anti-microbial effects, in reducing viruses, yeasts, and parasites, a common use of herbal medicines.

FOOD PLANTS THAT MAY HELP TO FIGHT INFECTIONS
Garlic, ginger root, onion, clove, honey, lemon, lime, cabbage, carrots, and turmeric.

ANTI-COAGULANT (thins blood and helps prevent blood clots):

Clots that form on damaged arterial heart tissue can cause a heart attacks by blocking blood flow to the heart muscle. One of the best known blood-thinners (anti-coagulant medicines) *is aspirin, an extract from the bark of white willow tree, and aspirin (as salicylates, such as contained in the herb white willow bark) has effects on pain relief and inflammation. Digitalis* from the foxglove plant has some anti-clotting effects but is used more to strengthen the heart; use digitalis and foxglove only under a doctor's supervision. The latest studies suggest that a balanced diet can have an enormous influence on blood clotting factors; in fact, there is some evidence suggesting that the major influences of diet on heart disease have more to do with blood clotting factors than with blood cholesterol. The benefits of eating good food and essential fats and oils and having a properly balanced diet can have an enormous effect on preventing blood clots and keeping *the river of our life* flowing freely.

FOODS THAT MAY HELP WITH BLOOD CLOTTING
Chili pepper, clove, fruits, leafy green vegetables, garlic, ginger root, grapes, olive oil, onion and yogurt.

Important Note: Herb expert says, leafy green vegetables are nature's best sources of vitamin K. that is essential to the liver's production of clotting agents. Taking anti-biotic drug regularly, can destroy the vitamin K that our body is needed for blood clotting.

ANTI-OXIDANTS: Are substances that destroy or counteract free radicals and prevents cell damage. Key anti-oxidants include vitamins C and E and beta-carotene (converted to vitamin A in the body), minerals zinc and selenium. All of these antioxidants exist in plant (and animal) foods and have powerful protective properties that can help keep our blood vessels strong and protect us from toxicity and inflammation.

FOODS THAT MAY ACT AS ANTI-OXIDANTS

Include, garlic, ginger root, onion, dark colored leafy vegetables such as (spinach, asparagus, broccoli, lettuce and cabbage family*) and dark colored fruits such as (blueberries, blackberries, cherries, raspberries, grapes/raisins), Indian gooseberries, pomegranate, quince, and vitamin E rich foods such as red clover blossoms tea. They are well known for containing a high concentration of anti-oxidants. For each herb, please consult with an experienced naturopathic doctor prior to use.

*Cabbage family/cruciferous vegetables: include broccoli, cabbage, cauliflower, watercress, mustard greens, radishes, and turnips.

Note: Fruit like wild blackberries are great to eat out of hand when fresh and mature for their antioxidant qualities.

Mulberry fruits, see Glossary, page 229

ARTHRITIS:
Is an inflammatory disease that causes swelling and pain in joins. Arthritis is made worse by excess weight and pressure on the joints. As the disease progresses the joints can become very painful, swell and become deformed. There are many herbs that help provide some arthritis relief, such as cat's claw, and nutrients like glucosamine and hyaluronic acid that support joint health. For each herb, please consult with an experienced naturopathic doctor prior to use.

FOOD THAT MAY EASE SYMPTOMS OF ARTHRITIS

Anti-inflammatory: Include dark-colored fruits, such as blueberries, blackberries and citrus fruits (such as oranges, lemons and limes that are rich in vitamin C)

Note: A regular gentle massage on affected joints with neem herb from India may help ease the symptoms of arthritis. Please check with your health care doctor if this herb is right for you.

BAD BREATH:
Certain foods, poor oral dental hygiene, gum disease and stomach problems can create bad breath and unpleasant taste in the mouth. If chronic bad breath persist consult a health care professional doctor.

FOOD THAT MAY PREVENT BAD BREATH

Chewing cardamom seed, anise seeds or mint leaves can help freshen breath.

BLOOD SUGAR *(diabetes):* Glucose, or blood sugar, is something that keeps us alive and feeds all of our cells. When it becomes too high because we are overloaded with dietary sugars or our pancreas and insulin are not working efficiently, it can become diabetes, *which is disease in which the body does not produce enough or properly utilizes insulin, a hormone that is needed to help the cells use glucose and regulate blood sugar in our body.* People with diabetes are at higher risk for cardiovascular problems and perhaps other diseases, such as cancer and bone degradation. Heredity (if one of our parents is diabetic, our chances of being diabetic by the time we turn age 40 years is about 40% likelihood) and obesity (primary caused by consistent over-eating) are major factors in development of adult onset diabetes. Other contributors to diabetes include being overweight, and the excessive consumption of fat, sugar, alcohol and some drugs. *The most common symptoms of juvenile or acute diabetes are excessive thirst, frequent urination, weight loss, increased appetite and food intake, and weakness (physically and mentally). Anxiety, stress and worry can also have an effect on metabolism and may cause sugar levels to rise and appear in the urine.* Persons with these symptoms or those with health history of diabetes should consult a health care provider for evaluation. Currently there is no cure for diabetes, but it can readily be controlled. For its treatment, a good diet, yoga and meditation also play a vital role with consultation and guidance of a health practitioner doctor.

FOOD THAT MAY HELP CONTROL BLOOD SUGAR IN A

NON-DIABETIC

Artichoke, bitter gourd, cinnamon, bilberry leaves tea, celery stalk, fenugreek leaves and fenugreek seeds (that may be of great value in the treatment of diabetes), *fiber rich foods* (high soluble fiber diet that contained traditional whole grains such as barley and oatmeal), *garlic, onion, jambul fruit and Indian gooseberry, low carbohydrate vegetables and foods rich in anti-oxidant* (such as vitamin C, E and beta carotene). Using these food with consultation and guidance of a health practitioner, is beneficial to our good health.

CHOLESTEROL: The main causes of high cholesterol include poor diet, obesity, hereditary, age and stress. *Cholesterol is an important molecule that is the precursor on most body hormones and helps in the healing of inflamed tissues. Too much of total cholesterol and certain sub-fractions in the blood stream can results in plaque deposits and obstruction of arteries that may result in a heart attacks or strokes*.* Generally high blood cholesterol does not have any symptoms and the only way to know if you have high blood cholesterol is by having regular medical checkup. Please consult with your health practitioner doctor and follow his guideline.

*Strokes are biologically similar to heart attacks, only instead of arteries blockage to the heart, there is blockage of arteries to the brain.

FOOD THAT MAY HELP LOWER BLOOD CHOLESTEROL

We may bring our cholesterol level down by the following:

a) Having herbs such as fenugreek, garlic, ginseng, hawthorn, saffron (each one needs approval of a health care doctor), nutritious food such as diet high in fresh fruits and green vegetables (there is no cholesterol in plant-foods).
b) Avoid fatty foods such as fried foods and meats containing high fat.
c) Maintaining a healthy weight, doing regular exercise and meditation by using yoga exercise (food for mind and spirit).

Herb experts say, having ½ a chopped clove of garlic in a glass of warm water (make a tea and drink in the morning on an empty stomach and in the evening) and eating green onion regularly may reduce cholesterol and combat the build-up of cholesterol in arteries.

COLD AND COUGH: often results from a viral (virus) infectious diseases of the upper respiratory system (nose, throat, and bronchial tubes). The symptoms of a cold include running nose, frequent sneezing, fever, headache, nasal congestion, sore throat or excessive phlegm. Consult a health care provider if symptoms do not improve or get worse.

FOOD THAT MAY EASE COLD AND COUGH SYMPTOMS

Taking herb teas may relieve cold and cough symptoms. Some of these include: ginger root, turmeric root, lemon and guava (because of high vitamin C present in lemon and guava fruits), rosehips, black elderberry, peppermint, astragalus, echinacea and golden seal. Each of these herb teas may help relieve the symptoms of the common colds, sore throats and coughing and enhance the function of the immune system.

Caution: Please consult with your health care practitioner prior to using the above herbal plants.

Herb experts say, for phlegm congestion make a "*fenugreek drink*" by placing ¼ cup washed fenugreek leaves and 1 cup of water in blender, blend and strain off the liquid and mix with ¼ teaspoon freshly grated ginger root juice and ¼ teaspoon honey (if desire) to make a soothing drink. Please consult with your health care practitioner prior to using herbal teas/drinks.

CONSTIPATION: Natural medicine practitioners often suggest that *Many Diseases Have Their Roots in the Digestive System.* Having a healthy stomach and proper digestion is essential for maintaining good health. Probiotic foods help promote friendly bacteria in the gut (intestinal tract) and provide nutrients that help our digestive track work properly. Constipation can cause discomfort, a bloated feeling and results in a painful bowel movement. In general drinking plenty of spring water and having sufficient fibers in our diet will prevent constipation and also helps cleanse the whole body system.

FOOD THAT MAY HELP PREVENT CONSTIPATION

High Fiber Fruits and Vegetables in the Diet is step number one. These include papaya, pears, prunes (dried plums), grapes, fresh figs, gooseberry (golden berries), dandelion, fennel, asparagus, broccoli and parsley. Foods that should be avoided if there are problems with constipation include: white flour, refined sugars, processed foods, hard boiled eggs and cheese. Some medicines increase the chance of constipation and you should check with your health care provider for how to best deal with it.

Note: Please do not take laxatives on a regular basis to prevent constipation unless recommended by your health care doctor. Continued laxative use may weaken the intestines wall and prevent normal bowel movements. It is best to treat constipation with a fiber rich diet of fresh fruits and green leafy vegetables along with moderate exercise. See your health care provider for chronic constipation.

DETOXIFICATION:
Many *toxins* we receive from air, water and food (and what we apply on our body and hair) and are substances that stress and adversely affect the integrity and function of body cells, and interfere with healthy brain function (especially in young children) and normal cellular activity, which is the basis of good health. Getting good food and adequate nutrient intake to keep our cells functioning optimally.

Cleansing herbs may help eliminate toxins: Some of these include parsley, garlic, nettle leaves, burdock root, dandelion root, echinacea root, licorice root, and yellow dock root.
Caution: For each herb, please consult with your health care doctor prior to use.
Note: Grilled/Broiled/Fried Foods (especially meat) add a lot of flavor and taste to our food but there is potential risk from toxic compounds that are generated by chemical reactions that take place during grilling or deep frying can expose human cells to damaging toxins. Eating boiled or baked food is my preference.

DIARRHEA:
May result from an infection that may be caused by an illness or from consuming contaminated water or foods. Symptoms include frequent loose watery bowel movements, abdominal pain, nausea and vomiting. Stress and emotional upset can cause the bowels (and the peristaltic action) to move too fast and lead to wetter stools where the body doesn't have the time to absorb the water back. Certain herbs and foods may help calm the loose bowels.

FOOD THAT MAY HELP PREVENT DIARRHEA

You may use banana, applesauce, cooked rice with coconut water, or cooked rice with plain yogurt (yogurt contain live bacteria that may help minimize some cases of diarrhea).
Note: Ancient Ayurveda practitioner used cinnamon bark as a treatment for fever and diarrhea.
Caution: With severe diarrhea and/or vomiting, fever and stomach cramp, one can lose a lot of body fluids which can lead to dehydration and even death. Call your health care doctor or go to an emergency room immediately if symptoms persist.

DIGESTIVE SUPPORT: A properly functioning digestive system is essential to good health. In other words good health depends on the power of good digestion. Incomplete digestion can cause abdominal discomfort and bloating. Sometimes this is due to eating too much of certain foods such as beans, lentils, cheese, potatoes, and cruciferous vegetables such as cabbage, cauliflower and broccoli. Digestion problems can also be caused by eating too fast, not chewing food properly, and possibly eating too many different foods at a time.

FOOD THAT MAY HELP PROMOTE HEALTHY DIGESTION

The following may help with digestion: Anise seeds, artichoke, bitter orange, cinnamon, cayenne, cumin seeds, dandelion, fennel, fenugreek, papaya* and the consumption of plum/lemon and ginger root.

*Papaya flesh contains **digestive enzymes** (enzymes are large protein molecules that break down proteins, starches and fats into smaller chemical elements that can be absorbed by the body. The process of converting food into energy is controlled by the activity of various enzymes).

Note 1: Some people are lactose or gluten intolerant and must avoid food containing them. One should always avoid a food that causes stomach distress such as heavy fried meal, highly processed food or very spicy food.

Note 2: Raw cabbage juice is an excellent source of glutamine and nutrients that aid the digestive tract and it is one of my favorite drink. To the blender I add ¼ cup cabbage (shredded), ½ teaspoon of ginger root (freshly grated), 2-3 plums (pitted and diced), ½ teaspoon kaffir lime leaf (bruised) and 1 glass of mineral spring water. I blend together and drink. Please read ***Chapter one, page vi,*** for safe use.

ELEVATE MOOD & BOOST ENERGY: Many scientists firmly believe that

"what we eat has a profound effect on our moods". In addition, a person's mood is influenced by many other factors (besides food and nutrition), including general health, adequate sleep, financial stress, etc.

Energy Boosting Support can be supported with foods, exercise, and herbs like garlic, ginkgo and ginseng and can help to reduce stress and create a steady and stable energy levels throughout the day. Foods high in sugar and caffeine can stimulate temporary mood swings and should probably be avoided because they can lead to an unhealthy food addiction.

Note: A healthy diet containing whole grains, fresh fruits and vegetables and dairy products, basically a well-balanced diet, consumed in a family-friendly, low-stress atmosphere is essential to body-mind health.

FOOD THAT MAY HELP ELEVATE MOODS & BOOST ENERGY

Lavender flower, lemon balm, licorice root, rosemary leaves, culinary rose, St. John's wort, garlic, gingko and ginseng tea can help elevate the mood to its optimal level.

Caution: For each herb, please consult with your health care/naturopathic doctor prior to use.

GALLSTONE: Gallstones form in the gallbladder; it can start as the size of a grain of sand and grow to fill the gall bladder. *At certain sizes, these stones can block the flow of bile that aids fat metabolism and can be extremely painful and requires immediate medical attention.* Consult with your health care doctor if you have severe abdominal pain.

FOOD THAT MAY HELP PREVENT GALLSTONE PROBLEMS

Adequate Fluid Intake: Radish and parsley juice, papaya and fig and consuming lemon-water each day.

Caution: For each herb, please consult with your health care/naturopathic doctor prior to use.
Note: Chinese medicine uses turmeric for treating mild gallstone problems (turmeric stimulates gallbladder function).

Lemon, see Glossary, page 227

HAIR LOSS: Over the centuries in many cultures, hair has been a symbol of strength, beauty and inspiration. A thinning hair line and hair loss is a mystery that may be caused by genetics and/or poor diet, deficiency (or excess) of certain hormones, poor circulation, lack of good sleep and rest, emotional stress, hair and scalp dryness or some unknown factors. If thinning hair continues, you may wish to contact your health care provider.

FOOD THAT MAY HELP PREVENT HAIR LOSS

Massaging coconut or rosemary oil onto the scalp and leaving on for 25 minutes before washing one's hair may help. Please consult with your health care doctor prior to use.

Herb experts say, using freshly ground green fenugreek leaves or grind fenugreek seeds with a little water to make a paste. Apply paste over the scalp and leave on for 25 minutes before washing out might help prevent hair loss. Please consult with health care doctor prior to use.

Note: Nettle tea, Vitamin B complex, vitamin C, zinc, iron and sufficient protein and a balance diet is recommended by health care doctors and may contribute to healthy hair growth.

HEART CONCERNS (*our living pump*): It is important to know that **oxygen*** is carried by the blood supply through the coronary arteries to the heart; when there is a blockage of the arteries supplying the heart, a heart attack results. *This is mainly due to plaque buildup in one of the heart's arteries. Warning signs for heart issues include: chest, neck, and jaw pain and tightness, heaviness (in the left side of chest), shortness of breath, fatigue, dizziness, and persistent headache, irregular heartbeats and sweating.* If any of these symptoms occur, stop what you are doing, call 911 and go immediately to an emergency room. *In general, we do not notice the danger of circulatory deficit (plaque buildup) until almost 80% of our heart arteries are blocked.*

*Oxygen is essential to energize and activate all body cells. *It is especially* important to have enough oxygen in order to keep our brain sharp and functioning properly.

HIGH BLOOD PRESSURE (*hypertension*):

Normal blood pressure is 120/80 or below. When blood pressure reaches 140/90 or more, it is considered to be high blood pressure and can leads to major complications and health problems such as heart-attack, kidney failure, strokes and vision impairment. High blood pressure can be caused by poor diet, heredity, and a hyperactive lifestyle, also related to stress, caffeine intake, and more. The symptoms of high blood pressure include: weakness, sleeplessness (insomnia), headache (especially the back of the head), dizziness, fatigue and sweating. Often there are no symptoms (that is why it is called "*silent killer*"). Adults should have their blood pressure checked on a regular basis by a health care provider and follow their recommendations. Of course, in caring for yourself, you can monitor your own blood pressure or do it in your local drug store.

INSOMNIA: Relates to sleeplessness or inability to sleep, either in sleep onset or with awakening during the night. A good night's sleep is necessary for our body cells to renew the cells and restore our energy. There are many things to do to improve your sleep, such as lowering caffeine intake, reducing stress, and possibly using many various natural treatments, herbs like lavender, valerian root or hops with approval of your health care doctor.

FOOD THAT MAY HELP RELIEVE INSOMNIA

A well balanced nutritional dinner and relaxing as you drink a cup of calming tea such as lavender may be helpful for a restful sleep. *Stress/anxiety circumstances and caffeine can interfere with a sweet-good-night sleep.*

Note: To mix yogurt with chopped cucumber, scallions and sprinkle with mint, salt and pepper is one of my favorite go back to sleep treat.
This calming exercise may help you for sleep: Lie on your back, place hands on your side and close your eyes. Slowly take deep breaths 8-10 times, with each breath say *"Thank God for my many blessing"* and then lie on your side and go to sleep.

INTESTINAL GAS PROBLEMS (FLATULENCE): Eating too much,
not chewing well, and certain foods that include such as beans and lentils, and veggies like cabbage can cause abdominal pain and bloating. Ask your doctor about herbs (carminatives) may help reduce or expel gas from the body and relieve flatulence.

FOODS THAT MAY HELP REDUCE GAS PROBLEMS OR FLATULENCE

These include many seeds like anise, caraway, dill, fennel, and fenugreek, ginger root, garlic, black cumin seeds, peppermint leaf teas and papaya.

LAXATIVE HERBS: Laxative herbs help prevents constipation, and help eliminate
the accumulations of toxic build-up within the intestines. Laxatives may be mild or strong. Mild laxatives are called simply "*laxatives*" such as aloe vera (please read page 319, Aloe vera). *Strong laxatives are called purgatives or cathartics as they stimulate the intestinal movement more extremely* such as senna leaf (please read page 278, senna). A person who usually has regular bowel movements may occasionally require a strong laxative. Chronic constipation, as well as

constipation in the elderly with its accumulation of gas and dryness in the colon should be treated by health care provider doctor.

Caution: One should not use laxative herbs without the approval of their health care provider.

FOOD THAT MAY HELP AND ACT AS A LAXATIVE

Figs and prunes may be used as a mild laxative. High fiber herbs such as alfalfa, flaxseeds, marshmallow root and yellow dock root are good with approval of your health care doctor.

Note: Figs have been thought to be a particularly effective aid to regulate bowel movement. Figs syrup is often given to children in the Middle East as a laxative. You may use fig, flaxseeds and other herbs as a mild laxative with consultation of health care provider prior to use.

VISION (*The eyes are our window to the world and to our soul. We should cherish our vision and protect our eyes.*)

A major cause of vision impairment in older adults is the formation of cataracts. Cataracts are an eye disease that happens when the lens of the eyes gradually becomes cloudy or opaque and vision is impaired. At some point, surgery may be required, and this has advanced to remove the cloudy lens and replace it with a new one that allows better vision. *Impaired vision can also be caused by diabetes, metabolic disorders, heredity, aging, exposure to radiation and reading or working in front of a computer for long hours.* Drugs, alcohol and smoking and any kind of work that cause *eyestrain* can contribute to vision problems. As you know, vitamin A and the carotenes found in many fruits and vegetables supports healthy eyes.

FOOD THAT MAY HELP IMPROVE VISION

(The value of vitamin A* rich foods for improving vision is essential).

Carrot, turnip, spinach, dark green leafy vegetables, citrus fruits, stone fruits (many of them contain beta-carotene that the body can convert to vitamin A) and dairy products. Please read *Chapter one, page vi,* for safe use.

*Vitamin A is a major dietary factor in good vision and foods containing it are essential to seeing well.

Beets (Beta vulgaris)

CHAPTER 7

INDEX OF RECIPES

Cucumber and pear smoothie, 19
Cucumber drink, 18
Cucumber pickling, 97

D

Dahi East Indian cuisine, 135
Dijon mustard dressing, 115
Delightful summery salad with peaches, 111
Dress-sauce dressing, 115

E

Easy appetizer with tomato and cheese, 8
Elegant turkey meatball (kofta), 73
Elderberry sherbet with agar agar, 47
Elegant tasty chicken salad with rice, 116

F

Fennel and mustard seed sauce, 136
Flavorful spicy potatoes salads, 117
Flaxseed pudding, 48
Fruit and carrot puree blend, 20
Fruit and herbal blend, 21
Fruity puree blend, 21

G

Ginger and tamari sauce (Korean style), 136
Grape juice dressing, 118
Green peas pesto with soft cooked eggs, 159
Green pesto sauce, 137
Green salad with kale, 118
Grilled chicken liver, 9
Grilled spicy chicken, 75
Grilled Tuna, page 57
Guacamole salsa, 137

H

"Haleemy oat" for good breakfast, 31
Herb seasoning dip, 55
How to make vegetarian soup/clear broth, Tips, 178

Perfect luncheon soup, 151
Persian rice golden cake, 108
Persian-style diamond cake, 39
Persian-style quince-lime drink, 22
Pickled cauliflower and carrots, 99
Pickled eggplant with herbs and spices, 100
Pickled onions, 99
Pizza desert with fresh fruits, 102
Pizza with herbs, 103
Popsicle with banana and kudzu root starch, 50
Porridge with chocolate topping, 32
Power snacks, 11
Prawns with coconut milk, 78

Q
Quinoa tabbouleh salad, 121
Quinoa with oat and chocolate, 33

R
Rice spaghetti, 92
Ricotta cheese light dessert, 51
Roasted cauliflower salad, 122
Roasted chicken with various spices, 79
Roasted tomatoes with garlic, 166
Robust flavorful dipping oil, 56
Romesco sauce, 139
Root vegetable casserole, 80
Royal rose salmon salad, 122

S
Salad dressing with mustard and honey, 123
Salad with red cabbage, 124
Sandwich with crimini mushroom, 81
Satisfying pea soup with herbs and spices, 152
Sauce with butternut squash, 140
Sauce with fresh herbs, 140
Sauce with lentils and herbs, 141
Sautéed Swiss chard green salad, 125

CHAPTER 8

ABU ALI SINA (AVICENNA)

(A brief history of master "*herbalist*" and "*doctor*", Abu-Ali-Sina)

(Pen drwing of Dr. Abu-Ali Sina, by Ju-lian Toh)
A very famous and brilliant Persian scientist, **Master Herbalist,** and *Doctor* Abu Ali al-Hussain ibn Sina
(980-1037), who cured people with herbal plants.
He was a great physician, philosopher, mathematician, writer, poet,
and musician with an international reputation.

Abu Ali Sina (Avicenna) was born near the city of Bukhara, part of Persia (now Tajikistan), and he lived in Isphahan Persia (now Iran) when he was seven years old. Abu Ali Sina had educated teachers at an early age, provided by his father while he was growing up. At the age of 14 he taught himself since he could not find a teacher to teach him more information than he already knew; he was a genius physician at the early age of 17. He spent fruitful years in reading and writing books in Persian and Arabic. He died at the age of 57 and was buried in Hamadan Persia (Iran). He was the king of *herbalist doctors* during the sixth century in human history for helping others.

"PERSIA THE IMMORTAL KINGDOM"
A manuscript written by Vladimir Minorsky and published by Orient Commerce Establishment, England 1971 states:
"His canon of Medicine was translated into various European languages and was used as a textbook at European universities. It remained as the standard source of medical knowledge in Europe for some four centuries." Because of his deep devotion, compassion, and immense knowledge, he stands out not only in Persian history, but in the world as one of the most glorious doctor in his time period. I feel it is my duty to name this noble person, so his hard work and contribution to the world cannot be forgotten.

A CELEBRATION WITH HERBS ON NEW YEAR....

A cultural tradition established for New Year 'No-rooz' goes back to Millennia.
To celebrate nature's revival, new life for good health and goodness.
My parents inspired me at the *New Year festival* to symbolize food with *seven letter* "S", which means seven food items start with the letter "S" and is called "*Haft-Seen*".
My mother said "*The use of natural herbal plants on New Year symbolized Persians big passion for cooking. No-rooz is a celebration of life to remember seven-day a week through the years for your well-being*".

STANDARD HERBAL ITEMS "HAFT SEEN" ARE:

1. **Apple** (*seeb*), symbolized beauty and wholesome diet;

2. **Sprouts** (*sabzeh*), made of sprouted wheat berries (new born seeds) to celebrate nature rebirth;

3. **Rejuvelac dessert** (*samanoo*), a simmered malt made of sprouted wheat/barley berries with flour;

4. **Jujube fruits** (*senjed*), an ancient fruit of love, enhance the metabolism;

5. **Garlic** (*seer*), a king in the vegetable kingdom with many benefits to limit illness;

6. **Sumac berries** (*sumagh*) to enhance good taste and flavor;

7. **Fermented grapes-vinegar** (*serkeh*) symbolized of age/patience and good health.

OPTIONAL ITEMS "GOD GIVEN ENLIGHTENMENT" ARE:

- **A Holy Book of Koran Karim** must be present and represents God's blessing in Muslim religion;

- **Mirror**, perfect of the universe reflected in its model of astronomical system as resemble of parents deed of actions reflected image of their own seeds;

- **Eggs, wholesome** eggs, a universal symbol of fertility corresponding to mother earth and children's enjoyment;

- **Seeds, Nuts and Fruits**, will grow only in a state of love;

- **Feasts and Presents**, compassion of family is natural medicine to celebrate and make soul youthful;

- **Candles**, keep your luminosity of wisdom at the forefront of your vision;

- **Joyous Fish,** the continuation of life cycle, keep alive effectively and fruitfully;

- **Coin,** prosperity and success in trade through good deeds;

- **Flowers**, such as "*hyacinth*" the sense of beauty and sweet fragrance in the air along with, music and dance to cherish nature reviving everywhere;

- **Wild-Rue** (*esphand*), **an aromatic seed,** traditionally burned on fire along with other seeds or roots to refresh air, praise (glorify) purifies soul to better love.

  Note: Please read sprouts (page 173), jujube fruit (page 224) and sumak (page 243) for information.

....HOW PERSIAN *(ARYAN PEOPLE)* NEW YEAR STARTS

The date of cultural Persian New Year is unknown;
but it is deeply rooted to traditions of Zoroastrian belief principals.
(A brief history of Ancient Persia)

"**Chaldean astronomers** believed that changes in the heavens revealed the plans of the gods. So they studied the stars, the planets, and the moon. They recorded what they learned. Once they understood the movement of heavenly bodies, they made maps that showed the position of the planets and the phases of the moon. They developed one of the first sundials, and they were the first to have a *seven-day week*."*

When Chaldea (Babylon) was conquered by Persia (about 539 B.C.), Persian astronomy with their accumulated wisdom, experience and intelligence of Aryan people, was developed and flourished.

Persian New-Year, *"No-rooz"* is the first day of spring during the equinoxes which means the sun is positioned above the *equator; day and night become equal in length* all over the world. The national celebration begins, and it goes back to **Zoroastrians** belief principals ascend over 2500 years ago, the time of **Cyrus dynasty** (about 532 B.C.). The Zoroastrian concepts had a significant affect on the enlightened of man and belief in the progressive revelation to the God Ahuramazda. The core of Zoroastrians was centered on ethics (moral principles). They consider planets as part of our vast universe and that planets exert their influence on humankind, moving according to the master plan of the universe. We all are connected to them, and part of God's immense plan.

During Cyrus dynasty, their philosophy, sciences and arts begin to flourish. Cyrus, the great king of Persia, was wise, generous and a benevolent king, he desire to do good to others and treated his people kindly. He starts the world's first declaration of "*THE RIGHTS OF NATIONS*". These are well-known historic writing about Persian King Cyrus. He was buried in Pasargadae, Persia (Iran).

*"Human Heritage A world History", a manuscript written by Cox, Greenblatt and Seaberg. Published 1981 by Bell and Howell in USA.

MY VISIT TO "AYURVEDA UNIVERSITY", JODHPUR, INDIA

On my fourth visit to India my life has been enriched by ancient traditional herbal food and teas (*the food free from preservatives*). This knowledge of herbal cures and their benefits was handed down from ancestral to younger generations through millennia. On July, 2015, when I returned from India, I planned to recreate some of the wonderful dishes I had enjoyed there and write on my special visit to "*Ayurveda University*". I would like to share my enthusiastic treasured experience with my readers.

Indians believe that using **AYUVERDIC** herbal plants (such as bitter gourd, curry leaves, Jambul fruit, lychee fruit and neem tree) as an initial holistic healing treatment that is recommended by health care practitioner and/or naturopathic doctor, whenever appropriate, can be very helpful to our body and mind.

Native of Indian Healer Believe:

- Our body's cell is like a seed, it will be constantly renewed by "*Mother nature*" to bloom again, if we treat it well. Using natural herbs, practicing yoga and meditation will bring balance into body and mind.
- The herbal cure are most beneficial when combined with a balanced diet.
- Many herbalists from India believe that the use of herbal cure for particular symptoms not only is beneficial but also can extend to unexpected other organs as well as one which was weak and the person did not notice it.
- Native Indian healers believed fresh fruits and vegetables, the most healing foods and their quality (locally, seasonally and organically) has greater benefit and makes our body-mind health stronger and many farmers enjoy growing herbs from organic seeds.
- The ancient Indians blend cumin seeds in their curry that can improve digestions, reduce flatulence, and cleanse body from toxins and various illness.
- Ayurveda means "*The Science of Life*". **Ayurvedic herbology** is a complete ancient medicinal healing science (the ancient Hindu art of medicine and the power of ancient wisdom), including the physical, psychological and spiritual aspects of prolonging people's life to rejuvenate body cell and mind by using "*right combination*" and "right usage" herbs of nature according to individual condition and needs with consultation of **health provider or naturopathic doctor.**

  Prof. Dr. Radhey Shyam Sharma states:
  > "*Ayurved is not only a medical science but moreover it is a life science of great human importance. It teaches us how to live and how to protect the precious humanity.*"

AN EXAMPLE OF AYURVEDIC HERB

(Neem tree)

Lychee fresh fruit, has a delicate
pulp with a floral smell and
fragrant and sweet flavor
(see page 273).

Neem tree (Azadirachta indica),
One of the world's most
versatile herbs
Ayurveda medicine believe neem tree
"cure all ailments".
It has been called the
"Village Green Pharmacy"
(See *"Neem tree"*, page 274)

Jambul fresh fruit, has rosy flesh
inside and dark purple outer
skin (see page 269).

Ayurveda a traditional healing system from India is an ancient "Holistic Health Practice."
This is only achieved through balanced dietary change and yoga and meditation.
(Please see "True Healing", page 313)

RAJASTHAN AYURVEDA UNIVERSITY, JODHPUR, INDIA

Front row: Professor, Dr. Radhey Shyam Sharma, Vice-Chancellor and Parisa Z. Ambwani
Back row: From left to the right: Professors, Dr. Chakrapany Sharma, Dr. Chandan Singh,
Dr. L. N. Sharma, Dr. Rajendra Purvia and Dr. Manoj Adalakha.

Prof. Dr. Radhey Shyam Sharma
Vice Chancellor

Office: Nagaur Road, Karwar, Jodhpur - 342037
Phone: 0291-5153701 (O), 291-2542200 (R)
E-mail: vd.rssharma@gmail.com
rau_jodhpur@yahoo.co.in

डॉ.सर्वपल्ली राधाकृष्णन्
राजस्थान आयुर्वेद विश्वविद्यालय
जोधपुर

Dr. Sarvepalli Radhakrishnan
Rajasthan Ayurved University,
Jodhpur

No   RAU/VC/15-16
Dated : 24th July, 2015

Message

Ayurved is not only a medical science but moreover it is a life science of great human importance. It teaches us how to live and how to protect the precious humanity. It emphasizes upon the lifestyle of human beings. Unfortunately lifestyle is being discarded away now a days by the new generation as a result of which various lifestyle related disorders are spreading in the society. "**Early to bed and early to rise makes a man healthy and wise**" this and these type of slogans have now just become a study material. The junk and fast food, late night parties, getting up late in morning, moving away from physical exercises are some of the examples of moving away from the lifestyle theory. Ayurved explains do's and don'ts in details in terms in terms of daily routine and seasonal routine.

Ayurved mentions Ahaar (Food), Nidra (Sleep) and Brahmacharya (Celibacy) as the basic pillars of life. Therefore Ahaar is also the main component of the survival of human life. Ayurved mentions the dietary theory and regimens in detail. Various herbs and medicinal plants are used in dietary supplements according to daily and seasonal basis. This way a human not only keeps himself nourished but also makes him secured from the seasonal diseases as these regimens are responsible for the strength of immunity system also. Ginger, Turmeric, Cumin, Pepper etc. are a lot of spices and other herbal supplements which are the part of food and function like the medicinal elements in the food. Therefore the knowledge of culinary regimens from Ayurved perspective is very much effective.

I am very much glad to know that Parisa Ambwani has come forward to publish a book in this regard.

I extend my good wishes for the success of this book.

(**Prof. Dr. Radhey Shyam Sharma**)
Vice Chancellor

WISDOM OF THE UNIVERSE

**The Universe will respond to you truly and accordingly
to your thoughts and your purpose in life.**

- Our thoughts are with us all the time in a continual process of thinking and making decisions. Our attention will be concentrated around our thoughts, and once a final decision is made, it becomes part of our destiny. Positive thoughts and loving communication in our inner mind allows the wisdom of the truth to shine, *"Truth is far more important than our personal desire when making decisions for our fabulous journey"*.

- Pristine love is a free gift from God, something unique generated within ourselves that we carry with us and that radiates warmth everywhere.

- Always be humble, down to earth as much as you can. Remember that all the water of rivers join at the oceans' edge (essentially the lowest point of the earth). Your devotion to being humble helps you relate to others at God's mighty ocean edge and enables you to make a lot of difference in this world.

- If you cannot agree with somebody and you are in conflict, you can eliminate all the hate that comes from unpleasant conversation. Just say "even though I do not agree with you, I still love you". You will be surprised at the emotional freedom you experience. The conflict you felt turns into love and peace, and you start to walk away from the old narrow minded street you were on to unlimited opportunity of a new life stream.

- The most precious legacy we can leave for our loving children is how much we care for their flourishing health and happiness and kindly giving them advice through our own experience *"Praise the law of Universe; it is wisdom of the truth"*.

- Four things you cannot bring back: A food after it was eaten, a speech after it was given, a time after it has passed, and an opportunity after it has gone (if you get a second chance, grab it with both hands).

Wishing you a life-long journey to your good health and happiness in celestial love and peace.

©*Parisa Z. Ambwani*

312

TRUE HEALING

(Live blossoms to your fullest potential)

True healing can come from yoga and meditation as we connect to a higher level of divine consciousness for support and we experience a greater spiritual awareness of love and peace. For therapeutic relaxation and energy renewal, we should spend quiet time, deep breathing (gentle yoga exercises) and meditating; our mind is clarified, relaxed and rejuvenated by ***positive thoughts***. We experience enormous benefits from improved blood circulation, functioning nerves and muscles with flexibility and balance, reduced body stress, release of chronic tension that may help to improve digestion, lower blood pressure, blood sugar and cholesterol. By continuing to practice yoga and meditation we will be blessed with mindful clarity, peaceful life and acquire a strong core of deeper love and peace.

ASSESS YOUR POSITIVE THOUGHTS!!

Some people may assess themselves psychologically for their own value by comparing themselves with others. With knowing this fact, essential to life is to find our own talent and acknowledge our unique true nature and learning who we are. Therefore we can feel exceptional and acceptable about ourselves and cultivate our natural ability in creating self-confidence. Facing the wisdom of the truth and choosing healthy life style patterns which take us to a whole new level of experience is part of growing and having a fruitful and joyful life.

Stunning lavender blossoms are one of the most loved herbs for beauty and relaxation, page 226.

©Parisa Z. Ambwani

Pristine Gift of Ancient Living Earth
When you are in love with nature, you live in the brightness of the majestic world
and you will find your strength in the shadow of the loving God.

As we journey through this glorious life, our knowledge of herbal plants ("*green pharmacy*") expands exponentially with spiritual motion, we are able to transform our brain in a positive way to appreciate *love of nature, wholesome food, and the whole world*. We want to share this experience of joy and peace with everyone by explaining what it means to be with nature:

BEING WITH NATURE

God is **our God**, not mine.

The space is **our space**, not mine.

The ocean is **our ocean**, not mine.

Let the sun's rays of reality shine on the land,

And break with light of freedom, love and peace.

Let us become one with each other, nature, and earth.

Let us comprehend the magnificent creation of living earth,

By keeping our earth, ocean and space clean and pristine.

The manifestation of this responsibility will flow beautifully through us,

By breathing precious air, we will create a soul symphony and live

A wholesome life in this sumptuous place – our God – given planet.

Good health is a foundation of our happiness. Quality food organically found in nature *~ Ancient living earth ~* provides us all the richness, benefits and nourishment that bring forth the essence of the human spirit on our healthy planet.

©*Parisa Z. Ambwani*

Special Announcement....

How does the food industry influence our nutrition and health?

Ju-lian Toh

We want our children to be sustained with indispensable wholesome living.

Today our shopping list includes carrots, apples, pears and lettuce.

Parisa Ambwani with Katherine Fulvio in the
Kitchen of "Cookery School".

Culinary Tour of Ireland, 2006

Lemon Blossoms, see Glossary, lemon, page 227

Olive, see Glossary, olive, page 232

Aloe vera also known as (Cape, Barbados, and Zanzibar Aloe)
You may have an Aloe vera potted in front of your kitchen windowsill.

You may cut off the thickest green part of leaves and squeeze out a small amount of clear Aloe vera gel onto *minor injuries* (for the person who does not develop an allergic reaction) to help wounds heal and prevent infection. Commercial Aloe juice may be used as a laxative herb to help constipation, but it may cause diarrhea and cramps or other unexpected problems (Please read Food Plants That May Help, laxative herbs, page 296).

Caution: Pregnant, breast feeding women, children and adults should avoid using Aloe vera. Please do not use Aloe vera internally without consultation with your health care or naturopathic doctor.

Tarragon, Basil (Thai), oregano, lemon verbena,
thyme (golden lemon) and rosemary.
(Please see Tips, bouquet garni with fresh herbs, page 173.)

A celebration with herbs on new year, page 306

LIFE'S DECISIONS

A woman came out of her house and saw 3 old men with long white beards sitting in her front yard, she did not recognize them. She said, "I don't think I know you, but you must be hungry...Please come in and have something to eat. "Is the man of the house home?" they asked. "No", she replied. "He's out". "Then we cannot come in", they replied.

In the evening when her husband came home, she told him what had happened. Go tell them I am home and invite them in. The woman went out and invited the men in.

"We don't go into the house together", they replied. "Why is that", she wanted to know. One of the old men explained: "His name is Wealth", he said; pointing to one of his friends, and said pointing to another one, "He is Success and I am Love". Then he added, "Now go in and discuss with your husband which one of us you want in your home."

The woman went in and told her husband what was said. Her husband overjoyed. "How nice", he said. "Since that is the case, let us invite Wealth. Let him come and fill our home with wealth". His wife disagreed. "My dear, why don't we invite Success?" Their daughter-in-law was listening from the other corner of the house, she jumped in with her own suggestion: "Would it not be better to invite Love? Our home will be filled with Love". "Let us heed our daughter-in-law's advice", said the husband to his wife. "Go out and invite Love to be our guest". The woman went out and asked the 3 old men, "Which one of you is Love? Please come in and be our guest".

Love got up and started walking toward the house. The other 2 also got up and followed him. Surprised the lady asked Wealth and Success: "I only invited Love, why are you coming in?" The old men replied together: "If you had invited Wealth or Success the other 2 of us would've stayed out, but since you invited Love, where ever Love goes we go with him".

Wherever there is Love there is also Wealth and Success!!!!!!!!!!!

Author unknown.

322

NOTES